The Other

Studies in Contemporary German Social Thought
Thomas McCarthy, general editor

Alfred Schmidt, *History and Structure: An Essay on Hegelian-Marxist and Structuralist Theories of History*, 1981

Hans-Georg Gadamer, *Reason in the Age of Science*, 1982

Joachim Ritter, *Hegel and the French Revolution: Essays on the* Philosophy of Right, 1982

Theodor W. Adorno, *Prisms*, 1982

Theodor W. Adorno, *Against Epistemology: A Metacritique*, 1983

Hans Blumenberg, *The Legitimacy of the Modern Age*, 1983

Jürgen Habermas, *Philosophical-Political Profiles*, 1983

Jürgen Habermas, editor, *Observations on "The Spiritual Situation of the Age,"* 1983

Michael Theunissen, *The Other: Studies in the Social Ontology of Husserl, Heidegger, Sartre, and Buber*, 1984

The Other
Studies in the Social Ontology of Husserl,
Heidegger, Sartre, and Buber

Michael Theunissen
translated by Christopher Macann
with an introduction by Fred R. Dallmayr

The MIT Press Cambridge, Massachusetts, and London, England

This book was typeset in Baskerville
by The MIT Press Computergraphics Department
and printed and bound by The Murray Printing Co.
in the United States of America.

Library of Congress Cataloging in Publication Data

Theunissen, Michael.
    The Other: studies in the social ontology of Husserl, Heidegger, Sartre, and Buber.

    (Studies in contemporary German social thought)
    Translation of: Der Andere.
    Includes bibliographical references and index.
    1. Husserl, Edmund, 1859–1938. 2. Heiddegger, Martin, 1889–1976. 3. Sartre, Jean Paul, 1905–1980. 4. Buber, Martin, 1878–1965. 5. Ontology—History—20th century.
6. Transcendentalism—History—20th century.
I. Title. II. Series.
B804.T4513   1984   111   83–16267
ISBN 0-262-20048-1

Contents

III
The Philosophy of Dialogue as the Counterproject
to Transcendental Philosophy: The Dialogic of
Martin Buber

Series Foreword

From Hegel and Marx, Dilthey and Weber, to Freud and the Frankfurt School, German social theory enjoyed an undisputed preeminence. After the violent break brought about by National Socialism and World War II, this tradition has come to life again, and indeed to such an extent that contemporary German social thought has begun to approach the heights earlier attained. One important element in this renaissance has been the rapid and extensive translation into German of English-language works in the humanities and social sciences, with the result that social thought in Germany today is markedly influenced by ideas and approaches of Anglo-American origin. Unfortunately, efforts in the other direction, the translation and reception of German works into English, have been sporadic at best. This series is intended to correct that imbalance.

The term *social thought* is here understood very broadly to include not only sociological and political thought but also the social-theoretical concerns of history and philosophy, psychology and linguistics, aesthetics and theology. The term *contemporary* is also to be construed broadly; though our attention will be focused primarily on postwar thinkers, we shall also publish works by and on earlier thinkers whose influence on contemporary German social thought is pervasive. Previous translations in this series have included works by such well-known authors as Adorno, Gadamer, and Habermas, as well as works by authors like Hans Blumenberg and Joachim Ritter who were thereby first made accessible to the English-speaking public. The present work by Michael Theunissen belongs in the latter category. I want to thank Dennis Schmidt for his invaluable assistance in editing the translation.

Thomas McCarthy

Introduction

Fred R. Dallmayr

Because the Cartesian *ego cogito* has served as a central metaphysical pillar of the modern era, twentieth-century efforts to move in a "postmodern" direction have typically been anti-Cartesian. The "picture theory" of the early Wittgenstein reduced the *cogito* to a boundary or extreme limit of the intelligible world, while his later conception of "language games" submerged the subject entirely in ongoing linguistic and cultural practices. On the Continent, the phenomenological movement heralded both a radicalization of the Cartesian legacy and its progressive transformation. Husserl's transcendental phenomenology was predicated on the cognitive potency of a refined, transempirical "subjectivity" or consciousness; but his lifelong ambition was to grasp the genesis of an "objective" or intersubjectively shared world and thus to elucidate the link between ego and alter ego, between subject and fellow-subjects. Recasting the Husserlian perspective during the interbellum period, Heidegger redefined the subject as a situated mode of being (*Dasein*) enmeshed in a setting made up of human and non-human components. Roughly at the same time, spokesmen of "dialogical" existentialism—foremost among them Martin Buber— portrayed the subject not so much as a fixed premise but as a derived category emerging through interpersonal encounter. The phenomenological-existentialist concern with intersubjectivity was continued in the postwar era by a host of French thinkers, notably by Sartre and Merleau-Ponty. More recently, the reversal of Cartesianism has assumed dramatic new forms. Launching a broad-scale attack on the traditional outlook, structuralist and poststructuralist writers have advocated a complete "decentering" or dislocation of the subject in favor of systemic correlations or the transpersonal interplay of "differences." Simultaneously, champions of "critical theory" (or a post-Kantian critical philosophy) insist on the need to replace the *cogito* by the notion of communicative intersubjectivity as the foundation of reflective thought.[1]

These trends, one might add, are not purely speculative. In large measure, the post-Cartesian turn to "otherness" is nourished by the broader mutations and dislocations of our age: dislocations manifest in the confrontation between Western and revitalized non-Western cultures on a global scale, and also in the clash between competing social classes and experiential life-worlds. Particularly with regard to the latter types of contests, the impact of otherness has frequently been thematized under such labels as "reification" and "alienation." Whereas Marxists have tended to associate reification or loss of autonomy with expropriation and the prevailing mode of production, existentialist writers have preferred to construe alienation more ontologically as involving an estrangement between man and universe or, more narrowly, between human experience and the imperatives of a technological civilization. Despite a certain commonsense plausibility, however, arguments of this kind lack theoretical cogency as long as the boundary between "I" and "Other"—between the indigenous and the alien—is not elucidated or is simply taken for granted. Contrary to the assumption of a fixed or easily defined boundary, there is a strong tradition in Western thought—stretching back to Hegel, Schelling, and beyond—according to which the linkage between I and Other is not a relation of exclusivity but one of mutual dependence. In light of this background, it seems desirable to differentiate between an alienation that is simply synonymous with oppression or repression and a more nuanced estrangement seen as a road to self-discovery. The second alternative has been powerfully reasserted by many post-Cartesian authors. Thus from the vantage point of dialogical existentialism, self-discovery presupposes the passage through otherness, specifically interaction with a different, nonobjectifiable "Thou." A similar insight is voiced in Adorno's later work. The theory of alienation, he notes in *Negative Dialectics*, confounds the legitimate yearning to comprehend the "heteronomous world" with the "barbaric" unwillingness or incapacity to respect and "cherish what is alien or different." Alienation, he adds, "would mostly cease if strangeness were no longer vilified."[2]

The present translation renders available to English-speaking readers
a milestone in the literature on otherness and intersubjectivity. First
published in 1965 and reedited in 1977, Michael Theunissen's *Der
Andere* is easily the most systematic and detailed study of diverse
treatments of the theme in our century. As the author rightly notes
in his introductory remarks, otherness "has certainly never penetrated
as deeply as today into the foundations of philosophical thought" —
to the point that it qualifies as a "topic of first philosophy." The chief
aim of the study is to unearth the basic metaphysical underpinnings
of approaches to intersubjectivity; accordingly, its investigations proceed
(in the words of the subtitle) on the level of "social ontology" rather
than that of concrete social or sociological theory. In its broad outline,
the presentation juxtaposes or opposes two major theoretical frameworks or conceptions: transcendental phenomenology, abbreviated as
"transcendentalism," and the "philosophy of dialogue" or "dialogicalism." Starting from the premise of the ego, the first position seeks
access to intersubjectivity by construing the Other basically as an
"other I" or alter ego, whereas the second position derives ego or self
in some manner from an original encounter with a "Thou." These
contrasting vantage points give rise to additional, more specific divergences. As articulated by Buber and other representatives, dialogicalism insists on the immediacy and reciprocity of interpersonal
relations and on the simultaneous genesis of both partners through
encounter (defined as an "in-between" realm) — features that stand in
marked opposition to the egological outlook of Husserlian transcendentalism and its stress on the relatively "mediated" and dependent
status of the alter ego. In the discussion of both frameworks, close
attention is given to the respective role and significance of estrangement
or "alter-ation" (*Veranderung*), in its varying meanings of reification,
alienation, and self-discovery.

The study is remarkable not only for its broad scope but also for
its philosophical subtlety and rigor. The author brings to his task a
solid background in the rich tradition of Continental thought, extending
from contemporary phenomenology and existentialism backward over
German idealism to classical Greek philosophy. Presently a professor
in Berlin, Theunissen received his training in philosophy, theology,
and German philology at the universities of Bonn and Freiburg. His
early writings established his reputation as a perceptive analyst of
existential philosophy and its historical antecedents. His first publication

in 1958 dealt with a central notion in early formulations of existentialism: the category of "seriousness" in Kierkegaard's teachings. During the same year Theunissen wrote a long essay on the "Kierkegaard image" as reflected in recent research and exegesis. Subsequent publications probed such topics as the linkage between Husserl and Heidegger, the relation between Kierkegaard, Schelling, and Hegel, and the significance of Buber's "negative ontology of the In-Between."[3] The present study was originally submitted as a *Habilitation* at the Free University of Berlin, where Theunissen began his academic career (and to which he eventually returned after interludes in Bern and Heidelberg).

As an examination of intersubjectivity in twentieth-century phenomenology *Der Andere* is too wide ranging and complex to permit easy summary. I would like, however, to highlight some particularly outstanding features and arguments. According to its basic design, the study places primary emphasis, in the discussion of each of the two contrasted frameworks, on one leading thinker or spokesman: on Husserl in the field of transcendentalism, and on Buber in the domain of dialogicalism. Subsequently attention is given to amplifications or modifications of a given framework by less prominent or else less typically representative authors. Under the rubric of transcendental phenomenology, the opening section offers a detailed and instructive account—hardly matched elsewhere in the literature—of Husserl's persistent attempts to formulate a coherent theory of intersubjectivity on transcendental-egological premises. The account begins with an outline of the philosophical or metaphysical "foundations" of transcendentalism, and moves on to a steadily more focused analysis of Husserl's conception of the "I-Other" relation. Among other things Theunissen discusses the reliance on an "extramundane" subjectivity or transcendental "facticity," the role of "phenomenological reduction" as a gateway leading from the "natural attitude" to eidetic intuition and transcendental reflection, and the stress on the "constitutive" or meaning-generating function of consciousness. With regard to the theory of intersubjectivity, the presentation concentrates chiefly on Husserl's *Cartesian Meditations*, especially on the famous fifth meditation, without neglecting prior or subsequent treatments of the same topic (in such works as the three volumes of *Ideas, Formal and Transcendental Logic*, and *Crisis*). After tracing the basic course of Husserl's theoretical effort, Theunissen himself offers a convenient brief synopsis of the five basic steps involved in the move from ego to alter ego. The starting point for Husserl, he notes,

> was my primordinal world as the pure thing-world transformed into phenomenon, the transcendentally reduced "mere nature," in whose midst I myself have been constituted as a primordinal, personal, psychophysical I, as the moving agent of my animated body from which I am, however, set at a distance. The first step toward the Other, in the first instance toward the Other in general, is the apperception of the (alien) physical body as an organic body on the basis of the analogy with my own body, which, in part at any rate, is constituted as a physical body. The second step is, in a psychological direction, the experience of the psychic life of the alien, while in a transcendental direction, it is the experience of the pure alter ego. Inasmuch as the vehicle of the first step is a quasi apperception of analogy, the second makes use of the purified analogizing as empathy. . . . So we come to the third step: the constitution of the objective world out of the identification of the primordinal worlds. In the objective world I apperceive—that is the fourth step—the Other as a unitary object complete in itself and situated in space and time. In this way the Other loses the meaning "Other in general" and becomes another human being. In the fifth and last step, I finally transfer the objective unity "human being" to myself in that I empathetically presentify myself how and as what the Other represents me.

Apart from outlining the various steps on the road to intersubjectivity, Theunissen accentuates a number of distinctive traits of transcendentalism as manifest in Husserl's perspective. A central trait is the "mediacy" or mediated character of the I-Other relation, a character deriving both from the focus on the Other's worldly or bodily appearance and from the constitutive role ascribed to egological empathy. "Quite generally," Theunissen notes, "it is the interest in the world, an interest bound up with the principle of transcendental philosophy, that drives Husserl to a 'thematization' of the 'Other.' And so it is also the world that, from the outset, prescribes the bounds within which the Other can become thematic from a transcendental-phenomenological standpoint." Due to the constitutive functions of "my" body and "my" subjectivity on the levels of analogical perception and empathy, however, meditation through the world ultimately coincides with mediation through the ego. Husserl's departure, in the fifth Cartesian meditation, from the ego's "primordinal sphere" entails

a number of further implications or distinctive aspects—among which
Theunissen mentions mainly these: the encounter of the Other as a
bodily phenomenon, situated in a "spatial world" and experienced
chiefly through visual "perception," a perception transforming the
Other into an object and, at best, into a nondescript fellow-being
among a multitude of similar beings. In the broader context of the
study, the last two aspects are particularly significant. For Husserl, we
read, the Other "never enters my awareness in the sense that I exist
for him: never does he figure as primordinal subject and I originally
as his object." Moreover, the Other as thematized from a transcendental
vantage point is "from the beginning only one among many others
who inhabit my world; he is not the unique individual related to me
in singular fashion. The distinction between the intimate Thou and
the world of strangers has no place in the sphere of primordial-
transcendental constitution."

Theunissen's comments on phenomenological intersubjectivity, it
goes without saying, are based on his broader assessment of transcendentalism and of Husserl's enterprise as a whole. Students of
Husserl are liable to find controversial several of the theses advanced
in the study; but they are bound to respect the author's scholarship
and his painstaking effort to substantiate arguments through reference
to primary and secondary literature. One of the more startling or
striking theses is the assertion that, far from forming a radical antithesis,
Husserl's conception of the "natural attitude" is itself overshadowed
by transcendental reflection or by a "transcendental-theoretical prejudgment"—in the sense that, by treating the partner in a natural
everyday encounter as an object in the world, Husserl's "understanding
of this alien experience [of the Other] is already guided by the transcendental interest, by the concern for the constitution of the world."
Coupled with this "prejudgment," in Theunissen's view, is a pervasive
parallelism and even "surprising identity of content" between the
transcendental-theoretical perspective and the "naturalistic attitude"
as practiced in the natural sciences. Equally startling and perhaps even
provocative is his thesis regarding the derivative status of the alter
ego and the final coincidence of the Other with "my" ego (in particular
with "my past ego"). Transcendental empathy, he writes, "does not
presuppose the alter ego, but posits it first of all." Just as in mediating
the Other's concrete existence, "my body . . . plays the 'role of the
originary body' (*Urleib*), so my I, as the mediator of all alien I-ness,

takes on the meaning of an 'originary norm' (*Urnorm*). In this way, however, the other I becomes an 'analogue' of my own. . . . Husserl tends to go beyond the representation of analogy and mirroring in the direction of *identity*. From the standpoint of experience, the I of the Other is my own I." These considerations undergird the author's views on solipsism. In rejecting the "equiprimordiality" of the Other, he notes, Husserl reveals the "undeniable limitations" of his attempt "to overcome . . . the 'transcendental solipsism' of 'pure egology' . . . through the theory of intersubjectivity."

The analysis of Husserl's perspective is followed in the second part by a discussion of two thinkers in whose writings transcendentalism was "further elaborated and transformed": Heidegger and Sartre. In Theunissen's presentation, Heidegger's fundamental ontology—as outlined in *Being and Time*—appears essentially as a "modified repetition" of the transcendental-phenomenological approach, particularly in the domain of intersubjectivity or "social ontology." Among the modifications or "seminal innovations" discussed are the following: the treatment of cobeing or "being-with" as a structural characteristic of existence or *Dasein*; the ontological rather than merely ontic-factual status of the I-Other relation; and finally, the rejection of the visual-perceptual paradigm. "Husserl," we read, "stands in the great and long tradition of those for whom truth manifests itself in the intuition of perception and in the view of theoretical knowledge. Heidegger, on the contrary, proceeds from the truth of observation back to the disclosure of inner-worldly beings in the course of practical interaction with them." None of these deviations, however, affects Heidegger's moorings in transcendentalism. According to Theunissen, the linkage is most clearly evident in the stress on the indirect or mediated character of interpersonal contact. "This is the most significant of all the points in common," he writes, "that, in [Husserl's] theory of intersubjectivity and [Heidegger's] analysis of being-with, the *immediacy* of the encounter with the Other is discounted in a similar manner because the medium of the 'world' is interposed between 'me' and Others." Radiating into other facets of the two versions of transcendentalism, the congruence is said to surface in the affinity between phenomenological "constitution" and the Heideggerian notion of "project," in the parallel between natural attitude and "inauthenticity," and also in the respective transcendence of everyday life through recourse to absolute subjectivity or "authentic" existence.

Somewhat more independent or unconventional arguments are found in Sartre's *Being and Nothingness*. The chief innovation in Sartre's approach, according to *Der Andere*, resides in his partial endorsement of intersubjective immediacy, in the sense of a direct impact of the Other on "my" experience. As delineated in the "dialectic of the Look," the Other originally approaches me as an alien reality or an "extramundane existence," completely immune from the grasp of phenomenological reduction. In contrast to Husserl's constitutive egology, Theunissen notes, "the primarily present Other is, according to Sartre, supposed to be a 'real being existing beyond this world,' that is, an entity that does not first achieve its fullness of being for me out of its world relation" and that thus imposes itself as an "immediate presence." To the extent that mediation plays a role, it operates in a reverse manner from Husserl's model: instead of being a medium of "my" world, the Other in the end "mediates me with myself." A similar reversal affects other facets of intersubjectivity. Thus, in opposition to transcendental phenomenology, the "passivity" of encounter or "my" alienation by the Other takes precedence over active-constitutive appropriation; as a corollary, far from being simply a derivative of the ego, the alter ego places its imprint on "my" subjectivity. While Husserl, we read, seeks transcendence in the confines of an immanent constitution, "Sartre . . . seeks absolute transcendence in absolute immanence. Figuratively speaking, he wants to push through the shell of immanence right to the transcendence concealed in it." As in Heidegger's case, however, Sartre's novel departures are insufficient to rupture the transcendentalist mold. Despite the mentioned differences, transcendentalism triumphs at last in the identification of "being-for-itself" with consciousness, in the stress on the "internality" of consciousness, and in the construal of intersubjectivity as an "internal negation." Thus the reversal of Husserl's scheme remains on the level of a "destructive repetition": "What remains in this inversion is the transcendental duality itself, the bipolar unity of world and 'world,' of the a priori project overthrow and the factically given, of the horizon and the horizontally appearing."

The third part of the study is devoted to "dialogicalism," chiefly as exemplified in Buber's writings. In a slight deviation from the book's guiding methodology—the initial focus on one leading spokesman of each framework—the discussion of Buber's work is interspersed from the beginning with references to a host of other authors active during the interbellum period. As spelled out in the introductory remarks, the reasons for the deviation have to do with the character of dialogicalism as a "trend of the time" and also with the comparatively subordinate philosophical stature of all its spokesmen, a circumstance that entails that dialogicalism is "less well represented, so to speak," in Buber's arguments than is transcendentalism in Husserl's opus. In line with these considerations the opening chapter offers, together with a brief synopsis of Buber's teachings, a delineation of the historical background and of the central thrust of dialogicalism or the "ontology of the between" as a broad intellectual movement. English-speaking readers will appreciate especially the careful portrayal of "historical contexts" and of the respective roles of such authors as Franz Rosenzweig, Hans Ehrenberg, Gabriel Marcel, Ferdinand Ebner, and Eugen Rosenstock-Huessey. In its overall thrust dialogicalism is presented as a counterpoint to transcendentalism, and particularly as an antidote to the notions of an abstract-general consciousness and of the constitutive function of subjectivity. Challenging these notions, Buber and other dialogical writers insist on the need to differentiate cognitive subject-object or "I-It" relations from genuine interpersonal contacts where "I" and "Thou" meet in an "in-between" sphere underived from egological intentions. While "I-It" connections are typically relations of domination and subordination rooted in the designs of subjectivity, interpersonal encounter yields an "immediate"—that is, egologically not mediated—human bond predicated on the complete "reciprocity" of engagement and the "equal primordiality" of partners.

Descending from the level of a broad overview, Theunissen subsequently examines the distinctive traits of dialogicalism and the concrete steps involved in its attempted "destruction" of the transcendentalist model. Of central significance for the entire endeavor is the linguistic construal of the "in-between" fabric of encounter. In contrast to the Husserlian and Sartrean focus on perception, he notes, "language is the home of the Thou"—a medium that, by its nature, "moves beneath that 'sphere of subjectivity' with which the model of intentionality stands or falls." In light of its linguistic character, the structure of encounter is most poignantly displayed in reciprocal speech or dialogue, in the interplay of address and response (an exchange that makes room for meaningful silence). In dialogue, the partners face each other in full temporal "presence"—as opposed to the past tense prevalent in "I-It" relations. Based on the linguistic medium of

encounter, dialogicalism's departure from the transcendentalist framework occurs in two basic, interrelated steps: namely, through the
removal of the "Thou" from the field of intentional objects, and through
the segregation of "I-Thou" contacts from the range of intentional-
noetic acts. In sharply differentiating between "It" and "Thou," Buber
formulates the contrast between the two modes of experience in terms
of a stark being-nothingness antithesis; in his own words (in Theunissen's
translation): "Whoever speaks Thou does not have something for an
object. . . . Where, however, Thou is spoken, there is no something.
Whoever speaks Thou has no something, has nothing." While the
objects of the "It-world" are firmly lodged in time and space, the
members of the "Thou-world" are temporally and spatially discon-
tinuous—a feature deriving from the Thou's "exclusiveness" and lack
of "fixity." With the transgression of the object-domain the I's engagement with the Thou loses the quality of an intentional act; more
precisely, the engagement eludes the distinction between active constitution and passive reaction (to objects). In Theunissen's words: "The
relation to the Thou disappears into a region that lies on the other
side of the difference between action and passion"—a region where
action simultaneously acquires new meaning. Differently put: through
encounter "my" activity comes into its own "in this way, that it gives
itself up as intention and becomes a doing that, at the same time, is
a not doing, to the extent that it is done to me by the Other." The
move beyond action and passivity can also be viewed as the coincidence
of freedom and destiny—to the extent that the latter is genuine destiny
"only as freedom," just as the former is freedom "only as destiny."

Several chapters have been omitted from the present translation
because of the relative distance of their content from contemporary
concerns in the Anglo-American context. These include a chapter
dealing with Buber's "theology of the in-between," which culminates
in the notion of an "eternal Thou" completely irreducible to worldly
objects. Also omitted are discussions of such dialogical thinkers of the
interbellum period as Rosenstock-Huessey, Marcel, and Grisebach and
chapters reviewing various types of rapprochement between transcendentalism and dialogicalism developed by writers initially influenced by Husserl's and Heidegger's arguments (Adolf Reinach, Karl
Loewith, and Ludwig Binswanger). Because of their relevance to ongoing philosophical and sociological debates, the translation does include two appendixes dealing with particularly prominent versions of

the mentioned rapprochement: the "social ontology" of Alfred Schütz and the communication theory of Karl Jaspers. In both cases the author underscores the precariousness of the effected symbiosis—a precariousness due chiefly to the pervasive impact of the transcendentalist legacy. There is also a third appendix contained in the present translation (attached as an excursus to the chapter on Sartre; see section 10 in chapter 6) in which the main themes of the *Critique of Dialectical Reason* are compared with the "dialectic of the Look" as outlined in *Being and Nothingness*.

Since its first publication, *Der Andere* has attracted a considerable amount of attention on the Continent. Different aspects of the study have been taken up and further explored by authors from various disciplines, including philosophers, social theorists, and literary critics. Owing to its innovative insights, primary attention has tended to be given to the discussion of dialogicalism in the third part, particularly to the analysis of Buber's "ontology of the between."[4] Among the more general concepts employed throughout the work, the category of "alter-ation" (in the sense sketched earlier) has found favorable reception for its assistance in clarifying the issues surrounding alienation and reification.[5] Despite its many virtues, the study has not been immune from criticism. Doubts have been raised regarding the book's general structure: the somewhat rigid bifurcation between the two frameworks of transcendentalism and dialogicalism. Rejecting the dichotomy as such, some authors and reviewers have in effect defended a closer interpenetration of transcendentalist and dialogical perspectives, citing as evidence the works of leading phenomenologists.[6] Even if one accepts (as I do) the general plausibility of the bifurcation as an ideal-typical tool, one may still question some aspects of the concrete implemention and the adopted classification scheme. Questions of this kind pertain primarily to the opposition between Buber's dialogicalism and Heidegger's fundamental ontology. Regarding the latter, despite remnants of transcendentalism, one can hardly overlook the persistent critique leveled in *Being and Time* at intentional constitution and the foundational role of subjectivity. If this aspect is taken into account and if, on the other hand—as Theunissen himself asserts—Buber's position remains tied in important ways to the transcendentalist model, the classifications of the two thinkers become more a matter of emphasis.

Notwithstanding the generally sympathetic treatment of his aims, reservations regarding Buber's approach—and regarding dialogicalism in general—are repeatedly voiced in *Der Andere*. Thus commenting on the distinction between "I-It" and "I-Thou" relations, Theunissen notes that both modes can be construed as ego-based "attitudes"— in the Husserlian sense of the term—in which "I am intentionally directed toward something. Everything antithetical . . . rests on the basis of this commonness." More pointedly phrased: "*I*, this human being behaving in such and such a way, am therefore the one who makes something into a Thou or an It." Thus intentionality "compels the Thou to adopt perspectival orientation to the I as the midpoint of the world." At another point the study detects the effects of transcendentalism precisely in its presumed negation or reversal. "It will now be shown," we read, "that, to a considerable extent, the ontology of the between remains, in its execution, a purely negative ontology. This means, above all, that Buber grasps the 'sphere of the between' only in abstraction from the 'sphere of subjectivity.' . . . Accordingly, he thinks of the I-It and the I-Thou relationships in a similar manner, after a model whose ontological basis can only be sustained by the I-It and not by the I-Thou relationship." However, quite independently of the "I-It" model, the conception of encounter as an "I-Thou" relation is not free from doubt. In particular, one may wonder whether the stress on the world-transcending immediacy of encounter and the treatment of the "Thou" as nothingness do not necessarily entail idealist and transcendentalist implications. This issue is acknowledged by Theunissen himself when he queries at one point "whether the conception of the relation to the Thou as the transcending of the It does not in the end follow from a transcendental understanding of being and out of an orientation toward intentionality." The same concern, one might add, has been voiced by Heidegger in his *Letter on Humanism*, where he questions the feasibiliby of grasping existence (*Dasein*) in either "It" or "personhood" categories. Only a properly ontological perspective, attentive to the "openness of Being," he states, brings into view "the clearing of the 'in-between' " in which subject-object (and subject-subject) relations can occur.[7]

The postscript, written after completion of the study (and included in the present translation), contains several afterthoughts relevant to the status of dialogicalism and the merits of competing frameworks. Despite a continued attachment to Buber's goals, the postscript reiterates and reinforces the mentioned reservations regarding implementation. Particularly striking is the author's self-distantiation from a certain existentialist "mood" prevalent at the time that was in danger of reducing dialogical tenets to slogans or "popular currency." On a more substantive level, apprehensions are expressed regarding the strict philosophical viability of dialogicalism when measured against transcendentalist standards. In light of the gulf between aspiration and implementation, one passage even speaks of "the impotence of dialogical thought in comparison with the power of the transcendental project." As Theunissen recognizes, these apprehensions stand in contrast to the confident outlook adopted in *Der Andere*, where, on the whole, transcendentalism is criticized from the vantage point of the "philosophy of dialogue." He writes that the work's approach "is supported by the belief that philosophy is in a position to overcome the de facto negativity of contemporary dialogic in every respect. This belief is not entirely broken, but only subsequently relativized, through a partial skepticism." The main outgrowth of this skepticism is a suspicion that the limitations or shortcomings of dialogicalism coincide ultimately with the boundaries of philosophy itself: "After long hesitation I have arrived at the view that the incapacity of dialogic to account for the origin of the I *purely and simply* out of the meeting with the Thou attests to a fundamental limitation of the philosophy. The philosophy fails, or so it seems to me, at the extreme point of the doctrine of the originality of the between."[8]

While expressing reservations regarding the dialogicalism of the interbellum period, the postscript hints at a new and more favorable assessment of Heidegger's approach (an assessment that may not mesh with the assumption of fixed limits of philosophy—especially if these limits are set by transcendentalism). As Theunissen observes, Heidegger's treatment in the study was prompted in large measure by the adopted scheme of interpretation: the confrontation of two ideal-typical frameworks. This confrontation, he admits, dictated a general "renunciation of all that which already corresponds to dialogical thought in *Being and Time*." Apart from these procedural considerations, the postscript attributes the same deemphasis also to the circumstance that "the positive relation of fundamental ontology to the philosophy of dialogue is not to be met with on the level of the analysis of being-with, but at the higher level of the question of being. The question of being, which guides and encompasses everything in *Being and Time*, must, however, for its part be given up, in order not to extend without limit the interpretation." One may question here the segregation of "being-with" or of interhuman relations from the broader fabric of *Being and Time* and especially from its "all-pervasive" ontological theme.[9] Yet given his methodological premises, one cannot doubt the fairness of Theunissen's comments regarding a certain "perspectival foreshortening" in his study: "While I consider Husserl's transcendental philosophy principally in its futurally significant aspects, I question Heidegger's fundamental ontology with regard to its past. . . . It is clear that, in this way, *Being and Time* cannot be fully evaluated." The postscript, one should add, also draws attention to the more intimate affinity between dialogicalism and Heidegger's later opus. The "substantive proximity" between the two modes of thought, we are told, resides chiefly in the fact that in both instances thinking is focused on language.

The skeptical afterthoughts on dialogicalism, outlined in the postscript, are meant to foster not an uncritical acceptance of transcendentalism but rather a tentative reconciliation of frameworks: "Now insofar as the present investigation wards off the claim to absoluteness on the part of the transcendental project of social ontology, and so establishes the impossibility of such a claim from the side of the philosophy of dialogue, it does in the end aim at *mediation*." In Theunissen's view, the most promising avenue in this direction resides in a genetic or developmental treatment of the I-Other relation, a conception starting from a transcendentally construed ego and leading through various steps to a genuine I-Thou encounter. The adopted starting point, we are told, is justified primarily by the ego's prevalence in a civilized setting; especially in light of the loss of (prereflective or prehistorical) "origins," one must "concede that for us there is no other reality than that which is transcendentally attainable." Once this premise is granted, a genetic approach renders possible an adjudication between the competing frameworks, "allowing us to grant to transcendental philosophy the originality of the beginning and to the philosophy of dialogue the originality of the goal, of the completed end. The beginning would be my individual I, the goal the self that proceeds from the meeting." For purposes of illustration and corroboration Theunissen refers both to some of Marcel's writings and also to Hegelian teachings. "In the ontological history of mankind that Marcel depicts in fragmentary fashion," he notes, "the transcendental relativization of the world is the first epoch, the mundanizing alter-ation of the relativizing subject the second, and the dialogical self-becoming is the third, conclusive epoch." In the context of Hegelian thought, the same genesis appears as the "history of the human spirit, which comes out of its being-for-itself into otherness, and eventually wins itself back again out of alienation through mediation with the Other. . . . On the first step, the I is nothing but an I; on the second, it is with the Other in such a way that it itself becomes an Other; and on the third, it is with itself in being-with-the-Other."

Theunissen's writings published since the first appearance of *Der Andere* elaborate further on intersubjectivity and related themes in a manner sensitive to these afterthoughts and reservations. A prominent common thread linking these writings is a steadily intensified preoccupation with Hegelian thought, a move designed to remedy both the philosophical weaknesses of dialogicalism and its neglect of "temporality," or the historical dimension of human interaction. A study published in 1969, devoted to an examination of the Frankfurt School and especially of Habermas's work, presented a Hegelian (or quasi-Hegelian) critique of the transcendentalist ingredients in "critical theory"—while simultaneously acknowledging affinities between "ideal speech" and dialogical encounter.[10] Theunissen's Hegelian sympathies, one should note, embrace not only the *Phenomenology of Spirit* but extend to Hegel's later work, including his *Science of Logic*. However, while Hegel's mature thought is frequently invoked in recent literature as an antidote to the "existentialist" leanings of the *Phenomenology*, Theunissen's approach never segregates conceptual "dialectics" too rigidly from dialogue and reciprocal struggle for recognition. Thus a study done in 1970 portrayed Hegel's theory of the "absolute spirit" as a "theological-political" doctrine, closely akin (in central aspects) to Buber's "theology of the in-between" and his notion of an absolute encounter.[11] Subsequent writings probed in greater detail the intersubjective elements in Hegel's philosophical outlook in an effort to reveal "the unity that overarches the contrast between dialogical immediacy and dialectical mediation" and to show that "dialogicalism thematizes what is tacitly presupposed in dialectics."[12]

In terms of both volume and depth, the high point of Theunissen's recent writings is a book published in 1978 whose title in English translation reads, *Being and Appearance: The Critical Function of Hegel's Logic*. Devoted to a detailed exegesis of the *Science of Logic*, the book presents Hegel's work not only as culmination of Western metaphysics but also in central portions as a critique of metaphysics: more specifically, of the metaphysics of "substances" as well as the metaphysics of (reflectively constituted) "essences"—perspectives marked respectively by the "indifference" or unrelatedness of elements and by their subordination to dominant categories. In contrast to both indifference and domination, Theunissen postulates as the "normative standard" of Hegel's logic the idea of "communicative freedom" or of a "complete unity of self-relation and other-relation." "Communicative freedom," he writes, "signifies that one part experiences the other not as boundary or limit but as the condition of possibility of its own self-realization." Under ideal circumstances, that is, in a "reality that would have found its substantive 'truth' and thus become fully real," he adds, "everything would be *relatio* to such an extent that the *relata* would not retain their separateness. True reality in this sense is characterized by the specific New Testament coincidence of love and freedom."[13] Although superbly developed in the *Science of Logic*, the idea of communicative freedom is probably not an exclusively Hegelian insight; as it seems to me, the integration of *relata* into a comprehensive *relatio* can also be found— though without the arsenal of conceptual dialectics—in Heidegger's later thought, especially in his notion of *Ereignis* signifying a "gathering" or "appropriation" that allows elements to come into their own without fusion or indifference. Heidegger's later thought—especially his view of the relation between thinking and "holiness"—also seems relevant to the concluding passage of the postscript, where Theunissen writes, that considered "as 'theology' the philosophy of dialogue . . . can only be the philosophy of the kingdom of God. But the kingdom is not God. In it, that thought that admittedly thereby already surpasses itself has an intimation of the splendor of God or of the Holy, which latter is revealed in the Thou without its revelation being able to be such as would permit philosophy to becomes genuine theology, or discourse about God Himself."[14]

Notes

1. See, for example, Karl-Otto Apel, *Towards a Transformation of Philosophy*, translated by Glyn Adey and David Frisby (London: Routledge and Kegan Paul, 1980); Jacques Derrida, *Writing and Difference*, translated by Alan Bass (Chicago: University of Chicago Press, 1978).

2. Theodor W. Adorno, *Negative Dialektik* (Frankfurt: Suhrkamp Verlag, 1966), p. 172.

Introduction

3. See especially Michael Theunissen, *Der Begriff Ernst bei Søren Kierkegaard* (Freiburg: K. Alber, 1958); "Das Kierkegaardbild in der neueren Forschung und Deutung," *Deutsche Vierteljahresschrift für Literaturwissenschaft und Geistesgeschichte*, 32:576–612 (1958); "Intentionaler Gegenstand und ontologische Differenz; Ansätze zur Fragestellung Heideggers in der Phänomenologie Husserls," *Philosophisches Jahrbuch*, 70:344–362 (1963); "Bubers negative Ontologie des Zwischen," *Philosophisches Jahrbuch*, 71:319–330 (1964).

4. See especially Jochanan Bloch, *Die Aporie des Du: Probleme der Dialogik Martin Bubers* (Heidelberg: Lambert Schneider, 1977); Hans Duesberg, *Person und Gemeinschaft* (Bonn: Bouvier, 1970); Gerhard Bauer, *Zur Poetik des Dialogs* (Darmstadt: Wissenschaftliche Buchgesellschaft, 1969). In part this literature is influenced also by another study that appeared almost simultaneously with *Der Andere*: Bernhard Casper, *Das dialogische Denken* (Freiburg: Herder, 1967).

5. See, for example, Jochen Hörisch, *Die fröhliche Wissenschaft der Poesie* (Frankfurt-Main: Suhrkamp, 1976).

6. See, for example, Bernhard Waldenfels, *Das Zwischenreich des Dialogs* (The Hague: Martinus Nijhoff, 1971); Ernst Tugendhat, *Der Wahrheitsbegriff bei Husserl and Heidegger* (Berlin: W. de Gruyter, 1967).

7. Martin Heidegger, *Über den Humanismus* (Frankfurt-Main: Klostermann, 1949), pp. 16, 36.

8. These comments are qualified by recognition of the greater intellectual courage of dialogicalism in comparison with traditional philosophy: "If philosophizing means to venture into the terrain of the as yet unthought even at the risk of shipwreck, then the impotence of dialogicalism is actually more genuinely philosophical than the power of transcendentalism, which yields less problematic conclusions only by taking fewer risks."

9. I have tried to present an interpretation of "being-with," or cobeing, differing from Theunissen's, in my *Twilight of Subjectivity: Contributions to a Post-Individualist Theory of Politics* (Amherst: University of Massachusetts Press, 1981), pp. 56–71.

10. Theunissen, *Gesellschaft und Geschichte: Zur Kritik der kritischen Theorie* (Berlin: W. de Gruyter, 1969).

11. *Hegels Lehre vom absoluten Geist als theologisch-politischer Traktat* (Berlin: W. de Gruyter, 1970).

12. "Vorrede zur zweiten Auflage," p. ix; compare, for example, "Begriff und Realität," in *Denken im Schatten des Nihilismus* (Darmstadt: Wissenschaftliche Buchgesellschaft, 1975), pp. 164–195.

13. *Sein und Schein: Die Kritische Funktion der Hegelschen Logik* (Frankfurt-Main: Suhrkamp Verlag, 1978), pp. 45–46, 49.

14. Compare Heidegger's comments in *Über den Humanismus*: "Only the truth of Being renders possible thought about the nature of the holy. Only the nature of the holy renders possible thought about the nature of divinity. Only the nature of divinity renders it possible to think and articulate what the term 'God' might mean" (pp. 36–37). Theunissen's postscript specifically refers to the notion of *Ereignis* as the gathering of earth and heaven, mortals and immortals.

The Other

Introductory Remarks on the Scope and Method of the Investigation

Thematic Scope

Few issues have exercised as powerful a hold over the thought of this century as that of "the Other." It is difficult to think of a second theme, even one that might be of more substantial significance, that has provoked as widespread an interest as this one; it is difficult to think of a second theme that so sharply marks off the present— admittedly a present growing out of the nineteenth century and reaching back to it—from its historical roots in the tradition. To be sure, the problem of the Other has been thought through in former times and has at times been accorded a prominent place in ethics and anthropology, in legal and political philosophy. But the problem of the Other has certainly never penetrated as deeply as today into the foundations of philosophical thought. It is no longer the simple object of a specific discipline but has already become the topic of first philosophy. The question of the Other cannot be separated from the most primordial questions raised by modern thought.

Generally speaking, "the Other" comprehends all those concepts by means of which contemporary philosophy has sought to set out the structure of being-with, or its original transcendental form. Thus, among other things, it comprehends the difference between the "Thou" on one side and the "alien I"—the "alter ego" or being-with-the-Other—on the other side. Concepts such as these already imply a decision with respect to what the Other originally is. The philosophers dealt with in the first two parts of this work belong to those who seek the most original being of the Other in the alien I, or in some existential modification of the alien I. In contrast, the thinkers presented in the third part are characterized by the fact that, for them, the Other is originally only to be encountered in the Thou, as the "second person" of the personal pronoun. For them, the original being of the Other is to be found in the one who is addressed, in the partner of discourse or of "dialogue." The extent to which this "philosophy of dialogue"—which, following one of its representatives,[1] and for the sake of brevity, will from now on be known as "dialogicalism"—is to be seen in opposition to the position of the philosophers discussed in the first two parts will only become apparent in the light of what Husserl had in mind when he called his thought "transcendentalism."[2] At this point we only want to stress that, on the basis of the difference between their starting points in the alien I and in the Thou, a distinction has already been established between transcendental philosophy and the philosophy of dialogue.

However abstract and formal these conceptual distinctions may appear, they do nevertheless provide an indication of the thematic limits of the investigation. Above all, they help to explain why, in the third part, philosophers such as Johannes Volkelt, Max Scheler, and Karl Jaspers are not taken into account. Although these thinkers do speak of the "Thou," they most certainly do not mean the Thou in the strict sense of dialogicalism, that is, the "second person." Jaspers is much more concerned with the "other self," and Volkelt and Scheler understand by the "Thou" solely and simply the "alien I."[3] Both the other self[4] and the alien I[5] keep the representatives of dialogical thought from the Thou.

But the contrast between transcendental philosophy and the philosophy of dialogue shows, at the same time, that those who see the Other as alien I have not thereby gained the right to be presented in the first two parts of our investigation. What justifies the inclusion of material in these parts is not its starting out from the alien I but from transcendental philosophical premises that are in any case necessary to the interpretation of the primordial Other as alien I or being-with-the-other. More exactly, the necessity in question springs from the peculiar conceptual approach of the modern transcendental philosophy inaugurated by Husserl. It is on account of its primary concern with the subjective constitution of the world that this philosophy is transcendental. Inasmuch as it poses the question of the Other in connection with the problem of world constitution, it can only grasp the Other as the alien I that exists, as does one's own, as the subjective pole of the world. Outside transcendental philosophy in this sense we find, in addition to the projects of Volkelt, Scheler, and Jaspers, the entire empathy psychology represented by such figures as Wilhelm Dilthey, Ernst Troeltsch, Eduard Spranger, and Max Weber, all of whom aimed to contribute to our understanding of the Other from the standpoint of a humanistic hermeneutics.

Thus transcendental philosophy and the philosophy of dialogue are not the only positions from which the thought of the first half of the twentieth century approached "the Other." Nevertheless, it still makes sense to undertake an investigation into both of these positions under the general rubric of the problem of the Other. For, to a certain extent, through their very antagonism, the standpoints that we have selected constitute the extreme limits comprising all the other possibilities of thematizing the Other that have actually been developed to date. But we should not be taken to mean thereby that, from now on, the horizon for any possible handling of the theme has already been marked out. On the contrary, the question has to be left open whether the disjunction of the Thou and the alien I suffices to cover the field in its entirety. There is no reason why the being of the Other should not be brought to light as something that cannot be fitted into the category of either the Thou or the alien I. However, in a historical perspective, that is, with reference to the present situation of philosophical thought, all nontranscendental and nondialogicalist attempts to develop a theory of the Other come across either as derivative modifications or as mixed forms of transcendentalism and dialogicalism. They can be either traced back to one of the two extreme positions or, in the final analysis, situated between them.

A few examples will help to illustrate the foregoing. Not only the doctrines of imitators but also those that can only be established on the basis of transcendental philosophy or the philosophy of dialogue are derivative. The posthumous publications of Ortega y Gasset[6] must be seen as a sheerly imitative reflection of the transcendental conception, inasmuch as they transfer Husserl's theory of intersubjectivity to the plane of Heidegger's analysis of being-with. On the other hand, both empathy psychology and the humanistically oriented hermeneutics of the Other are original constructions, which, although they did in part emerge before the transcendental philosophy of the Other, nevertheless could only be properly justified with reference to the latter. The social philosophy of Alfred Schütz, which is discussed in appendix I as an illustration of the impossibility of developing a dialogical philosophy on a transcendental basis, serves as a noteworthy example of the attempt to bolster up a hermeneutics of the Other—which had already been developed before the transcendental philosophy of the Other in a form given to it by Max Weber—with the resources made available by transcendental philosophy.

In the third part of our investigation, we take note of systems based upon the philosophy of dialogue. Even thinkers whose positions are to be located at varying points between the two extremes, thinkers such as Georg Simmel and Johannes Volkelt, will be touched upon. To what extent Jaspers belongs here will be more exactly specified in appendix II. Whereas he, from a historical perspective, already distances himself from dialogical thought, Scheler and Volkelt, despite their starting point in the alien I, are well on the way to this position. Indeed, they approach it precisely through their affirmation of interpersonal immediacy, whose very denial separates Jaspers from dialogicalism. Once a supporter of that extreme mediation founded in an inference from analogy—a position that was attacked by Theodor Lipps at the same time that it was rejected by Husserl[7]—Volkelt later accords to the experience of the "Thou" an immediacy that is intended to render redundant not only any mediation through inference and explicit reproduction but also the kind of mediation through association assumed by Husserl.[8] Over and above the recognition of this complete immediacy, Scheler takes a further step in the direction of the philosophy of dialogue. With his descriptions of sympathetic joy and sorrow, love and hate, he penetrates through to the concrete richness of what Buber called "the dialogical life." And there can be no doubt that with phenomenal analyses of this kind he goes beyond his own point of departure in the alien I.

Although our investigation into transcendentalism and dialogicalism can, to a certain extent, throw light upon the entire field of interpersonal philosophy, nevertheless, the area of research that lies before us will be restricted by limits quite other than those introduced by the limitation of the theme to the extreme positions. In particular, supplementary limitations are to be found on three scores. First, on the score that even the material that does fall within the province of transcendental or dialogical philosophy cannot, by any means, be fully taken into consideration. The reader will find many names missing, particularly the names of non-German authors, and much of the material will only be sketched out. This is the reverse side of the method set out below. In principle, it is a matter of a deliberate refusal to undertake anything like a history of the problem, which is still far too close to us to be treated from the remote standpoint of the historian. Even the presentation of dialogicalism, which, given the inclusion of less well known writers, might appear to be historical in character, cannot in reality, and on account of its overall design, support such a claim.[9]

The refusal of any historical presentation accounts for a second limitation that can also be explicitly stated. This second limitation consists in the fact that the present investigation does not really attempt to go back to the historical roots of the modern philosophy of the Other. Such an attempt would require a historical study reaching back to the nineteenth century, and even to the eighteenth century. Even the philosophy of dialogue, which, on account of its contempt for Scholastic metaphysics, could pretend to disregard tradition, was nurtured on the linguistic philosophy of Hamann, Jakob Grimm, and Wilhelm von Humboldt, as well as on Jacobi's philosophy of faith, Fichte's ethics, the insights of the Romantics, the early thought of Hegel, and Feuerbach's "philosophy of the future."[10] The present investigation was originally so broadly conceived as to include all these attempts. After the extent of the material had forced a restriction to the twentieth century, a neglect of earlier periods was the price that had to be paid for the composition of the work in its present form, that is, in the form of a systematic presentation.[11]

Even as a systematic presentation this work is subject to an essential limitation that is listed here as the third and last but is in reality perhaps the most important of all. In coming to terms with this limitation we shall at the same time be fulfilling the task of specifying more precisely just what is meant by the term "social ontology" in our subtitle. The limitation in question will be both clarified and obscured by this title. More exactly, it will be brought into focus insofar as we mean social *ontology*—whereas it will run the risk of losing this focus insofar as we mean *social* ontology. The term social "ontology" not only serves to express the fact that the Other has today gained access to first philosophy. It should also suffice to distinguish the theme of our investigation from the subject matter of social philosophy in general and from the individual social sciences. However, the very distinction that we have established here can easily be obscured by the nomenclature "social" ontology, since contemporary linguistic usage tends to reserve the concept of the social for that kind of societal phenomenon with which sociology in particular is concerned. Thus it is all the more essential to establish, from the beginning, that the present investigation is aimed at something different from the sociologically significant phenomenon of the social. Our objective is certainly that "bilateral bond" of which Simmel speaks in his "sociology," but not the social reality of the objective structure that, according to Simmel, gets built up on the basis of the "bilateral bond." Indeed, it is our conviction that an accessible path to the constitution of the social structure can be opened up from neither a transcendental nor a dialogical standpoint. For this reason we bring our analyses to a close at the point where those thinkers who followed this theme tried to pursue such a course. To this extent, the social ontology delineated in our investigation stands in contrast not only to empirical sociology but also to every attempt to establish a philosophical foundation for sociology. Of the earlier attempts of this kind, that undertaken by Simmel probably stands closest to our own, precisely because Simmel always respected the qualitative difference between the bilateral bond and the social group, while Alfred Vierkandt already saw in the bilateral bond the focal point of social objectivity.[12] Leopold von Wiese, on the other hand, actually reduces the objectivity of the social structure to the peculiar processional nature of bilateral bonding.[13] However, the limits of Simmel's theory of elementary relations are also clearly drawn in that these relations will not be considered here from the standpoint of their contribution to social solidarity.

As a result of the above, a question clearly arises as to why the analyses that we are about to offer should be presented as "studies in contemporary social ontology." Three answers to this question are in order. In the first place, a widely diffused linguistic usage can never, for all that, take on the character of a binding norm. In the second place, it is perfectly appropriate to accord the concept "social" a meaning that enables it to be extended to every type of relation to the Other, including the presocial. And in the third place, two thinkers who play a critical part in the present investigation, namely, Husserl and Reinach, do actually interpret this concept in this way. If they call an act "social," they do so not with reference to its formative social function but simply because it is directed toward the Other in an original manner. Nothing stands in the way of our following them and so christening a philosophical science with the name "social ontology," a name that would otherwise have to be transcribed by means of long-winded formula.

Method

What remains to be said on method to a certain extent continues our account of the limits of the investigation. It has already been emphasized that this investigation makes no claim to complete historical coverage. We must now explain the positive meaning behind that claim. In the first place, it means that our primary concern is with the reflective positions we have typified. These positions will have to be developed out of the wealth of available material. Thus in the first part we shall not report on a whole range of theories constructed on the same basis as Husserl's theory of intersubjectivity. Rather, Husserl's theory will have to represent all the others in an exemplary fashion. Then, instead of painting a complete historical picture of the repercussions of Husserl's theory of intersubjectivity in the second part, I am simply going to sketch the creative innovations to which it gave rise, and that solely with a view to offering some idea of how the transcendental philosophical project of social ontology is sustained through the variations of philosophy of consciousness and existential philosophy. The third part proceeds in a similar way. In the first chapter we limit ourselves to an interpretation of the position opposed to transcendental philosophy, taking as our guide one single instance of a philosophy of dialogue, namely, that of Buber.

It should immediately be apparent to the reader that the third part of the investigation does not conform to the methodological principles we have laid down as strictly as does the first. Here both chapters contain numerous allusions to convergences and divergences between Buber's dialogical philosophy and the other approaches to a philosophy of dialogue. This, in a certain respect methodologically inconsistent, procedure is motivated by the same circumstance as that responsible for the third part of the work conveying in part the impression of a historical presentation, namely, that "dialogicalism," to a much greater extent than transcendental social ontology, constitutes a current of thought in which many minds participated. If the rejection of history also excludes consideration of dialogical thought from the standpoint of its historical impact, unearthing parallels should at least make it possible for the reader to gain a general impression of the appeal of the "dialogical principle" to the thought that followed World War I. The extensive treatment of the I-Thou philosophers who were prominent alongside Buber's dialogical philosophy is necessitated by what was mentioned above. While the transcendental project of social ontology is the work of a few exceptional philosophers, the more numerous thinkers through whom dialogical philosophy was taken up again during and after World War I are of lesser importance. Judging by purely philosophical criteria, even Buber himself belongs to the lesser spirits. Consequently the philosophy of dialogue is, so to speak, more poorly represented through Buber's dialogicalism than is transcendental social ontology through Husserl's theory of intersubjectivity. On the other hand, it also follows therefrom that the interpretation of the former position, in contrast to that of the transcendental standpoint, demands the inclusion of other modes of realization.

A further discrepancy between the method of the first two parts and the third part follows from this. Insofar as Husserl's theory of intersubjectivity is relatively well adjusted to its corresponding "ideal typification," we can allow our presentation of a transcendental theory of intersubjectivity to be stated in its own words. On the other hand, for the reasons mentioned, we cannot allow our own idea of a philosophy of dialogue to be drawn from what Buber has to say. Rather, Buber's dialogical philosophy must be formulated in the context of an idea of the dialogical in general that cannot be derived from it. Nor can this idea be derived from any other extant philosophy of dialogue. Thus it remains to reconstruct it out of one's own insight. This will, as a matter of fact, be attempted in the third part of the investigation. The idealized, radicalized, and purified goal toward which the philosophy of dialogue progresses serves there as the yardstick of the presentation as well as of the criticism. It should also be stated that the idea to be constructed is by no means the subjective product of the interpreter. However, while it might be impossible to read an "ontology of the between" *off from* any historically developed philosophy of dialogue, it will still be possible to read it *out of* the totality of these philosophies, namely, as that principle to which the thinkers in question themselves conform.

In accordance with this procedure of presenting reflectively formalized positions from more or less representative models, the interpretion of an author is, in both parts of the investigation, oriented once again around one particularly exemplary text chosen as a model from the complete works of the author. However, in this connection, a distinction should be drawn between the foundational character of the first two chapters and what is constructed on this basis in the third. With regard to the fundamental significance of Husserl and Buber, the totality of their writings is evaluated throughout. In the case of writers handled in the second chapter, this is in general not necessary, since, in most cases, each author's social ontology was published in a single text. But even here, where several works of a social-ontological character are available, I select—when there are no other grounds for not doing so—only one, namely, the one that seems best to meet the function of providing a model.[14] The difference between this procedure and that employed in the foundational chapters, in which the relevant complete works provide the requisite documentation, is quite insignificant in view of the generality that must be assumed insofar as the interpretation of Husserl and Buber is also undertaken in accordance with a model text. The interpretation of Buber's dialogical philosophy can therefore, thanks to its unity, be carried out in the form of an analysis of his main philosophical work, and in such a way that citations from other writings simply serve to strengthen and support the interpretation. In the course of the critique of Husserl, on the contrary, it is necessary to go into a variety of texts in separate analyses, due to a certain lack of unity in the transcendental theory of intersubjectivity, which Husserl developed in a whole series of approaches.[15]

The orientation toward, or rather the limitation to, a single model text is justified, above all, by the advantage that arises out of the renunciation of any summary survey. On the positive side, instead of a summary survey, close attention to specific texts, to whose style our interpretation attempts to adjust, allows for the possibility of a differentiation that would never be achieved if the details were ignored. Not least of all, this possibility must be seized upon simply because it is only by this means that the danger of schematization can be resisted, a danger that arises out of that very same procedure. It alone is capable of protecting the individuality of the thinker against the consequences of the thought process.

In any case, in order to enjoy this advantage, we should have to suffer the disadvantage of excessive length and breadth. To be sure, the disadvantageous consequences could be diluted by an artificial device that might be called "change of tempo"—if such an arrogant expression is to be permitted. By this it is meant that the comprehensiveness of the treatment of the basic positions is balanced, to a certain extent, by the brevity of those passages in which secondary positions are dealt with or a parenthetical glance is cast over the multitude of historical forms of development. While the investigation into Husserl's theory of intersubjectivity or Buber's dialogical philosophy proceeds with appropriate slowness, the pace of our presentation with respect to Heidegger and Sartre is rather swift. Still, the need to linger on the texts sets lower bounds on rigor. Thus the most complete brevity can only be achieved where the principle of textual interpretation is dispensed with. On the other hand, even the analysis of secondary positions brings with it a certan lengthiness, insofar as, and to the extent that, the reproduction of the thought is guided by the inner movement of a work that is complete in itself.

Such a movement arises principally out of a distinction intrinsic to the work, the distinction between intention and realization. In proportion to the height of the claim and the real finitude of philosophical thought, the realization falls short of the intention, not just occasionally but of necessity. Accordingly, it seems to me that the interpreter must first bring the intention to light as such and then evaluate the distance between it and the realization. This distance is itself continually varying. A philosophical text subsists in a continual movement in the direction of its intentions, which it not only either realizes or fails to realize but which it can approximate to varying degrees and from which it can retreat in a variety of directions. At times it is faithful to its intentions; at times it subverts them. The supposition that all of this is essential to the understanding of the text is perhaps the most important methodological presupposition of the following interpretation.

I

The Original Transcendental Project of Social Ontology: Husserl's Theory of Intersubjectivity

1

The Basis of Husserl's Theory

1 The Fundamental Determinations of Egological Subjectivity

Edmund Husserl's social ontology, which makes its appearance as a theory of transcendental intersubjectivity, occupies a special place in the system of his phenomenology. It forms one of the two basic disciplines into which phenomenological philosophy is divided;[1] moreover, it is the second in order and so constitutes the keystone of the system. It seeks to answer the questions that "egology" leaves in its train, the very egology with which phenomenology takes its start. Before we present, interpret, and examine the presuppositions of this social ontology, we must therefore gain an insight into this egology and so into the whole of transcendental phenomenology. This will be the task of our first, introductory chapter.

The most exhaustive treatment of Husserl's theory of intersubjectivity is to be found in the fifth and last of *Cartesianische Meditationen* [*Cartesian Meditations*] (CM). Consequently, it behooves us to present the fundamentals of this theory as the guiding principle behind that idea of phenomenology that is programmatically sketched out in the four previous meditations. This does not mean that we are going to limit ourselves to one single interpretation of the *Cartesian Meditations*. It does mean, however, that other earlier and later writings will only be taken into consideration to the extent that they agree in principle with the systematic outline that lies at the root of that main work (CM XXVII).

Husserl formulates that idea of phenomenology unfolded in the *Cartesian Meditations* in a particularly fruitful way in a passage that is worth noting, since it leads immediately on to the problem of inter-subjectivity. Here we read,[2]

A science whose peculiar nature is unprecedented comes into our field of vision, a science of concrete, transcendental subjectivity, as given in actual and possible transcendental experience, a science that forms the extremest contrast to sciences in the hitherto accepted sense, positive *objective* sciences. Among the latter there is indeed a science of subjectivity, but it is precisely a science of objective subjectivity, the subjectivity of men and other animals, a subjectivity that belongs to the world. Now, however, we are envisaging a science that is, so to speak, absolutely subjective, whose thematic object exists whether or not the world exists. But more than this. It seems as though my (the philosopher's) transcendental ego is and must be not only its initial but its (that is, phenomenology's) sole theme. (CM 68–69:29–30)

In the context of the present investigation we shall not be able to explain to what an extent Husserl's phenomenology is scientific and yet to be distinguished from any positive science.[3] On the other hand, in the interests of an attempt to lay the foundation of the theory of intersubjectivity, the question arises, What is at issue with this sub-jectivity that Husserl represents as the all-encompassing object of his phenomenology? In line with the above-mentioned text, it is, first of all, quite independent of the decision with respect to the being or nonbeing of the world. We shall see later that this statement is specious. The following claim, however, is not specious: the theme of phenom-enology, which, as the most remote counterpart to the objective sci-ences, must also be opposed to the objective sciences of worldly subjectivity, is that subjectivity that *does not belong within the world*. To belong to the world means to be encountered within the world. The phenomenon of phenomenology is, as Husserl says, "extramundane" subjectivity, that subjectivity that is not to be encountered in the world. This, in itself purely negative, determination is of the first importance for Husserl's approach as well as for the entire first part of our in-vestigation. Husserl's whole attempt to recover a truly subjective sub-jectivity, or to keep it "pure," works on the assumption that subjectivity must be freed from all "worldly" elements. And his radicalization of the Cartesian problematic consists essentially in the correction of the "mistake" that Descartes committed when he effectively envisaged the "ego," once again, as a "little residual of the world" (CM 63–64:23–24).

In the text under consideration, Husserl calls worldly subjectivity "animal." This "psychic" subjectivity is endowed with *anima* and *animus*, with "soul" and "spirit." According to Husserl, Descartes reified the "ego" by characterizing it as *mens sive animus* (CM 63:24). In this respect he fell under the traditional sway of psychology, which considered itself as the science of animal subjectivity. According to *Die Krisis der europäischen Wissenschaften und die transzendentale Phänomenologie* [*The Crisis of European Sciences and Transcendental Phenomenology*] (K), however, the object of psychology is an abstract residual, that which, in pre-Cartesian physics, remained over after the sheerly physical body had been subtracted from human being.[4] So human subjectivity is mundane. On the other hand, the subjectivity on which phenomenology is constructed forfeits both its worldliness and its humanhood. To be sure, it is, just like Descartes's "ego"—at least in a certain, still to be specified, sense—an "I." But *this* "I" is not a piece of the world. To say "I am, *ego cogito*" does not therefore mean I, this human being, am (CM 64:25).

Phenomenological subjectivity is not to be found in the world and is not I, this human being. I, however, who write this, am to be found in the world. So is phenomenological subjectivity something like a supraindividual, not empirically perceptible, "subject in general," a "universal subject" set over against myself and yourself and all other empirical subjects? The answer to be found in our text is no: "It seems as though my (the philosopher's) transcendental ego is and must be not only its initial but its (that is, phenomenology's) sole theme." Admittedly, the sentence is ambiguous. Is it apparently or only seemingly so? Both. In relation to "the individual object," "it seems" has this meaning: it is only seemingly so. So much is clear from the further course of the text. To Husserl's way of thinking, my transcendental ego is not, in reality, the only object of phenomenology because, so far from remaining an egology, phenomenology, as a theory of intersubjectivity, draws the "alter ego" into the investigation (CM 69:30). However, my ego is certainly its "initial" object. Section 95 of *Formale und transzendentale Logik* [*Formal and Transcendental Logic*] (FTL) bears this title: "The Necessity of Starting Out from One's Own Subjectivity."[5] This point of departure never exceeds the bounds of phenomenology as long as it remains an egology. The critical question whether—as Husserl believes—it exceeds these bounds in the theory of intersubjectivity will have to be held over for a later clarification. What is certain is that, according to Husserl, "intersubjective phenomenology" does not leave the basis of one's own subjectivity, even when it transcends it. With equal certainty one can say that when the alter ego is thematized, this basis is not transcended in the direction of a supra-individual "universal consciousness" or a "universal subject."

The most important of the preconditions that have to be fulfilled in order that "the Other" should become a philosophical problem is that the subjectivity that is made the object of philosophical reflection should be my own.[6] In the horizon of a supraindividual, universal subject, the Other cannot become problematic, precisely because its existence is already included therein. In any case, in the particular social ontologies with which we shall be concerned, ownness is understood in a variety of ways, and this variety is itself constitutive of the difference between the particular projects. Ownness in Husserl means something fundamentally different from, for example, ownness in Heidegger. We shall soon be in a position to bring this difference to light. First, however, we must become better acquainted with Husserl's basic approach to ownness. We find it even before early phenomenology gets set up explicitly as "egology." Book I of *Ideen [Ideas]* (Id.I)— which, of the three moments of intentionality, *ego-cogito-cogitatum*, only thematizes the *cogito-cogitatum* in the unity of "consciousness" and largely screens off the ego[7] — already grasps consciousness as "my own consciousness."[8] However, ownness is so fundamental to the explicitly egological phenomenology that without it, it would not be entitled to the name. Egology is called a "self-contemplation" (CM 179:153), a *"self-explication of the ego"* (CM 118:86). This latter is, however, necessarily a "self-explication of *my* ego" (CM 118:86), or a self-investigation of "the knower with respect to itself" (K 100:97).

To be sure, with the characterization of subjectivity as "my own," its presentation as "consciousness in general" or "universal consciousness" is still not denied. It could well be that I have to undertake a self-investigation only because the subjectivity that is to be found in me is the same as that in every empirical subject. In other words, the subjectivity in question could be my own and, in spite of that, a universal subjectivity, provided my individuality did not extend right into it. According to Husserl, even the subjectivity that is responsible for the phenomenal character of phenomenology is mine in the sense that it is "just such an *individual* being" (Id.I 70:112).[9] In it is to be found a "concrete ego existing with an individual content made up of subjective processes, abilities, and dispositions" (CM 67:29). The entire life of consciousness centered on the ego is investigated by phenomenology in its individual being (K 181:178). Thanks to its individuality, the "pure" ego, that is, the ego that has been purified of all "worldly" content, is "in principle different from each stream of consciousness" (Id.I 138:173). One cannot emphasize strongly enough the significance that this supposition has for social ontology. In the first place, it opens the way for a conception of "the Other" as one who is not merely different from me in being this or that other (person) but who, as the I that he is for himself, is quite different from the I that I am for myself. We can also characterize Husserl's insight into the individuality of the pure ego as the recognition of the fact that there is an *extramundane* individuality. Only on this account is Husserl at all able to speak of an experience in the transcendental sphere. For, according to his own established terminology, experience can only have individual being for its object. Just as the characterization of egological phenomenology as "self-explication of the ego" attests to its ownness character, so too does the terminologically determinate title "transcendental experience" (CM 68–70:29–31c, 60:20, 65:26, 67:28) bear witness to the individuality of transcendental subjectivity.

Even the attempt to dull the edge of ownness by reducing extramundane subjectivity to a simple *ideal* possibility of my ego misses the mark. Not only am *I* this extramundane subjectivity, I also *am* it—I, in my factical existence. It is not only distinguished by ownness and individuality but also by *facticity*: "Each of us, as Cartesian meditator, was led back to his trancendental ego . . . as this factical ego." (CM 103:69). Just like the individuality of the transcendental ego, this transcendental facticity is also otherworldly.[10] The "fact of the transcendental ego and the special mode of givenness of its transcendental field" (CM 107:73) is not a mundane fact. The "factualities of the transcendental ego" (CM 104:70) are, as such, necessarily distinct from all worldly facts. It is a question of the specific "facticity of universal transcendental subjectivity itself" (K 181:178). All the subsequent stages of our investigation will be concerned with this extramundane facticity. In the last analysis, any real "progress" that the social ontologies to be discussed later make with respect to transcendental phenomenological social ontology consists in the penetration, domination, and deepening of the extramundane facticity that Husserl brought to the assessment of subjectivity.

In its very unworldliness, phenomenological subjectivity enjoys its own *fullness*, a fullness that precisely does not stem from the world. This fullness encompasses more than merely facticity and individuality. To be sure, it is also true of this individuality that it establishes itself in me before all mundanity. My mundane individuality is due to causality, localization, and temporalization.[11] But if one eliminates all the individual determinations that come to me thereby, there still remains over the "uniquely *original* individual" (Id.II 301—italics are mine). For precisely because the extramundane ego possesses "individuality in itself and through itself. . . . not individuality through causality," the positions that I adopt as "this human being" in "space and time" "do not make the slightest contribution to its being as an *ens per se*. As such it already has in itself its uniqueness" (K 222:218). But it would have no fullness if it were only the momentary experience of an I as "identical pole" of an actually operative *cogitatio*. This momentary I is also already individual in an original way, but it is still relatively empty. It only first acquires fullness when it is extended into its own past and future, when, before all worldly time, it is itself temporal. In the course of this time "habitualities" grow up in it, that is, unworldly "properties of the I" that it fills out in itself. (CM 100–101:66–67). In other words, it becomes historical, though, once again, not world historical, but historical in its own individual sense: "The pure ego of the actual *cogitatio*, which is itself an absolute individual in itself, already possesses individuation. But the ego is not an empty pole, but the bearer of its habitualities, and, for this reason, it has its individual history" (Id.II 299–300). Alongside transcendental ownness, individuality, and facticity, "transcendental *historicality*" (K 212:208—italics are mine) has also to be ascribed to phenomenological subjectivity.[12] This determination is as essential to it as the others. For although, in the aftermath of Cartesian reflection, phenomenology is confronted, in the first instance, with the momentarily actual, pure I of ongoing lived experience, as the apodictically certain, from this point it is still obliged to question back into the streaming *life* of inner time consciousness, in which the individual lived experiences are themselves constituted. So its theme is "the Heraclitean flux of constituting life . . . in its individual facticity" (K 181:177). This flux, the temporally immanent extension of subjectivity, is *one*, and certainly an important, side of the "infinite field of transcendental experience" (CM 69:31), a side that merits phenomenological explication. Only when phenomenology moves beyond the punctuality of the still empty I pole to "explore the tremendous realm of transcendental experience" (CM 68:30) is it able to appropriate for itself the preworldly being of subjectivity. In this way, phenomenology takes an essential step beyond Descartes, whose attempt to grasp the ego as a little residual of the world was doomed to failure precisely because he took the ego, at the same time, as his point of departure, with a view to encompassing outer reality within it (CM 63:24; see also CM 66:27, 69–70:31).

Thus far we have simply expounded a *problem*. The problem is, how phenomenological subjectivity can be I myself in my individual and historical facticity, although it is not what I am, a human being manifesting itself in the world. Clearly, the problem is sharpened by the introduction of a further determination, that of the *absolute*. The object of egology is my factically individual, historical, and, at the same time, absolute subjectivity. For this reason alone phenomenology is, as Husserl puts it in our text, "a, so to speak, absolutely subjective science." This means that it is the "science of transcendental subjectivity as the only absolute entity" (FTL 240:272). But how can I be the absolute entity in my individual and historical facticity? A conclusive answer to this question, as also to the question of the unification of the ownness, individuality, facticity, and historicality of the transcendental ego with its unworldliness and its unhumanness, can only first be attempted in the next section of this chapter. Here it is only possible to prepare the way.

A first hint is already provided by the term "absolute subjectivity." In accordance with this term, absoluteness is not something that hems subjectivity in, but precisely something that breaks out in the most extreme radicalization of subjectivity. Subjectivity is only absolute insofar as it, together with the science that studies it, is absolute subjectivity, that is, ultimately radical subjectivity. But then, what does the concept "absolute" mean? Nothing but that *particular mode of ownness* that Husserl had in mind.[13] My transcendental ego, "this factical ego," is, as such, and in no way in spite of its facticity, "the one and only absolute ego" (CM 103:69). The addition "the one and only" is decisive. It tells us what absolute means. And, at the same time, it reveals how ownness is, and is not to be, understood. Ownness is not to be understood as personal. Phenomenological subjectivity is certainly my I, but this I stands in no relation to a Thou and is not a member of a We. For, just as it transcends the whole of humanity, along with the entire world, so it also transcends "the entire order and division of personal pronouns" (K 188:185). Its absoluteness, or, what amounts to the same thing, its "uniqueness," is also, from a negative point of view, its "personal indeclinability" (K 188:185). Husserl makes the same point when he says that "I," as the *fundamentum inconcussum* of "strict science," am not "one," namely, one I among others: "I am not *an* I that, in a natural sense, still always has its Thou and its We and its community of fellow subjects" (K 188:184). More than this we can say—that I do not communicate with just any Others that are also "I's" for themselves. In the last analysis, we find the following: that I—as absolute subjectivity—*have no knowledge of my equivalent.* The mine of mineness cannot be set off against thineness, his or herness, or ourness.

This brings out the fundamental difference between Husserl's and Heidegger's concepts of mineness. According to Heidegger, the term "mineness" comprises a "statement to the effect that a given I and no other is this entity (that is, *Dasein*)."[14] The words "and no other" are intended to express the differentiation of the I from the (consequently presupposed) Others. My very own *Dasein* is, in its being, one with another *Dasein*. Accordingly, Heidegger grasps mineness as the very personal mineness that Husserl refused on account of its transcendental origin. Of this fact Heidegger himself is aware: "Because *Dasein* has in each instance *mineness*, one must always use a *personal* pronoun when one addresses it. 'I am, you are' " (SuZ 42:68). Heidegger is also perfectly aware of the fact that he has, in this way, located mineness on the ontic plane. To be sure, mineness is in his eyes reckoned among the "fundamental determinants of *Dasein*" (SuZ 117:152). But while existentiality qualifies *Dasein* ontologically, mineness remains an ontic characteristic of *Dasein*, one that is, in the course of the analysis, overlooked to a remarkable degree. So Heidegger explicitly labels the conclusion drawn from this (that *Dasein* is "an I") an "ontic . . . statement" (SuZ 114:150).

In contrast, Husserl's mineness appears as *ontological.* In a more positive way this is brought out by the fact that I and *the* I fall together purely and simply. As absolute subjectivity I am *the I,* or, as Husserl says, the "originary I" (K 187–189:184–186). The originary I is identical with the "absolute" or the "one absolute" ego of earlier writings.[15]

Its absoluteness consists in its "solitude" (K 188:184)—admittedly a solitude that, because there is no I alongside of me, is also free of any longing for community. Precisely for this reason, however, Husserl observes that the ego of egology "is actually called 'I' only by equivocation, although it is an essential equivocation, since, when I name it in reflection, I can say nothing other than: I am it" (K 188:184). This dialectic necessarily belongs together with ontological, transcendental, or absolute mineness. Absolute subjectivity is actually "I" only by equivocation for the same reason that it merits the title "originary I"—because it is not an I and consequently not that which I usually mean when I say I. Whether I am myself authentically or not, I am nevertheless the "sole absolute entity" in my individual, historical facticity.

Among the attributes that, in our text, Husserl ascribes to subjectivity, we have mentioned in our previous reflections unworldliness (which brings unhumanness along with it), mineness (implying individuality, facticity, and historicality), and absoluteness (signifying asociality).

The concepts of the *concrete* and the *transcendental* still await elucidation, however. Phenomenology is "the science of concrete, transcendental subjectivity." Both concepts point in the same direction— and indeed in a different direction from all the determinations that we collected together above. Certainly they too receive their meaning from the relation to the world. But from the standpoint of the concrete and the transcendental, this relation now has to be seen in a positive light. Phenomenological subjectivity has a negative relation to the world insofar as it is not to be encountered in the world. The relation is positive insofar as it is phenomenological subjectivity that first *projects* the world. Husserl calls such a projection "constitution." Its vehicle is "intentionality." Hence the task of phenomenology is the "systematic disclosure of constituting intentionality" (CM 119:86).[16] Inasmuch as constitution means nothing other than "meaning giving," the disclosure of constituting intentionality comes down to the same thing as the "explication of meaning" (CM 119:86).[17] From here we arrive at a conclusive definition of the initial stage of phenomenology as a "consequentially executed self-explication in the form of a systematic egological science, an explication of my ego as subject of every possible cognition and, indeed, with respect to every meaning of what exists, which latter can only have meaning for me, the ego." (CM 118:86).

For this reason, the "science of concrete transcendental subjectivity" is at the same time the "science of the totality of beings" (K 6:8). As apodictically grounded, it is also universal science. For it brings to light *every* meaning of being, of beings that I can only grasp through meaning. We shall see that the universal meaning, a meaning that comprehends those of all individual beings, is the "world-meaning." The science of truly subjective subjectivity is also, accordingly, philosophy as worldly wisdom.[18] It is able to assume such a role precisely because it insists upon the unworldliness of subjectivity. Because it does not take subjectivity to be something individual in the world, to be a subjectivity of the world, it is able to comprehend the entire world as a world of subjectivity. Hence the world is not a supplementary theme situated alongside or following upon subjectivity. Indeed, in connection with the world that belongs to it, Husserl speaks of "subjectivity" and not of the "subject." The subject, which is also admittedly subjective, stands over against the world; subjectivity itself, however, is its world.[19] The concept of the concrete now has the function of accentuating this worldliness. The ego is not already concrete as individual, factical, and historical, but only first insofar as it includes within itself the entire world as its *constitutum*, that is, as "intentional objectivity" or objectivity in the mode of meaning: "From the ego as identical pole, and as substrate of habitualities, we distinguish the ego, taken in full concreteness (the ego taken in full concreteness we propose to call by the Leibnizian name, monad), in that we take, in addition, that without which the ego cannot after all be concrete. The ego can only be concrete in the flowing multiformity of its intentional life, along with the objects meant, and, in the final analysis, constituted as existent for it, in that life" (CM 102:67–68).

While the concept "concrete" only indicates that the world falls within subjectivity, the concept "transcendental" expresses the fact that it is subjectivity that constitutes the world. In accordance with the meaning of the word, it is founded upon the peculiar characteristics of "transcendence," characteristics that we shall have to analyze more closely and that mark out that world dependent upon my meaning-giving activity: "If this '*transcendence*' belongs to the proper sense of the world . . . then the I itself, which bears the latter within itself as an accepted sense and is, on its side, necessarily presupposed by it, should be called *transcendental* in the phenomenological sense. Accordingly, the philosophical problems that arise out of this correlation are called transcendental-philosophical" (CM 65:26). Husserl is only able to say that the world-meaning presupposes the I because he assumes that, conversely, the I in a certain sense also presupposes the world. Without the world, the I cannot be what it is, namely, "concrete transcendental subjectivity." We already noted that, for Husserl, the I cannot be concrete without the objects that are constitutive for it. Now we know that without the world there would be no transcendental I. With hindsight we can see that, at the beginning of our interpretation, we did not account correctly for the thesis that the concrete, transcendental subjectivity is, in its being, "independent of the decision with respect to the being or nonbeing of the world." The ego of egology is not independent of the world purely and simply because it is only concrete inasmuch as it *projects* the world.[20] The dependence of the world on it, as the dependence of the constituted upon the constituting, implies its dependence upon the world, as the quite differently disposed dependence of the constituting upon the constituted.

Insofar as Husserlian phenomenology has to do with the transcendental as world-constituting subjectivity, it is essentially transcendental philosophy; indeed, it is the completed "final form" (K 71:70) of it, in Husserl's sense. I shall utilize this concept of transcendental philosophy, a concept developed out of the world relation, whenever I speak of it in the following investigation. Husserl himself gives me the right to include even non-Husserlian philosophies under this concept. For he himself draws our attention to the fact that he uses the concept of transcendental philosophy, as also that of the transcendental, with an extension that permits this concept to characterize not only a single system, that of Kant and the Kantian school, but also the basic tendency of contemporary philosophy in its entirety (K 100–101:97–98). For my part, I restrict the range of the validity of this concept somewhat further. It is intended to cover all modalities of those forms of thought, but only of those forms of thought that thematize the projection of the world out of subjectivity in such a way that the world becomes its explicit object. The philosophy of the last few centuries since Descartes was certainly always already directed toward the subjective grounding of the world. But Husserl was the first to bring the constitutive relation of subjectivity to the world *as such* into the very center of philosophical attention.[21] According to him, "the whole transcendental problematic" turns upon the relation of my pure I to my worldly subjectivity, to my "soul," and so, in the end, upon "the relation of this I and my life of consciousness to the world itself" (K 101:98).

In the next section, it will be necessary to show how I, the beginning philosopher, am brought face to face with my world-constructing subjectivity. This way is the method of the phenomenological, transcendental, or transcendental-phenomenological "reduction." Insofar as it leads me from my mundane to my extramundane being, it will also become clear how mineness, individuality, facticity, and historicality are compatible with unworldliness and unhumanness in the origination of the world. Whether, and in what way, the starting point in mineness and the determinations implicit in it can be aligned with the method of eidetic reduction will then be investigated in the third section, which, because it is intended to secure our presentation of egology against possible objections, has more of the character of a simple appendix. The theme of the last section of this chapter comes to grips more immediately and more substantially with the explanation of the phenomenological reduction. In the next section we shall take up the world in the way in which the phenomenological reduction has predisposed us to do it. We shall have to describe in outline those features that are responsible for the constitution of the world by me and without the cooperation of the Other. Thereby we shall fix the point egology is able to reach, at which the further work (of constitution) is handed over to a transcendental theory of intersubjectivity.

2 The Phenomenological Reduction as the Discovery of World-Constituting Subjectivity

Reduction[22] means leading back. In the phenomenological reduction we are led back to the origin of something.[23] We know what the origin is: concrete transcendental subjectivity. We must now come to terms with what it is that is reduced. First, however, a word on the act of reduction itself. As regression to the origin it has no simple meaning, not even one that is primarily negative (Id.I 67:110). To be sure, it is made clear that that which has to be reduced is not itself the origin. However, in that the reduction brings it back to its origin, it helps it to become what it is. As regression to the origin, it also does not actually posit one thing as antithetically set over against another. For that to which the reducible is brought back is *its own* origin. These preliminary remarks are necessary because Husserl's nomenclature readily lends itself to an impression of something negative. In *Ideas* he identifies the phenomenological reduction with the *epoché*. However, he translates these concepts, taken over from Stoic and Skeptical texts, by means of expressions in which the negative connotation predominates almost exclusively. The *epoché* is a disconnection (Id.I 65:109), a bracketing (Id.I 109), a making no use of (Id.I 65:109), a setting out of action (Id.I 65:109), a play (Id.I 72:114), a positing of value (CM 53:12). Moreover, in other places, Husserl distinguishes between reduction and *epoché*. The identification and the differentiation of the two are equally possible because reduction and *epoché* are two sides of one and the same reality. The reduction is a reduction *to*, and so emphasizes the origin to which it leads back. The *epoché* is a holding off . . . *from* (Id.I 66:109), and so is immediately directed to that which is reduced. Since the entire movement is directed from that which is reduced to its origin, Husserl, in *Crisis*, takes the *epoché* to be the presupposition that makes the reduction possible (K 154). Hence the positive aspect of the reduction, in the broad sense, gravitates around the reduction in the narrow sense, while the negative aspect characterizes the *epoché*. Consequently, thanks to the dual aspect (positive-negative) of the *whole* movement, the *epoché* also participates in the positive aspect, while the reduction, which is quite distinct from the former, also participates in the negative aspect.

A more concrete understanding of that which is initially only abstractly outlined as the unity of the positive and the negative becomes available to us when we look beyond the formal character of the act and take into consideration what has to be reduced. At first this unity is disclosed by Husserl in the guise of a contradiction. On the one hand, Husserl wants that which has to be reduced to be "radically altered" (Id.I 63:107; see also EP.II 10–11, K 151:148) in the course of the regressive movement. On the other hand, we are told that "we alter nothing" (Id.I 65). That which has to be reduced will be radically altered insofar as it has been divorced from the origin and yet, at the same time, makes itself out to be the origin. Insofar as it does this, it is called the *natural attitude*. The reduction maintains a purely negative relation to the natural or "naive" attitude. As the discovery of the origin, phenomenology remains an overcoming of naiveté as the forgetfulness of the origin. On the other hand, that which has to be reduced is not in any way altered insofar as it is only that which has arisen from the origin and is therefore still retained within it. The

only effect that the reduction has upon it is that it locates it in the
origin in which it is intrinsically rooted. This positive kernel in the
negative shell of the *epoché* brings Husserl by diverse, but not always
entirely perspicuous, means to say that as "suspension of judgment"
the *epoché* is compatible with the conviction of the validity of the
judgment from which it withholds judgment (Id.I 66:109). That which
is bracketed remains as it is between brackets (Id.I 65:108); that which
is suspended is still there outside the configuration of the connection
(Id.I 65:108). Most appropriately, Husserl formulates the state of affairs
in a continually recurring phrase: that which has to be reduced does
not "disappear" but is recovered as "phenomenon" (K 155:152). As
phenomenon, it is that which has been brought back to the origin,
and so it has become original itself, manifesting itself in an original
way. This regression to the origin is accomplished as a purification of
that which has to be reduced from what the natural attitude added
to it, that is, a spurious originality accorded to it out of a forgetfulness
(Husserl says "anonymity") of the true origin. It is important to hold
on to this because it can all too easily be lost sight of as a result of
Husserl's own formula, more particularly as a result of the frequently
recurring assurance that, as phenomenon, the reduced content is retained exactly as it was for me before the reduction (K 155:152). If
this were the case, the phenomenon to be recovered would be the
same as the object of the natural attitude, which cannot be the case
if phenomenology as σωζειν τα φαινομενα is truly to overcome naiveté.

What is to be reduced, in the neutral sense of that which has sprung
from the origin, has to be everything that is "transcendent" for concrete,
transcendental subjectivity and its conscious life. Herein belong, alongside the individual realities encountered in the real world, all idealities,
all universal objectivities (Id.I 140:175), together with logic (Id.I 142:172,
CM 53:13), the positive sciences (CM 53:13), and the ontologies (Id.I
143:178) related to them. Since, according to Husserl, the ideal world
is grounded in the real, the logical and idealizing sciences are also
grounded in everyday life, the very life in the course of which we are
preoccupied with individual objects in the real world. In the first
instance, this world has to be described as it is naively referred to in
Ideas as the *world of the natural attitude* (Id.I 57:10). At no point in the
text does Husserl delineate, in so many words, the schema that we
are working out. Rather, we must piece it together out of the totality
of the individual statements. Nevertheless, the key to the doctrine of

the reduction in general is to be found in this schema. More important, in the further course of our investigation this schema will clarify the dominant role played by the theory of intersubjectivity in the overall framework of the problem of the natural attitude.

I—"this human being," one among the "human beings of natural life"—experience the world as "surrounding world" (Id.I 57:101). This does not mean that I only experience a segment of the world. In a certain sense, the entire world, that is, being as a whole, is known to me through and through. But this whole can never be objectified in all its parts at one and the same time and in one and the same manner. For that would only be possible if I were located outside of it. But I stand within the totality of the world. Wherever I go, wherever I stay, I am always at the center of the world. The term "surrounding world" expresses precisely this: The world is always around me. It is necessarily centered upon me. Husserl reads this orientational character primarily off the spatial perspective of the world of things, the totality of "things pure and simple" (Id.I 59:103). The thing that I actually perceive is continually surrounded by a "perceptual field" as the "central environment" (Id.I 58:102). To this region there belong all objects that, admittedly, are not perceptible from the standpoint of my present location, but that I more or less clearly and explicitly "know," so that, at any time, I can direct the ray of my attention upon them. But even with the copresent "circuit," the resources of the surrounding world are still not exhausted. Rather, this circuit is once again "surrounded by an undetermined actuality of which one is hardly aware" (Id.I 58:102). For me, the world is just this whole made up of the actual perceptual field, the surrounding circuit of the copresent, and this horizon. Accordingly, the world, insofar as it is my "natural environment," is, as it were, ordered around me, the center, in concentric circles. However, it has such a structure not only in its spatial extension and not only as pure thing-world. From a temporal perspective too I constitute the center point of my now-existence, which is first of all encompassed by the present in a broad sense and then by the known past and the living future as also, in the end, by the unknown, no longer immediately apprehended past and the lifeless, not yet anticipated, future (Id.I 59:103). Similarly, the surrounding world is, as "world of values, world of goods, practical world" (Id.I 59:103) oriented around me. "Use objects" (Id.I 59:103), for instance, are at any time at hand or not at hand. The same goes for the common world, the world in which I circulate every day with my fellow human beings. It is divided up into the narrow world of relatives, acquaintances, and friends and the featureless world of strangers (Id.I 59–60:103). Just as things are near or far, so one's fellows are also near or far. So they too are subject to the (not only spatial) law of perspectivity as the fundamental law of the actually experienced world. In this perspective, however, the world reveals itself as a world that is *dependent* upon me, the subject of experience. How, and in what perspective, objects appear to me depends upon me. Only because, at this moment, I am here, where I am, do they appear to me in the way in which they do. Should I change my perspective, the aspect of things would also change. *I* decided what, in general, an object should explicitly be for me. And it is also up to me to decide what, in each case, the perceptual field, the copresent and the indefinite horizon, amounts to.

The "world of the natural attitude" possesses another feature that is radically opposed to this dependence upon the I. I "find it before me in an immediately intuitable manner as existing" (Id.I 57:101). It is the "totality of that which I find before me in the natural attitude" (Id.I 62:106), or, as it is called in *Crisis*, the "universe of the present at hand" (K 153:150). Even as this universe, it also, alongside "mere things," encompasses "all other human beings who present themselves in my surrounding world" (Id.I 61:104). According to Husserl's intention, the concept "present at hand" is directed toward a fundamental in-dependence of the world from the I. The things of the world are *"present at hand* whether I pay any special attention to them, whether I am involved with them in a perceiving, thinking, feeling, willing manner or not" (Id.I 57:101).

That the world should be both dependent and independent of the I is not a contradiction for the natural attitude itself. It is not disturbed by it because it has always already committed itself to the priority of independence. It is thereby committed to the priority of the world over the I, the only one that it knows of. The world is dependent upon me to the extent that I *bring order to* it. However, I, the I of the natural attitude, understand by the independence of the world from me not just this, that prior to and in the absence of my ordering activity the world is present at hand. Far more, I envisage it as the fact that *I have my place in the world*. For this reason, the characteristic in question, the being present-at-hand of the world, takes on the character of being prior to me. I not only find the world, I find *myself* in the already existing world. In the unity of a dependence and an independence of the world upon the I, the world of the natural attitude is "the world in which I find myself, which is at the same time my surrounding world" (Id.I 60:103). Finding myself in the world, I posit my ego as itself belonging to the world (Id.I 63:106), as a worldly being amidst other worldly beings or as a member (Id.I 59:103) of the world. I also represent my relation to the world in the same manner: "In this manner I find myself in wakeful consciousness (at all times and without being able to change it), standing in relation to . . . the world. It is continually present at hand for me, and I am myself a member of it" (Id.I 59:103). "I am continually present to myself as someone who perceives, represents, thinks, feels, desires, and so forth, and thereby I find myself related, in present experience, to the fact-world that is constantly about me" (Id.I 60:104). This means that inasmuch as I conceive of myself as part of the world order, I have to recognize that my ordering activity is part of the world order. I look upon my relation *to* the world as a fact that belongs *in* the world order.

This integration in the world order is what makes me into a *human being* and my consciousness into a *soul* (EP.II 71). Consequently it makes me into what I, as a transcendental subjectivity, am not, into a non-transcendental, natural, I. As a result, it (this integration in the world order) is the basic event of the natural attitude itself. It does not appear as a subsequent addition to the natural consciousness of the dependence of the I and to the naive belief in the independence of the world from the I, but, from the first, determines the specifically natural meaning of the dependence of the I upon the world, as well as the independence of the world from the I. Just as it gives the meaning of being-before-me to ego independence, so it qualifies the dependence of the world on the I as being the dependence (circumscribed by the world totality) of beings (confronting me in the world) upon me as an equally worldly being. In this way ego dependence, the relativity of worldly appearances, will be ascribed to the psychophysical constitution of this being, human being. The world itself, however, will be disburdened of it. In this way the natural attitude is liberated from the problem that the universality of ego dependence poses. Even if the *whole* world, as surrounding world, *appears* in a perspectival orientation, it still rests completely independently "in itself" as that which is clearly first and most primordial.

This is the "world of the natural attitude" whose "general thesis" has to be suspended by means of the *epoché*. As the *general thesis*, the natural attitude *itself*, that is, the *whole* naively apprehended world, is that which has to be suspended:[24] "We put out of action the general thesis that belongs to the essence of the natural standpoint; we place in brackets whatever it includes with regard to the ontic. This entire natural world, therefore, which is continually 'there for us,' 'present-at-hand,' and will ever remain there, is a 'fact world' of which we continue to be conscious, even though it pleases us to put it into brackets" (Id.I 67:110). The totality of the natural world lends itself to an *epoché* from a particular point of view, and Husserl characterizes this point of view in the quoted passage with the concept "fact-world." The concept of the fact-world is admittedly ambiguous. It signifies that which has to be overcome just as well as that which has to be recovered, the naively apprehended and the entirely different transcendental reality that alone "remains" after the reduction. The naively signified reality is, however, the being-before-me whose being present-at-hand is qualified by my integration in the world. This being-before-me is therefore the inhibited fact-world: "I inhibit the being-for-me in advance of the world" (Id.I 68:111; see also 67:110, K 153:150). Consequently, my integration also belongs to it. The transcendental reduction purifies "the psychological phenomena of what is conferred upon them by reality, and, therewith, integration in the real 'world,' of what is conferred upon them by a real world in general" (Id.I 6:44). However, inasmuch as this integration not only psychologizes my consciousness but also humanizes my ego, through the *epoché*, I also, and above all, forfeit my humanness. Through the phenomenological "rendering inoperative of the being status of the objective world," consciousness loses "the meaning of a real layer of human reality belonging to the world and already presupposing the world" (Id.I 72:113). On this basis alone does it become clear that, with the disconnection of reality, the *fact-world*, the *entire* natural world, succumbs to the *epoché*. Even the dependence of the world upon the I, a dependence that is a feature of the surrounding world, succumbs to the *epoché*, insofar as the former is understood as dependence upon a human reality that already presupposes the world.[25] Husserl talks quite deliberately of the *epoché* as "rendering inoperative of the being status of the *objective* world." The concept of "objectivity" states even more explicitly what is already intended by the concept of the fact-world. But even this concept is two-sided. The objectivity that is naively believed in is of a different kind from that which is legitimated through a phenomenological analysis of constitution. The "*naiveté* of the talk about 'objectivity' " (K 99:96) has to be overcome, but phenomenology is required to render "transcendentally intelligible" (K 193:189) what objectivity originally is. The origin of objectivity, just like the origin of anything else, is, however, in truth, subjective subjectivity. On the other hand, it is that which is free from all subjectivity that is naively presented as objectivity. As long as naiveté is nothing other than forgetfulness of original subjectivity, the naively apprehended world and the world that, in this sense, is taken to be objective are the same. The *epoché* amounts to a suspension of the world of the natural attitude, or a "rendering inoperative of the being status of the world." The significance of Husserl's identification of natural world and objective world finds its most direct expression where Husserl calls the naively intended object the object "pure and simple" (Id.I 222–223:261, 325:370, 333:378, CM 91:56, K 157:154). The natural object is purely and simply, or only, an object because there is nothing subjective about it.

At the same time, this terminology once again brings to mind the point at which the *epoché* is established as being negative: the belief in the being present-at-hand of the world that I naively interpret as independence from me and, in the light of my being integrated in the world, as an unequivocal expectation with respect to the presence of the world. This is the very point that the positive sciences interpret positively. It is for precisely this reason that they are called objective sciences and for this reason that phenomenology—as Husserl says in the *Cartesian Meditations*—constitutes the "extreme contrary" to it. As sciences "ignorant of the worldhood" (CM 183:157), they want to carry through and secure that objectivity whose understanding of the life-world is naive (K 193:189). Thereby, however, they prove themselves to be guilty of a naiveté of a "higher order" (CM 179:153). In extreme opposition to them, phenomenology takes up a positive stance with respect, so to speak, to the other end of the life-world—to the natural consciousness of the relativity of all objects of experience with respect to me, the subject of experience. Just as in *Crisis* a reduction of the objective sciences to the life-world is explicitly carried out, so here the way to transcendental reflection is prepared by means of a reflection upon the relativity in question (CM §38). With a view to providing an introduction to the "sciences of concrete, transcendental subjectivity," it engenders a "science of the universal means by which the world is given in advance" (K 149:146). From this it transpires, admittedly, that the former is, as such, not yet the latter. The life-world's knowledge of the relativity of appearances is still naive. But its naiveté consists exclusively in this, that it is subordinate to the preceding belief in the nonrelativity, in the independence of the world from the I. Under the influence of this belief, the I of the natural attitude takes relativity, as we have seen, to be, first, something that does not disturb the being-in-itself of the world, and, second, a psychophysically conditioned relation to itself, a human being integrated in the world. Inasmuch as phenomenology suspends both presuppositions, relativity is taken account of. To the absolutization of the objectivity of the life-world, as the nonrelativity presumed by the positive sciences, it opposes the ultimate radicalization of the subjectivity of the life-world, as the relativity of the world with respect to the ego that experiences it. In *Crisis*, the dialectic that governs this opposition between an objective science and an absolutely subjective science is brought to light. The absolutely subjective science strives after a radicalization of the relativity of the life-world, in the direction of "a total transformation" of "the natural world-life" (K 151:148), whereas objective science does not need such a transformation because, with the absolutization of the objectivity of the life-world, it stands opposed to the innermost tendency of the prescientific, natural world-life. Whereas, as a matter of fact, through this absolutization the world (existing in itself) (K 270–271) of objective science de facto absolutizes the life-world (which remains "subject relative" even in spite of all its objectivity) (K 127:124, 141:138, 168:165) and in this way brings the objective sciences themselves to a "crisis" and the life-world into forgetfulness (K 48–50:48–50), phenomenology, by getting outside the life-world, is able to confer upon the latter its own truth.

That phenomenology latches onto the relativity of the life-world in a positive way can also be read out of the observation that the radical alteration of the naive "attitude of immediacy" (K 146:143) has already become a thinkable prospect on account of the "anthropological relativism" of the classical skeptics (K 71:70). Accordingly, phenomenology itself could be called a *transcendental relativism*.[26] Admittedly, for subjectivity of this transcendental-type (K 70–71:69–70) relativity signifies more than just relatedness to; it signifies the constitution of the world *through* an I that is itself unworldly. The totally relativized world is the world "as phenomenon," that is, purely as a correlate of the subjectivity from which it derived its meaning, on the basis of whose validity it "exists" in general (K 155:152).

We have now reached the goal to which we pointed in the introductory paragraphs and to which the phenomenological reduction should have led us. At the same time, light has been thrown upon the difficulty created for us by the unity, given in the pure ego, of extramundane unhumanness and factically individual mineness. The thesis that, as a pure ego I am not human loses its strangeness with regard to the meaning to which my "self-apperception as a human being" is restricted by Husserl. For, according to Husserl, to grasp oneself as a human being amounts to nothing other than to allow oneself to be fitted in as one worldly object among other worldly objects. As a reversal of this integration, the phenomenological reduction is both a derealization and a dehumanization in one. But it is also clear that thereby the I in no way loses its factically individual mineness. On the contrary, it first achieves it in this way. For the individuality, facticity, and mineness that it has, as an object integrated in the world, are not determinations that belong to it as an I. Its worldly and human individuality does not distinguish it, in the last analysis, from all other worldly objects, inclusive of the inanimate, which, simply on account of their integration in the world, are individual. Its worldly and human facticity is a simple occurrence that is experienced in an external way and not out of the inner perspective of the I itself. Its worldly and human mineness pertains to it solely insofar as it is one among others and not an I that is beyond compare. With respect to its incomparable character, "its uniqueness and its personal indeclinability" (K 188:185), the *epoché* brings the I back home to itself: "The *epoché* generates a uniquely philosophical solitude" (K 187–188:184), a solitude that, as absoluteness, that is, as release from all otherness and all Others, throws the I back upon itself and upon its own individual facticity. The reverse side of absoluteness, however, is the radical relativity of the world with respect to the I that constitutes it. It is the two together, the relativity of the world and the absoluteness of the I, that first grounds its "solitude." This solitude is the necessary uniqueness of the center point that, solely because it is what it is, relegates everything else to the periphery. It is the solitude of the

constituter who does not know his equivalent because he only encounters what he has constituted.

Doubtless, one can and one even should distinguish between the I
that carries through the reduction and the I that is discovered in the
reduction and that constitutes the world. Nevertheless, it is significant
for our interpretation that in the *Crisis*, where Husserl speaks of solitude,
he places no value upon this distinction. The solitude that consists in
the fact that I can always only carry through the reduction for myself
is, as a matter of fact, for him the solitude of the constituter. This last
we shall meet again at the end of our interpretation of Husserl, after
we have followed the theory of intersubjectivity through to its goal.
Nevertheless, the solitude of the I that practices the *epoché* in the
"Cartesian" manner is still greater than that which we shall encounter
again. The latter is mitigated by the discovery of transcendental intersubjectivity. This in no way implies that it takes no notice of those
Others who make their appearance in the world. Whatever is valid
of the rest of worldly being is unquestionably valid of the Others, of
my fellow human beings, even when they remain "contained between
brackets." In the final analysis, they lose their status as objective
existents and, just like nonhuman worldly objects, are transformed
into pure "world phenomena," that is, into objectivities of the acts by
which I constitute them. But these beings constituted have to be distinguished from their constituting capacity, thanks to which they are
incorporated within *transcendental* intersubjectivity. In accordance with
Husserl's own insight, the Cartesian method of reduction, which we
have patterned on the description in book I of *Ideas*, bypasses transcendental intersubjectivity because, through a direct abandonment
of the universal "ground of the world," it proceeds *immediately* to the
last foundation, to the "originary I." This "leaping over" transcendental
intersubjectivity appeared to the later Husserl as the principal error
of the "Cartesian way," which he attempted to avoid through the new
way of the "phenomenological-psychological reduction": "The advantage of this second way into transcendental intersubjectivity over
the Cartesian way is that it gives us the means of tying intersubjectivity
into the reduction" (EP.II 313 B).[27] This is supposed to happen in the
following manner: a reduction operative with respect to particular acts
and so not suspending the world as a whole is directed first upon my
"pure psyche" and solely from there out upon my absolute, unique
ego. The "pure psyche" is the I that will be laid out in the third

chapter of the present investigation, when the I is integrated within the transcendental community of monads.[28] Only it is certainly not a matter of accident that the method of reduction as it is originally conceived and still practiced in the *Cartesian Meditations* leaps over transcendental intersubjectivity, just as it appears to be no accident that Husserl (whose confused expositions in the second part of *Erste Philosophie* [*First Philosophy*] (EP)[29] prove the point) never arrived at a clear understanding of the "new way." So long as the phenomenological reduction represents a radical relativization of the world, the tendency to an exclusion of transcendental intersubjectivity belongs to its essence. With the recognition of the Other's constitutive capacity came the admission that Others, for their part, relativize the world with respect to themselves and thereby fit me into their world. In this way the "uniqueness" of the middle point of the world that I am by virtue of the transcendental reduction is endangered. What Husserl has to say in *First Philosophy* is pertinent to this in the strictest sense: "The self-reflection that the philosopher has to carry through at the beginning *must* be carried through not in the natural attitude of communication but, so to speak, in the solipsistic attitude" (EP.II 59—italics are mine).

3 The Starting Point in "Mine-ness" and the Problem of Eidetic Intuition

What in the *Cartesian Meditations*[30] Husserl calls eidetic intuition (CM 106:72) he elsewhere designates as *"eidetic reduction"* (for example, Id.I 6:44). The agreement with respect to the principal title "reduction" is evidence for the connection between the theme of the previous paragraph and that of this paragraph. What cannot be glossed over, however, is the fact that the connection is extremely problematic.[31] Thanks to the reduction, phenomenology is eidetic, or a "science of essences," and that means that it is not a "factual science" (Id.I 6:44). The transcendental reduction does, however, bring one "fact" to light: the fact of my individual historical ego. How is this fact to be reconciled with the required essence? How is its individuality to be brought into agreement with the generality of the essence? And finally, can one claim without further ado that the object of egology, in toto, is "my ego" when the *"eidos* ego" now shows itself to be its object? With respect to the laying of the foundations of the theory of intersubjectivity, this last question is the most important.[32] We must therefore pay special attention to its clarification.

For this reason, we are compelled to proceed beyond what is literally set down here and there in Husserl's text and, on the basis of relatively infrequent indications, to draw consequences that Husserl did not draw. The need to proceed in this way results from a circumstance that can hardly be contested, namely, that Husserl neglected to rethink radically the method of eidetic intuition (which was developed before the discovery of the phenomenological reduction) on the basis of the presuppositions of a situation that was radically altered when that method later became the decisive means of approach to it. In the final analysis, its importance diminished in exact proportion to the increase in the importance of the phenomenological reduction—until finally, in *Crisis*, it is no longer mentioned at all. This might mean that the mineness, individuality, and facticity of the pure ego appear to be of less importance to transcendental philosophy than the universal validity, generality, and ideality of the essence, which, in the Platonic ontology of *Logische Untersuchungen* [*Logical Investigations*], was brought into battle against psychologism. However, the responsibility for this also lies with the lack of clarity essentially inherent in the relation of these two determinations to one another. I do not mean that what Husserl neglected to do can be done over again. But, at the very least, we should attempt to place the "eidetic reduction" on that basis that was provided by the "transcendental turn" of phenomenology.[33]

In the text of the *Cartesian Meditations*, it is already difficult to determine the *systematic* relation of the two reductions.[34] Husserl places the eidetic *after* the phenomenological; but immediately afterward he indicates that this is done only for didactic reasons, to make it easier to understand (CM 103:69). " 'In itself,' the science of essence should precede the science of transcendental actuality and first make it possible as a science" (CM 106:72). Again, that does not mean that the phenomenologist, who does not have to take any pedagogical precautions, should carry out the eidetic *before* the phenomenological reduction. Rather, it only means that the former is always already *implied* by the latter, and in such a way that both reductions necessarily have to be carried out *as one*. In the course of the phenomenological reduction, Husserl himself, as he admits, has "unintentionally" made use of eidetic intuition, even before he introduced it (CM 104:70; see also CM 103:69). So its introduction only has the meaning of a "clarification"

(CM 103:69) of something that was previously practiced without awareness of the method involved. However, Husserl does not tell us *why* the phenomenological *epoché* can only be correctly practiced by means of eidetic intuition. Our explanation for this is that the factual, which as mundane is distinguished from its *eidos*, is, in the final analysis, as transcendental, one with the *eidos* itself.[35] The following presentation of the "method of ideation" (PP 86) will have to prove this.

I perceive a table. This is the example that Husserl uses to illustrate the method of ideation and that we shall stick with. The phenomenological reduction has suspended the naively assumed objectivity, the actuality or the facticity, of the *table*. Therewith the object pure and simple is suspended; that is, the "thing out there" (Id.I 225:264), the real table that is exposed to real changes in the world. Insofar as eidetic intuition, even if it is not called by this name in the *Cartesian Meditations*, also has the character of a reduction, does it not also have to suspend something? And if so, what? The facticity of the *perception of the table*: "In other words, while retaining its existential status, we change the fact of this perception into a pure possibility" (CM 104:70). Properly speaking, this suspension is to be strictly distinguished from the suspension of the mundane facticity of the perception of the table, which belongs to the phenomenological reduction as a psychic act. We look upon the perception of the table as a transcendental *factum*, which has to be converted into a pure possibility. In accordance with the structure of intentionality, this takes place in the alteration of that which is factically perceived as such, as well as in the ideational alteration of the perceiving I, "the coposited, factical ego" (CM 104:70).

Let us undertake right away the ideation of the factical as the perceived table. What makes this, as also any other, ideation possible is "fantasy" (CM 104:70, PP 72). By this means, we must "vary" or "imaginatively transform" the perceived object, the table (CM 104:70). According to Husserl, the imaginative transformation remains, on the one hand, "entirely at our free discretion" (CM 104:70) or our caprice (PP 72), and is, on the other hand, appropriately regulated (PP 76). The capricious element has to do with the relative indifference as to the direction in which I undertake the imaginative transformation and the number of the fictions that I run through. The fantasy is regulated, however, by a preview of the *eidos* that it seeks to recover (PP 76). In our case, it is a question of the intuitive apprehension of the *eidos*, "the perceived (thing) as such." Therefore, with respect to the factically perceived table, I am entitled to transform everything except its being perceived and its being a thing (CM 104:70). Supposing that I start off by transforming its color and its shape, I can, in the end, even abstract from the fact that it is a table. I let the most varied imaginative constructs go through my mind and only hold on to the fact that they are essentially perceivable things. As pure fictions, all such imaginative constructs stand out in contrast to the original perceptual object, the table, inasmuch as they are not actually given. However, like the latter, they are individually determined. They are certainly freed from "every kind of facticity" (CM 104:70), but not from every kind of individuality. For fantasy is not an abstraction, but an entirely perceivable representation of something individual.[36] Still, in the course of a variation of the individual, the "general type" (CM 104:70), or the *eidos*, "perceived thing as such," manifests itself as that which belongs to everything that can be conceived insofar as it is intended to be a perceivable thing. In this same way, that which is factically perceived is regulated by the *eidos*. With regard to the fiction from which I started out, I grasp it as a "simple example of a pure possibility" (CM 105:71), which, together with that which has really been transformed and all conceivable possibilities, makes up the ideal extension of the *eidos*, "perceived thing as such" (CM 104:70, PP 86).

A question arises as to how the phenomenologist could know *what* he had to hold on to as the typical form of the kind sought after *before* the onset of the process of variation. If one does not want to accuse Husserl of a petitio principii and say that he presupposes what allegedly should first be brought to light through the variations, only *one* answer is forthcoming: Already in the confrontation with the transcendental *factum* that the phenomenological reduction makes available to me, I am intuitively directed solely to the *eidos* of this *factum*. The *eidos* is that which belongs to the perceptual table-object, insofar as it is perceived and, more exactly, perceived as a thing. That which is perceived exists as a special mode of the constitutive relation to myself. In its turn, the being of the thing prescribes a specific how for this special mode of relation, that is, for the relativity of that which is perceived. This is precisely what I see when I am presented with an actually perceived table as the "residual" of the phenomenological reduction, of the process of transcendental relativization. In consequence, I am directed exclusively toward its *eidos*. Certainly, the perceptual object, the table, is individually determined. It has its particular colors, its particular form, and so on. Still, in the transcendental attitude, it is not this color that interests me, but the way in which it establishes a relation to me, that is, the way in which it is given perspectivally. The particular form is of no interest to me, but rather this, that the table (which as table is of no account) as an extended thing in general has to be given to me in an essentially regulated manner, and in a manner that accords with the law of perspective. This latter manner remains identical to the former, no matter how and into what I may imaginatively transform the perceptual table-object. And even with fictions, I am not interested in their individual being but only in "the perceptual thing as such."

Admittedly, in its turn, this answer raises a question, the question why the process of variation should be necessary at all. It is necessary in a sense that was set out in the beginning, a sense that the introduction of the method of ideation brings with it: as an explication of that which is already implicit in the phenomenological reduction. In order to see this one has to realize that the alteration that produces eidetic intuition is brought about not so much by a progress from fact to fiction as far more by a regress from fiction to fact. This alteration consists in the fact that the original fact loses its exceptional appearance and takes on an exemplary one: it becomes, as we learned earlier, a simple example of pure possibility. This means: The true object of the attitude that is only attained through the phenomenological reduction, the *eidos* of the transcendental fact, explicitly separates itself from the facticity of this fact, from that which is irrepeatably individual about it. The method of ideation really only accomplishes the destruction of the specious claim that the object of the attitude that is brought about by the phenomenological reduction might be the momentary transcendental fact in its individual determinateness. For this reason, it stands in need of variation. For only in the light of fictions that, as determinate, are susceptible to a differentiation that is regulated by a typical identity does it become apparent that the *eidos* is bound neither to facticity nor to the particular existence of the transcendental *factum*. This is how it is originally recovered *as eidos*.

This interpretation has certainly saved the *eidos*, but at the expense of the individuality and the facticity of the perceptual object. The phenomenological reduction should be compatible with eidetic intuition because, already in accordance with the inner tendency of the phenomenological reduction, it does not depend at all upon that individuality and facticity that is intrinsic to the original perceptual table-object. On the contrary, it requires a special redirection of attention to seize upon individuality and facticity as that which is really significant and so to set up phenomenology as a transcendental factual science. How little it depends upon facticity in particular is apparent from Husserl's claim that phenomenology could just as well start out from an imagined entity as from one that is actually perceived and perform the transcendental *epoché* with respect to it. Specifically, *the* individuality and facticity that we spoke about in the introductory paragraphs are those of the *perceiving ego*. It is, however, by no means settled whether the individuality and the facticity of the perceived object coincide with the corresponding characteristics of the perceiving ego. The individuality certainly does not. To be sure, the facticity of the perceived object is, in certain respects, identical with the facticity of the perception and, to this extent, also with that of the ego as the subjective pole of perception. But it is questionable whether, with this facticity, the facticity of my ego is at all exhausted. We shall have to test this when we go on to investigate the ideation of the factical ego that is "coposited" in factical perception. Only in the course of this investigation will it become apparent whether the ego loses its individuality and facticity through the process of ideation. Above all, however, we shall thereby first be able to pose the central question concerning the relation of *eidos* and mineness. It has to be decided, first, whether my very own subjectivity really is—as Husserl claims—the necessary starting point and, second, whether it remains the sole object of egology.

Inasmuch as I imaginatively transform the factically perceived table-object into all kinds of fictive constructs, I have to imagine an ego actually corresponding to these constructs. I have to do this because, through the ideation of the factical perception of the thing, I intend to attain the "general type," thing-perception. I do not intend simply to represent *something* in fantasy, but imaginatively to include myself in a *perception*. I presentify something as something perceived and thereby also the ego that perceives this something.

The problem is now, what kind of being attaches to this ego that is imaginatively included in this way? To start with, is it my ego or not? Undoubtedly, I can represent anyone else as the perceiver. But (and this is alone important for our question) the variation of my factical ego does not require me to presuppose the Other: "It should be noted that in the transition from my ego to an ego in general, neither the reality nor the possibility of an inclusion of Others is presupposed. In this case the scope of the *eidos* ego is determined by a self-variation of my ego. I imagine myself as if I were someone else. I do not imagine Others" (CM 106:72). So every "ego in general," that is, every conceivable ego in general, is, in this case, *mine*.

Admittedly, just as the originally perceived object loses its determinate individuality through variation, so also does the ego that is posited in correlation with it. It loses its *determinate* individuality—a determinate individuality that, as we say, is quite distinct from that of the perceptual object—but does not lose its individuality as such (no less than does the perceptual object). I imagine myself as being an Other; that is, I change my particular being into that of an Other.

And what happens to my facticity? The ego that I imagine as perceiving is doubtless not my actually perceiving ego. Still less can it be identical with the actually imagining ego, since it is far more its intentional correlate. Further, it is not that ego that is factically present. However, it is present. For it is represented as perceiving now. Therefore it also cannot be my past or future factical ego. In other words, it is not at all my *factical* ego. The facticity that accordingly has to be withheld from the imagined ego is one with the facticity of the perceptual object that, in the course of imaginative transformation, likewise has to be given up. Husserl's own statement proves helpful in coming to a more precise determination: the imagined perception stands "out of all relation to our (that is, in this case, actually, my) otherwise factical life" (CM 104:70). It is not only the case that the ego that is imagined along with the imagining of a perceptual object is not my factical ego—though it is mine. Inasmuch as it is not my factical ego, it also has no relation to the particular circumstances that led me to the perception of this table, and to the situation in which the perception of the table actually takes place. In order that I should now be able actually to perceive the African elephant that I have imaginatively constructed out of the table, my "otherwise factical life" would have to be different from what it actually is. In this way, the meaning of being an individual in this and some other way gets clarified. The imaginatively transformed existence is that of a determinate life that, as a matter of fact, is my own, and the being otherwise into which I transform it is, in its turn, the particular life that I must assume in order that I should be able really to perceive the fictive perceptual object.

Every ego that is at all conceivable, insofar as it is, on the one hand, *mine*, and yet, on the other hand, is not my *individual factical* ego, stands for a "pure transformational possibility of my factical ego" (CM 105:71). As such it is, at the same time, a pure possibility of the *eidos* ego corresponding to which every perceptual object that is at all conceivable also incorporates a pure possibility of the *eidos*, perceptual object. Indeed, the agreement of the "objective" and the subjective sides of the process of ideation goes still further. Just as all conceivable perceptual objects, along with that which is factically perceived, belong (as an example of a pure possibility) to the ideal scope of the *eidos* perceptual object, so there also belongs to the ideal scope of the *eidos* ego, determined "through a self-variation of my ego," not only all pure possibilities of my factically individual ego but also this latter itself. The eidetic researches of phenomenology are "disclosures of the universal *eidos*, transcendental ego in general, which comprehends within itself all transformational possibilities of my factical ego, and this latter itself as a possibility" (CM 105–106:71).

Insofar as the scope of the *eidos* ego is determined through the self-variation of my ego, my ego comprises the *eidos* ego itself. Insofar, however, as the *eidos* ego includes within itself my factical ego, the latter is comprised within the former. If one sticks exclusively by the second state of affairs, one appears obliged to concede that Husserl's conception of egology, in accordance with which my factically individual ego is the sole all-encompassing object, gets stranded on the requirements of ideation. It is not my individual-factical ego that is all-encompassing but the *eidos* ego, within whose compass my individual factical ego is only a very small part. At the same time, my ego encompasses the *eidos* ego. There is no contradiction between these two statements because "my ego" is not identical with "my factical ego" but, in addition to the latter, also includes within itself all its transformational possibilities. Both phenomena, the encompassing of my individual factical ego by the *eidos* ego and the encompassing of the *eidos* ego by my ego, Husserl pulls together in the unity of a *single* sentence, at a place in the *Cartesian Meditations* that comes after the passages we have interpreted. There he says, "The phenomenological self-explication that went on in my ego" has, in the methodical form of an eidetic a priori self-explication, a bearing upon my "factical ego only insofar as the latter is one of the pure possibilities to be acquired by its free fantasy-variation (fictive changing) of itself. Therefore, as eidetic, the explication is valid for the universe of these, my possibilities as essentially an ego, my possibilities, namely, of being otherwise" (CM 117:84–85). This sentence says everything that is of relevance to us: the *factical* (not necessary) starting point of phenomenology from my factical ego, the setting aside of my determinate individuality and facticity through the eidetic apprehension of my phenomenological self-explication, the thereby positively instantiated, differentiation of my individual-factical ego in the universe of pure possibilities of the *eidos* ego, and finally—the most important of all—the retention of this universe in my ego, which bears within itself the pure possibilities of the *eidos* ego as *its* possibilities. The "ego in general," which is in question here, *I am myself* as the universe of my possibilities among which my factical ego constitutes the actualized possibility translated back into its pure possible being by means of ideation. So it is *my* ego and nothing else that is the universal "*eidos*, transcendental ego in general, which includes within itself all pure transformational possibilities of my factical ego, and this latter itself as a pure possibility." In this way the orientation toward mineness is plausibly connected with the directedness toward the *eidos* ego. My concrete subjectivity is the necessary starting point and the sole all-encompassing object even of *eidetic* phenomenology.[37]

Now we can take an essential step in the direction of an eidetic-phenomenological recovery of my individuality and facticity. If my ego, as the universe of my possibilities, is to be legitimately called "mine," then it must also be individual and factical in a sense other than that which has been employed hitherto. I can only speak of myself as the individual that I am in fact. I am also the individual that I am factically as the sheerly possible ego, insofar as this latter is really only *my* possibility. My possibility belongs, just as does my reality, to my being, which has been factically determined in this and not some other way. One way to differentiate *this* individuality and *this* facticity from the individuality and the facticity that is set aside by the process of ideation is indicated by the account given above. Through ideation I imaginatively transform my specific, factical "life." The fact that I now perceive a table also falls within this life. Should I, in the course of representing myself in fantasy, perceive, instead of the table, an African elephant, I would presentify my life as one that was not factically mine. By contrast with my actual existence, this particular existence is something other. However, as we said before, in the being other of my nonfactical existence, I remain the same individual that I actually am in my factical existence. Certainly, according to Husserl, the fact that my life takes such and such a determinate course makes of me—as we shall see later—a "person," but not that individual that I am insofar as I am an "I" at all. The individuality and facticity that necessarily belong to the ego *as mine* and that, in consequence, cannot be suspended by any ideation are therefore, in relation to that individuality and facticity of my ego that can be imaginatively suspended, a priori characters of being. We may also say with regard to a distinction that is not derived from Husserl but appropriate to him that they comprise, in opposition to those purely *ontic* determinations, the *ontological* constitution of my very own ego. However, in the introductory sections of this chapter we have already depicted as ontological the mineness whose moments are transcendental individuality and facticity. The thesis advanced there, that the necessary starting point and, up to the theory of intersubjectivity, the sole object of phenomenology should be my individually factical subjectivity, not only holds good in the confrontation with the doctrine of eidetic intuition; starting from the latter, it is possible to make progress toward a better understanding of the thesis itself. More precisely: the explicitly executed ideation strips away from my ego the still ontically determined individuality and facticity and clarifies the ontological meaning that, in phenomenological self-explication, is hazily present to me as the specific meaning not only of mineness but also of the individuality and the facticity of my transcendental ego.[38]

4 The Transcendental Differentiation of the World

The phenomenological reduction to be carried out in eidetic intuition opens up a field that has to be worked out in constitutional researches. The movement of constitution runs to some extent in the opposite direction from that of the reduction. Whereas the latter results in the *de*struction of the objective world of the natural attitude, the former is the transcendental *con*struction of the objective world, or its construction in a transcendentally justified form. The construction takes place in the two steps of egology and the theory of intersubjectivity. The systematic laying of the foundation of this construction has, for this reason, to be tied at least to an outline sketch of egological world construction. Therefore, with a view to the necessary abbreviation of the material, we place ourselves upon a level that will be supported by the operations of the self-constitution of consciousness in immanent temporalization—upon the level of individual lived experience that juts out of the endlessly flowing stream of consciousness as an already immanently constituted unity.[39] We shall, in turn, pursue the "intentional analysis" of lived experience in a "noematic orientation." Starting from the object of individual lived experience, we shall in the end come up against the egologically constituted world as a whole. This world—the world that still does not need the Other for its constitution—is the thing-world in its pure thinghood. That very lived experience with respect to which Husserl chiefly demonstrates the constitution of things and of the thing-world is perception. Accordingly, we shall also follow the egological constitution of the world on the basis of "the lived experience of the perception of the thing" (Id.I 111:148) to the extent that it is of interest to us.[40]

Husserl prescribes the point from which we have to set out and from which we have to allow ourselves to be guided: "Intentional analysis is guided by the fundamental cognition that, as a consciousness, every *cogito* is indeed (in the broadest sense) a meaning of its meant. However, at any moment, this something meant is more (meant as more) than what is meant at that moment explicitly" (CM 84:46). The *cogito*, the lived experience, as intentional act, is, for this reason, essentially a *"meaning more"* (CM 84:46). In *Crisis* Husserl gives us the commentary to this concept: "Things seen are always already more than what we 'really and truly' see of them" (K 51). What is really seen when, for example, seeing a house as a house is that part of the house that is immediately turned toward me, the front, for instance, along with one of the two sides. Even this I only see in the actual moment from a particular distance and perspective, in an adumbration that is conditioned by the perspective, and in varying degrees of clarity. With respect to the house, what faces away from me "in the actual moment" presents itself, first of all, as that which is additionally intended (in our example, the back side). Even this is "seen," insofar as I ever see a "house." Admittedly, according to Husserl, it is not, as is the front, "absolutely originally given" but simply "cogiven," not "originally present" but "appresent" or "appresented." This distinction names a difference within the present whose temporalization is presented by perception and so also within that "originality" that is ascribed to perceptual experience. The present that is presentified in the total experience of perception is the "concrete" present, which, to be sure, Husserl also envisages as "the now," from out of which, however, Husserl disengages, as its "innermost core," the "limiting point of the pure now" (EP.II 175). The "absolutely original phase, the moment of the living now" (Id.I 183:221) is "the actual moment" in which that which is immediately present is immediately present. It has a "flowing" (EP.II 175) character. In Husserl's sense, the perception of the house is no momentary, static act, but a process in which I experience the house in the original meaning of the word; that is, I let my glance roam in the different directions, approaching nearer, going around the house, and so on. In the course of this process I can bring to absolute givenness what initially is only cogiven. At all times, however, the perceived, or to be perceived, object remains centered upon the living, originary now, on the basis of which I appresent what is cogiven, which, by comparison with the perceived object, already falls back into the past or the future. That is, I hold onto the perceived object in the circuit of the concrete present. The two modes of such holding onto are "retention," as preservation of the immediate past, and "protention," as a reaching out to what is immediately coming up (EP.II 175, K 163:160). They are to be distinguished from remembrance and expectation in that they do not, as do the latter, make the wholly past (equally the pure future) present in the manner of independent acts, but, as dependent moments of the act of perception (which is carried over along with the analogizing transposition of perception into remembrance and expectation), they make *co*present what is not, or is no longer, absolutely present (K 163:160).

This difference between what is originally present and what is appresent lays the foundation upon which the transcendental theory of intersubjectivity will be constructed. It arises out of the transcendental relativization: A mode of givenness, which is to some extent nonperspectival and which ignores the relation to the I, is ascribed to the naively intended "object pure and simple." But this transcendental relativization differentiates the "object pure and simple" into the originally present and the appresent, that is, into what is accessible *here* and *now* and what is not accessible here and now but can only be made accessible to me *then* and from *there*. As the typical result of a transcendental relativization, this difference does not just happen to materialize once in a while; rather, it wholly dominates the entire experience of the worldly. The specific evidence that belongs to this experience—whether it is originary or not—and that stands over against the "apodictic" evidence of pure self-experience is determined by this originary presence-appresence distinction. As "inadequate" evidence, it rests upon the "essential one-sidedness" of the givenness of things that can never show themselves from all sides with absolute originality (CM 96:61). Because the meaning of what is not absolutely originally given is, as meaning more, primarily a meaning in advance (K 51:51), Husserl identifies inadequate evidence with the presumptive (CM 96–97:61–62). The evidence of the experience of worldly things is, so to speak, a premature certainty that is founded in anticipation and that, for this reason, can at any time, in the course of the presentation, come to grief on the "really and truly" given. And it *stays* that way. If I am also able to bring what is now simply cogiven to absolute givenness, it too, as absolutely given, will have its "train" of the cogiven, to which what is now absolutely given belongs retentionally and to which what I perhaps now do not even anticipate belongs protentionally. The one-sidedness of the givenness of things cannot be done away with; the process of the experience of worldly things cannot be concluded.

That the difference between the immediately appearing and the cogiven, between the originally present and the appresent, as a trait essential to the perception of things, does, according to Husserl and in conformity with this model, dominate every intentional experience of worldly things points to the typification of intentionality as "horizonal intentionality" (CM 83:45). For the horizon implicit in outer perception is, in Husserl's nomenclature, a "horizon of inauthentic cogivenness" (Id.I 100:137). It bears upon the appresented that surrounds the originally present. In conformity with the spatial placement of the appresented as the periphery of the here, "horizon" means the same as "field" or "background" (Id.I 202n:240n). In conformity with the temporal centering of the appresented upon the originally living now, it even has a retentional-protentional constitution, a "horizon of the before" and a "horizon of the afterward" (Id.I 199–200:237–238). Further, in contrast with the complete determination of the originally present, the appresent is relatively undetermined. While I have the front of the house in all its particularities before me, I can only represent the back side in rough outline. Precisely this interval between inexhaustible fullness and abstract emptiness distinguishes the horizon. It is predelineated as "an indeterminateness that possesses a determinate structure" (CM 83:45). Consequently it possesses the trait of "openness" (CM 83:45). However, the presentation of the appresented, the carrying over of the relatively undetermined into the complete determinateness of what is explicitly at hand, is, as the disclosure of "the potentialities of the life of consciousness," nothing other than the "laying out of the horizon and the ever new horizons that are continually awakened" (CM 81–82:43–44). Consequently Husserl talks of the *"horizon structure of all intentionality"* (CM 86:48) with regard to the same phenomenon that led him to the definition of intentional lived experience as "meaning more." The more is the sheerly cogiven, and this enters into consciousness as the horizon.

To be sure, the more is still something else. I "really and truly" see *the house as such* just as little as I do the back of the house. Indeed, in contrast to the back side, the house itself can never be made absolutely present on a par with the front. I can only be directed toward it and can never bring it before me as something present at hand. This "intentional object as such" (CM 79:41, 87:50), the "cogitatum qua cogitatum" (CM 82:45) or—as Husserl also says in our text—the "objective meaning" (CM 75:37, 80:42, 82–84:45, 91:56) functions as the "objective unity . . . of a multiform and variable multiplicity belonging to determinate modes of appearance" (CM 77:39). The immediately appearing in the "multiplicity of modes of appearance" is the "complete *noema*" to which the "complete *noesis*" stands in relation (Id.I 223–225:262–264). Just as the noematic multiplicity is "centered" on the sense, so the noetic multiplicity is "centered" on the ego as the "I pole" of intentionality. I projects itself away over the correlation of *noesis* and *noema* toward the sense, and *this* relation alone (Id.I 318:363), the self-relation of the I to the sense, is the intentional relation that characterizes consciousness as meaningful possession (Id.I 223:261). The constitution of the object is the synthesis (CM 77–79:39–41) of the multiplicity of modes of appearance with regard to the likewise predelineated (CM 83:45) sense. But "the goal (its forehaving) striven for" (K 174:171) by the experiencing I is the objective sense in an even more fundamental sense than the appresented. It is already predelineated in every intending of what lies explicitly at hand, so much so that this latter could not be available as that which it is if I had not always already projected its meaning. With respect to our example, the front could never appear to me *as* the front (of a house) if I did not have the house as such in mind in advance. Likewise, the fore-having of the objective sense guides the laying out of the horizon, just as, admittedly from the opposite standpoint, the objective sense first "gets clarified" through the laying out of the horizon (CM 82–83:45).

The differentiation that has been duplicated in this manner is carried over by Husserl from the individual thing in the world to the world as a whole. The world is, in the first instance, "world horizon" (K 146:143, 255:251, 267:263). What has hitherto been called "horizon" Husserl separates off as "inner horizon" from the "outer horizon," that is, from the simultaneously appresented environment of the actually intended thing, wherever he has the world in mind as well as the individual object. The world is first brought into the field of attention inasmuch as this outer horizon, for its part, is brought to consciousness as a "segment" of the world (K 165:162), as the world horizon that encompasses all other horizons. However, just as the meaning of the individual object gets clarified in the laying out of the inner horizon, so the "world-meaning" is disclosed in the laying out of the world horizon (Id.I 356:403). In both interpretations, that of the enclosing horizon and that of the enclosing sense, the world is brought to consciousness together with the consciousness of worldly things. It is the world horizon because it is not stuck on to the inner and outer horizons from the outside but is implicated in them with necessity, so that "anything given in a worldly manner brings the world horizon with it and can only thereby be brought to consciousness as worldly" (K 267:264). In the end, the difference between what, with respect to the thing, is explicitly present at hand and what is horizonally present proceeds on the basis of the distinction between the former and the totality of entities that are given along with the horizon. Likewise, in the presentification of individuals, the world sense is copresent because, as the universal "cogitatum" it includes within itself all particular "cogitata," therefore the very sense of individual being (CM 80:43, 75:36). And so, in the difference (which has been more fully gone into earlier) between what is immediately present at hand in the thing and the thing's most fundamental sense, the immediate present-at-hand and the world sense get differentiated. What Husserl says about the "world itself" applies quite truly to the latter: It "does not exist like an entity" (K 146:143), and it "is not there as a thing" (K 254:251).

The world that is transformed into meaning is the "phenomenon" to which the world of the natural attitude is brought back by the phenomenological reduction: the "meant world purely as such" that remains over as the noematic correlate of the pure life of consciousness (CM 75:37). However, although the world described here is one that has already been transformed into meaning, a noticeable distance still obtains between it and the former world, which is supposed to count as the phenomenon disclosed by the reduction. And this not only because it is exclusively a thing-world but also, and before all else, because it is lacking in genuine "objectivity." Genuine objectivity, that is, objectivity that has been purified of its naive interpretation and "rendered transcendentally intelligible," is drawn from the purely "egological" or "solipsistic" constitution. For instance, even if the thing that is objective in the transcendental sense is not "independent of the I," in the manner in which it is naively supposed to be, still, it transcends my ego in a much more radical manner than the egologically constituted thing. To be sure, there belongs to the latter a transcendence that is proclaimed in the first section of the present chapter, a transcendence whose thematization makes of phenomenology a transcendental philosophy. It is not immanent to consciousness, if immanent is supposed to mean really (*reell*) immanent (Id.I 141–143:282–284). In contrast with the *noesis* and the *hyle* of the content of sensation, it does not really take place in consciousness—which, in the language of the *Cartesian Meditations*, means: "Just as the reduced ego is not a piece of the world, so, conversely, neither the world nor any worldly object is a piece of my ego" (CM 65:26). However, it certainly is "intentionally or ideally" immanent (CM 80:42), namely, with the ideality of the meaning that is the intentional object. So it is simply an immanent transcendence. All the same, in *certain respects* one must characterize *every* transcendence as immanent, insofar as it turns out to be transcendental at all, and so also "objective transcendence" (CM 136:106), the transcendence of the transcendental phenomenon of the *objective world*: "Transcendence, in *every* form, is an immanent existential characteristic, constituted within the ego" (CM 117:83–84—italics are mine). As transcendental, the transcendence of the objective world is also immanent insofar as it is constituted in the ego. Correspondingly, one must say that the objectivity of this world, as an objectivity that has to be transcendentally justified, is, at the same time, insofar as it is constituted in the ego, subjective. In this very way it is to be distinguished from the naively intended objectivity that is incorrectly derived from subjectivity, in that it is presented as totally unrelated to it, and as presupposing the world. The transcendence of the egologically constitutable thing-world is even more genuinely immanent than the "objective." For in contradistinction to the immanence of objective transcendence, its immanence consists in this, that it belongs inseparably to my concrete subjectivity as that intentional objectivity without which my subjectivity cannot be concrete. In this ideal manner, only that sense can be a part of my subjectivity itself that functions as the synthetic unity of a multiplicity of appearances. This amounts to the same thing as the statement that from the "external world" only the thing-world, reduced to its pure physicality, can be egologically constituted. For "mere things" are, according to Husserl, unities of a multiplicity of appearances and everything constituted as such a unity is a "mere thing." The only constitution that can be clarified on an egological basis is nothing other than the "passively operative synthesis" (CM 79:41), a unification already occurring originally in life itself, a unification of determinate modes of appearance directed toward an objective sense that is preserved as the identical through change. The only constitution that can be clarified on an egological basis is *the* constitution that I am able to carry through for myself as transcendental "solus ipse." On the basis of the self-evident distance between what is constituted by it and what has been conceded in advance by the phenomenological reduction as the goal of its constitutional analysis, the phenomenologist is driven to the supposition that the latter, the phenomenon of the *objective world*, demands a constitution in which, aside from myself, those others also participate who have to be taken into consideration as constitutional sources; namely, the other transcendental subjects.

So egology refers beyond itself and on to the transcendental theory of intersubjectivity, whose telos is predelineated by means of a task that egology is not in a position to carry through. The theory of intersubjectivity proceeds on the basis of a clarification of the constitution of the objective world as objective,[41] or, what amounts to the same thing, of the clarification of the real, of the transcendentally transcendent in a transcendentally possible understanding, or, what once again amounts to the same thing, of the overcoming of "transcendental solipsism," the "transcendental solipsism" in which the incapacity of egology to make the objectivity of the world intelligible is rooted. Admittedly, it is now already possible to establish, with respect to that immanence by which even transcendent transcendence remains ensnared as a result of its transcendental constitution, what will become ever more significant to us in the course of our interpretation of Husserl: that the intersubjectively constituted objective world is not only constituted in me alone insofar as it is not *immediately* constituted in me alone. It is mediately constituted through and through in me alone, namely, in that mediation, through an intersubjectivity inclusive of me, in which it is immediately constituted. In other words, it is, in the last analysis, constituted in me alone again because even those others by means of which it is so constituted are constituted in me.

This preliminary sketch of the theory of intersubjectivity presented here persists from its first working out—according to Husserl's own indications in the Göttingen lectures of the 1910/1911 winter semester[42]—through to his latest presentation. To be sure, in book I of *Ideas* (1913) we do not find, in the words of the epilogue, "the explicit taking up of a position with respect to the problem of transcendental solipsism, for example, to transcendental intersubjectivity, to the essential relatedness of the world that counts as objective for me to those who count as Others for me" (Id.III 150). However, wherever in book I of *Ideas* Husserl still touches upon the problem of transcendental intersubjectivity,[43] at that point the connection with the question concerning the constitution of the objective world also comes to the fore. At the very least, it engenders a demand for a description of "the intersubjective constitution of the 'objective' thing-world" (Id.I 374:421). Nevertheless, he puts off answering this demand until book II, which was written in the years 1912–1928,[44] but which never appeared during his lifetime (Id.III 150).[45] In this work he tries to clarify "how the relation to a multiplicity of reciprocally interacting human beings enters into the apprehension of the thing and is constitutive for the apprehension of the thing as 'objectively real' " (Id.II 80). *Formal and Transcendental Logic* (1929) sketches out, in an outline of steps that are differentiated in a methodologically strict fashion, the "intersubjective constitution" of the objective world that Husserl, in a note to the lectures on *First Philosophy* (1923/1924), depicts as "the task of phenomenology" (EP.II 395 B), and to which these lectures themselves make essential contributions. It strives after "the clarification of that very intersubjectivity that functions for the objective world as constitutive of its sense" (FTL 209:236). In concise strokes it outlines "the developed transcendental problematic of intersubjectivity and therewith the categorial form of 'objectivity' for the world" (FTL 210:238). In the "Fifth Cartesian Meditation" (French edition) Husserl finally develops its themes in detail. This is by far the most comprehensive meditation and the one upon which the weight of the whole book rests. It presents a "transcendental theory of the experience of the Other" as the foundation of a "transcendental theory of the objective world" (CM 124:92).

With this goal continually in mind, we want to present Husserl's theory of intersubjectivity in the following chapter in a manner that is as faithful to the text as possible. The more penetrating interpretation we leave to the third chapter, and the disclosure of the fundamental presuppositions to the fourth. Admittedly, even this presentation, which is oriented around the "Fifth Cartesian Meditation," will already be an interpretation in two ways: first, insofar as it pursues more precisely what we claim that Husserl meant over and above what he said; and second, insofar as it brings together into a unity that which is presented separately in the text. In omitting everything that plays only a peripheral role on the way to the genuine goal, we restrict ourselves, in essence, to an explanation of §§50–56 of the text. However, that which is insufficiently explained there and is, at the same time, of "teleological" significance will be set out more exactly with reference to other writings. We thereby draw in only such passages as correspond to the fundamental position of the "Fifth Cartesian Meditation." The proposals that diverge from this or move out beyond it are first taken account of in the later chapters.[46] In this way, the latter also completes the "presentation" of the theory of intersubjectivity. We are entitled to propound the form that Husserl gave to his ideas in the "Fifth Cartesian Meditation" as "the" theory of intersubjectivity because, in the scope of our theme, it is representative of all those thoughts that Husserl brought to complete clarity.

The Course of Husserl's Theory

1 The Reduction to My Transcendental Sphere of Ownness

At the outset of Husserl's theory of intersubjectivity we find a new reduction: the reduction to my "primordinal" or "ownness sphere," called, for the most part, "primordinal reduction" in what follows.[1] In contrast with the eidetic-phenomenological reduction this one is, according to Husserl, a "new kind of *epoché*" (CM 126:95) in two respects: first, insofar as I, as already "transcendentally instated," carry it through on the basis of the phenomenological reduction and "within" the transcendental "sphere of universality" (CM 126:95) that is uncovered by its means; and then, insofar as, in accordance with its intent, it is what the phenomenological reduction precisely is not— "abstraction."[2] As a "peculiar kind of thematic *epoché*" (CM 124:92), it lays bare a particular "layer" of the totality of the transcendentally reduced world by means of an abstraction from everything else. Consequently, its objects are also distinct from those of the phenomenological reduction. That which the latter reduces, namely, the world of the natural attitude, I no longer confront in the carrying through of the primordinal reduction. Its content is far more that to which the phenomenological reduction has reduced the natural world—the world as phenomenon. That to which the primordinal reduction is directed is only a part of that to which the phenomenological is directed: "a unitary, coherent stratum of the phenomenon-world" (CM 127:96).

That from which the primordinal reduction abstracts is "what is now in question" (CM 124:92). In the theory of intersubjectivity it is the "transcendental meaning of the alien subject" (CM 124:92) that is primarily in question. And so it is, above all, the constitutive achievement of that intentionality of mine that is directed toward alien subjects that is covered over (CM 124:92), that is, not this intentionality itself, but "the reality of the alien for me" (CM 125:94) that precisely presents the constitutive performance of the intentionality of mine that is directed toward it. Thanks to this performance, alien subjects are there for me *as such*, or as intentional objects that are subjects at the same time. Accordingly, the primordinal reduction abstracts from "that which gives men and animals their specific sense as, so to speak, I-like living beings"[3] (CM 126:95). Certainly, as we have seen, Husserl inquires into the transcendental sense of other subjects with reference to the transcendental sense of the objective world. Even this sense belongs to what is in question, and indeed essentially so. As a consequence of the foregoing, the primordinal *epoché* likewise excludes everything in the "world of phenomena" that attests to "the Other" as the constitutive condition of its possibility, all "cultural predicates," and, above all, the "surrounding world for everyone," which gives the world the aspect of an intersubjective objectivity (CM 126–127:95). Thus, in the end, there remains only "that which is my own," as the residuum of the abstraction from all "aliens" as "nonalien" (CM 126:95).

Before we pass judgment upon Husserl's *positive* determination of this nonalien, we should at least get clear in passing about the methodological function that, following upon what has already been said, the primordinal reduction appears to have. This function evidently consists in a more radical repetition of the work that has been carried out up to now by the Cartesian meditator, and in securing the field that is to serve as the point of departure for the theory of subjectivity. And so the primordinal reduction is also, in a certain sense, and in spite of the acknowledged difference, a "repetition" of the phenomenological reduction that is described in the *Cartesian Meditations*. More exactly, it brings to light the "solipsistic" tendency that adheres to that reduction insofar as it abstracts from transcendental intersubjectivity. The primordinal and the Cartesian-phenomenological reduction appear to be different if one considers the latter only from the standpoint of its claim to reduce the naturally intended "Other" to the "phenomenon Other." For the "phenomenon Other" is the Other as Other, and therewith that from which the primordinal reduction abstracts. However, insofar as the Cartesian-phenomenological reduction leaves transcendental intersubjectivity out of consideration, it also already secretly abstracts from that which, in a transcendental sense, first makes of the Other an Other, namely, its constituting capacity. As a result one can say that primordinal reduction is a repetition of the Cartesian-phenomenological reduction to the extent that the latter is an implicit anticipation of the primordinal.

The repetitive character of the primordinal reduction will be still clearer in the light of the positive determination of "that which is my own." My "ownness" coincides, in fact, with the scope of that which has already been disclosed by egology under the auspices of the phenomenological reduction as the constituting, on the one hand, and the constituted, on the other. On the side of the constituting, we find the flowing life of consciousness with all its actualities and potentialities (CM 131:100); on the side of the constituted, we find the world that belongs to me as intentional immanence, the totality of objects that are only transcendent in contrast with the real (reellen) immanence of my consciousness, and that are constituted as synthetic unities of a manifold of sensible modes of appearance (CM 134–135:104). The primordinal world is accordingly—and here too its identity with the egologically constituted world is evident—a "bare nature" (CM 128:96), a world of things that the act of abstraction has artificially reduced to its pure corporeality. Husserl characterizes it explicitly as "immanent transcendence" (CM 136:106, 140:110) in contrast with the sought-for transcendence of the "alien," whereby we are to understand, as the immanence in question, that very ideal belonging of the egologically constituted world to myself, which was referred to at the end of the preceding chapter. It is "a determining part of my own concrete being as ego" (CM 136:106). In the unity of the constituting and the constituted, my ownness is therefore my concrete, transcendental subjectivity itself, the "domain of my very own essentiality, of what I am in myself, in my full concreteness, or, as we may also say, in my monad" (CM 135:105).

At the beginning of the "Fifth Cartesian Meditation," Husserl goes beyond the constitutional analyses of the first four in one point alone. Namely, he directs the attention of the reader to the circumstance that the I that governs in my body, an I that is, as such, to be distinguished from my originary I, stands out in relief at the center of my primordinal world (CM 128–130:97–99). The corporeality of my body, which is thereby separated off from everything around me, is present to me straight away, inasmuch as I experience it at one and the same time from within, as the field of my sensations and as the immediately disposable organ of my dealings with the "outer world."[4] In this entanglement with my body, however, I am myself an embodied or psychophysical I, an I that Husserl calls "my personal I," although it is not personal in any human sense.[5] Before the constitution of my objective and worldly humanhood, which is itself also "in question," my transcendental originary I constitutes itself as the bodily acting center of its worldly sphere of ownness. But this is not the place to explicate this constitution more exactly.[6] It should only be noted that with his (highly cursory) outline of it, Husserl adds something that itself falls within the thematic circle of "transcendental solipsistic" phenomenology. That, however, it is first announced now, at the beginning of the "Fifth Cartesian Meditation," is on account of its direct relevance to the theory of intersubjectivity. This will be immediately evident when we turn our attention to this theory.

2 The Constitution of the Alien Body

The clarification of the goal that Husserl's transcendental theory of intersubjectivity has in mind, namely, the constitution of the objective world, occupies, in the "Fifth Cartesian Meditation," a relatively small place in comparison with the thoroughgoing description of the means by which this goal is supposed to be attained. The reason for this lies in the topic, namely, that the first, merely introductory, step "creates the genuine, and by no means slight, difficulties," while the possibility and necessity of the last, in themselves much more difficult, steps are immediately evident once these initial difficulties have been overcome. The first step is "the step to the Other (or Others)."[7] Since these Others are supposed to be the condition of the objective world, they themselves cannot yet belong to the objective world. Insofar as Husserl grasps "human beings as worldly objects," this means that the Others to which the first step in the theory of intersubjectivity leads are not yet the other *human beings*, still not my fellow human beings (CM 137–138:107–108).

How and as what do I now experience the Others? Everyday language—"what we generally say in the case of the experience of a human being"—attests to a state of affairs that is positive and negative at the same time. Positively, it indicates to us that there really is an *experience* of Others—indeed, an experience of *Others* and not of some kind of a thing from which we subsequently infer an Other on the basis of a consciousness that somehow inhabits it. Negatively, however, this experience reveals itself to be sheerly *mediate*: we concede straight off that, where we experience an Other, we still do not experience him *himself*, not his I, his experience, his appearances. Before all else, his body is, so to speak, constructed; it alone appears to be *immediately* experienced. This is what reveals and at the same time conceals the Other, for the simple reason that it precludes any direct access to the interiority of the Other. Husserl interprets this *"mediacy of intentionality"* on the analogy of the experience of a thing. In connection with the "experience of the Other," it is a matter of a "kind of making copresent, a kind of appresentation." Just as only the front of a thing is present, its back, on the contrary, being merely appresent, so it appears that the interiority of the Other can only be appresented in the presentation of its body. It is "there along with" and not "there itself"; nor can it ever be. In this way, according to Husserl, appresentation in the experience of the Other is fundamentally distinct from that of the experience of the thing. In contrast with the appresentation of the thing, the appresentation of the Other never, in the course of experience, goes over into an absolutely originary presence. That is "excluded a priori." The fundamental character of this difference attests to the distinction, in principle, between the mediacy of the experience of the Other (alien experience) and that implicit in the experience of the thing. The mediacy of the experience of the Other must be still more mediate than that which attaches to the experience of the thing. To what an extent this is the case is apparent when we interpret what is indicated in everyday speech on the level of the primordinal world, therefore from a transcendental standpoint (CM 139:109).

With this change of perspective the situation is transformed in one essential respect. The "organic body" (*Leib*) of the Other now no longer appears as immediately present, but simply his "physical body," and even that not as the physical body of an Other but solely as *a* physical body in general (CM 140:110). It cannot be the body of an Other because it has yet to receive this meaning. As *a* body, however, it is one thing among other bodily things that we characterize as "simple" things. It is constituted in exactly the same way as the latter: as the synthetic unity of a multiplicity of modes of appearance. And so not just a "kind" of appresentation is to be found in its experience, but the same appresentation that is at stake in the presentational experience of every other thing. Like every thing, "the (physical) body (of the Other to be)" (CM 147:118) has its unseen sides, which I can bring immediately into view in a verificational presentation. As a thing in my primordial world, it is, however, so little the Other itself that it rather belongs to *me*, to me as concrete subjectivity (CM 140:110).

While the preliminary orientation toward everyday discourse gave rise to the impression that I first arrived at the Other "itself" in the transition from the alien body to the alien psyche, the transcendental attitude reveals the step from the (physical) body (of the Other to be) to its (organic) body as the authentic step to the Other. The "difficulties" of which Husserl spoke are concentrated upon *this* step. Its most prominent difficulty, however, is to be found in its mediacy, and only this mediacy is the specific mediacy of alien experience, which far surpasses that implicit in the experience of the thing. My organic body functions as mediator. The motivational basis of mediation forms a "similarity" between my organic body (*Leib*) and the physical body (*Körper*) of the other. On the basis of this similarity I carry over from my body the meaning "organic body" (*Leib*) to the physical body (*Körper*) of the Other, which thereby becomes the body of an *Other* and is taken out of the plane of equality with "simple" things. The apprehension of a physical body as the body of an Other is accordingly an "*analogizing*" or "*assimilating apperception*" (CM 140–141:110–111).[8]

It is important to get clear in what the mediacy of analogizing apperception essentially consists, and in what it does *not* consist. In order to be able to see in what it does not consist, we need to be made aware of the method applied by Husserl with respect to the interpretation of alien experience. Husserl emphasizes that "it is a matter here not of disclosing a genesis going on in time but of a static analysis" (CM 136:106). This holds for the *whole* theory of intersubjectivity, from the experience of the primordinal world to the constitution of the objective world. What is set out thereby in individual steps is, "in reality," that is, for "the real and so at any time realizable experience of the Other" (CM 150:121), present at *one* blow. With regard to the analogizing apperception of the body of the Other this means that it is—as Husserl emphatically points out—"in no way an *inference* from analogy" (CM 141:111—italics are mine).

That the analogizing is carried out unnoticed and in a single moment without any mediating thought act is something Husserl demonstrates with respect to the role that it plays in all understanding of pregiven objects and so also in everyday experience, in the apprehension of the pregiven world. Every object whose sense is understood for the first time functions here as "the primal instituting original" (*urstiftende Original*), whose sense I transfer to the objects of a similar sense that I encounter thereafter. It is so little the case that this transfer takes place "in explicit reproduction, comparison, and drawing conclusions" that it is far rather the reason why we apprehend a world of pregiven objects "at a glance" and are able to understand it "as a matter of course" (CM 141:111).

For all that, the analogizing apperception of the alien body is, in another sense, a highly mediated experience, even an experience whose mediacy is completely unique. The first condition for the apprehension of its mediacy is insight into its distinction from the analogizing apperception of pregiven objects to which we have just referred. It cannot be subsumed under the latter by any means because the analogizing apperception of pregiven objects is inserted within possible primordinal experience, even though it surpasses the primordinal sphere, or, to speak more exactly, is the surpassing of the primordinal sphere. Husserl is perfectly well aware of the difference contained therein: "Ultimately we always get back to the radical differentiation of apperceptions between those that, according to their genesis, belong purely to the primordinal sphere and those that present themselves with the sense 'alter ego.'" Concretely, the everyday apperception of the thing is to be distinguished from the experience of the body of the Other, in that the "primal instituting original" is, in the former case, past, and, in the latter, present. Even if the former requires no "explicit reproduction," still, it is directed toward an implicit remembering that transcends the domain of what is presently at hand. In the example given by Husserl of the scissors whose functional sense has for the first time been appreciated by me, I no longer perceive the scissors themselves in that instant in which I transfer this sense to a sensibly present pair of scissors. I saw them "already before" and now do not see them. On the other hand, my body, on the basis of which I apprehend the physical body (of the Other to be) as an organic body, is itself present in the accomplishment of this apprehension. Alongside the nonpresentability of the appresented, it is the "peculiar characteristic" of the analogizing apperception of the alien body "that here the primally instituting original is always livingly present." This, however, is the foundation for something more than merely a specific difference in the proximate genus of "the analogizing apperception of pregiven objects." The presence of the "primally institutive original" is proof of the analogical apperception of the alien body of the Other in its essential distinction from everyday apperception of things (CM 141–142:112).

Up to this point, our understanding of the matter is unequivocally supported by Husserl's text. We have simply articulated the radicality of the "radical distinction" a little more sharply than Husserl. Now, however, Husserl's interpretation of the analogizing apperception of the Other's body becomes problematic. According to §51 of *Cartesian Meditations*, and on the basis of the peculiarity that the primally institutive original is present in it, this apperception is supposed to be a special case of "pairing." The entire Husserl literature has uncritically accepted this. In contrast, I would like first of all to venture the negative thesis that, on the basis of Husserl's presuppositions, analogizing apperception of the Other's alien body cannot be thought of as pairing. This thesis is not on that account purely destructive, but forms a part of the "presentation" of Husserl's theory of intersubjectivity because it makes room for the positive determination of the relation of the experience of the alien body to the pairing association and because it allows one to see that Husserl himself corrects his initial classification in the direction of this positive determination.

In its universal transcendental signification, pairing is an originary form of the passive synthesis of association. In "the most primitive case," two data (in higher-level cases more than two) stand out in consciousness as similar: the purely passively registered similarity of the data motivates their association as a pair, that is, a "reciprocal overlapping with respect to the objective sense" (CM 142:112). Now we have already said that what enables Husserl to spell out the analogizing apperception of the alien body as a pairing of this kind is the *presentness* of my functioning body as the primally institutive original. In opposition to the analogizing apperception of pregiven objects, both members are present in pairing. However, in the experience of the alien body, the fact that something functions there as the *primally institutive original* militates against its subordination under pairing. In this manner, a one-sidedness of the transfer of meaning is posited that stands in strict contradiction to the reciprocity of pairing. It is completely impossible to force this reciprocity upon the experience of the alien body intended by Husserl. Were it a matter of genuine reciprocity, Husserl would already at the outset have run counter to his precept to disregard all the constitutive operations of the Other. The transcendental conception that prescribes the starting point from the primordinal sphere itself demands the separation of the experience of the alien body and pairing association.

Now, in a positive vein, it is my opinion that pairing, without including analogizing apperception of the alien body within it, has a twofold relation to the latter. On the one hand, it precedes and makes the experience of the alien body possible; on the other hand, it succeeds the experience of the alien body and is made possible by it. The preceding pairing is admittedly different from the succeeding ones. This means that its members are to be distinguished from those that follow. Husserl does not explicitly take account of this difference. However, he describes that pairing, which he interprets as the analogizing apperception of the alien body, so differently that one can say that in fact he has in mind two different phenomena.

We turn first to the pairing that *follows* upon the understanding of the alien body. Husserl focuses upon it with the affirmation "that ego and alter ego are always and necessarily given in an original pairing" (CM 142:112). If we consider this citation in its own right, three interpretative possibilities offer themselves, corresponding to the threefold meaning of the "ego." The ego could first of all be my absolutely unique ego; second, my primordinal ego; and third, my personal-human objective I. The first two possibilities fall away. To be sure, the alter ego is always and necessarily given on the basis of my absolutely unique ego and my primordinal ego. But my absolutely unique ego would not be absolutely unique if it were only given in an original pairing with the alter ego. And, in the same way, my primordinal ego would not be primordinal if it needed the alter ego as a condition for its own givenness. In consequence, the third possibility alone remains. If we understand the ego that is under discussion to be my human-personal, objective I, the statement introduced above turns out, as a matter of fact, to be meaningful. It then becomes clear that it anticipates Husserl's doctrine that we have still to account for, and in accordance with which I, who constitute the Other as Other in general, and as an other human being, take on, from the Other, the meaning of an objective, personal, very own I. Two further remarks of Husserl leave no doubt that the statement is to be understood in this way. After

Husserl has said in connection with the analysis of the empathizing apprehension of psychic contents that each successful empathic comprehension of the Other opens up new associations, he continues, "Just as conversely, since every pairing association is reciprocal, every such comprehension uncovers my own psychic life in its similarity and difference" (CM 149). The similarity and difference accentuate the unity that is uncovered at the beginning of the next chapter, the unity of positing on a par (*Gleichstellung*) with me and positing in opposition (*Gegenüberstellung*) to me, which characterizes the personal mineness of the psychically mundane I. It is directly thematized by Husserl when, after the thesis that the Other constitutes itself as a modification of my self, he adds, in brackets, that "this character of being *my* self it gets by virtue of the contrastive pairing that now necessarily takes place" (CM 144:115). Here, as a matter of fact, we do find reciprocity and also, therewith, pairing. But this pairing is not the analogizing apperception of the alien body but rather already presupposes it. As the originary constitution of the Other, the analogizing apperception of the alien body must already have done its work in order that "ego and alter ego" can make their appearance through pairing.

The pairing that precedes and makes possible the understanding of the alien body associates my body and the physical body (of the Other). Two points can be proved: that the text provides a handhold for such an understanding and that wherever this handhold is provided, the qualitative difference between such pairing and the analogizing apperception of the alien body shows through, in contrast with the initial subsumption. Already toward the end of §51 we find that "now in case there presents itself, as outstanding in my primordial sphere, a body 'similar' to mine, that is to say, a body with determinations such that it must enter into a phenomenal pairing with mine, it seems clear, without more ado, that, with the transfer of sense, this body must forthwith appropriate from mine the sense-animate organism" (CM 143:113). In the first place it is evident that the members of the pairing referred to at this spot are the physical body (*Körper*) (of the Other to be) and my *physical body*, therefore neither my ego in any of its interpretations nor—what with respect to the relation to the understanding of the alien body is decisive—my *organic body* (*Leib*). So it then transpires from the statement cited that Husserl himself has come up against the difference in question. Evidence for this is the little word "forthwith." The gap that it brings to light is still further deepened by the "seems." It is only seemingly clear that without more ado. . . . In reality, all the intermediate determinations that Husserl introduces in the further course of the investigation still have to be noted. In continuing he also clarifies what is said here. At the beginning of §54 he first describes pairing more exactly as pairing of my physical body (*Körper*) and that of the Other: "The body that is a member of my primordinal world (the body subsequently of the other ego) is for me a body in the mode 'there.' Its mode of appearance does not become paired in a direct association with the mode of appearance actually belonging at the time to my organic body (*Leib*) (in the mode 'here'). Rather, it awakens reproductively another, an immediately similar appearance included in the system constitutive of my organic body as a body in space." Appended to this, however, we find this: "Thus the assimilative apperception becomes *possible* and *established* by which the external physical body over there receives analogically from mine the sense, organic body." Far from being itself a pairing, the analogizing apperception of the alien organic body really presupposes the physical body pairing. For here also—as in what follows—Husserl talks not of an associative apperception by analogy but of an "associately *awakened* apperception" (CM 147:117–118—italics are mine).

Against Husserl's theory of the experience of the alien body it has been objected that no similarity at all exists between the physical body (*Körper*) (of the Other) and my organic body (*Leib*). Insofar as the physical body (of the Other) is perceived externally and my organic body, on the contrary, primarily experienced from within, the latter is "as dissimilar as possible" from the former.[9] This is undoubtedly correct. In accordance with our presentation, however, it is just as indubitable that the objection does not touch Husserl. It could only be raised because Husserl's reference to the difference of physical body pairing and the analogical apperception of the alien organic body had not been sufficiently attended to.

This difference also justifies the recourse to the reciprocity implicit in pairing. The reciprocity of the pairing of "ego and alter ego" is in agreement with the starting point from my primordinal sphere because it first enters into effect after it has been surpassed. The reciprocity of physical body pairing fits in with this because it still takes place within the peculiarly reduced world. Strictly speaking, the Other is not even taken account of there. He is simply the physical body (of the Other to be), which, "as primordinal, is naturally only a determining part of myself" (CM 140:110). To that extent, the constitutive "operation" that starts out from him does not start out from the Other. If we now ask what its constitutive operation is, the significance of the disagreement (which is fundamental for Husserl's theory), fixed in the expression "physical body" (of the Other to be), is revealed. Insofar as the other physical body that enters into the pairing with my physical body still belongs to the *Other* to be, the Other already, at the same time, has an effect upon me with it. His constitutive capacity, that is, the constitutive capacity of his perceptual act, is of the same order as the effect that—in accordance with our next chapter —the Other exerts upon me. That is to say, it already has the character of "alter-ation" (*Veranderung*). We can characterize it more exactly as *physicalization of my organic body*. The failure to thematize this embodiment is presumably responsible for Husserl's initial positing of the organic body of the Other on a par with the pairing of the physical body. In order to throw more light on this, one has first to consider to what an extent a purely solipsistic constitution of my physical body is possible. Even this is only touched upon briefly in the "Fifth Cartesian Meditation" (CM 143:113). More exact information is provided primarily by *Ideas*, where it is said that my organic body can only be *partially* constituted in the "solipsistic attitude," as a visually perceptible physical body (Id.II 145, 157–161). I can look at my hands while I move them, peer at my legs while I walking, inspect the place where I feel the pain; but, in primordinal viewing, I can never represent my body to myself as a whole. Precisely this makes the perception of the physical body of the Other possible for me—thereby enabling me to transcend the purely solipsistic attitude. It changes my body into an outer thing. The purely solipsistic constitution of my physical body is incomplete, however, because my so constituted body is tied down to the "central here" (CM 145:116) of my organic body. Therefore my organic body can, in pairing, only be embodied in this way: that the view of the (alien) physical body that is to be found "in the modus there" also places it in the there. Once again, this can only happen in the manner described by Husserl. The mode of appearance of the (alien) physical body "awakens reproductively a similar appearance included in the system constitutive of my animate organism as a body in space. It brings to mind how my body would look *if I were there*" (CM 147:118). Admittedly, an "explicit reproduction" is left entirely out of account. I do not, in an explicit remembering, recall my having been there then. Rather, the mode of appearance of the (alien) physical body reminds me of it. It awakens, reproductively, a similar appearance of my physical body. But even this, as it were, passive memory is included in the presentness of the incomplete experience of my physical body. Only a comprehensive presentness allows for the application of the category "pairing." Still, the contribution of memory to (physical) body pairing shows that even this already brings with it difficulties for the subsumption under the universal transcendental phenomenon "pairing." With a view to the physicalization of my organic body, the present primordinal experience of my physical body and the memory elicited by the view of the (alien) physical body have to work together. Only with regard to their cooperation does the whole range of the mediacy of the understanding of the alien organic body reveal itself. This collaboration is itself the most primordinal mediation. The physicalization (*Verkörperung*) of my organic body that results from this then mediates the embodiment (*Verleiblichung*) of the (alien) physical body. In spite of all these mediations, the understanding of the organic body of the Other is still free, however, of the mediacy of that inference that Husserl denies to the analogizing apperception of pregiven objects and to pairing association.

Hitherto the analysis of the experience of the Other has only been presented to the extent that it seeks to clarify the possibility of the apperception of a primordinal body as *organic* body. Since the physical body (of the Other to be) emerges in the primordinal world as a thing like any other thing, one can say in a very general way that in the preceding reflections it was a question of proving how, at the lowest level (that of the organic body), an experience of the Other as an Other contrasted with things, or as a nonthing, is possible.

To the same problematic there belongs the question how such an experience can be confirmed in the further course of experience, that is, by what means the organic body of the Other can be verified in its nonthingness. From what has been said, it is clear that this cannot happen through fulfilling presentation. And yet the verification of the embodied character of the Other's body is founded in this mode of verification. For insofar as it is the gradual presentation of what is at first appresented that, above all, distinguishes the experience of the thing, so too it guides the course of the experience of the physical body apperceived as organic. However, just as the first presentation of the alien physical body, together with the appresentation of that which is presentable by means of analogizing, also appresents an element of the unverifiably embodied, so each further step in the process of perception (which transforms what is at first only appresented on the body into the physically presented with new horizons of the sheerly cogiven) likewise appresents, by means of analogizing, new sides of the unpresentably embodied. In this manner, the synthetically harmonious running off of the fulfilling verifying presentations of the physical body "indicates" an originally inaccessible system, which holds out through fluctuations in comportment as the unitary "behavior" of the organic body (CM 143–144:114).

Now, however, an answer is also required to the question how the alien body, which is accordingly verified as nonthing, gives proof of its difference from *my* body. Having hitherto considered solely the question of what makes the alien body into an organic body, we should now ask with Husserl, "What makes the organic body into an *alien* and not into a second own body?" (CM 143:113—italics are mine). While the question, as a question, extends beyond the problematic developed above, Husserl still draws the answer to it from insights that are already familiar to us. To put it more exactly, he gives two answers. The alienness of the alien body, as of the Other in general, is first assured through the nonpresentability (in unity with the verifying indication of the appresented) of the fulfilling progress of the experience of the physical body: "The character of the existent 'alien' has its basis in this kind of verifiable accessibility of what is not originally accessible. Whatever can become presented, and evidently verified, originally is something I am, or else it belongs to me as peculiarly my own. By virtue of this, whatever is experienced in the founded manner that characterizes a primordinally unfulfillable experience, an experience that does not give something itself originally but that consistently verifies something indicated, is alien" (CM 144:114). Second, the alien body gives proof of its alienness through the "coexistence" (CM 148:119) of its being-there with my being-here. To be sure, thanks to the possibility of "crossing over" (CM 146:116) that adheres essentially to me, I can at another time be there where the other body is, but not *at the same time* as my being-here. In this way, the being-there-now of the other (organic) body attests to something that its being-there alone could not make credible: that it is not my own, not a "duplicate" (CM 146:116) of *my own* body (CM 148:119).

With this proof of the alienness of the alien organic body, a problem nevertheless arises that still has to be resolved before the sphere of embodiment is abandoned. How can the physical body, which is primordinally constituted by me in the modus "there" and which I apperceive as alien (organic) body, be *identical* with the physical body that, as this other organic body, must appear to the Other itself in its own world in the modus "here"? When taken seriously, does not the alienness of identity conflict with ownness? Not according to Husserl. According to him, the essence of that very appresentation whose positive and negative connection with the presentation attests to the alienness of the alien (organic) body also guarantees its unity with the corresponding physical body of my primordinal world. This identity is due to an essential unity that holds appresentation and presentation together and that lies at the root of the law of the nonpresentability of the bodily appresented as well as of the schema for the verification of the bodily appresented in process of presentation. As simple "co-perception," which can never be separated from "authentic perception," appresentation is not possible without a "core of presentation." However, the identity of the *object* lies in the fact that presentation and appresentation "stand in general in the functional community of *one* perception," which is presented appresentatively and appresented presentatively. Just as for anything else, this also holds for the perception of the Other. So the appresented organic body of the Other is also, as the physical body constituted by the latter, one with the physical body primordinally presented by me, a body that, on the basis of its similarity with my own, is indicative of alien embodiment. By virtue of the relation of the presented and the appresented to one and the same being, this indication is "not simply an indicator" in the sense of a reference of something to something else, but is, so to speak, a self-indicator. The physical body that is primordinally perceived is "the physical body of the Other itself" (CM 150–151:121–122, 153:124).

3 The Empathic Experience of the Alien Soul and of the Alien I

We have completed our analysis of the theory of intersubjectivity, that is, the constitution of the alien (organic) body. In accord with Husserl's observation that the real difficulties lie at the beginning, everything else presents itself as a direct consequence of the foregoing. For once a (physical) body has been apperceived as alien (organic) body, everything that makes it into an organic body is also given in and with it: in a psychological direction the alien "soul," which is bound up with it "in the unity of a psychophysical reality" (CM 153:124), in a transcendental direction the I of the alien ownness sphere, which "governs" in it (CM 143:113, 151:122), and, finally, the "pure alter ego."[10]

In accordance with the transcendental orientation of his theory, Husserl only briefly touches upon the psychological side. In essence, he limits himself to the remark that psychic contents are indicated in "the behavior of organic bodies in the outer world." These contents are intelligible to me (as is embodied behavior itself), thanks to analogizing apperception. Since we intend to follow the most direct route to the transcendental terminus of the theory of intersubjectivity, we shall forgo a detailed presentation of the material sketched out here through the introduction of citations from other works.[11] In the interest of a clarification of the basic principles, our attention need only be drawn to one thing. According to Husserl, such self-revealing moods as anger or joyfulness, which are disclosed in the behavior of the alien body, are intelligible "from my own behavior under similar circumstances," and even the style of the higher psychic occurrences should be understood through associative connection with my own empirically familiar life style in its roughly typical form. It should be noted here that, from a psychological standpoint, the past components enter by themselves and therefore stand out much more strongly than on the plane of pure embodiment, where the implicitly remembered — as we saw — remains restricted to the present of the perceived. My own behavior "under similar circumstances" is normally completely different from my present behavior, normally not at all my present behavior but that behavior that I once exhibited on the day that I was angry or joyful. And my familiar life style is the style of the life I have already lived out. However, this means that the psychological understanding of the Other is what the understanding of the alien body precisely is not, that is, *pure* analogical apperception (CM 149:120).

This stipulation is also important for the understanding of the goal of the theory of intersubjectivity. For it applies in a similar manner to the transcendental alter ego. Husserl uses the term "empathy"[12] to name the innovation both with regard to the experience of the alien soul, as also that of the pure alter ego, in opposition to the appresentation of the alien body. Therefore it is necessary to dwell on this term for a while. That it is by no means self-evident, even in Husserl's eyes, can be gleaned from a remark in *First Philosophy*. There Husserl finds the "recently" discovered description of alien experience as empathy hardly satisfactory (EP.II 63). In agreement with this, Husserl introduces the concept of empathy in the "Fifth Cartesian Meditation" as completely synonymous for the "experience of the Other" by speaking of "so-called" empathy (CM 124:92, 173:146). In the passage before us, however, where he *only* means the experience of the alien soul, the word "empathy," which was first used in the previous connection, is brought out in italics, without any apostrophizing (CM 149:120). In just as positive a manner, Husserl employs this word as the title for the specific experience of the transcendental alter ego. In the Paris lectures, it is a matter of the "transcendental operation of empathy" (CM 34:34). Husserl is thinking primarily of the discovery of *this*, the transcendental operation, when in the "Fifth Cartesian Meditation" he says "that the problem of empathy first received its true meaning and the true method for its solution through constitutional phenomenology" (CM 173:147).[13] If, nevertheless, he completely refuses the identification of empathy and the experience of the Other, it is only because he did not want to characterize as empathy that appresentation of the alien body that belongs essentially to the experience of the Other.

The context in which the remark from *First Philosophy* cited above is set also attests to the same thing. The "experience through interpretation" in the name of which alien experience emerges there means, upon closer investigation, the "perception of the alien body." This is "perception through original interpretation," or the "originally interpretative regard." Empathy stands out in clear contrast to such a regard, whose originality is, according to Husserl, precisely grounded in the immanental present of the "regressive relation to my own original embodiment" (EP.II 63). To be sure, the direction of the act is the same to the extent that it is the Other whom I regard as well as experience empathically. However, while that which I *see* in the Other I read off of the Other (even if in the mediate manner of an analogically mediated appresentation), that which I empathically experience in him is through and through my own soul, or my own ego. In empathic experience I try to understand the Other in such a way that I "put myself in his place" and so "am absorbed in him." "I put myself in the other subject" (Id.II 274–275 — italics are mine), and in so doing I make of myself not only a means to the understanding of the Other (as is the case with the perception of the alien body) but also its object, an object that, admittedly, only represents what really has to be understood. It is clear that in this way the mediacy of alien experience is heightened once again. In the purely and simply "mediate mode of experience of 'empathy,' "[14] even the relative immediacy of the regard is obliterated.

Nevertheless, in relation to the alien I and the alien soul, Husserl also speaks of "appresentation." Indeed, the scope of the concept of appresentation, a scope that is presupposed as self-evident and that reaches into the psychological and transcendental sphere, conditions the possibility and the legitimacy of Husserl's endeavor to adduce the reasons for the alienness of the alien body and for its enduring identity with the body of my primordinal world, and is now introduced for the purpose of proving the corresponding state of affairs on the plane of the psychological and transcendental alien experience. Let us restrict ourselves, from now on, as does Husserl himself, to the transcendental problematic. The alienness of the alter ego is once again guaranteed through the incompleteness of the appresentation and through its coexistence with my ego (CM 144:114, 148:119). The alien ego is, however, just like my own, a concrete monad, and therefore is the I of a primordinal world. With its alienness, the alienness of its sphere of ownness is therefore equally guaranteed. Likewise, the unity of the appresentation with the founding presentation grounds the identity of my and the alien primordinal world in its broadest scope: "Through the appresentation itself and the unity that it, *as* appresentation, necessarily shares with the presentation cofunctioning for it (thanks to which an Other and, consequently, his concrete ego are there for me in the first place), the identity sense of my primordinal Nature and that of the presentified Other is necessarily brought forth" (CM 152:124). Identity does not mean here, however, that the Other is nothing other than my sphere of ownness. For in that case, the identity would set aside the alienness. That my and the alien primordinal world are identical can, on the basis of the alienness of the alien, rather only mean that in it there appears, to me in this way and to the Other in another, one and the same world—"*the*" world.

4 The Intersubjective Constitution of the Objective World

In this way we have already reached our goal with one mighty leap, which, admittedly, has jumped over a great deal. We now have to go the last bit of the way, once again, step by step. Let us first of all bring to mind the meaning that the concept "alien" has in the train of thought that has been set out. Alien means there: not own. However, to that which is own, there belongs my entire primordial world. With the demonstration of the alienness of the Other a being has been indicated that "wholly and entirely transcends" my primordial world (CM 135:105). With this we have been put on the track of "authentic" (CM 136:106) and "genuine" (FTL 213:241) transcendence: "That which in a subjectivity can only be constituted through apperception, but not through perception, is also no longer immanent in it, neither actually (*reell*) nor ideally (*ideell*) immanent. All such transcendence, all such surpassing and going out over subjectivity beyond itself, rests upon empathy. Here is the sole authentic transcendence, and everything else that is still called transcendence, like the objective world, rests upon the transcendence of alien subjectivity" (EP.II 495 B note 2).

Even the objective world, which is supposed to be constituted with the help of the alter ego, is "transcendent" transcendence. This corresponds to the circumstances that even Husserl's concept of the alien is related as well to the alter ego as to the objective world: "The fact of the experience of something alien (not-I) is present as the experience of an objective world and others in it (non-I in the form other-I)" (CM 136:106). The other I is only the "intrinsically first alien" (CM 137:107). However, the concept of the alien must have another meaning in relation to the objective world than in the relationship to the alter ego. What is common to it in both areas is only the negative signification of the not-own. However, the alter ego is the not-own because it is an other ownness. The objective world, on the other hand, is, as the not-own, also not the own of the Other. The own of the Other excludes the my-own, and vice versa. The objective world, however, is neither the my-own nor the own of the Other because it includes both within itself. It is to be identified neither with the latter nor with the former because, as has already been indicated, it is that which is identical in both. So its alienness, in opposition to the "pure" alienness of the alien subjectivity, is mediated by identity. As mediated in this way, however, it posits over against (merely) "my" world and the world of the Other, a third—a third that, according to Husserl, first emerges out of the latter through "identification" of the primordinal worlds.

Transcendental empathy, as "appresentation" of the alter ego, is supposed to be the organon of the constitution of the objective world out of the identification of the primordinal worlds. In the conventional understanding, "empathy" (*Einfühlung*) means: feeling oneself into. . . . In this way I feel my way psychologically into the psychic life of the Other, into his moods and experiences, into his character and his habitual, solidified behavioral traits. But it is obvious that, prior to any such empathy, that toward which it is directed must already be constituted in its being. As constituting, transcendental empathy cannot, therefore, in the first instance, possess its usual meaning. At root, it is not a feeling oneself *into* an alter ego but the empathy *of* an alter ego.[15] Nevertheless, it would remain without reality and without confirmation if it did not also feel itself into something. The essential determination of the transcendental alter ego bears witness to this something. In the same way as the transcendentality of *my* I, that of the alien I is also grounded in the constitution of the world. That constituted by the Other is, in the first place, its primordinal world. Hence the empathy of a transcendental ego is carried out as a feeling oneself into the alien primordinal world.

This world is, as we know, characterized by the difference between the noematic appearance and the intentional sense that lies at the root of that appearance as synthetic unity. Correspondingly, transcendental empathy must be differentiated into the apperception of the appearance of what is alien and the presentification of its synthesizing unity. What characterizes transcendental empathy in general also holds of the appresentation of the alien appearance. It is bound up with the first apperception of a physical body as an alien organic body: "To the sphere of that which is appresented with the seen organic body there belongs also the system of appearances in which an outer world is given to these subjects" (Id.II 168). The physical body that arises in my sphere of ownness and is apperceived as alien organic body appears to me in the modus there, so that this there is determined out of the central here of my organic body. So the union of the appresentation of the alien appearance with the appresentation of the alien organic body confers the highest significance upon the here-there relation (which already played a dominant role at the level of embodiment) for the transcendental empathy. This "putting oneself in the place of" that is proper to all empathy takes transcendentally the form of a putting oneself into the there, and, on this basis, each putting oneself in the Other, even when it is no longer articulated in an immediately spatial manner, receives the character of a putting oneself in the "standpoint" of the Other. I apperceive the Other empathically not "with spatial modes of appearance that are mine from here, but . . . with such as I would likewise have if I were to go over there and be where he is" (CM 146:117).

As different as is the there from the here, however, are the apperceived appearances of the Other from those that are now present to me. To be sure, I do have (under the assumption made in the text of the integrity of the sense organs) the same appearances as the Other now has, if I have actually gone over there and now stand "there." However, as these appearances are then for me orginally present and no longer merely appresent, they are also no longer those of the Other but my own. But, at the same moment, the Other again necessarily has other appearances and, indeed, with the same necessity with which we, thanks to the spatiality of our body, are separated in a real or worldly way from one another (CM 157:129), so that my standpoint is exclusive of the Other's and the Other's of mine, at one and the same time (CM 148:119).

This difference obviously also obtains when I and the Other observe one and the same thing. Then we observe it precisely "from different sides." Indeed, in the *Cartesian Meditations* this is Husserl's preferred model. Husserl only comes to speak incidentally of the possibility that even the objects really perceived by the Other are not the same as "those presently perceived by me" (CM 152:123). But whether we are now directed intentionally toward the same object or not, the difference between our appearances that is implied thereby is indicative of the same *alienness* as that which has already been demonstrated in the physically-organically embodied here-there difference, in which the former is rooted. It is a matter of the alienness of the sphere of ownness of the alter ego, in contrast with my sphere of ownness. Therefore as long as one grasps transcendental empathy only as "appresentation" of alien *appearances*, it remains unintelligible how it is supposed to effect the transition from the primordinal world to the *one* objective world.

This transition is first brought about by the empathic presentification of the intentional sense. In conformity with the anticipated thesis, whereby the objective world is constituted out of the identification of the primordinal worlds, that which is identically intended by the Other, on its side, must be identical with that which is identically intended by me. According to Husserl, this higher identity is coexperienced in the empathic act itself. This is most clearly the case with respect to Husserl's preferred model, that of the intentional directedness of ego and alter ego toward the same thing. For, with respect to it, Husserl also demonstrates most precisely the identity of intersubjective experience: "The things posited by the Other are also mine: through empathy I take part in the positing of the Other. I identify the thing, for instance, that I have over against myself in the mode of appearance α with the thing posited by the Other in the mode of appearance β" (Id.II 168). The thing that previously was for me only the, so to speak, *subjectively* identical thing is now, as the objective sense of a manifold of appearances inherent in my concrete subjectivity, "*the intersubjectively identical thing*, a constitutive unity of a higher order" (Id.I 372:420). Only, it simply looks as though the experience of intersubjective identity can be most easily exhibited in the common directedness toward *one* thing. When I, as the correlate of my own and the Other's perception, appeal to one and the same thing, I have already presupposed precisely what has to be proved: the intersubjective identity of the thing. On what basis, then, do I know that the Other really is oriented toward the same thing as myself? With what right, therefore, do I identify the thing that is the synthetic unity of "his" appearances with the thing that is, for the Other, the synthetic unity of "his" appearances? Why should the appearances of the Other alone be alien and not also his intentional objects, which certainly belong just as well to his ownness sphere and so are for me the not-own, that is, purely alien?

In order to be able to grasp the problem fully, one must bear in mind that the intersubjective identification of the thing is bound up with the empathic act itself and does not subsequently enter into the appresentation of the alien sphere of ownness (CM 152:123). To be sure, subsequently, and without further difficulty, the identity of the intended can be sought through "reciprocal understanding" (Id.III 2, K 166:163) and "agreement" (Id.II 133–134:327), just as can the particular content through which what appears to the Other is concretely distinguished from what appears to me. Again, each of us can subsequently become convinced of the correctness of what is verbally communicated in this way thanks to the "possibility of exchange through change of place" (Id.II 168; see also FTL 209:236). Still, the intersubjective identification of the thing comes before all change of place and all verbal expression. Indeed, in one place in book II of *Ideas*, it is said that "between different human beings it is only through understanding that the possibility exists of *knowing* that the thing that one sees and that the Other sees are *the same* (Id.II 85). In this way, however, only *the* meaning to which Husserl in general limits its constitutive operation will be attributed to speech, namely, to bring to clear knowledge what is already prepredicatively constituted through conclusive fixation upon explicit objectivity. In this sense, understanding certainly brings the world of intersubjective identification to *completion*, but precisely for this reason the latter is already presupposed as a specifically prepredicative experience.

The attempt, in the next chapter, to interpret the intersubjective constitution of the objective world more originally with reference to *Crisis*, more originally than is possible with the help of the representation of identity, cannot ultimately be justified by the difficulty that attaches to this doctrine of the identification of the primordinal world. To be sure, Husserl himself, in the "Fifth Cartesian Meditation," believes he can get on top of this difficulty through the regress to an identity (grounded in a functional community of presentation and appresentation) of the physical body of sphere of ownness apperceived as alien organic body with the physical body of the Other as that which partially constitutes his organic body in his sphere of ownness. With this identity, the desired identity of both primordinal worlds is supposed to be given already. According to Husserl, the sense of identity emanates from the isolated point of the "alien body" in which, at the same time, my own and the alien sphere of ownness intersect and on to the totality of both ownness spheres. The governance of the other I "in this body there is directly apperceived, and indirectly its governance in the nature that appears perceptually to it—the same nature that belongs to this physical body over there, the same as that which is my primordinal nature. It is the same only in its mode of appearance, as if I were to stand over there in the place of the alien organic-physical body. The physical body is the same (given to me as there, to him as here) as the central body, and 'my' *whole* nature is the same as that of the Other" (Id.II 85). Formulated more pointedly this means that as a consequence, "my" whole nature is the same as that of the Other (see also Id.III 109 B)—admittedly, in a sense of consequence that cannot first be envisaged as an inference. Negatively, it should also be emphasized that the intersubjective identity should not be carried over from the commonly observed individual thing to the whole of the primordinal world. Rather, there exists in this respect a priority of the "*whole* of nature" over the individual thing, as the alien body from which even the individual thing first of all receives the sense of the intersubjectively identical, which sense is then communicated to the primordinal worlds. Only for this reason can the objects perceived by the Other and that do not lie in my field of observation be posited as intersubjectively identical, through empathy, in as original a manner as the objects intended in common.

The rank ordering in the intersubjectification of the world, sketched above from the alien physical-organic body through the "aggregate nature" up to the individual natural object, confirms the construction of the objective world described in the text as constituted out of intersubjective identification. The object that is in itself primary (in the transprimordinal sense of intersubjective objectivity) is, accordingly, the alien physical-organic body: "The experiential phenomenon, objective nature, has, besides the primordinally constituted stratum, a superimposed, second, merely appresent stratum originating from my experience of someone else; and this fact concerns, first of all, the alien physical-organic body, which is, so to speak, the intrinsically first object." At the same time this implies that the objectivity of the alien physical-organic body directly excludes the objectivity of the whole of nature. However, with the objectivity of nature, the objectivity of each thing appearing in nature is also posited: "From that, as is easily understandable, every natural object experienced or experienceable by me in the lower stratum receives an appresentational stratum . . . a stratum united in an identifying synthesis with the stratum given to me in the mode of primordinal originality: the same natural object in its possible modes of givenness to the Other" (CM 153:125).

I have already emphasized that the identity of the primordinal worlds, as the ground of the objective world, which, however, like the the alien primordinal world, is supposed itself to be "authentically" transcendent, must preserve the character of alienness in itself, an alienness that distinguishes authentic transcendence. That which is identically meant by me and by the Other in the change of actual appearances is "the same" not because it is unitary, but because the same appears in it. According to Husserl, the objective sense that already holds together what appears to me in one intentional unity also becomes the appearance of the objective entity that, in a similar manner, is supposed to make known to it how it is itself present in the manifold of noematic appearances. This applies just as well to the objective sense of the individual thing as it does to the world whole, and indeed this primarily concerns the latter. The constitution of the alter ego in empathy brings about a "universal superaddition of sense to my primordinal world, whereby the latter becomes the appearance of a particular *objective* 'world' as the identical world for everyone" (CM 137:107). At the same time, however, . . . an essential result of the transformation of the world as a whole is that even that which "was already a real thing, but for *one* pure I that has still not carried through an empathic interaction, now becomes a . . . mere 'appearance' " (Id.III 110 B). For "each one, what each originally actually experienced as a perceptual thing is transformed into a simple 'representation of,' 'appearance of,' the one objective entity" (K 167:164).

5 Understanding the Other as a Human Being and Humanizing Self-Apprehension

We are coming to the ultimate and the penultimate points in the transcendental doctrine of experience of the alien, which we shall take as the point of departure for the following interpretation, and which, for that reason, we shall only handle briefly at this point. According to that part of Husserl's theory that we have just drawn upon, the objective world has been constituted through an empathic relation with "the Other in general." Insofar as this world has received its objectivity from the alien physical body, the Other itself now takes over the sense of an objective entity from the objective world. The Other is fitted in as an intersubjectively constituted object in the objective world, constituted by means of its mediation. Admittedly, this does not mean that after the objectification of the alien physical body featured at the beginning, the other part of the Other, which, in the deepest sense, is its pure ego, should now be objectified. Rather, the objectification of the Other is to be sought first of all precisely in this, that that which was split up by the primordinal reduction into alien body and alien I is brought into one unitary object: to "the Other." This unitary object is called "human being." It is therefore from the objective world that the Other is first constituted as "the objective human being" (Id.III 112 B): "In this world (that is, the objective) all egos again present themselves, but in an objectifying apperception with the sense, human beings or psychophysical human beings as worldly objects" (CM 137:107).

According to Husserl, "the alien human being is constitutionally the intrinsically first human being" (CM 153:124). He is this in distinction from me, the last human being. Already thereby it is decided that I can only be constituted as a human being through the Other, therefore never in solipsistic experience: "In solipsistic experience we do not reach the natural object, 'human being' " (Id.I 161:199; see also Id.II 89–90). This thesis is developed positively in the theory of the "transference" to me of the objective unity "human being" read off the Other, that is, to the whole of that which primordinally falls apart into my body and the "personal" I that governs therein: "Only with empathy and the constitutional direction of experiential attention upon that which is appresented with the alien organic body and the psychic life continually taken up in conjunction with the organic body does the completed unity human being get constituted; and this latter I carry over subsequently to myself" (Id.II 167).

In many places Husserl describes how this transference proceeds in a highly insightful manner.[16] It is grounded in the fact that I empathically presentify not only how and as what the things that surround the Other and myself are given to the Other but also how and as what *I myself* appear to him. However, in principle I can only appear to the Other as he appears to me, hence, in the first instance, appresentatively as an I that is localized in a physical body to be found "there," therefore in the horizon of the objective world as a unitary object, "human being," whose spatiotemporal position is determined by the now-there of my physical body. Inasmuch as I transfer myself over to this alien "representation of myself," I must make sure that the one as which I shall be seen over there is quite other than I myself, that is, than the "I" that I discover in direct inspection (as the I that stands over against my body). On the other hand, however, the evidence of the experience of empathy compels me to identify myself with the alien representation of myself. For what I contribute to the Other in and through empathy, namely, the transformation of his ego, which corresponds to his own body, into the world object "human being," now has to be allowed to happen to me on the basis of the self-appresented similarity of the mode of being of ego and alter ego. I have to grasp myself as a human being: "The comprehensive representation that Others have of me, or could have, serves to make of myself a social 'human being,' and this in quite another way than by a directly apprehended inspection" (Id.II 242).

With this we have succeeded in getting to the end of our presentation of the transcendental doctrine of alien experience. Let us remind ourselves of the course of the individual steps.[17] The initial basis was my primordinal world as the pure thing-world transformed into phenomenon, the transcendentally reduced "mere Nature," in whose midst I myself have been constituted as primordinal, personal, psychophysical I, as the moving agent of my animated body from which I am, however, set at a distance. The first step toward the Other, in the first instance toward the Other in general, is the apperception of the (alien) physical body as an organic body on the basis of the analogy with my own body, which, in part at any rate, is constituted as a physical body. The second step is, in a psychological direction, the experience of the psychic life of the alien, while in a transcendental direction, it is the experience of the pure alter ego. Inasmuch as the vehicle of the first step is a quasi apperception of analogy, the second makes use of the purified analogizing as empathy (*Einfühlung*). The empathy of a pure alter ego realizes itself, however, as a feeling oneself into the alien sphere of ownness, which, like mine, consists of a world differentiated in accordance with its appearance and its sense. While empathy into the alien appearances really only brings alienness to light, the making present of the synthetic unities of these appearances does, according to Husserl, make it clear that the Other only has "the same" in mind, but from the standpoint of another side. So we come to the third step: the constitution of the objective world out of the identification of the primordinal worlds. In the objective world I apperceive—that is the fourth step—the Other as a unitary object complete in itself and situated in space and time. In this way the Other loses the meaning "Other in general" and becomes another human being. In the fifth and last step, I finally transfer the objective unity "human being" to myself in that I empathically presentify myself how and as what the Other represents me.

3
The Goal of Husserl's Theory

1 The Intersubjective Constitution of the Objective I

In this chapter we shall undertake what might be called a "deepening interpretation," that is, a think-through of Husserl's theory of inter-subjectivity with a view to its goal, the constitution of the objective world, thereby to view the objective world not so much as a transcendental phenomenon but rather as the world of the natural attitude. Behind such a view we find the supposition that, together with the constitution of transcendentally demonstrable objectivity, Husserl entrusts the Other with another constitution, which differs from the former in a certain respect. In what follows, it must be shown whether, and if so to what extent, this supposition holds good.

Within certain definite limits this supposition is already supported by the last-mentioned point of the transcendental theory of intersubjectivity: by the doctrine of the empathic transference of being human from the other to my own I. The so constituted I also appears to be the "objective," "real," or "empirical" I that I observe in the natural attitude. This natural I is precisely the human I that, at the same time, is no longer apprehended as *the* I, but as *an* I, and, indeed, as a *mundanized* I. In order to prove that the natural I is constituted in its naturalness with the help of the Other, we must first explain more clearly how I, as the human being that the Other makes me be, am *an* I and, to boot, an I that has become a worldly object.

On closer inspection we find that the constitution of my self, as a human being, through the mediation of the Other is carried out in two steps. Husserl has the first in mind when he says, "I arrive at the apprehension of human being through a comprehension of the Others in relation to my self, namely, insofar as I not only comprehend them as central with respect to their surrounding worlds but also with respect to my organic body, which is a worldly object for them" (Id.II 242). Accordingly, the first step is empathic insight into the alien presentation (fundamental for the appresentation of my organic body) of my physical body as a part of the alien sphere of ownness. Through this empathic insight the embodiment of my organic body is first completed, that embodiment that reaches far beyond the limit of what is solipsistically possible through the pairing of physical bodies. Whereas in the solipsistic attitude I could only take account of the physicality of my organic body in an incomplete manner, the look of the alien physical body already completes the constitution of my physical body. However, the physicality of my body is accentuated yet again for me when, in empathy, I take part in the alien primordinal positing of my organic body as a pure physical body. Only now can one truly say that my body is a thing like any other thing. It is for the Other an "environmental object," in no way different from the chair and the table, next to which it makes its appearance in the alien surrounding world. Husserl thinks of this worldliness primarily as spatiality in the sense of being tied down to a particular place. Inasmuch as I presentify the there of the alien physical-organic body as the here that it is for the Other, "I can now regard my organic body as a natural object; that is, from the standpoint of this 'here,' it is 'there,' just as the alien organic body from my here is situated at a point in objective space and is regarded by me as an other thing" (Id.II 169).

The consideration of my body as an ordinary physical body certainly *makes possible* my humanizing self-apperception; it is still not the latter itself, however. As long as I only apprehend my body as an other thing, I can always take up a position over against my mundanized being. It is the mundanization of my *I*, however, that first makes of me a human being. This is the second and decisive step in the constitution of my human being. That the Other understands me as a human being means therefore that he constitutes me as a unitary object. And that in turn means that he coposits my I in that worldly object that he at first only has before him as my organic body. As a human being my I is in itself a "human I," which it can only be as a "mundanized I in the spatiotemporal world" (K 209:205). This, my worldliness, leads Husserl back just as explicitly as my humanness to the encounter with the Other: "To the extent that we have taken alien subjects into our surrounding world," to that extent we have thereby "*eo ipso* taken ourselves into our surrounding world" (Id.II 347 B). Ourselves means: our own I. Feeling myself into my being human, I understand myself as an I that "exists in the world" (Id.III 114 B).[1] And together with my I, I also empathically apperceive "each of my lived experiences as a component part of the 'world' (the objective spatiotemporal sphere of reality)" (Id.II 200).

In that I become a human being through the Other, I not only become a worldly I but also "an" I in the specific sense in which the naturally intended I is such. My human I is worldly insofar as it is "integrated" in the objective world. However, it is integrated therein in a twofold manner. For the Other, and therewith also for myself, who feel my way into the alien "representation of myself," I "am this human being, one human being among human beings and animals, among other realities all of which go to make up the world" (FTL 222:251). "Being integrated" means: to be situated "among" other beings. As a human being I am, however, first, a worldly being among worldly beings whose mode of being is not human ("among other realities"), and, second, a human being among human beings. I am, on the one hand, the "human I that appears as a member of the personal human world" (Id.II 204). As a member of the natural world, I fit myself into the whole of natural occurrences. As a member of the personal human world, "I fit myself into the association (*Verband*) of humanity" (Id.II 242). In the association of humanity, however, I am necessarily a human being, "a human being among other human beings" (CM 158).

The nonhuman worldly object is also fitted into the world in both ways. This table there is, on the one hand, a table among chairs, beds, and "other realities"; on the other hand, it is "one" table among other tables. However, my integration in the association of mankind is to be distinguished from the integration of an exemplary thing into its species in two essential respects. While the individual table is from the first "a" table, I have first to be made into a human being. So the association of mankind is a community in opposition to the totality of tables. As human I am always already "a" human being because human being "already as an individual carries with it the sense of a member of the community" (CM 157:129). Through this relation to the community, the concept of the person, relevant to book II of *Ideas*, distinguishes itself from the primordial concept of the person in *Cartesian Meditations*. Precisely on the basis of this original communalization, Husserl, in book II of *Ideas*, identifies the "human being" with the "person," the human with the personal I.[2] And only because the human association is a "human community" (CM 157:129) is it possible to talk of it as of the "personal world of mankind."

All the same, Husserl principally thinks of my integration in the association of mankind in accordance with the same schema as the integration of an exemplary thing in the appropriate species. A table is of another kind than a chair and a bed, but of the same kind as all other tables. Similarly, as a human being, I am of another kind than a tree and a stone, but of the same kind as all other human beings. Hence Husserl is able to say that the constitution of my self as a human being "brings with it an objectivating equation of my existence with that of all Others; consequently, I (or anyone else) am a human being among other human beings" (CM 157–158:129). The event through which I become "a" human being is precisely the event (understood as bringing about) of this equation. Out of the unique and incomparable "originary I," which, as the sole originary ground of the world, does not know its equal, I become "someone" who is like "everyone," one who is equated with all others. The (statically understood) equation is then also the form of the human community. The latter is a community of the "we," or, as Husserl occasionally (for example, K 186:182) says, of "all of us." In transcendental empathy I recall that I am for the Other "alter ego," as he is for me, and, in the same way, each Other for every Other, so that the "everyone" preserves its sense just as does the we and the I as " 'one among Others,' as included in 'everyone' " (FTL 210:238). However, the human community may arise constitutively out of a "reciprocal being for one another" (CM 157:129), in which I, as subject, encounter the Other as object; it is, in its developed form as we-community, an association of equally posited or, so to speak, collaterally ordered, subjects that, in any case, are, as a whole, objectified subjects. As a subject objectified in this way, however, I am not only "a" *human being* but also "an" I. All of "us" are "we with many I's," among which I am "an" I (K 186).

The task of demonstrating my becoming human (a process mediated by the Other) as the transformation of my absolute I into "an" I is thereby completed. Because we are dealing here with a point of special importance for our interpretation, it is appropriate at the same time to articulate the preceding thoughts a little more and so guard against misunderstanding. As a supplement to the thesis in accordance with which I, by means of empathy, fit myself into the alien "representation of myself" as a human being in the association of human beings, Husserl continues: "Now for the first time I am truly an I in opposition to the Other and can now say 'we.' Now for the first time I also become an 'I' and the Other precisely an Other. 'We' are all human beings, similar to each other, equipped as human beings to meet in concourse with one another and to enter into human associations" (Id.II 242). Although the statement confirms the thought of equalization in some parts, it seems to contradict it in its basic tenor. Not equalization but the confrontation (*Gegenüberstellung*) of myself and the Other first becomes possible through my becoming human. However, while the transformation of my absolute I into "an" I appears, under the aspect of equalization, as a deprivation of my I, it first allows me to manifest myself as I (as also the Other as an Other), as the condition of the possibility of confrontation. Inasmuch as I am equated with the Other, I am one among them, therefore precisely not the I as the unique non-Other. Inasmuch as I confront the Others, I am still the Other of the Others, hence "truly" I.

The appearance of a contradiction persists because two different concepts of the I are in play. In accordance with one, the only I that is truly I is the one to which uniqueness can be attributed in the transcendental sense. For the other I simply names the personal "de-clinable" I, the partner of an Other and member of a community. The interpenetration of both concepts has already been met with once,[3] on the opposite side as it were. The same I that, according to the first concept, is the "absolute" or the "originary I," Husserl will not even characterize as an I in the orientation toward the second concept. How it is that I become an "I" has to count as a deprivation of my I in accordance with the former linguistic usage—in accordance with the latter, as its authentic birth. Herewith I is first "an" I. The most suitable title for this I is "someone." For someone is, as the personal counterpart to the pure thingly something, a worldly object or that something that, as object, is, at the same time, subject. The opposition that is presupposed by my integration in the human as-sociation is therefore the opposition of myself as someone and "someone else." Insofar, however, as someone only manifests itself as a (determinate) someone in general when he distinguishes himself from others, it is indeed true that I first truly become an I on the basis of my integration in the human association. It is just as evident that this confrontation is grounded in the above-mentioned equalization. As someone, I am, in my entire difference from someone else, just like this Other, who is likewise someone. Here, too, the analogy of the relation between the individual thing and the general essence helps to make things intelligible. "A" table can only be posited in opposition to another table because both are "a" table and to that extent posited as the same. The agreement in the same *eidos* upholds and comprehends all individual differences. Of course, it should be borne in mind here that "human association" means "human community." Inasmuch as equalization, as collectivization, is an integration in the we, confrontation appears within the horizon of the community as an I-Thou relation. That confrontation presupposes equalization therefore means, from a personal standpoint, that only as a member of the "us-all" can I be the I of a Thou. For the I of a Thou is constantly "an" I. However, I am "an" I only as one among the many that, in their totality, make up the universal we of the human association.

What we have hereby pointed out in this matter, namely, that the Other, in constituting me as human person, at the same time makes my I into that "objective," "empirical," or "real" I that I take myself to be in the natural attitude, is what Husserl explicitly proclaims on many occasions. This is what is in question, for example, in the first draft of book II of *Ideas* (from the year 1912), which we have already cited repeatedly. My I "becomes in the course of an intersubjective exchange of experience an objectively real I. . . . I apprehend myself no longer as the pure I of my pure *cogitationes*, but I apprehend myself as if I were an objective human being in the objective world, with an objective soul and so also as an *objectively real I*" (Id.III 114 B; see also Id.II 111, CM 129:98).

2 The Intersubjective Constitution of the Objective I as Substantializing and Personalizing Alter-ation

A question now arises as to the unitary and basic feature of the alteration that my I undergoes through the Other. We said that through the Other I become that objectively real I that I find myself to be in the natural attitude. As an objective I, I am a human being, and, as a human being, I am, on the other hand, a human being among human beings. Let us look more closely at both these ways of "being integrated" into the objective world. That, as a human being, I am a worldly object among nonhuman worldly objects follows from the unification (derived from the alien I under the presupposition of the objective world) of my I with my physical body, which appears to the I as a spatiotemporally localized worldly object among other worldly objects. In accordance with Husserl's own words, however, I empathically regard my physical body "like an *other* thing." In that, thanks to empathy, "my organic body acquires the ontological status of a physical body *among others*" (K 109:106), it is appresentatively given to me as a "transcendent *external* object" (Id.II 169). Therewith I also, as a human being, am an external object, a thing like any other. Through empathy into the alien representation of ourselves as human beings, we attain "the givenness of ourselves as a spatial thing like all others" (Id.II 161). Even as a human being I see myself "from the standpoint of *external* perception" (Id.II 169—italics throughout are mine). Mundanization in the most radical form of a reification is transposed from the physicalization of my organic body to the humanization of my I. Taken as reification, however, the alteration that I undergo through the Other is, according to everything that has been brought in here, a *becoming-something-other*.

In contrast, thanks to my integration in the human association, I become *an* Other. In the we, I am, as Husserl said, "I as *one among others*," as included in "everyone." In empathy I regard myself accordingly not only "as an other thing" but also "just like every other" (Id.II 114 B). This *becoming-an-Other* is what is intended, in the last analysis, when Husserl speaks of the objectivizing "equalization of my *Dasein* and that of all Others."

Terminologically, we bring this becoming-*an*-Other and becoming-*something*-Other down to one common denominator, in that we characterize the alteration that I undergo through the Other, in the here as in the there, as "alter-ation" (*Veranderung*). As reification, my becoming human is a substantializing alteration; as communalization, it is a personalizing alter-ation. Husserl himself does not employ this term, though he does use concepts that have a similar meaning. With respect to the substantializing alter-ation at least, it provides for a clear and unambiguous expression of the issue that is thereby confronted.

Already in book I of *Ideas* (131:165) he notes that consciousness is, in the realization brought about through empathy, "developed into an (that is, something) Other, into a component part of nature." Furthermore, he has his own title for personalizing alter-ation, namely, alien-ation (K 189:184). At this point, where it is a question of *my* alien-ation, the hyphen is not supposed to give the word the meaning of a suspension of alienness. Rather, it has the function of articulating the alienness that comes over me in alter-ation, as the only operative alienness, as that of the "alien" in the sense of the alter ego. The concept of alien-ation is therefore precisely aimed at the becoming-*an* (someone)-Other.

The alteration that I undergo through the Other is, as alter-ation, a depotentialization in the negative sense, a disempowerment of my I. For integration takes from my I the power that it has as an ordering I. In its original purity, the constituter of all others is, through alter-ation, turned into the one constituted among all others. This depotentialization has the form of a *decentering*. My I loses its world-instituting power, in that, through Others, it is thrown out of that middle point of the world that it occupies in its transcendental originality and that Husserl, on the plane of the primordinal world, names "the central here." It is decentered in this way in the substantializing just as well as in the personalizing alter-ation. As a thing among nonhuman things it is similarly confronted with this "anywhere" and "at any time," without there being an integral ordering of a world around its spatial and temporal location. This is how I stand as "an" I, and "a" human being, completely leveled down in the range of other human beings. I am simply a "member" of a chain that neither begins nor ends with me.

3 A Preliminary Determination of the Alter-ation Character of Empathy in General

We now want to expand the scope of our interpretation of this problem so that it is covered by the theory presented in the previous chapter. Hitherto we have meant by alter-ation solely the intersubjective constitution of the objective I. Hence the thesis that I undergo alter-ation through the Other was only an abbreviated expression of the complete state of affairs that, in its unabridged form, can be reproduced as follows: Through an empathic relation with the Other I grasp myself as an objective I. A certain alter-ation is now, however, to be found already in the empathic relation as such, before any transference of the alien "representation of me" already in the empathic appresentation of the alien perception of a thing distinct from myself. This is Husserl's own opinion. For empathy as such is named "alien-ation" in the passage cited from *Crisis*. In addition, the subject matter itself also attests to empathy as alter-ation. Empathy is "putting oneself in the standpoint of the Other." I can, however, only put myself in the standpoint of the Other inasmuch as I make myself into this Other. Which means, psychologically speaking, "I not only feel myself into his (that is, the Other's) thinking, feeling, doing, but must follow him therein, his motives becoming my quasi motives. I have to '*go along with*' them in thought" (Id.II 275). In transcendental empathy, however, I act as if the there, which is the central here of the Other, were my here. In so doing, I act as if I were the Other that is transcendentally defined by means of his now-being-there. This alter-ation, like that of the constitution of the objective I, is a disempowering decentering. To the putting oneself into the there, there necessarily corresponds a putting oneself out of the central here. The disempowerment consists in the fact that the I, that I am in the there, is only a quasi I. In reality, I am here and not there, which, more sharply articulated, means that I am only here, but not, in reality, an I there. In any case, over there I am also only a quasi Other. Since I am only a quasi I because I act "in place of" the Other and thereby as the Other, I am equiprimordially only a quasi Other because in all "putting myself in the there" I still remain that I that, on this, the primordinal, level is never able to lose its central here.

This already shows, from one particular side, the difference of the two alter-ations. In contrast with the alien representation of an object distinct from myself, the empathic relation to the alien representation of myself effects a more complete and more radical alter-ation. First of all, with empathy as such, it is a matter of personalizing, not of substantializing, alter-ation. I make myself into *an* Other, not into something other. The condition for personalizing appears to be met insofar as I empathically become a "persona," in the old, theatrical sense of the "role" that I play. However, in that I only play the role of an Other, I am not really an Other. On the other hand, insofar as I identify the alien representation of myself with myself in humanizing self-apperception, I posit myself therein as the real Other that I am for the Other. So the alter-ation that has now also been thematized as personalizing falls short of the authenticity of the personalizing alter-ation of humanizing self-apperception.

The distinction between the alter-ation of empathy in general and the alter-ation of humanizing self-apperception makes itself known in this way through determination of the occasional relation of activity and passivity. Both moments are contained in a fundamental way in both alter-ations. In accordance with its general structure, this pertains to not only alter-ation, namely, that I become an Other, or something Other, but also the circumstance that I become this *through the Other*. To this extent alter-ation is something that continually happens to me as becoming alter-ed. Nevertheless, Husserl presents me as the executive organ of my own alter-ation and, indeed, just as much in empathy in general as in the alter-ation that takes place in humanizing self-apperception. As far as this is concerned, the concept self-apperception already points toward my activity. I myself apprehend myself as one among Others and as something among Others. I can only do that by relying upon empathy. Even this empathy is my act. Thereby it is already implied that I myself also carry out my alter-ation, an alter-ation that is brought about by the empathic relation to the alien representation of an object distinct from myself. Indeed, this alter-ation is not only actively determined but is even so essentially. For it is wholly and entirely contained in my act. Correspondingly, the passive moment in it has relatively slight weight. Through the Other I am only so far alter-ed that his factical appearance brings about my act of empathy. I would not empathically put myself into the there if there were no Other, if he did not factically exist over there. In contrast, in the constitution of the objective I, the passive moment comes into its own. That the Other sees me falls, as his act, entirely outside the scope of my own act. It is a fact removed from my freedom that I can neither make use of nor prevent. This becoming seen is already, however, the authentic alter-ation. The contribution of my activity is restricted here to bringing to mind my being-an-Other, which, in the first instance, is only for the Other. Here, therefore, with respect to activity and passivity, the respective weights are distributed inversely from the way they are distributed in empathy in general. There, in the constitution of the objective I, activity outweighs passivity. There I essentially *make* myself into an Other; here I *accept* myself as the Other that an Other has made me into.

Activity, however, reveals the power of the I, passivity the power of the Other, which is at the same time the powerlessness of the I. In this respect, the constitution of the objective I proves, in relation to empathy in general, to be the more radical alter-ation. Empathy in general is, so to speak, alter-ation to the first power, while objectifying self-apperception is alter-ation to the second power. The latter, however, includes the former. Insofar as my objectifying self-apperception presupposes empathy, in transposing myself I have to make myself into an Other in order to be able to accept myself as the Other that an Other has made me into. In other words, alter-ation to the second power is not possible without alter-ation to the first, even though alter-ation to the first power is possible without the second. Although alter-ation to the first power remains inferior to alter-ation to the second power in intensity, it still has the advantage of greater universality.

4 A Preliminary Indication of the Constitutional Interconnection of Empathic Alter-ation and Naturally Intended Objectivity

In this universality, transcendental empathy is the vehicle of the constitution of the objective world, that is, of the objective I as well as of objective things. It plays a "constitutive role in 'objective' experience" (Id.I 373:420), and indeed precisely insofar as the "external" thing proves itself to be "an objective reality . . . only through empathy" (Id.III 110 B). Empathy is therefore "one of the basic forms of experience even for external thinghood." This, however, means that the precondition for the constitution of the objective world is alter-ation to the first power. In what follows we want to investigate whether this is confirmed by the naturalistic being-status of the "objective world" and the "objective thing."

Let us stay with Husserl's preferred model. I see a thing and feel myself into the representation of this thing via an Other located over "there." We know how and as what the thing is given to me before the emergence of the Other. It differentiates itself into the originally present appearing and the simply appresented horizon that announces its objective sense. Now that which is originally present owes its original presence to the circumstance that it is directly visible from my central here, just as, on the other side, the appresented is simply appresented because it cannot "itself" be seen "from here." The necessity of the appearances of a thing in the difference between absolute presence and simple horizonal cogivenness is therefore grounded in the essential perspectivity of the transcendentally and primordinally reduced world "oriented" around my central here.

In contrast, in the second section of the first chapter we have already drawn attention to the fact that the natural-objective world as "world pure and simple" and the natural-objective thing as "object pure and simple" are, to some extent, given without perspective. The natural objectification of the world is, to a certain extent, its deperspectivalization and therefore also brings with it the suspension of the difference between the immediately appearing and the horizonally cogiven. But my alter-ation to the first power now appears as the condition of this deperspectivalization or dedifferentiation. That the appearing thing falls apart transcendentally into the originally present and the appresent because it is perspectivally related to my central here means, upon closer examination, that I still only have the thing in the difference between the presently appearing and the horizonally cogiven because, in being here, I cannot *at the same time* be "there." If I were there at the same time, together with the immediately present front of the thing, the presently not-present back would also be immediately present. The appresent would be present just like the present, and so the difference between presence and appresence would be suspended. Now, however, I transpose myself empathically into the there in which the Other encounters me simultaneously with my being here. But it still remains the case that I cannot "actually" be here and there at the same time. However, this is possible in the special manner of empathy, in that, namely, a quasi being there intervenes in my being here.

With the intervention of this quasi being there, the difference between the originally present and the horizonally appresent seems to be suspended because, with empathy, it is not a question of appresentation in the primordinal sense, but of the fictive representation of the presentation of the Other. I complete what is present to me through what is present to the Other. Looked at in this way, objectification consists in the disappearance of appresence. The objective thing is the thing appearing without a horizon. But it goes without saying that the present is also no longer the actually present. What is present to the Other is not so to me because I only represent it to myself as present. And

that which is present to me is also not so any longer because I—as
has been said—can only transpose myself into the there insofar as I,
so to speak, transpose myself out of my actual here. Thereupon it
becomes possible to understand what Husserl means when he says
that "the thing (that is, the objective) is truly that which no one has
actually seen" (K 167:164). That, however, the actually appresent, just
as well as the actually present, disappear is grounded in the forgetfulness
of their distinction (from each other). This, in its turn, is, as deperspectivalization, grounded in the decentralization that alter-ation is
negatively presented as being. Accordingly, what already emerged as
a formal consequence from the insight into the alter-ation character
of empathy appears, as a matter of fact, to be confirmed by phenomena.
The condition of the constitution of the natural-objective world is the
alter-ation located in empathy in general. The world of the natural
attitude is constituted in an I that has been alter-ed in the empathic
manner.

5 A More Precise Determination of the Alter-ation Required
as the Constitutive Condition of the Natural-Objective World

It only looks as though we have already attained our goal.[4] For the
quasi I that I am when I transpose myself into a quasi Other in the
there does not yet satisfy the claims that should be brought against
such an I, which should, in truth, count as the immediate constitutional
source of the natural world, a world that has ceased to be differentiated
in the above-mentioned sense. The I described is still quite incapable
of accounting for the dedifferentiation that has been entrusted to it.
Indeed, it falls short of this task in two respects. First, it was not
capable of reconciling within itself both the moments that were furnished, in a similar manner, as the condition of a dedifferentiation:
decenteredness and being-here-and-there-at-the-same-time. In that
the world, as dedifferentiated, can only be apperceived by one I, which
is decentralized as well as being here and there at the same time,
decenteredness ought not to be a complete departure from the here;
for being-here-and-there would then not be possible. Being-here-and-
there should not, in its turn, be so understood that the I could be in
the there *without prejudice* to its being in the central here. Now we
have indeed attributed both the decenteredness and the being-here-
and-there-at-the-same-time to the I described. But it is not clear how

this I, in spite of its being here and there at the same time, should be decentered and therefore not be in its central here.

In yet a second respect, the I that I make myself into, in that I make myself into an Other, falls short of the task expected of it, the task of dedifferentiating the world. The dedifferentiation that it brings about can never be total because the there into which it empathically transposes itself is still only an *individualized* there, that is, the there of the individualized Other to which it relates empathically. We have been in error in this respect, that we viewed the difference between original presence and appresence as already suspended in that I, by means of empathy, represent as originally present what is originally present to the Other, instead of appresenting it in the primordial sense. In reality, however, I still am not able to bring about the complete disappearance of appresence through the transposition of myself into an individualized there, since, in the representation of the alien presentation, I corepresent the horizon appresented by the Other. So the world not only reveals itself from my here as differentiated into the originally present and the appresent; it also does so equally from every individual there. Even from this there the seen divides itself up into the immediately given and the simply cogiven.

These negative assertions nevertheless admit a conclusion with respect to the positive constitution of that I that demands the natural-objective world as its immediate constitutional ground. First, this I in being there must at the same time be here in such a way that its being here is not to be distinguished as here from there, but simply as one arbitrary spatial position among others. Only then could it reconcile, each with the other, the seemingly exclusive moments of decentering and of being here and there at the same time. It would be here and there and, for all that, decentered, that is, thrown out of its "central here," which as "central" or "absolute" is precisely not one spatial position among other spatial positions. Second, in order to be able to level down wholly the difference between original presence and appresence, this I has to be not only here and there at the same time but also, together with this there, there from where the now merely represented, as appresented, could in its turn be represented as originally present. So it must have transposed itself not simply into one individual there but into all possible standpoints and, therewith, so to speak, be "everywhere." For solely out of the synthesis of all possible standpoints does the world really and completely present itself as derelativized.

But do these indications not lead in a completely different direction from the one we have been pursuing? Have we not maneuvered ourselves into a situation from which there is no way out? The thesis to be verified was one to the effect that the natural-objective world is constituted through that alter-ation as which empathy has already disclosed itself in advance. What had to be proved was not that the objective world is constituted through empathy. That had already been accepted in the preceding chapter as Husserl's opinion, as an opinion that, admittedly, now requires interpretation. What requires justification, rather, is the supposition that the constitution of the natural-objective world out of empathic relations presupposes its alter-ation character. The interpretation of the natural-objective world as a de-perspectivized, dedifferentiated world should help us with this justification, so much so that it should be clear that this world demands, as the constitutive condition of its possibility, an I that has itself been alter-ed in the empathic manner. Now, however, it has been shown that it demands an I that is completely different from the quasi I of empathy. So it looks as though we shall have to get used to the idea that precisely that very meaning of the objective world upon which we have relied has led our thesis astray.

However, this is not at all the case. For alter-ation has most certainly informed us as to the route to be entered upon as the constitutive condition of the natural-objective world. We know the transcendental connection of the "here" and the "I," of the "there" and the "Other." When the objective world gets constituted in an I whose here is distinguished from the there no longer *as here* but still only as one arbitrary spatial position from another, it subsequently gets constituted in an I that is *one among others.* For, as an arbitrary spatial position, the here is precisely a there, *one* there among others. In this transference of the here-there relation to the relation of the I and the Other, the being everywhere, which is the second condition of the objective world, discloses itself as the integration of all Others in the one Other that I have become myself. As one among others I have somehow to be at the same time *all others.* However, I am that in every case in which I am one among Others, and already solely by virtue of being this. For, as one among Others, I am a "member" of an "association." As a member, however, I can only realize myself consciously in that I realize the entire association whose member I am.

Now, an I that has become an Other in such a way that it has become *one among* Others is undoubtedly more radically alter-ed than an I that is only an Other because it has put itself in the position of an Other. If one therefore concedes that in the regression to the natural, existential status of the world, the specified "alter-ation to the first power" has not come to light as its presupposition, one has then immediately to add that an alter-ation has disclosed itself as this presupposition that far exceeds the former in its radicality. One can go further: If that which has just made its appearance is not the above-described "alter-ation to the first power," Husserl will still recognize it as the alter-ation that is involved in "empathy in general." Accordingly, it is by no means our intention to correct the thesis whereby the constitution of the natural-objective world presupposes the alter-ation character of empathy, but solely our initial determination of empathic alter-ation, and only because this determination was still too timid. The alter-ation involved in empathy in general is alter-ation in a yet more radical sense than we had supposed: In it I do not simply make myself into an Other; I become far more, one among the Others that, at the same time, I am. This is the reason for which our initial definition becomes more urgent. We have characterized the alter-ation involved in empathy as such as not substantializing but as personalizing. For all that, there belongs to the complete concept of personalizing alter-ation not only the circumstance, which was the sole circumstance taken into consideration above, that I am transformed into an Other. Rather, to it there also belongs, and indeed essentially so, that I become one among Others. For only as one among Others am I a person, since I am only a person insofar as I take my place as a comember of a community.[4]

6 Verification of Our Hypothetical Approach in Husserl's Own Interpretation of the Being of the Natural-Objective World

It now has to be confirmed that the I that has been alter-ed into one among Others, and that, from now on, in accordance with our rad-icalized thesis, has apperceived the world immediately as objective, has been taken into consideration by Husserl himself and provided with a corresponding function. That is all the more important as this I, which has suddenly become the crux of our entire interpretation, remains unsecured in a double respect. In the first place, we have not discovered it directly, but simply constructed it on the way out of the objective world, where it is present in the natural attitude as its constitutive condition. Second, the meaning given to the natural-objective world, and from out of which we enquired back into the I (itself not expressly posited by Husserl but only discovered through interpretation) was that of a world that is deperspectivized and leveled down in relation to the difference between presence and appresence. And so it first has to be investigated to what extent the being that the natural-objective world possesses, according to Husserl's own determination, refers back to the I that has been transformed into one among Others. So it has to be determined how Husserl thematizes this I.

"To the being-sense of the world and, in particular, of nature as objective . . . there belongs the *there for everyone*, as that which is constantly cointended by us when we are talking of objective reality" (CM 124:92). The objective world is the "world for us all" (FTL 209:236). As the world of the natural attitude, which we are considering it as here, it is that, however, *from the outset*: "Each and every consciousness of the world is already beforehand consciousness . . . of one and the same world for all" (K 257:254). Accordingly, in the natural attitude I do not experience the world first as a world that would only be for me, in order, incidentally thereafter, namely, through "contact" with Others, to learn that it is a world "for everyone": "In that I am directed toward things of the world as things for everyone, it is not a matter of a thing being able to be real for each and every person in the sense of being completely self-given, as if each could have it for himself or could attain it as it is itself, after which people standing in relation would be convinced that each had known the same—as it is itself. Rather, things are, from the outset, and in accordance with their being-sense, things for everyone" (K 468 B). And so, even when I experience the world with Others "for myself," that is, without actual communalization, I do not experience it as it is for myself but as it is for all. I overlook, so to speak, its simple being for me and "see" only its being-for-everyone, which I am convinced of before any actual seeing.

This, however, is only possible in that I also, in my experience of the world—in the solitary experience that is not in fact accompanied by any Other—am "at least implicitly, continually related to the Other as corepresenter, ultimately coknower" (K 468 B). In other words, the being already from the outset for everyone of the objective world demands, as the subjective condition of its possibility, the always already having been communalized of this experience (which precedes every factically communalized, as also every factically solitary, thing-experience) whose universal object is the objective world. Husserl states this condition quite clearly. When the objective world is the world of the natural attitude, its corresponding noetic experience is the experience of the "natural" attitude. This is, however, according to Husserl, identical with the "communicative attitude" (EP.II 59), the natural experience identical with the "communicative experience" (EP.II 394 B). We not only speak but also think where we naively live— "in the communicative plural" (EP.II 59).

What is valid of the natural experience is also automatically true of the I that has such an experience. The I that experiences communicatively before every actual contact with the Other is, however, distinguished in the first place by the fact that all Others are integrated in the horizon of its world experience. With the sense "there for everyone," it can only apperceive the world if it is itself, in a certain respect, "everyone." In itself, and as its horizon, "a sense of 'everyone' must already be constituted in order that an objective world can be so constituted in relation thereto" (FTL 212:240). It can, however, in turn, only realize everyone as horizon of its world experience in that (in the second place) it is "included in 'everyone' " and therefore is "one among Others" (FTL 210:238). In that Husserl ascribes both to the communicatively experiencing I, this I, to which the objective world refers back, in accordance with the sense explicated by Husserl, fulfills the two presuppositions that it must fulfill according to our own hypothetically postulated meaning of the objective world.

7 The Alter-ed Ego as the Transcendental Phenomenon of the I of the Natural Attitude

In order to be able to convey how, and as what, Husserl conceived the communicatively experiencing I, we must first determine, at least in outline, the systematic place of this I. Without further ado, the following results from our discussions: it is *the I of the natural attitude*. As such, it is to be distinguished from the "natural" I that Husserl calls the "objective," "real," or "empirical" I. For the latter is objective precisely because it belongs in the objective world, the world that the I of the natural attitude has before it. The I of the natural attitude apprehends the world as objective and *itself* as object in the world. However, it is thereby not itself this object but the subject that apprehends itself in this way. The difference is most immediately evident when one pictures the relation of the objective world to the objective I and to the I of the natural attitude. While the objective world has a precedence over the I as objective, the I, as I of the natural attitude, has a precedence, even if of a completely different kind, over the objective world. To be sure, the objective world comprehends the objective I, but, together with the objective I, it is comprehended by the I of the natural attitude, the I that first of all makes the world objective and makes itself into an object appearing in that world.

In spite of its difference from the natural, qua objective, I, the I of the natural attitude must nevertheless also be a natural I. What is natural about the natural attitude does not lie in any continuing state of an object independent of it, but in the naiveté of what is posited by it. The I of the natural attitude is naive and thereby itself natural. Indeed, insofar as its object is not in itself natural, it is more truly natural than the objective I.

Clearly, its naturalness also results from the fact that the way in which it experiences the world as objective is not the way in which, according to the "Fifth Cartesian Meditation," the objective world is constituted. We know that, according to the "Fifth Cartesian Meditation," the objective world is constituted out of the "identification" of my and the alien sphere of ownness. This means that "I" henceforward *first* experience "a world for myself," which "I" then *subsequently* apperceive as the intersubjectively identical world. I therefore have an experience that I precisely do not have as the I of the natural attitude. What Husserl energetically rejects with respect to this attitude, namely, that the world might first give itself for knowledge in actual connection with Others as "world for all," precisely this characterizes the constitution of the objective world out of the identification of the primordinal worlds. Now, the way that is pursued in the "Fifth Cartesian Meditation" is quite certainly not the way of the natural I. Through the reduction to my ownness sphere, "I have lost my natural sense of an I" (CM 129:98), and even when my ownness sphere is surpassed, the brackets, in which previously the phenomenological reduction already set the natural I, still remain. In contrast, were one to apprehend the I that apperceives the world immediately as objective, as a natural I, the difference between its way and the way of the "Fifth Cartesian Meditation" can be explained without difficulty. For the "Fifth Cartesian Meditation" describes its transcendental genesis, which it itself no longer brings to completion, precisely because it is its product. The I that apperceives the world immediately as objective is an I that is always already communalized. Its transcendental genesis is therefore a communalization as that kind of alter-ation through which it becomes one among others. In order to be what it is, it does not need first to communalize itself, precisely because, as that which it is, it is always already communalized. On the basis of its always-already-being-communalized, it also knows nothing of the transcendental communalization through which it became what it is. In this way it reveals itself as a natural, that is, self-forgetful I.

But one need only reflect upon the fact that the I in question has to be the one that "apperceives the world immediately as objective" in order to arrive at the knowledge that it belongs just as well in the transcendental sphere. Its dual configuration (natural-transcendental) only corresponds to the ambiguity of its objective correlate. The objective world is itself the world of the natural attitude *and* the transcendental phenomenon to which the phenomenological reduction traces the natural world back. In this tracing back, the reduction (thoroughly thought through and freed from the narrowness of the "Cartesian way") uncovers, at the same time, the transcendental phenomenon that, in truth, the I of the natural attitude is. The reduction of the natural-objective to the transcendental-objective world is accomplished, as we know, negatively, as suspension of the naively intended objectivity, as "independence of the I," and positively, as disclosure of the true objectivity, as intersubjective identity. This reduction is in itself already, from a negative standpoint, the overcoming of that self-forgetfulness that makes the *I* of the natural attitude into a natural I and is responsible for its naive faith in the world's "independence of the I." From a positive standpoint, it is the disclosure of the I of the natural attitude as a transcendentally communalized I whose transcendental communalization makes possible the apperception of the world as intersubjectively identical.

8 The Theory of Transcendental Intersubjectivity as the Preworldly Alter-ation of My Absolutely Unique Ego

Having outlined the systematic position of the I in question, we now want to develop the part of Husserl's theory that draws this position into the coordinate system of transcendental philosophy.

The point of departure for Husserl's reflections is formed by the fact (evidently demonstrated in experience of the alien) that there is a plurality of concrete subjects, of monads. The monadic *plurality* must, however, according to Husserl, be a monadic *community* (CM 166:139). This is no metaphysical postulate but the immediate consequence of the experience of the monadic plurality itself. The latter is, from the outset, only given as a community because the subjects of which it consists are only given as ones that constitute the objective world in common and in such a way that, through empathy, my constitutive performances reach intentionally into those of the Other and those of the Other into mine (CM 157:129).[5] It is the "absolute functioning community of subjects out of whose communicative intentional performances the objective world 'is constituted' " (K 416 B), an "essentially unique connectedness, an actual community and precisely such a one as makes transcendentally possible the being of the world, a world of human beings and of things" (CM 157:129). The human world is made transcendentally possible, however, by the monadic community in such a way that the latter is realized in it. The human community that we talked about at the beginning of the chapter only therefore posits the mundanized form of the monadic community that we are now talking about. The monadic plurality is "an explicitly or implicitly communalized one; this involves an objective world constituting itself in such a plurality and in it—as animal, and in particular as human beings—spatializing itself, temporalizing itself, and realizing itself" (CM 166:139). Just as my ego, by means of empathy, is "objectified" into that of a human being in the "alien representation of me," so the entire human association is a copresent objectification of the monadic community in empathic consciousness. The latter is, however, as a community of *transcendental* subjects, itself a *transcendental* community. Here we first find the very transcendental intersubjectivity that Husserl is searching after in the end. To the community of human beings there corresponds, "in transcendental concretion, a correspondingly open monadic community, which we shall characterize as transcendental intersubjectivity" (CM 158:130).

Already as a consequence of this correspondence, the monadic community must also have the form of the *we*. The title "transcendental intersubjectivity" refers to a transcendental "we-community" (Id.III 153). However, I am myself included in the we-community. It is a "unique generality that includes me in itself" (CM 167:140; see also CM 137:107). Inasmuch as it includes me myself, however, I am, as a transcendental I, a link in the chain of transcendental Others, or one among them. And only as an I altered in this way can I—in this connection Husserl now says as much quite directly—experience the world in the sense of the objective world: "My ego, given to me apodictically—the only thing I can posit in absolute apodicticity as existing—can be a world-experiencing ego only by being in communion with others like itself: a member of a community of monads, which is given out of its own perspective" (CM 166:139; see also, K 175:172).

According to our preparatory analysis, the objective world can only be immediately apperceived as such by an I that, as one among Others, at the same time integrates all Others in itself. Even this second presupposition is, according to Husserl, given with the communitarian character of the monadic plurality. This is already indicated in a treatise from about 1924, in which it is said that "the community is not a simple collection of individuals existing outside and alongside one another, but a synthesis of individuals through interpersonal intentionality" (EP.II 198). The concept of synthesis "of the on-going synthesis specific to the I and the other I (each purely as I)" is the title under which Husserl takes up the problem of intersubjective integration in the *Crisis*. Although in the treatise from 1924 it still remains uncertain whether this concept of synthesis also characterizes the *transcendental* community, it is in any case in *Crisis* precisely the latter, the transcendental community, whose ontological constitution Husserl seeks to grasp as "we-synthesis" (K 175:172).

Husserl in the *Crisis* characterizes as "we-synthesis" the fact that the subjects in which the objective world is immediately constituted "are all 'united' not externally but internally, namely, through the intentional interpenetration of the communalization of their lives" (K 258:255). The "intentional interpenetration of the subjects and their transcendental lives" (K 262:259) can, however, only be conceived as the "implication" of all Others in the "horizon" of my subject (K

259:255).[6] Of my subject—this means not only that "I" implicate all
Others in my horizon but also that, conversely, each Other implicates
"me" as one among the Others in his horizon (K 262:259). This horizon
of mine is, however, an "empathic horizon" (K 258:254). Husserl therefore himself sees that empathy can only become the vehicle for the
constitution of the objective world by way of the transcendental communalization of the empathizing I. Before the constitution of the objective world, and as its condition, empathy is constituted through it,
as the horizon that embraces all Others in itself, an empathy that, on
the one hand, insofar as it is *my* horizon, is comprehended by me,
but, on the other hand, also comprehends me as one among the
Others. It is the "constitution of the personal (pure egological) horizon
in which each I knows itself" (K 175:172).

From the standpoint of the objective world, each I knows itself
already from the outset in the horizon constituted through empathy
that precisely functions as the a priori of its immediate world understanding. In such a way, the Others are implicated in this horizon
from the outset. Husserl emphasizes "that in the living, flowing intentionality in which the life of an I subject consists, each other I is
already implicated intentionally from the outset in the manner of
empathy and the empathic horizon" (K 259:255). The corollary "already
from the outset" attests to the fact that the "I subject" that is in
question here takes up the "systematic place" that we have attributed
to the I of the natural attitude as transcendental phenomenon. As
communalized "already from the outset," it can neither fall into the
objective world, since it is supposed to be its transcendental *pre*supposition, nor be my *absolute* ego, my originary I, since the latter is
precisely not already communalized from the outset. Rather, it is itself
first constituted by my unique, absolute ego in a constitution established
before that of the objective I. My originary I constitutes, more exactly,
first, the transcendental community of monads (CM 158:130, FTL
212:240), second, all Others as its comembers (FTL 210:237, 212:239,
K 416 B), and third, my self as one among these Others. Or in the
inverse order: I as originary I constitute "myself and my horizon of
Others, and the homogeneous we-community, in unity therewith" (K
416 B).

As the condition of the possibility of the objective world, this constitution is preworldly, as a transcendental occurrence prior to the
constitution of the world that is always already apperceived as objective.

According to this manuscript, which Husserl probably composed just a year before his death, "the I community that is constitutive for the world is always prior to the constituted world." The constitution in which I am myself transcendentally communalized is "*not world constitution* but the performance that can be characterized as the *monadizing of the ego*—as the performance of the personal monadizing of the monadic pluralization."[7] The monadic pluralization, which is positively characterized by Husserl as the preworldly alteration of my ego, is, however, nothing other than what we called "alter-ation." It is indeed that very alter-ation that is alone possible in the transcendental sphere: the personalizing but not the substantializing whose personalization is also established prior to the humanizing.

9 Unanswered Questions Concerning the Transcendental Genesis of the Natural Attitude

Herewith "the distinction between the unique, absolute ego . . . and the, so to speak, self-declining I" (K 417 B) has found clear expression. The distinction between the self-declining I, as transcendental phenomenon, and the same I, as natural I in the role of the I of the natural attitude, remains, on the contrary, remarkably unnoticed in Husserl. As a natural, unreduced I, Husserl, on the whole, only contrasts the transcendentally communalized I with the mundane I, which the I of the natural attitude apprehends itself as being. Here we find a lacuna in Husserl's thought that is of fundamental importance. Already in the second section of chapter 1 we have allowed ourselves to follow Husserl in saying that it is the task of phenomenology to make the naturally meant objectivity of the world "transcendentally intelligible." This task, which egology could not fulfill, has been accomplished by the theory of intersubjectivity insofar as it has disclosed the phenomenon that, in truth, lies at the root of the naturally meant objectivity: the being-for-all of the world, which, on its side, is grounded in the always already being communalized of the world-experiencing subject. Thereby "render transcendentally intelligible" was made to mean: to lead the naturally meant objectivity back to something that is something other than objectivity in its natural meaning. However, surely the naturally meant objectivity also has to be rendered transcendentally intelligible in *the* sense that it must be made clear how it can be brought to a natural apprehension of objectivity. This is the requirement that

that constitution of appearances, thanks to which the objective world ultimately appears as independent of the subject, should be followed up. In other words, what is in question there is the constitution of the objective world as the world of the natural attitude, or the *constitution of the natural attitude itself.*

The lacuna that is noticeable in the inattention to the distinction between the transcendentally communalized ego and the same ego as the I of the natural attitude consists, essentially, in this, that Husserl did not work out this question for himself, much less explicitly answer it. Nevertheless, it is tied to the question he did pose concerning the transcendental phenomenon of the objective world, and the answer that he gives to this question already contains in itself the possibility of an answer to the question into the transcendental ground of the natural attitude. For the truth of the objectivity disclosed by it, namely, intersubjective identity, itself motivates the apparent objectivity as the supposed independence from the I of a world that confronts me in its occurrence. To make this more apparent was a principal goal of our reflections in this chapter. We sought to achieve it by going back to the world experienced as intersubjectively identical, to the being-always-already communalized of the immediately experienced subject. At the same time, we discovered in it the suspension of the difference between originary presence and appresence. It is indeed the naturally objective world, the world that is taken to be being-in-itself, which, from the standpoint of the transcendentally relativized world, presents itself as a deperspectivalized world, as a world that has been leveled down with respect to the difference between originary presence and appresence.

However, that the natural attitude should proceed from transcendental alter-ation corresponds to its innermost essence. For the self-insertion of the I in the natural attitude is, as forgetfulness of its own authentic being, itself an alter-ation, and indeed an infinitely heightened one, which ultimately works its way out in the most radical alter-ation, that of human development in abstraction from the world. Human development in abstraction from the world is the extreme end of the movement in which my I falls away from its origin through the "fault" of the Other. The falling away of my I from its origin is manifest in the movement out of its transcendentality, that is, in the self-insertion in the natural attitude. But if, in general, this leaving of the transcendental sphere of origin itself has a transcendental ground, then it can only lie in a falling away of my I from its deepest origin, a falling away that already takes place within the transcendental sphere of origin. This first stage of the movement of alter-ation—the pre-worldly personal, world-conditioning "pluralization" of my most original I, of the "originary I"—is, however, grounded, as are all further stages, in the fact of the transcendental Other. Thereby the Other is itself also the authentic ground of the natural attitude, of naturalness in the sense of the self-forgetfulness that necessarily precedes naturalness in the sense of worldliness, of being integrated-in-the-world. As for forgetfulness of my incomparably unique I, naiveté is only possible because the fact of the transcendental Other already makes my transcendental I into one among Others and so robs it of its incomparably unique I-ness.

4
The Presuppositions of Husserl's Theory

1 The Simultaneity of Objective Being in the World and Subjective Being for the World as the Transcendental Clue

In the preceding chapter alter-ation (in its various modes and degrees) was disclosed as the "effect" that the Other has upon me. What still remains questionable is the mode of being that Husserl ascribes to the Other, that Other that is operative upon me. Accordingly, the question that has to be answered in what follows runs: *Which* Other alters me? How is the Other, through whom I will be altered, in the mode of alter-ation, to be apprehended in advance? So we are enquiring into the concept of the Other that lies at the root of the theory of intersubjectivity and that is unquestionably presupposed by Husserl himself.

The theme of the interpretation of the previous chapter was the *goal* of Husserl's theory of intersubjectivity, the constitution of the objective world. Corresponding to the direction of the enquiry that now has to be undertaken, the *way* to this goal, that is, the experience of the alien itself, was presented in chapter 1, while the exposition of this transcendental experience of the alien constituted the main part of chapter 2. Husserl's doctrine of alien experience has to provide the material investigated by the transcendental-phenomenological concept of the Other. The answer that this investigation provides has already been prepared by our exposition in the second chapter. According to Husserl, the Other is essentially characterized by the *mediacy* of its encounter. For mediacy has emerged as the basic unitary trait of the alien experience explicated by Husserl. Thereby the route that runs through alien experience and that we have followed step by step represented an advance into ever deeper mediacy, but in such a way that already, at its outset, a thesis (supported by everyday discourse) materialized, the thesis of the essential mediacy of alien experience. This initial mediacy will occupy us right away in the first part of the present chapter. It will preoccupy us in the sense that we shall analyze the presuppositions that led Husserl to decide in favor of it. We shall therefore go still further back behind the obvious beginning of the way to this goal to the place "from which" it arises. That "from which" it arises is, however, necessarily determined by that "to which" it leads, in this case, by the goal of the constitution of the objective world. Quite generally, it is the interest in the world, an interest bound up with the principle of transcendental philosophy, that drives Husserl to a "thematization" of the "Other." And so it is the world that, from the outset, prescribes the boundaries within which the Other can become thematic from a transcendental-phenomenological standpoint.[1] The world into which the course of Husserl's doctrine of alien experience leads is, by the same token, that "from which" it arises, that is, the space that Husserl breaks out of to reach his goal. This means: the mediacy that is already at work from the beginning is the (in itself multiform) mediatedness of the Other through the world. And only because Husserl, with reference *to* the world, at the same time thinks the Other *out* of the world, is mediacy for him the essential trait of *all* alien experience.

That the theme of the "Other" in Husserl is stamped with the universal theme "world" just as much as it is hemmed in by it is demonstrated by the "transcendental clue" in accordance with which Husserl orients his theory of intersubjectivity (CM 43). I take "the experienced Other just as he is given to me straightforwardly and in depth in his noematic-ontic content" (CM 122–123:90–91). Later we shall have to concern ourselves with the question on what level the ontic-noematic form is to be encountered.[2] For the present, we need only hold onto the following: in accordance with their ontic-noematic form, the Others originally confront me in an essential ambivalence, on one side "as world objects," on the other as "subjects for this world" (CM 123:91, 34:34). The unity of the intrinsically ambivalent presence of the Other accordingly founds the world.

If we explicate the state of affairs with the help of that distinction between the objective and primordinal worlds first arrived at in the theory itself, the following picture emerges. In relation to both worlds, to the objective and to the primordinal, the Other appears as world object just as well as world subject. As world object he comes to prominence *in* the world, whether this is the intersubjectively objective or my primordinal world. He is, in the one case, just as in the other, something "worldly" (K 410 B), worldly by the standards of the worldliness of the objective and the primordinal worlds. In the phrase "world object" the "object" is also, just as is the "world," so broadly fixed that it can mean not only entities in the strict sense of "objective" world but also entities of the primordinal world. Accordingly, the Other is, as world object, not already necessarily intersubjectively objective. However, in a quite different and much stricter manner, he is certainly more in unity with the intersubjectively identical world object that I represent him as being in the framework of the objective world than with himself qua primordinal world object. The Others *themselves* emerge in the objective world, in general and as a whole, as world objects, so much so that I represent their subjectivity in an objectively mundane manner. At the very most, I restrict their "genuine" objectivity to their physicality with which they are so intrinsically interwoven that they, in their turn, become objective as "souls": "Interwoven with bodies in a quite peculiar way, they are *in* the world as psychophysical objects" (CM 123:91). In contrast, the primordinal reduction reduces the inner-worldly objective being of the Others (abstraction made of the fact that it draws its intersubjective sense therefrom) to the pure physicality of the alien body. With respect to Others, everything that does not belong to this pure physicality falls on the other side of their being, in accordance with which they (admittedly in a broad sense equally objectified, but no longer mundanely objective) exist as subjects for the world. As such they are in themselves nothing worldly, that is, "nothing that is found in the world" (K 410 B). However, as those who "have" the world intentionally, they are certainly "the correlates of all that which we call worldly entities" (K 270). To be sure, they are not what they are as worldly objects, namely, "members of the outer world" (Id.II 163), but they are *poles* of the outer world and *only* that. To this extent, the consciousness of Others is nothing more than "experiencing consciousness of Others as having a world" (K 258:255). Were one to strike out their relation to the world, they themselves would disappear by the same token. They receive their fullness—for me who experience them—solely out of the world to which they are related. As indicated, Others are, in their turn, just such empty subject poles "for" the objective as well as "for" the primordinal world. To be sure, *the* primordinal world whose subjects they are is their own and not mine. But it is the same world that I also experience, and, in this identity, it is the objective world.

I experience Others as world objects and *at the same time* (CM 123:91) as subjects for the world. So Husserl does not say that there are two different experiences of Others, one that brings these before the self as world objects and another that intends them as subjects for the world. Rather, the noematic correlate of each alien experience is supposed to be an entity that is a world object and, in conjunction therewith, a world subject. Even though the Other may at one time stand before me more as a world object and then again more as a world subject, this "at-the-same-time" cannot be suspended.

Mediacy as the mediatedness of the world cannot therefore be suspended. It appears in many different forms. The experience of the Other as a subject for the world is mediate because I can only experience the Other itself by means of the experience of its world apperception. Another mediacy is to be distinguished from this one. It consists in the fact that the alien is a subject for the world only as a world object. Husserl has this in mind at the beginning of the section referred to from the "Fifth Cartesian Meditation." In the reduction to my sphere of ownness, only the physical body, which I present as a world object, mediates the experience of the alien subject. Finally, a third mediacy is to be found in the fact, which is taken for granted, that the Other is an object in the world. Husserl does not go into this at all, perhaps for the reason that it offers no specifically distinctive trait of alien experience but is equally valid of the experience of things. I experience each worldly object merely mediately insofar as it is mediated by the world whose object it is. This mediacy exhibits in turn two aspects. Essentially, it is the mediation of the world object through the world sense ultimately imparted by me and through the world horizon in which it appears. Inseparable therefrom is its mediation through the other world objects circumscribed by the same horizon, with which it enters into causal relations or upon which it "impinges" in any form. As certain as it is that this third mediacy inhabits our experience of things as world objects, it is still not at all self-evident that it also regulates every experience of Others. What cannot be doubted is simply that it regulates the experience of Others when these are regarded with Husserl as world objects.[3]

2 The Primordinal Situation

In order to grasp the limited character of Husserl's statement, one must bear in mind what the "transcendental clue" excludes a priori. The *im*mediacy that is reflected back from the three modes of mediacy as an equally threefold inverse possibility is only a name for an experience that, in a similar manner, is distinguished thereby in that it envisages the Others neither as subjects nor as objects and therewith also breaks through the unity (which is only the simultaneity of opposed moments) in the direction of a totality that is not put together. The smallness of the basis of experience upon which the theory of intersubjectivity stands becomes even more noticeable when we consider what the primordinal situation, projected in accordance with the transcendental clue, presupposes as self-evident. Above and beyond the general presuppositions contained within the transcendental clue itself, five implications are, above all, to be named.

1. The world in which I encounter the Other originally is, in accordance with its constitutive meaning for the encounter, a *spatial world*. It is, so to speak, reduced in advance to its pure spatiality. This holds, above all, for the primordinal world in which I perceive the physical body (of the Other to be). With the body, however, the Other is itself brought under the category of the spatial. As long as his body is "there," he appears as "coexistent ego in the modus 'there' " (CM 148:145). The foundational function of the here-there relation for the alien experience is unequivocal testimony to the sovereignty of space in the primordinal sphere. The identification of primordinal world and primordinal space also further betrays the fact that, in his description of the constitution of the objective world, in the "Fifth Cartesian Meditation," Husserl certainly acknowledges the constitution of objective time that is carried out along with it, but not, on the contrary, that of objective space (CM 156:153).[4] Admittedly, in the transformation of the primordinal into the objective world, time *and* space are coobjectified. Still, because Husserl conceives the primordinal world from the outset as spatial, he does not need to mention the transformation of primordinal into objective space, on its own merits.

Herewith, the congruence of *objective* world and *objective* space manifests itself in the manner anticipated. Correspondingly, the spatialized
interpretation of the alien-personal being is also carried through on
the level of the objective world. In accordance with the clue given in
the *Paris Lectures* (CM 34:34), which—as we shall see more clearly—
is taken from the experience gained in the objective world, I experience
the Others, insofar as they are world objects for me, as "appearing
psychologically interwoven in a natural connection in space." The
"separation of the apart" of which *Crisis* speaks (259:255) (characterized
in the "Fifth Cartesian Meditation" as spatial separation), and that is
insurmountable with respect to human persons, stands in relation to
the objective (as already to the primordinal) world. It is the "real
separation, the worldly separation of my psychological existence from
that of the Other, a separation that presents itself as spatial on account
of the spatiality of the objective (organic) bodies" (CM 157:155).

However, the tendency to an equalization of the intersubjectively
constituted objective world with objective space betrays itself not only
in concealed observations. Rather, it comes openly to the fore in the
terminological interpretation of the world constituted *primarily* through
intersubjectivity as "nature" (CM 149:146). In that it is nature, the
initially constituted objective world comes together with the primordinal. The conceptual overlapping is, however, in fact an agreement
in a specifically spatial being-sense. Within the intersubjectively objective sphere, Husserl distinguishes the primarily constituted nature
from the personal culture world (CM 159–163:157–159) whose constitution, as he says, engenders "relatively few difficulties" (CM 157:154)
and can, of course, very easily be clarified (CM 159:156).[5] He can,
however, only be of this opinion because he also operates in the field
of the cultural world with spatial categories under which the intersubjective constitution of the objective nature is carried out. He can
treat the constitution of the personal culture world as a pure supplement
to the constitution of objective nature because, although the latter is
certainly to be distinguished, formally, from the objective world, which
is its initially constituted step, it nevertheless, and precisely on account
of its originality, subjects the entire objective world to the laws of its
transcendental constitution. In any case, behind the fleeting sketch of
the culture world given in the "Fifth Cartesian Meditation" stands
that which Husserl already, in book II of *Ideas*, describes as the correlate
of the personal attitude and what he later, in *Crisis*, thematizes under

the title "life-world." The question whether, here, he gets free of the spatial orientation is still not answered with the recognition of the dominant role of space in the "Fifth Cartesian Meditation." However, the foundational relation holds firm: objective nature, as the primarily intersubjectively constituted spatial world, founds the world of the personalistic attitude as well as the nature projected by science that, as the correlate of the natural attitude, first arises through abstraction "from the personally engendered predicates of the objective world" (CM 127:95).

2. In the primordinal situation, there is a presence of the Other for me only in the form of his corporeal actuality. Only the Other who stands before me "corporeally" (CM 139:136) is actually present. So Husserl reduces the fullness of possible modes of presence of the other person in advance to the single modus of the factically present. This is clear from the primordinal situation itself. It is the transcendentally modified and even primordinally reduced form of a determinate everyday situation. I find myself in a region at first wholly void of human beings and am then, through the factical emergence of an other human being in my perceptual sphere, torn away from my solitude: "Let us suppose that another human being enters our perceptual sphere. Primordinally reduced, this signifies: In the perceptual sphere pertaining to my primordinal Nature, a body is presented that, as primordinal, is, of course, only a determining part of myself" (CM 140:137). Without this bodily appearance, I could not experience the Other.

3. Implied in the fact that the actual appearance of the Other in my perceptual sphere is the condition of the possibility of his being encountered is the following: According to Husserl, the Other originally encounters me only in an outer perception. The perception that discloses the Other in the primordinal situation, Husserl restricts, in turn, to sensible seeing. As appresentation of the alien organic body, experience of the alien is "an interpretative perception" and, as such, the "spatial seeing and originally interpretative envisioning that is connected with the apprehension of an alien embodiment" (EP.II 63). So it is, for example, impossible to accomplish the sense constituting experience of the Other in hearing. Just as little, according to Husserl, does speech, as enunciative discourse, contribute anything to the primary constitution of the Other.[6] To be sure, once in a remark at the

beginning of which Husserl refers in another connection to the fact that he has not taken into consideration "the essential role of enunciation," he says, with regard to this lack, "This also is lacking in the originally projected doctrine of empathy, which has first to be worked out. According to my observations, it appears in children that the self-generated and then analogically heard voice furnishes the bridge for I objectification: for example, the formation of the 'alter,' and already before the child has and can have a sensible analogon for the similarity of its visual body with that of the Other" (Id.II 95). Still, from this psychological observation, Husserl has drawn no philosophical consequences. In the sphere of the relation of different subjects he introduces enunciation—as linguistically articulated reciprocal understanding—and from now on right up to the end of his life, he only brings it into play when the visually directed empathy has already done its work.

4. Beyond the general subject-object givenness of the Other, the primordinal situation prescribes, in more detail, that I, as subject, first run into the Other as object and only become aware of alien subjectivity on the basis of this objectification. As subject, the Other is, in my eyes, certainly no simple something in the sense of the thingly present at hand, but is still "someone." And "someone" is itself something that exists *for me*, a being known to me and for me and on the basis of me (K 410 B—italics are mine). So, according to Husserl, I never become conscious of him in that I am *for him*. He is never initially a subject, nor am I initially his object. I first discover myself as his object at an essentially later stage, and, indeed, on the detour by way of empathic insight into his world apperception. Even then I am nothing like the special object of the Other, but solely one among the many who manifest themselves to him in his world. Besides, according to Husserl, the experience of my objective being for the Other remains continually included in the experience of the objective being of the Other for me. According to Husserl, I can only experience myself as object of the Other when I have the Other in mind at the same time as my object. This, at the same time (*Zugleich*), is itself only a special case of the universal at the same time that binds together, in one act, the experience of the Other as a subject for the world and that of the Other as an object in the world.

5. The first of the levels at which, on the underlying basis of my primordial world, the objective is constituted is "the constitutional level of the Other or Others in general" (CM 137:107). At this point, we need not be concerned with the "in general," but with the interchangeability of singular and plural. Even where Husserl clarifies the meaning of the phrase "in general," he speaks on one occasion of "*the* pure Others (which still have no worldly meaning)" and on another occasion that "*the* Other has not yet arrived at the meaning human being" (CM 137–138:107 — italics are mine). The one Other whose givenness he explicates is precisely from the start only one among many others that appear in my surrounding world. He is not the only one who belonged to me in a unique manner. The distinction between the intimate Thou and the alien, in the innermost sense of that word, has no place at all in the sphere of the original constitution of the Other. As anyone, the "Other in general" is continually an "alien," an alien, admittedly, with respect to whom the contrast of the nearest is lacking, just as is the characterization as remote. This statement corresponds to the previous equalization of the presence of the Other with its corporeal appearance in the world. That the intimate is *there for me* in a manner other than that of the mass of those who also stand in contrast not only to me but also to him as "Others" can carry no weight in laying the foundation of alien experience because existence is regarded as the being there, the presentness, of the Other, which is insensitive to such differences.

3 The Difference between Transcendental and Natural Experience of the Alien and the Immediacy of the Natural

In addition to the five specified predeterminations that already form the basis of the point of departure for the theory of intersubjectivity, many others can still be enumerated. One has only to think of the bracketing of ethical phenomena and their constitutive meaning for the consciousness of the Other.[7] However, we cannot go into this. We have only introduced the five above-mentioned points because they bring to light the peculiar character of Husserl's statements in contrast with other possibilities of treating the theme, as we shall come to see in the further course of our investigation.

Now, however, we must clearly delineate the limits within which alone the indications laid down express something about the "pe-

culiarity of the Husserlian statement." We have tested the situation
in which the experience of the alien of the "Fifth Cartesian Meditation"
is carried through. This experience of the alien is, however, transcendental in character, and the transcendental is not the factical of
which we have experience every day in the natural attitude.[8] So, with
respect to transcendental experience of the alien, its validity does not
also bear upon the natural experience unless it could be proved that
Husserl interprets the latter by the standards of the former.[9]

That this is not entirely the case is indicated, for example, in point
5. As a coworld, the world of the natural attitude is, according to book
I of *Ideas*, always and essentially a socially differentiated world. They
(that is, Others) are my "friends" or my "foes," my "servants" or my
"masters," "strangers" or "relatives," and so on.[10] Admittedly, insight
into this fact is to be distinguished from its transcendental grounding.
Precisely here Husserl reproaches himself with being unable, through
his transcendental theory, to render intelligible something that he
recognizes as a life-worldly fact. Similarly, this insight bespeaks the
necessity of at least separating Husserl's description of the natural
experience of the alien from his description of the transcendental
constitution of the Other.

But Husserl does not, as a matter of fact, just describe the natural
alien experience here and there as something different from the transcendental. In two points, the natural alien experience must be distinguished from the transcendental. First, for the I of the natural
attitude, Others are always already present, that is, before any actual
communalization. In opposition to the transcendent alien experience,
therefore, the natural does not first take place because an Other, or
Others, appears bodily in my perceptual sphere. In place of the *ontic*
presentness that, in the primordinal situation, exclusively determines
the sense of the presence of the other person, there arises, in the
natural sphere as its transcendental condition, a certain *ontological* presentness, the present of the Other not in the world but in my world-
embracing horizon.

The second point of difference is even more significant. It specifically
bears upon the basic presupposition contained in the transcendental
clue itself. As long as I experience the Other as, at the same time,
object in the world and as subject for the world, I do not experience
him in original unity. Although experienced, *at the same time*, that is,
in the unity of *an* act, as object and subject, the Other is still, in

accordance with its mode of being, torn apart into subjectness and objectness. Nevertheless, I evidently make this splitting apart retroactively, in that I apperceive the Other in the course of the constitution of the objective world as "other human beings." For this is a unifying operation. I posit the Others in the objective world as the "closed unity human being." Even as one human being, however, I experience the Other in the natural attitude. Thereby the natural experience of the alien seems also to have overcome mediacy. For mediacy is to be found in the dividedness of the Other between the subject for the world and the object in the world. Conversely, the apperception of the Other as an original unity means nothing other than to experience him immediately. Insofar, however, as mediacy thoroughly determines the character of transcendent experience of the alien, there arises a gap, in principle, between the transcendental and the natural experience of the alien.

In the previous chapter we referred to places in the text where Husserl interprets the natural alien experience as the accomplished experience of factically present things in the horizon of nonfactically present Others. Similarly, he meets the second requirement that follows from his thinking: Insofar as he considers the natural alien experience as the apperception of an other human being, he, in fact, ascribes to it an intention to absolutely original unity. More important than anything else in this connection is the analysis of the personal attitude in book II of *Ideas*.[11] The personal attitude is precisely the one in which I grasp things as the motivational use objects of an understandingly projected "surrounding world" and grasp Others as human beings communicatively bound to me. In both respects, in that of the things and that of the Others, it is related inversely to the natural attitude, for which things are inanimate substrates of properties and Others "unities" of body and soul. In the personal attitude, where I live in a "comprehensive" consciousness of other human beings, I experience "not the natural unity between body and soul, much less the things that are natural things and that we see there as environmental things." The naturalistic unity is, however, a unity only in the sense of the joint occurrence of two entities, of which one—the soul—is one-sidedly dependent upon the other—the psychically signified body. The body as material body furnishes the basis on which the soul is suspended. In contrast, the personal experience of the Other is directed toward an original nonsynthetic unity, which is "the human being." "We" find there not two things outwardly interwoven with each other: bodies and personas. We find *unitary* human beings who interact with us and the bodies included in the human unity. The original unity of the human being Husserl also terms, in contrast with the naturalistic, "comprehensive" or "intuitive": the "thoroughly intuitive unity that presents itself whenever we grasp a person *as such*." "Everything is intuitive here, external world and the body just as the physical-spiritual unity of the human beings existing there" (234–236).

The difference between the naturalistically secondary and the personalistically primary unity of the Other reveals itself most remarkably when we start out from the difference of the acts in which the unity is given in such and such a way. In the naturalistic attitude, the act directed toward the Others already comes to a halt, as it were, with the alien physical-organic body. This is its direct and authentic object, and the soul is so only insofar as it represents the nonintuitive end point of the line that my act prolongs over and beyond the truly perceived physical-organic body. From the standpoint of the natural sciences, the soul is a "simple layer of real events in bodies" (175), which, for their part, belong to the foundational layer of material physicality. It is simply a "bodily annex" (209). As such it is posited behind the body, stuck inside it. This is what is meant by the concept "introjection" (166, 175–177), the term Husserl uses to characterize the naturalistic understanding of the soul (*Seele*). In a scientific perspective, I am required "to stick the alien soul in the alien body, to 'introject'" (167). When, on the other hand, in my personal environment, I enter into relation with a human being, I am in no way directed toward a body, still less toward a purely physical body. Just as little am I directed toward the 'spirit,' the form in which the I, reduced by natural science (qua psychology) to a soul, is preserved in a personal manner. Certainly, the human being with whom I enter into relation has, and even has for me, a body and a spirit. But he himself is neither spirit nor body but their unitary ground. I look down at this ground without any intermediary instance, and I only see the alien body in such a way that I see down through it—to the ground:

I see a human being and in seeing him I also see his (organic) body. In a certain respect, the apprehension of a human being goes through the appearance of the physical body, which the organic body is there. In a certain regard, it does not stay with the physical body, does not direct its glance upon it but through it—and not even to a spirit bound up with it, but precisely to the human being. And the human appre-hension, the apprehension of this person there who dances and enjoys himself, laughs and chats, or discusses science with me, and so on, is not the apprehension of a spirit fastened to an organic body but the apprehension of something that realizes itself through the medium of the appearance of the physical body. (240)

The human experience of other human beings is now, according to Husserl, distinguished by its pure *immediacy*: "If we look each other in the eyes, subject meets subject in an immediate interaction. I speak to him, he speaks to me. I command him, he obeys. These are im-mediately experienced personal relationships, which attest to an immediate experience of Others" (375 B).[12] This experience is im-mediate in the threefold sense that corresponds to the three meanings of mediacy. It is immediate, first, because it does not bring the Other before itself through the detour across the empathic insight into his world apperception. When we "look an Other in the eye," just such an empathy is in play. In which case, the Other is not directed toward the world but toward me. However, that I am not in this situation an object encountered in the world is due to the "each other." The each other articulates the equality of level in the confrontation and thereby excludes that subordination characteristic of my relation to the Other when I am his mundane object. The communicative experience of other human beings is immediate, second, insofar as it does not allow its correlate to be mediated by the alien (physical) body. It is immediate, third, because it does not enclose the Other as worldly object in my world projection and does not posit him in a mediating connection with other world objects. For this would contradict the eye-to-eye in exactly the same way as the reverse situation, which turns me into the worldly object of the Other.[13]

We have documented Husserl's concern with the naturalistic human apprehension with long citations because, in spite of its literary ob-scurity, it does, in fact, bring with it almost as fundamental a meaning as does the insistence upon the mediacy of transcendental experience of the alien. Inasmuch as the personal apperception of one's fellows is a discarding of mediacy, it not only abandons the transcendental clue but also, along with it, all those laws that dominate the primordinal situation projected in accordance with the transcendental clue. This is demonstrated by Husserl's exemplification of human-personal re-lationships. To be sure, I also see "human beings." But, on the basis of the personalistic and, more generally, the natural attitude, this seeing is no longer the sole mode of disclosure. For instance, hearing accompanies it. Already as the hearing of steps (I hear their approach) it is immediately a hearing of *human* steps. An even more important role is played by that kind of hearing that belongs to speaking, as the immediate understanding of words. Hearing and speaking are, however, from the outset, hearing *one another* and speaking to *one another*. The concept of language (inclusive of hearing) in this sense of discourse is,[14] alongside the communicating agencies, one of the two phenomena by means of which personal communication is gradually concretized. Discourse is differentiated, however, according to the communicative situation. He who "chats" with me speaks differently from the one who "discusses science" with me. And this situated determinateness of speaking is itself immediately coexperienced in the hearing of the spoken.

In book II of *Ideas*, all the other places at which Husserl wants to "presentify personal relations in a lively manner" refer to the same phenomenal sphere (182). In connection with a general characteristic of the natural attitude, he writes, "The personalistic attitude in which we are situated at all times is quite different when we live with one another, shake each other's hands in greeting, when we relate to each other in love and aversion, in act and intention, in affirmation and response" (183).[15] We find ourselves in this attitude when, for example, "we deal with other persons, turn to talk to them and them to us, receive orders from them, fulfill them, and so on" (234), when we, for example, "speak as person to person or listen to their speaking, work together with them, watch their actions" (236). This working together does not get associated with the above-mentioned acts of communication in an incidental manner. Rather, this practical association is a principal medium of the personalistic attitude. Whether those acts are realized in work or in play, however, they continually give rise to a situation that is to be distinguished from the primordinal in all five points. Not only has seeing lost its preponderance. Even space is incapable of dominating the world, insofar as it is a personal world. The personal present is not dependent upon the factical encounter with an alien (physical) body. That transcendental relationship that, at least at the beginning, is the sole normative relationship of me to the Other must, in the interhuman sphere, accommodate the original orientation of the Other to me, alongside or even across itself (see also Id. II 234). And out of the undifferentiated multiplicity of the Others who arise in my primordinal world, personal intimacy emerges as that relation in which I deal with one particular Other as with no one else.

4 The Abandonment of Natural Immediacy and the Twofold Character of the Personalistic Attitude

As weighty as Husserl's thematization of personal immediacy might have been, it is still only an exceptional sortie that is quickly abandoned. The taking back that concerns us here does not lie in the reduction of the natural to the transcendental experience of the alien but in a transformation of the meaning of natural alien experience itself. This will become clear from the passages referred to hereunder. These references should not, however, be taken as the establishment of purely individual deviations from the systematically prescribed way of phenomenology. Rather, we take them as the expression of a substantive intention that, just as much as its opposed intention toward immediacy, is motivated by the transcendental laying of the foundation of the natural experience of the alien. The theory of the constitution of the other human being legitimates the change of transcendental mediacy into natural immediacy as a closed unity. The self-suspension of natural immediacy is precisely set up in this theory, namely, in this, that both sides of the "other in general"—alien body and alien I—can only be unified in the entity "human being" in the manner of objectification. The Other is a closed unity only as a unitary object in the strict sense of intersubjective objectivity, whereby this objectivity also qualifies its subjectivity.

In Husserl's work this state of affairs corresponds to the general, and at the same time tone-setting, description of the natural experience of the alien.[16] What is disclosed there is not the original unitary being that reveals itself to an immediate encounter, but precisely this at-the-same-time of mundane objectivity and coobjectified subjectivity to which the transcendental theory adheres.[17] But the conception of the "personalistic attitude" expounded in book II of *Ideas*, in which the thought of communicative immediacy takes shape, falls away from this principle because Husserl interprets the personalistic act on the basis of an act directed toward one's fellows as *empathy*. In an appendix, Husserl, on one occasion, still attributes immediacy to empathy (375).

But here the immediacy is relativized through the contrast with the naturalistic mode of experience. Only in a comparison with it can personalistic empathy be called an immediate experience of the other. We shall soon see that Husserl undertakes just such a relativizing transformation of personal immediacy. In an absolute sense, however, empathy is as such essentially mediate. This interpretation is also advanced by Husserl in book II of *Ideas* (199) as elsewhere. Inasmuch as he grounds the personalistic attitude in empathy, he takes away from it the immediacy that, in other places in the book, he attributes to it.

In that it is empathy, the personalistic apperception of the alien human being comes together with the naturalistic. The sharply articulated difference of both attitudes (210), conceived in outline as the opposition of extreme mediacy and genuine immediacy, is, with regard to the relation to one's fellow human beings, reduced to the difference between two modes of empathy. Naturalistic experience of the alien is empathy of a particular kind known as introjection (228);[18] personalistic empathy is, on the one hand, empathy as understanding of alien personal motivations, and, on the other, of the sense with which the alien (organic) body is invested (224). The direction of the movement of the introjecting act is already familiar to us: it stops at the alien (physical) body and posits the alien soul behind it as something functionally dependent upon the former and upon material nature in general. The personalistic opposition to this procedure will, on account of the interpretation of personalistic experience of the alien within the horizon of empathy, not be touched upon. However, the dynamic direction of acts that Husserl positively counterposes to the naturalistic is altered thereby. Out of the stream of consciousness that is directed through the transparent body immediately upon the unity that holds body and spirit together, there develops an act that, so to speak, leaps over the alien body into the alien act center (the spirit), in order to come back out of it to the objects appearing to the other subject and, thereby, to me. This is what the new opposition of the naturalistic and the personalistic attitude looks like: "On the one hand, the alien I, lived experience, and consciousness are introjectively posited, built upon the basic conception and position of material nature conceived as functionally dependent on it and resting upon it. On the other hand, the I exists as person, as 'purely and simply' posited, and thereby posited as the subject of its personal and thingly surroundings" (228).

Being the subject of a personal and thingly environment, of a "sur-rounding world" that is at the same time structurally coordinated with that of others, defines the concept of the "person" thematized in *Ideas*, book II (see 182, 185–186). Thereby the "surrounding world" is the world "for me," the universal noematic correlate of my intentional life (186, 218). This determination makes it understandable why Husserl can elevate "motivation" to the "fundamental law" of the spiritual-personal life.[19] For motivation is the affective substrate of the intentional relation in which objects are the noematic correlates of acts carried out by a person (189). It is not, as is the causality governing between human beings and things, a relationship of "real subjects to real objects" (232–233), but a relationship present "only in the purely intentional sphere" (189) "between subjects and thing *noema*" (233). As an object already intentionally pre-viewed, a thing motivates me to those acts in which I can then grasp it expressly. It "awakens" my interest and "thanks to this interest, a tendency to turn toward" (216), a tendency that, admittedly, I can resist just as well as give in to.

However, I am motivated not only by things but also by persons, and thus especially by this, that in my deeds I am *directed toward them*: "When I do something because I hear that an Other had behaved in such and such a way, my doing is motivated by hearing and knowing" (231). Across the intermittent, occasional relationship to a particular Other, this motivational lawfulness regulates the entire personal life as an existence essentially dominated by the "one": Alongside the tendencies that emanate from other persons, we find, arising in the intentional form of indeterminate generality, the claims of custom, of usage, of tradition, of the spiritual milieu: 'one' judges in this way, 'one' holds one's fork in this way, and so on; the demands of the social group, of status, and so on" (269). Here Husserl imputes an even greater weight to those interpersonal motivational relations in which one person determines the other to adopt an attitude, in that one deliberately *turns to* the other and addresses himself *to* the other in linguistic enunciations, as well as in the expectation of an encounter: "There is yet another form of the action of persons upon persons. In their spiritual activities they are directed toward one another (the I toward the Others and vice versa); they carry out acts with a view to being understood by their opposite number, and to prompt it, through its understanding of these acts (expressed in such views), to certain personal modes of behavior" (192). These "*specifically social, communicative acts*" in which, according to Husserl, real sociality is first constituted (194),[20] are found again, in Adolf Reinach, under the same title. We have, however, already come across them in the course of our present reflections. In them, that communication is developed that is included under the title "immediacy," the reciprocity of dialogical partnership. Interpersonal motivation is disclosed as the intentional foundation of the "immediacy" of natural experience of the alien. Even in this connection Husserl speaks of immediacy, though in apostrophe: "Human beings exercise upon one another an 'immediate' personal action, an intuitive action. They have a 'motivating power' for each other" (192).

Have we not therefore been confronted once again with personal immediacy? The question must be answered in the negative insofar as Husserl subordinates empathy to the interhuman motivational relation. As the organ of the personalistic attitude, empathy should not consist in the understanding of alien motivations, at least, from the standpoint of its essential constitution. It is, however, one thing to be motivated to action by one's fellow; quite another to feel oneself into his being motivated. The former is an immediate, the latter a mediate experience. Even when one interprets the understanding of alien motivations in such a way that I empathically put myself into the act of that alien person motivating me, it remains mediate. It is, however, the empathy so determined on which Husserl grounds the motivational "action" exercised upon me by the other person. So he grounds the social act that, in and for itself, would be immediate, upon a mediate act. Thereby the immediacy of the social act itself becomes mediate — an immediacy in parentheses.

The seeming-immediacy of the personalistic attitude (which is even further removed from the substantive concept) has to be distinguished from this. As we have already indicated, it is in reality a mediacy, and simply appears as a form of immediacy in relation to the extreme immediacy of introjection. Its analogy to true immediacy is restricted to the fact that I, in the personalistic attitude, apprehend my fellow human being immediately, or "without further ado," as the *subject* of its surrounding world (191). However, the genuine, communicatively immediate act does not, as we have seen, intend the alien spiritual subject, but the *unity* of spirit and body given in the human being. With the foundation of the personalistic attitude in empathy, there transpires the abandonment of genuine immediacy in the subjective-objective bifurcation of the Other, or, what amounts to the same thing, in its world-relatedness.

For although I understand my fellow human being in the personalistic attitude "without further ado," as subject, he is for me at the same time an object—only I demote his being an object, by comparison with his being a subject, to the inessential moment; just as conversely, in the naturalistic attitude, I degrade his subjectivity to the status of an appendix to his objectivity. That I, as a person, experience the other person also as an object is indicated by the second determination of personalistic empathy: as understanding of the sense with which the alien body is invested, or as *expressional understanding* (236, 282–283). The latter at first retains the same direction that also characterizes the empathic consummation of the world-related act of the alien subject. Just as here I interact with the Other and from him on the objects that appear to him (myself included thereunder), so over there I interact with the movements in which the alien spirit expresses itself corporeally. But my understanding act grasps this direction first in a regressive move that is essentially preceded by an intention that runs from the alien organic-physical body and to the alien spirit. The alien physical-organic body is, so to speak, the pregiven material that I interpret with regard to its spiritual meaning. However, the expressional understanding structured in this way also lies at the root of the empathic relation to the alien person and in such a way that the latter is in general first inferred through the expression (245). Implied by the primary project of expressional understanding, personal empathy therefore also runs in both directions. The cooperating *with* and imitating *of* the acts of the alien subject presupposes a putting oneself into the latter. However, I can only put myself into the alien subject in that I transpose myself across the alien physical-organic body. The mediation of empathy in the alien subject through expressional understanding is indicative of the mediation of the alien subject itself through the alien (organic) body and, in the last analysis, the alien (physical) body. The latter, however, I also grasp in the personalistic, or (what ought to be the same thing) the humanistic attitude as an object, as an objective thing appearing in the world: "But inasmuch as I am in the humanistic attitude . . . this physical-organic body is, just like everything else that is not spirit, part of the surrounding thing-world. It is a thing that has a spiritual meaning that serves as a means of expression, an organ for a spiritual being, a person and its spiritual behavior" (204). Therewith, in fact, not only one's naturalistically but also one's personalistically apprehended fellow human being is, at one and the same time, subject and object.

Husserl characterizes human beings naturalistically as "unities of things and subjects with their psychic life" (162). But even the *personally* experienced organic body of the Other is as "fact"—according to the meaning of this concept (190)—a thing. It is a thing in the "factual world," therefore, itself, something worldly. Even in this it is not to be distinguished from its naturalistic caricature. Naturalistically, the following holds: "In my physical surrounding world I confront organic bodies" (164). This is supposed to mean that "the 'objective' physical totality, nature, is there for us, and dispersed throughout it are organic bodies, sensibilities, and psychic lives founded in it" (182). Together with the bodies, the souls that are functionally dependent upon them, and so the human beings themselves, are localized and temporalized in the actual worldly locations in which the bodies appear (177–179). Human beings themselves stand "in spatial connection among (viz., mere) things" (167), given like these as a "multiplicity" of objects, (162).

This is how Husserl describes "human apperception" when he remains in the natural attitude. However, all these categories recur in more or less modified form in the description of the personalistic human understanding. As a person, I confront a "multiplicity of persons" (207) who are fixed "in the spatial and temporal world" (202). To be sure, the theory of the connection of the personal spirit to the spatial and the temporal place of the body should be more indirect than the corresponding dependence of the natural soul, which, as such, itself belongs to the spatially and temporally differentiated nature. As a matter of fact, Husserl defines the former with the same concepts as the latter. That "spirit, human being as a member of the personal world," has a location should only mean that "it stands in a continual functional relation to a body" (204). However, Husserl also says of the soul that it is only "in a manner of speaking" spatially and temporally situated, namely, simply "through a functional connection" with the body (167). Personal spirit and natural soul are therefore both temporalized and localized because they stand in a functional relation to the body. The spatiotemporal ordering of the spirit is, however, an ordering in the world. Together with the alien physical-organic body, I also confront the personal subjectivity of the Other in my surrounding world: "The subject finds himself in his surrounding world, face to face not only with things but also with other subjects" (190). The latter are drawn into the mundane facticity that adheres to their bodies as "objects *in* the world."

Regardless of the foregoing, they are in themselves, as emphasized above, "subjects *for* the world." "Spirits" are distinctive in that "as I subjects they have their own being and, as essential to this, exist as counterparts to thinghood (that is, for the world)" (191). In this way, this formulation betrays the contradiction in which Husserl's conception of the personalistic attitude gets entangled through the orientation toward the being of the subject. Other persons have their own being insofar as they are more alien and more original than what accrues to them out of their placement in the world (298–299). As "counterparts" for the world, however—and they are that insofar as they are "subjects"—they precisely do not have their own being, no being that belongs to them over and beyond their relation to the world. In that the world depends on them as their surrounding world, they themselves fall into a dependence upon the world without which they would not be what they are: subjects for the world.

5 Transcendental Theory and the Natural Attitude

The last reflections have led us to an important result. We can now answer the question as to where Husserl gets the "transcendental clue" on which he establishes his theory of intersubjectivity. He believes it to be possible to read off the twofold mode of givenness of the Other, as an object in the world and a subject for the world, from that natural experience of the alien that factically occurs in the life-world. This point of departure from the natural attitude is indeed the general methodological principle of phenomenology. That, with respect to the transcendental laying of the foundation of experience of the alien, Husserl allows himself to be guided by its factical everyday accomplishment is unmistakably evident from the many passages of the "Fifth Cartesian Meditation": "The fact of the experience of the alien (not I) arises as the experience of an objective world and therein of Others" (CM 136:106). The recognition of what is given in advance constitutes the beginning of the theory. The latter is itself only "the interpretation of the intentional conditions that, in fact, reside in the world existing for us" (CM 138:108). It proceeds "just as the facts warrant" (CM 143:114). Accordingly, even in its development, it remains under the direction of the fact of the life-world. Just as in his first step, Husserl will disclose, of the transcendental clarification of the appresentation of the alien body, only "the truly complicated intentional operation of the actually resulting appresentation" (CM 140:110), so he is, in general, of the opinion that we can only then take account of the Other as a phenomenon in the phenomenological sense "when we hold onto the actual experience of the alien that can therefore come about at any time" (CM 150:121).

But does Husserl really hold onto this? One may doubt this with a certain justification. Inasmuch as Husserl posits an object in the world as the correlate of the actual experience of the alien, an object that is at the same time a subject for the world, his understanding of this alien experience is already guided by the transcendental interest, by the concern for the constitution of the world. As a result, the actual alien experience cannot be represented as what it is, namely, a *natural, life-worldly fact*. The deflection of the intention toward immediacy attests to this. In support of this, however, yet another systematic proof can be adduced. The transcendental interest is a theoretical one. That Husserl's understanding of the natural experience of the alien, insofar as he uses it as a clue for the transcendental theory, is itself, in turn, prompted by his transcendental interest; this means therefore that the natural alien experience is being considered from a theoretical standpoint. In consequence, there exists at least the tendency to seek it out there where it already possesses a theoretical form in itself.

In the framework of the natural attitude, experience of the alien does, however, possess a theoretical form as naturalistic. While, of both modes of the natural attitude, the personalistic is essentially practical, so that in it even theory appears as a form of praxis (189–190), the naturalistic is theoretical from the ground up, so that in it even praxis is theoretical.[21] For this reason, the formal equalization of the personalistic and the humanistic attitude has, in fact, another meaning than the correlative identification of the naturalistic and the scientific attitude. The naturalistic attitude is, from the outset, and as such, scientific. The personalistic, on the contrary, only first becomes humanistic through a subsequent scientification of the life-world that is the original point of orientation. Even the humanistic sciences that give it its theoretical form are not entirely theoretical, insofar as they have to elaborate the practically based structures of the life-world and the personal motivations of the world-related subjects. Whether and how this can happen is not the question here. For the moment we are only concerned with the theoretical character of the naturalistic attitude insofar as it continually endangers the transcendental theory by aligning itself with natural and not with personal experience. In fact, it can be shown that the construction of the transcendental experience of the alien follows the course of naturalistic comprehension as a result of a certain predilection (and we are only speaking of this).

If we test the relation of the personalistic and the naturalistic attitudes to the transcendental, it seems, at first in any case, that our suspicions are unjustified. On the contrary, the naturalistically instituted presents itself to us as that from which the truth of the transcendental attitude has entirely vanished, whereas the personally instituted lives near the transcendental origin. To be sure, both move in the natural attitude, but clearly the personalistic is, so to speak, transparent to the transcendental attitude. Indeed, if one takes a look at its universal object, the world as surrounding world, one might sometimes believe one were confronted with the world reduced to phenomenon. So the surrounding world is expressly characterized as the noematic correlate of my intentional life. Likewise, it looks as though I, the person related to the surrounding world, took the Other, to the extent in any case that I apprehend him as a person or as the subject of his surrounding world, not really as he is naively taken to be, but as he stands there in transcendental reflection. For I consider him as a subject for the world, which, as such, does not appear in the world. This is not so far removed from the concept of the transcendental alter ego, but it is entirely distinct from the natural concept of the Other as the fellow human being who generally, and as a whole, exists in a worldly manner. The demonstrable nearness of the personalistic to the transcendental attitude is expressly announced in the incidental description of the personalistic as the "egological attitude" (230). Admittedly, the personalistic attitude is not egological in the strict sense. All that is meant thereby is that the world discloses itself to it in its original relatedness to the I experiencing it. Correspondingly, the Other is known to me in it as the one who centers the world, qua his surrounding world, upon himself. In contrast, the alienation of the naturalistic attitude from the transcendental origin consists in this, that here the ego relatedness of the world is overlooked. Thanks to such an abstraction, the world then becomes "the 'objective,' physically natural totality" (182), as a world "in itself." The abstraction now presents itself as abstraction from the personalistic attitude, the forgetfulness of the I and its world-founding operation as the self-forgetfulness of the personal I that the natural scientist is, and still remains, in his scientific activities. Thus Husserl arrives at the insight that "the naturalistic attitude is subordinated to the personalistic and, through an abstraction, or rather through a sort of self-forgetfulness of the personal I, achieves a certain self-sufficiency, thereby at the same time illegitimately absolutizing its world, nature" (183–184).

Hence it appears that the parties to the contradiction that, according to our introductory exposition, characterizes the natural attitude are divided between the personalistic and the naturalistic attitudes. The personalistic attitude confirms, or so it seems, the essential relatedness of the world to the experiencing I. The naturalistic, in contrast, makes the world into an absolute, into something detached from the I. The personalistically experienced relatedness, however, is, if not the true transcendental relatedness, at least the basis on which the transcendental is to be discovered through carrying out the reduction.

This image reveals itself to be a misleading one as soon as we complete the presentation of the personalistic attitude. We said that the "surrounding world" to which the personalistic attitude is related is *my* surrounding world; it is as I actually experience it. It is, however, at the same time *common* to persons: "To each person there belongs their surrounding world, while, at the same time, several persons, communicating with one another, have a common surrounding world" (185). This means that each of the persons communicating with one another has the world in the same way as all the persons with whom they communicate: "In the communicative community everyone sees what I see, everyone hears what I hear" (198). Now I communicate as a person, but only occasionally with other persons. Even here an extension of our former conceptual specification is necessary. As a person in the sense of the personalistic attitude, I am not only the subject of a surrounding world but also "a *member of the social world*" (175), a "person in a personal association" (191). So, in the personalistic sphere, I always already communicate with other persons and, as a consequence, also always already have a common world. For "we are in a relation to a common world—we are in a personal association: this belongs together" (191). Accordingly, just as there are not in part persons who live for themselves in the world and in part persons who communicate with one another, so there are not, on the one hand, solitary, and, on the other, common surrounding worlds. That "several" people communicate with one another and only have one common world is, just like the being alone of persons shut out from it, and from any determinate community, an ontical fact based upon the ontological constitution of the person, in the light of which each person is always already communalized and has a surrounding world that has always already been communalized. Before any participation or nonparticipation in this or that personal association I am, the human person, integrated in the universal personal association of the human totality in which the "transcendental I-totality" is objectified (FTL 237:268). The surrounding world that is constituted in this collective with the "others" is the collective world that Husserl names the "*communicative*" (193).

It is easy to draw the consequences of the foregoing. The communicative world cannot exist *alongside* my own, or first get built up after it, through actual communalization. Rather, the world of the personalistic attitude is, from the outset, the communicative world and no other. The surrounding world that belongs to me and is bound to me, in the sense of the world of the personalistic attitude, is therefore an abstraction. In reality, we have here to do exclusively with "the 'egoistic world' of the person thought in isolation . . . the person who, in its world relatedness, is so abstractly thought that it includes no relation of understanding with other persons (nothing of a social association)" (193). Husserl carried out this abstraction in the textual passages interpreted above. It is a kind of primordinal reduction that is clearly only distinguished from the "genuine" in that it is enacted on the basis of the natural attitude. For all that, the abstraction set up in the framework of the personalistic attitude also truly suppresses the natural sense of being. The natural-objective world is precisely the communicatively experienced world and the natural-objective subject, the subject integrated into the personal human association. That Husserl thereby gets entangled in a contradiction is precisely what should be shown. Even in abstraction from the communicative world, he claims to describe the personalistic attitude and is unable to do so because he brackets, through abstraction, the natural sense of being that inhabits the personalistic attitude as the original modus of the natural.

The, at first compelling, proximity of the personalistic and the transcendental attitude thereby becomes deeply questionable. Wherever
this proximity announces itself, the personalistic experience is no longer
itself. It has already been altered in the direction of the transcendental
experience. Only in this altered form is it an "egological" attitude.
The sense of this designation first gets clarified with respect to the
abstraction from the original communicative form of the world. To it
there corresponds the meaning of the term "egoistic world." As the
latter, the thingly world, whose subject is the person, is identified with
my sphere of ownness in the transcendental "phenomenon world."
Husserl says himself "that the thingly, at times intuited or intuitable,
surrounding world of the person falls together with the world as it
appears to the solipsistic subject: things appearing in multiple ad-
umbrations group themselves around a central here" (202). Indeed,
precisely this change of proximity into identity is suspicious. It betrays
the fact that Husserl does not at all *confront* the personalistic and the
transcendental attitude but surreptitiously carries over the former into
the latter. Thereby it becomes difficult to make out in which individual
cases he carries out the primordinal abstraction and in which he does
not. Presumably, the difference between the recognition of communicative immediacy and the interpretation of personalistic experience
of the alien as an empathic relation to the subject of the alien surrounding world is to be traced back to the distinction between an
abstractive analysis and a nonabstractive analysis of the personalistic
attitude. Where Husserl abstracts, he regards its correlate as the immediately intuitable unity of human being. However, insofar as he
also takes the expressional and the motivational empathy to be a
personalistic alien experience, our objection is justified: the objection
that he transforms the immediacy of the *factical life worldly intercourse*
with one's fellows into a mediacy. That he takes possession of this
mediacy only in a quasi-transcendental attitude proves what it is supposed to prove: the preconception of that factical experience of the
alien that is set up as a clue for the transcendental theory is determined
out of a transcendental prehension in the natural sphere. Through
this prehension, through abstraction (set up on the basis of the personalistic attitude) from the preceding communalization of the person
and its surrounding world, however, the most genuine part of the
personalistic attitude—and this is decisive for us—is lost.

In opposition thereto, a remarkable relationship is established between the transcendentally reduced and the naturalistically disclosed
world, which does not first take place through a modification of the
content of the latter. We can easily read off the similarity from the
text of book II of *Ideas*. It is by no means simply limited to a convergence
of particular sections from the passage about the world of the natural
experience of the alien with other sections in which particular features
of the transcendentally reduced or even "genuinely" primordial world
are brought to prominence. Rather, that passage (162–172) contains
the entire theory of intersubjectivity (admittedly only in its crude outlines
and in a methodologically less differentiated structure), in the manner
in which, in the "Fifth Cartesian Meditation," Husserl developed it
out of the primordial world. If we divide up—as we are told at the
outset—the factically pregiven "human-apperception," "we have, at
the lowest level, the material physical body that, as a physical thing
like any other, has its place in space" (162). It is "originally perceived"
or given in "original presence." In contrast, the "innerness" of the
"subjectivities" is exclusively appresented (162–163). Upon "this fundamental distinction between originary presence and appresence,"
Husserl also grounds all further steps here. The goal, just as in the
"Fifth Cartesian Meditation," is the constitution of the objective world
as an intersubjectively identical nature in whose horizon the Other is,
in the end, itself constituted as the self-contained unity human being,
which I carry over to myself (171).

This entire genesis proceeds, as Husserl expressly observes, "in the
sphere of original constitution" (162). Accordingly, the intersubjectively
identical nature to which it is directed is "nature in the first and original
sense" (163), which, according to the system of the "Fifth Cartesian
Meditation," is neither the personal culture-world nor nature as correlate of natural science, but lies at the root of both as the "first to
be constituted in the form of the community" (CM 149:121). According
to the outline of book II of *Ideas*, however, it has at the same time to
be the nature of natural science. In this book, the passage that we
briefly summarized is the fourth chapter of the second part dealing
with "the constitution of psychic reality in empathy." The personalistic
attitude is first introduced by the third part, which follows immediately,
and by the last part, which follows the "constitution of the spiritual
world." The first part (on the "constitution of material nature") and
the second, whose general theme is the "constitution of animal nature,"

agree in this, that they stand in relation to nature in the sense of natural science: "We begin," so reads the first sentence of book II of *Ideas*, "our new discussion with nature as *the object of natural science*" (1).

The undoubtedly surprising similarity of content of the naturalistic and the transcendental-phenomenological attitude now, however, betrays the nominal and the systematic construction of the text—and not merely behind Husserl's back. Husserl himself also says as much. At the beginning of the first chapter of the third part he looks back at the already accomplished work. "The conclusion reached in the preceding sections in purely phenomenological analysis" he characterizes in the very next sentence as descriptions in the natural attitude: "We carried out our analyses in it (that is, in the natural attitude)" (174). In this way, the question arises whether Husserl explains the transcendentally given as an object of natural science or, conversely, transposes the object of natural science into the transcendental sphere. According to the context, he does the latter. He proceeds: "It is easy, however, to understand that the whole investigation takes on a purely phenomenological character in that we carry out the phenomenological reduction in a suitable manner." Easy—that means: the intentional object of the naturalistic attitude is not altered by the reduction. What emerges for the first time in the field of awareness is only an attitude that is itself correlated with it (174). To be sure, it thereby looks as though the similarity of content of "pure phenomenological analysis" and "the naturalistic attitude" now only appears to be settled. Clearly, the pure phenomenological attitude cannot be conformable with the natural attitude if the former also has the latter for its object, together with the object of the natural attitude. Nevertheless, according to Husserl, the subject of the natural attitude is identical with the pure I, which, in a quite peculiar manner, is identical with that pure I that is "the subject of all eidetic phenomenological research" (174). To add to what he has already said, and to bring the methodological reflections to a substantive conclusion, Husserl says, "As the subject of the naturalistic attitude, we then have the pure I." Therewith the natural attitude is itself identical with the transcendental in a manner that is admittedly not entirely of one kind. It coincides with the latter insofar as, to some extent, it prepares the world as "nature in the first and original sense" for the pure phenomenological analysis and, over and above that, indicates, in advance, the formal structures that, with respect to this nature, will be brought to light through the reduction.

The point, however, in which both attitudes do fall together, is their theoretical character. The natural attitude prepares the basis for the transcendental theory because it is already theoretical and interprets the world in a theoretical manner: "We proceeded from the natural (scientific) attitude in which nature as physical, corporeal, psychic nature achieves givenness and *theoretical knowledge*" (208). The theoretical knowledge of natural science—this is, at the same time, supposed to be the *"experience"* in which things and other human beings alike are *"originally given"* (162—italics are mine).

6 The Asociality of the Natural Attitude Required by Transcendental Theory

Our task is now to demonstrate the extent to which the translation of the natural into the transcendental experience of the alien is in principle possible. Without doubt there is a problem. For it only looks as though the same happens with the naturalistic experience of the alien as happens with the natural attitude in the execution of the phenomenological reduction. We have already observed, on several occasions, that in the phenomenological reduction, the world toward which the natural attitude is directed is certainly retained insofar as it is brought to its transcendental truth, but that the natural attitude itself is not retained but is overcome. In the translation that now presents itself for discussion, the natural attitude itself is "retained" along with the "world of the natural attitude" (174). What therefore has to be resolved is the contradiction that the naturalistic attitude is converted into the transcendental although, as natural, it excludes the transcendental. It can really only be resolved through the supposition that the naturalistic attitude is, in a certain manner, precisely not "natural," that is, that it is not so constituted as to make the natural attitude natural. This constitution is, as we have seen, a priori sociality. The task of providing for the condition of the possibility of the translation of the naturalistic into the transcendental also obliges us to disclose the fundamental asociality of the natural attitude that precedes all actual communalization and, at the same time, to render intelligible to what extent Husserl can then regard this attitude again as natural. The naturalistic attitude can only be shown not to be communalized if one is able to point out that its world is not communalized or that the scientific objectivity, which, according to Husserl, is of the highest and strictest kind,[22] is not an *intersubjective* objectivity in the sense that is constitutive for the natural attitude.

Now Husserl certainly *calls* the nature of natural science physical nature in its exemplary purity, just as he calls the initially constituted intersubjective nature and the personal life-world *intersubjectively* objective (88). But behind the same word a fundamental difference of meaning lies hidden. The objectivity of the primarily objective nature and the personal life-world is intersubjective because it is *constituted* through intersubjectivity; that of natural science, on the contrary, is so because it is *universally* valid. As "logical" objectivity, it consists in the universal validity of the insights at which I arrive in theoretical thought. These insights are from the very outset evidence for everyone, more exactly, for "every rational subject" (131). They can be carried out by all those equipped with the faculty of knowledge. In this and only in this understanding, scientific objectivity *implies* intersubjectivity: "For logical objectivity is *eo ipse* also objectivity in the sense of intersubjectivity. What a knower in logical objectivity knows, any knower is equally capable of knowing, provided that he meets the conditions that *every* knower of such objects must fulfill" (82; see also FTL 200–201:225). Precisely for this reason, however, scientific objectivity is not *constituted* through intersubjectivity. For I alone attain to the logical insights that Others can only *subsequently* carry out, but do not have to carry out in a *co*constitution. This means, however, that the world of the natural attitude is, in that meaning of this word employed by us, not at all "intersubjectively objective."[23]

This state of affairs is obscured by the circumstance that Husserl also accounts for the objective nature of natural science as constituted through intersubjectivity—whereby the concept "constitution" has a completely different and indeed inauthentic sense. Constitution is here not the inner genesis of the thing, but the outer *motivation* in relation to the thing, through which the thing enters into the field of awareness. Besides, this motivation is of a purely negative kind. The progress toward logical objectivity allows for the knowledge that the intersubjectively identical world is, at bottom, just as relative as the subjectively relative. It is precisely relative to the community of subjects in whose experience it proves itself to be identical (208). Therefore the physical thing is the logicomathematically determined *thing* "in *abstraction* from this (that is, intersubjective) relativity" (82; see also 78—italics are mine). What forces physics in a mathematical direction is the "question, how, in opposition to this relativism of the 'objectively existing,' that is, constituted through an intersubjective relation, the *objectively true* can be worked out" (Id.III 126 B). Within the horizon of the objectively true, which is the truly objective, intersubjective objectivity, in its relativity, now counts as fortuitous (Id.III 63–64). Its fortuitousness lies, more precisely, in the appearing character of the "merely" intersubjectively objective thing. In that natural science constructs the "thing in itself" through mathematization, the intersubjectively identical thing, which, for its part, has already degraded the purely subjectively identical to appearance, is itself again reduced to appearance. It is turned into the appearance of the "thing in itself" (171,207, Id.III 62–64).

In reaction to the relativity of the intersubjectively objective, natural science grasps the mathematicophysically objective—which already betrays the designation "thing in itself"—as the purely and simply irrelative. It is neither simply for me nor simply for all. Rather it is for everyone, and indeed solely because it is for no one, if the "for" is supposed to indicate the relativity of a relation. That it implies, but does not presuppose, intersubjectivity is also attributable to its irrelativity. It is "intersubjectively objective (that is, irrelative, and thereby, at the same time, intersubjective)" (84). Thereby the conception of the mathematicophysical world as purely and simply irrelative precisely brings out the naiveté of natural science. It is the reason why natural science is also "objective" in the sense of "natural." For the natural scientist thinks in the anonymity of the constitutive operations of his pure I (171). Transcendental reflection would like to bring him to recognize the fact that there is no "thing in itself." For it would like to bring him to awareness of the fact that the logically objective stands in relation to the logical acts from which it is derived. Transcendental reflection therefore restricts the putatively absolute irrelativity to the meaning of an independence from *sensible* experience.

With this in mind we must now determine more precisely the intersubjective quasi constitution of the nature of natural science. It has been disclosed as the motive for the break into the logically objective. The motive for scientific research is the insight into the relativity of the intersubjectively objective. However, this relativity is sensible relativity, the dependence of the intersubjectively identical thing upon the sensibility of the experiencing subject. It is the "real possibility and actuality of subjects endowed with diverse sense faculties, and the knowledge, present in every individual, of the dependence of the sense qualities upon physiological processes," that leads to a "consideration of precisely this dependence as a new dimension of relativity and a construction of the pure physical thing through thought" (86). This stepping beyond the dependence of the thing upon the sensibility of the experiencing subject is the ground for the physically fundamental division of "primary" and "secondary" qualities. The secondary qualities are the sensible ones, the real properties "that have not yet set aside the relation to the accidental subject, for example, to an accidental sensibility." The primary qualities, on the contrary, are the "geometrical determinations of things" that belong to "physical nature in itself" and that do not, like the sensible qualities, "belong in the sphere of phenomenal nature." They are thereby, in the mathematicophysical sense, "objective" properties (76–77, Id.III 62).

If we look more closely into the matter, even the intersubjective "constitution" of scientific nature, in the sense of the described motivation, becomes problematic. The intuitable thing is sensibly relative not merely to a plurality of subjects but also, and indeed principally, to the individual subject. Does the motivation of the discovery of logical objectivity stand in any need of a plurality of subjects? Husserl's answer to this question is already predelineated in the assertion that the real possibility and actuality of subjects endowed with sense faculties leads to the theoretical construction of the physical thing. In this way, Husserl addresses the problem of "anomalies."[24] An anomaly can, in the manner peculiar to consciousness, only be constituted on the basis of a "normality" (CM 154:125). On this basis, however, the solipsistic subject can already be aware of it within certain limits. Within certain limits — this means that it may only be *partial*. For example, should only *one* sense organ be abnormal, the appearances that are dependent upon it will be corrected through the perceptions of the other senses. The other organs are then constituted as functioning normally in that they at the same time bring to light the anomaly of the one (74–75). On the other hand, the solipsistic subject could not be aware of a *total* anomaly. It can only be constituted through intersubjectivity. In this case, the alien systems of appearance take over the corrective function. They prove my sense activity to be abnormal when the appearances relative to me diverge from them in any way that cannot be justified through the difference of the standpoints (206–207).

That the breakthrough to logical objectivity is motivated by the insight into the sensible relativity of the intuitable thing means that

it is brought about by the knowledge of the possibility and actuality
of the anomalies of sensible experience. For it is the possibility and
actuality of the anomaly that first renders relativity suspect. It is in
thinking about it that sensible experience loses its reliability. If this is
so, however, then the constitution of the physical thing is already
possible for the solipsistic subject. For it has the possibility of discovering
anomalies with respect to itself. On the other side, the intersubjective
world of experience does *not necessarily* motivate the constitution of
the physical thing: "On the one hand, there already exists, at the
solipsistic level, the possibility of pushing through to the constitution
of the 'objective' (physical) thing. On the other hand, even at the
intersubjective level, there does not exist the unconditional necessity
of pressing on so far" (89). The constitution of the physical thing is
possible for the "solipsistic" subject—above all, this is supposed to
make the positive point that this constitution *can* be brought about
here. However, it can also not be brought about. In that the discovery
of the physical thing is *only* possible for the "solipsistic" subject, it is
also, at its own level, not necessary. It is not necessary because a total
anomaly is just as possible as a complete normality (78). The possibility
of complete normality also leads Husserl on to the establishment of
the nonnecessity of intersubjective motivation. It permits the thought
of a world in which there are no anomalies at all, no illness, no illusions,
no hallucinations (89). For all that, Husserl places more positive worth
in the nonnecessity of intersubjective motivation, that is, in its pure
"possibility." That intersubjective experience motivates the step over
to the logically objective through the sensible relativity of its results
is not only possible but factically actual. As an addition to the cited
passage, we find "that, *in fact*, the constitution (that is, of the physically
objective thing) is carried out intersubjectively."

On what basis, however, can we ground the priority of the intersubjective motivations as actual over the mere possibility of individual
subjectivity? One is at first tempted to say, on the possibility of a total
anomaly on the part of the individual subject. However, a total anomaly
of all subjects who could ever enter into an intentional community is
also conceivable. Although Husserl does not mention this possibility
in our connection, it is hardly more fictive than the fiction of a complete
normality of all subjects. However, the thought of a total anomaly or
normality of the individual subject is already a fiction. In fact, the
individual subject, just as well as the totality of subjects, is, on the

basis of normality, partially abnormal—assuming that one allows the concept of "anomaly" the breadth that it has with Husserl (see the above-mentioned examples).[25] To this extent, the individual subject and the totality of subjects stand under conditions that are in principle the same.

The facticity of the intersubjective instigation to the constitution of the physical thing must therefore be rooted elsewhere. In the final analysis it can be explained in this way: that the instigation takes place in the natural world, qua life-world. As the subject of natural experience, the one engaged in scientific research is already communalized. Thus the world that motivates him is also intersubjectively objective—even when he turns to it in solitary experience. That "the experiencing subject is in truth not solipsistic but one among many," this is the condition under which "the *factical* constitution (that is, of the physical thing) stands" (78).

Just as the concept of the intersubjective constitution of the physical thing is "factically" ambiguous, so too is its supplementary determination. Doubtless, this means negatively that the intersubjectively objective world does not bring about the constitution of the physical thing with necessity. Still, it is in no way a denial of the fact that the constitution of the physical thing, when it actually occurs, is intersubjectively motivated by necessity. In any case, it is a matter here of operating under the assumption of the originary fact of the life-world. The necessity of the intersubjective constitution of the motivation that is itself not necessary and that leads to the constitution of the physical thing is the necessity of the sociality of the life-world. It is not a transcendental necessity, insofar as the "solipsistic" subject—abstractly, that is, thought in abstraction from the fact of the life-world—has the possibility of "thrusting through to the constitution of the 'objective' (physical) thing."

In sum, we may conclude that the mathematicophysical objectivity of the thing is, in a genuine sense, not constituted through intersubjectivity. Its constitution on the basis of individual subjects is entirely intersubjectively motivated. And even this motivation is only a factical one, in the sense outlined above.

In this way we have documented the asociality of the scientific attitude and pointed to the condition of the possibility of the immediate conversion of this attitude into one that is transcendentally concrete. However, the question has still to be answered, to what extent Husserl can impute the naturalistic attitude to the natural, and even define it as the height of naiveté. The justification for this is given to him in a certain respect by the circumstance that *one* object of scientific nature is really (that is, in the genuine sense of constitution), and with necessity, constituted intersubjectively: the scientist himself, who is fitted into this nature: "The solipsistic subject could indeed be confronted with an objective nature (that is, in the scientific sense), but *he could not envisage himself as a member of the natural world* . . . in the manner in which it is operative upon the intersubjective plane of experience" (90). The naturalization of the self as an alter-ation effected by the Other is, however, the last and most radical step in the intersubjective constitution of the objective world as *the world of the natural attitude.* Insofar, therefore, as the scientist envisages himself as an object in nature, conceived in the manner of the natural scientist, his attitude is natural. In this way, the reference of his self-objectification to intersubjectivity does not imply any reference of the naturalistic world to the personalistic. His self-objectification is different from the personalistic and also belongs in the world of the naturalistic attitude. Just as he regards the Other naturalistically, the Other by means of which he apperceives himself as a member of the objective nature, so similarly he himself becomes a human being as a "material thing" upon which the "psychic" layer is built up (161).

This state of affairs obliges us to limit the statement that the scientifically objective world is not (in the genuine sense) intersubjectively constituted. Only on the assumption of this limitation can Husserl's thesis be sustained, the thesis whereby the objective world is, in general, intersubjectively constituted. At the same time, the limitation changes nothing with regard to our interpretation of the naturalistic attitude as acommunicative and, to that extent, unnatural. Because the objectively natural I is not identical with the I of the natural attitude, the scientist, for the reason that as an objective I he is intersubjectively constituted, does not, as the subject of the natural attitude, need to be communalized at all. The subject of the naturalistic attitude is, as a natural subject, characterized by self-forgetfulness, that is, forgetfulness of the transcendental I. This self-forgetfulness, which is generally characteristic of the natural attitude, takes, as we have already discovered, the specific form of a "self-forgetfulness of the personal I" (184). The scientist does not pursue his science self-forgetfully because he is quite unaware of himself. For he is indeed aware of himself, namely, as a thingly member of the nature conceived by him. But precisely in that he only sees himself in this way resides the self-forgetfulness of his self, as the one for which the nature of natural science, together with all its members, exists. It is primarily the self-forgetfulness of the one pursuing natural science. The pursuit of natural science is theoretical praxis. The practical I is, however, the personal I. In this way, the subject of the naturalistic attitude is constituted, as Husserl says, out of the self-forgetfulness of the personal. Now this self-forgetfulness is, as Husserl says in the same place, "abstraction." The personal I, however, is, as a person among persons, the essentially communalized I. Therefore the subject of the naturalistic attitude is a product of an abstraction from its sociality, that is, from the sociality that it possesses as a personal I. The subject that, in fact, is intersubjectively motivated to scientific research is still "one among many." His noematic correlate is still the communicative world, and he himself is the subject of the personalistic attitude in which alone it is possible to talk of anything like "motivation." Insofar as he is established as the subject of the naturalistic attitude, however, this original sociality in him is effaced, just as is the "developed" objective nature whose subjective pole he then is.

7 The Reification of the Other through Interpreting Our Understanding of the Alien as Appresentation

We return to the text of the *Cartesian Meditations* presented in the second chapter, and so to the problematic of *transcendental* experience of the alien. The question whether the lines of direction provided by the "transcendental clue" are also valid for *natural* experience of the alien led us beyond the former problematic, which, however, we have never relinquished. The theme of the last paragraphs was the *relation* between the transcendental and the natural experience of the alien.

We shall now exclude the natural once again and consider the transcendental for itself. What pertains most truly to it, however, has by no means been articulated in the previous analyses devoted to its presuppositions. With reference to the report on the "Fifth Cartesian Meditation" undertaken earlier, we said that mediacy is the basic trait of the transcendental experience of the alien. Up until now, we have only apprehended this as the mediatedness of the Other through the world. One can easily represent to oneself how little it is exhausted therein by reminding oneself of the three principal levels at which it was brought to light, little by little, in the second chapter. The first level was the mediacy of the experience of the alien body as unpresentable appresentation; the second, the mediacy of the experience of the alien body as an "analogical apperception" of a peculiar type employed in the service of appresentation; and the third, the mediacy of the empathy that posits the alien I in which the analogizing apperception comes to prominence purely for itself. World mediatedness alone is simply the mediacy of appresentation as such. In contrast, what is new at both higher levels is to be sought in the mediation of the Other through *me*, that is, at the level of the perception of the alien body, through *my* body, and at the level of empathy, through the own I.

Now we have frequently emphasized in our presentation that the analogizing apperception (so-called) first grounds the *specific* mediacy of experience of the alien. So what pertains most truly to the transcendent experience of the alien is the mediatedness of the I. For all that, the thesis propounded at the start of the preceding chapter, namely, that Husserl's image of the Other is transcendentally determined through and through by a relation to the world that is in itself multifarious, entirely retains its validity. For, in accordance with our exposition in the second chapter, the mediacy of alien experience becomes, on its way through the three levels, not only ever more specific but also ever more radical. To the extent, however, that mediacy as such increases, it also increases in the particular form of world mediatedness. In that it is the mediatedness of the I, the mediacy of empathy is therefore, at the same time, the most radical mediatedness of the world.

In the interest of the attempt to get a hold on the special character of transcendental alien experience, we shall, in what follows, turn to the implications of the doctrine of empathy. In this way we also grasp the distinctive trait of the perception of the alien body insofar as it is an analogizing apperception. We only want to touch briefly upon the perception of the alien body as appresentation, and in the following manner: on the one hand, retrospectively, insofar as it confirms the naturalism of the transcendental theory; on the other hand, prospectively, and with regard to the fact that the systematic problem, which will become quite serious on the empathic plane, is already evident therein.

The appresentation of the alien body mediates the Other through the world in the sense of worldly being. This being, the pure (physical) body (of the Other to be) is mundane in the sharpest possible form of mundanity. It is nothing but a thing.[26] That world mediatedness that belongs to the experience of the Other insofar as the latter is an "object in the world" presents itself, in consequence, as the mediatedness of the thing in transcendental purity. Now one can perhaps already see in this an analogy to the natural experience of the alien. From a naturalistic viewpoint Others are material things through and through, upon which an animal layer is built up. Analogy is first brought to bear through the application of the category of appresentation to the presence of that in the Other that is not thing-like. In this way, Husserl (Id.I 101n1) still subordinates the non-thing-like (in accordance with his own interpretation) to the supremacy of the thing. For appresentation is originally, and in truth, the coperception of what does not appear with absolute originality in the thing. Counter to the indubitable intention to justify the precedence of the "subject for the world" over the "object in the world," the naturalistic understanding of the Other accordingly comes to prevail, that understanding whereby alien subjectivity is itself physicalized from out of the objectivity of the alien thing. It is not accidental that the doctrine of the appresentation of alien "innerness" springs up even in the explication of naturalistic alien experience in *Ideas*, book II.

Inasmuch as the category of appresentation now, to a certain extent, delivers over the Other to the thing-world, it endangers the realization of the most essential task that the transcendental theory of alien experience is, according to Husserl, supposed to accomplish, namely, the certification of the character of the Other as transcendent transcendence. For, that the Others are given to me in transcendent transcendence means, negatively, that they are "not given to me in perspectival unities, not in ideal immanence like thing objects" (EP.II 483 B). Considered in this way, the task of the theory of experience of the alien therefore consists in bringing to light the distinction between the mode of being of the thing and that of the Other.[27] However, the use made of the category of appresentation, which levels down the Other and the thing, stands in its way. Certainly Husserl limits the appresentation of the Other, in contrast with the appresentation of what appears horizonally in the thing, through the reference to its nonpresentability. However, the purely negative circumstance that the former excludes what this permits is too feeble to be capable of seriously impeding the leveling down.

8 The Resolution of Transcendent Transcendence in the Identity of Own I and the I of the Other

The immanent transcendence of the thing-world is only immanent because it does not overstep my "I-self." On the other hand, the specific transcendence of the Other is transcendent or "authentic" transcendence because the Other is entirely distinct from me. The attenuation of the distinction of transcendent and immanent transcendence disclosed in the application of the category of appresentation to the givenness of the Other therefore, at the same time, obscures the difference of the Other from me. This tendency comes into full operation in the theory of empathy.

If we test alien experience as transcendental empathy, the correctness of the expression that was only formally justified above is immediately confirmed, namely, that even world mediatedness is completed at the highest level of mediacy. While the Other, at the level of the appresentation of his body is principally present as "object in the world," transcendental empathy explicitly posits him as "subject for the world." Since it is itself constructed on the basis of the appresentation of the alien body, it also contains in it itself the peculiar mediacy of this appresentation: the mediatedness of the thing. There belongs hereto, however—and indeed as the more important moment—the mediation of the Other through the image of the world that he constructs for himself. Transcendental empathy is carried out as feeling oneself into the world that exists for the alien subject.

That I experience the Other as "object in the world" and, at the same time, as "subject for the world"—this, as the essential content of the "transcendental clue," is Husserl's cardinal presupposition. From the side of subjectivity that presently lies in our field of attention, the clue presupposes in particular that the Other is an Other I. He is the "not I in the form: other I" (CM 136:106). The taken-for-granted character of this statement is unmistakably conveyed in the circumstance that Husserl believes he can draw it straight out of language: "The meaning of the word Other can offer us a preliminary guide—other I" (CM 140:110). That the word "Other" means "other I" is so self-evident for Husserl that he does not take it to be necessary to justify it in the analysis.

The view that the Other is an other I and the supposition that the Other is made accessible originally only in empathy (EP.II 176) correspond. The other I calls for empathy as the means of access and empathy is necessarily related to an other I. Now our attention has already been drawn to the fact that transcendental empathy, as the empathy of an alter ego, is not a feeling oneself into an alter ego. It does not presuppose the alter ego, but posits it first of all. But where does it get it from? The answer is clear. As a purified analogical apperception it must be allowed to proceed from my ego. Just as my body, as mediator of all alien embodiment, plays the "role of the originary body" (EP.II 61), so my I, as the mediator of all alien I-ness, takes on the meaning of an "originary norm" (CM 154:125). In this way, however, the other I becomes an "analogue" of my own (CM 126:94, 35:35), in the same way as the alien body is the analogue of my body, thanks to analogizing apperception. Everything alien in the sense of belonging to the Other and, therefore, together with the alien I, its entire primordinal world as well, is "only thinkable as the analogue of that which is characteristically own" (CM 144:114).[28]

An analogue is not a "duplicate" (CM 146:117). Therefore, in that I empathically posit, in the alien body, an analogue of my own I, I do not duplicate myself. I do not appear once again where the alien (physical) body is to be found; rather, someone appears there who is as I am. He is I but not me. Nevertheless, according to Husserl, there exists, between the I of the Other and my I, a connection that, at bottom, binds the former still more closely to the latter than the concept of "analogue" is able to express. *For this reason*, and not because he wanted to weaken the analogy with respect to the self-sufficiency of the Other, Husserl does away with this concept again. In its place, he first sets the word "mirroring" (CM 29:28, 35:35), which, in its relation to empathy, means the mirroring, and, in its relationship to the correlate of empathy, means the mirror image. My mirror image has a likeness to myself that far surpasses the likeness between the analogue and its originary norm. For example, it also surpasses the likeness between the alien and my physical body. However, in the end, Husserl will not even seriously acknowledge the concept of "mirroring." The other I is a "mirroring of myself and yet not really a mirroring, an analogue of myself and yet again not an analogue in the usual sense" (CM 125:94). The connection between my I and the I of the Other is indeed, in Husserl's eyes, still closer than the relation between me and my mirror image. Only the enhancement that Husserl has in mind does not consist in a raising of likeness to complete similarity. If the I of the Other were completely similar to my own it would be my double, therefore the duplicate that it is not supposed to be. Husserl tends to go beyond the representation of analogy and mirroring in the direction of identity. From the standpoint of experience, the I of the Other is my own I: "Alter means alter-ego, and the ego that is implied herein is I myself" (CM 140:110).

But then, is the Other not I? No. I am identical with the I that is the Other, but I am not identical with the Other. The Other is certainly something more than merely I. Insofar as he is something more than merely I, he is also other than I. The Other (that the Other) is over and beyond his being I appears in transcendental purity as his physical body. His physical body is, however, distinguishable just as much from a transcendental standpoint from my physical body in that he is not here but there. When the Other is other than I therefore, insofar as he is other than I he is distinguished—this is Husserl's thesis—from me through his now being there. Whereas I am myself the ego in the alter ego, the alter in the alter ego is the there copresent with my here. So, as alter ego, the Other is not identical with me for this reason because what I would have been in myself, in the here, is modified through the there. In this way the "other is phenomenologically constituted as a *modification of my self*" (CM 144:115; see also K 189:185). With regard to his now-being-there, he is "an appresented I that I myself am not, but, relative to me, a modification, an other I" (CM 145:116).[29]

Still, the difference between the Other and me does not, properly speaking, fall in the sphere of our I. Does not Husserl himself, as we are aware, expressly emphasize that localization (just like temporalization) does not concern the Other as subject, but solely his physical body, which only colocalizes his subjectivity indirectly. In that Husserl ascribes the difference between the Other and me to the here-there difference, he reduces it—in contradiction to his postulate of the absolute individuality of the very own I—to the pure mundane differentness (*Verschiedenheit*) of mutually exclusive spatial things. The identity of the *I* in the Other with my own *I* is not in any way troubled by the "modification." The I in the Other—this is indeed the Other itself, the Other in his "very own" being. Consequently, the attempt to grasp the specific transcendence of the Other as transcendent transcendence breaks down. Insofar as I myself am the ownmost being of the Other, the Other is nothing other than what the thing-world is, with respect to which Husserl also says that it is "I myself." Indeed, the supposedly transcendent does, in a certain way, penetrate still deeper into immanence than the thing-world. The latter is still a transcendence, even if also immanent. The I of the Other posited in empathy has, however, with its distinction from my own I, altogether lost its transcendence.

9 Immanent Alter-ation as the Foundation of the "Transcendent"

The basic question of this chapter runs: How is the Other who alterates me (*verandernde*) to be grasped in advance? Husserl has now given us the answer. The Other who makes me into an Other is the one who, in the heart of his being, is made into my I. With regard to the double meaning of the word "alien-ation" (*Ent-Fremdung*) (as estrangement and as suspension of alienness) one can also say, the Other who alienates me (in the first sense) is the one who (in the second sense) I have dis-alienated. The empathy characterized by Husserl as "alienation" is, even if Husserl himself only has the first meaning in mind, in actual fact, both *my* being made alien and the suspension of the alienness of the *Other*. However, just as the immanental character of the Other is made known by the fact that I myself am the I of the Other, so my being alienated through the Other is an expression of his transcendence. For just as I have subjected the Other over there to me, so, over here, the Other demonstrates his power over me. In this, that I myself am the I of the Other, which in the actuality of empathy is the basis on which my alter-ation is played out, Husserl also delivers over the transcendence of the Other along with my alteration to immanence. We have already encountered the essence of alter-ation, hovering between immanence and transcendence, in the circumstance that I am certainly continually alter-ated *through* the Other, but am not, for all that, any less responsible for carrying through alter-ation myself.

The foundation of alter-ation in immanence can, however, be read off from a further, and most important, state of affairs. Husserl grounds the alter-ation stemming from transcendent transcendence upon an immanent alter-ation. Every presentification operative within the bounds of my own I reveals itself as such an immanent alter-ation, whether it takes the form of recollection or of expectation. The primally institutive original (*urstiftende Original*), or the originary norm for all presentification, is the presentation that is realized in perception. Correlatively, the present is itself the original and the prototype of the past and future. This state of affairs enables Husserl to set up an "analogy" between the relation of my present to my past and future, on the one hand, and the relation of my I in general to the alien I, on the other (CM 144:114, EP.II 175–176, 497 B, K 189:185). Just as the Other—as an other I—is an "intentional modification" of myself, so too are the past and future "intentional modifications "of the present, as "past" and "future present."[30] This analogy is an analogy between analogical relationships. An analogy between the relationship of the present to the past and future and my relationship to the Other exists insofar as the Other is the analogue of my self and past and future are the analogues of the present. In the analogy of analogical relationships, my relationship to the Other can only be the analogue of the relationship of the present to the past and future. The latter cannot, on the contrary, be the analogue of the former. For my I is the "originary norm" for the Other, and his experience of himself, the source of his experience of the Other. As the basic form of my stream of consciousness, however, it comprehends the entirety of my present, past, and future. In this way, the experience of my past and future on the past of my present is the "originary norm" for my experience of the Other. However, as empathy, the latter is alter-ation. Herewith empathic alter-ation gets grounded in immanent presentification.

We should not call immanent presentification an immanent *alteration* right away, simply because past and future are constituted as "intentional modifications," just as are Others, or, more precisely, because Others are constituted as intentional modifications, just as are past and future. What first gives us the right to such a characterization is much more the fact that, according to Husserl, I myself, in my relation to past and future, relate to my self as to an Other.[31] My past I that, in remembrance, I remember along with my past lived experience, is, on the one hand, identical with my present I, insofar as the latter holds out through time as one and the same. On the other hand, it is different from it. For it *is* no longer. In relation to my present I, it is therefore an Other I, in contrast with my I in general:

"The same I that is now actually present is, in every past that is its own, in a certain respect an other, precisely as that which was and so now is not, and yet in the continuity of its time remains one and the same self that is and was and has its future before it" (K 175:172). To be sure, I cannot encounter my past or future I as another I in the sense of transcendent transcendence. For, as transcendent transcendence, the Other has to fulfil the condition of being-*now*-there. My past or future I is, however, an Other precisely insofar as it is not now, and so also not now there. However, inasmuch as it is in no way a *transcendent* Other, it is still an Other, namely, an immanent Other.

Accordingly, recollection and expectation are modes of immanent alter-ation. We next establish that Husserl actually thought of them in this way. The alter-ation effected "through" the transcendent Other in different grades of explicitness, and to which we, for the sake of brevity, give the admittedly erroneous and imprecise name "transcendent alter-ation," is still, independently of its (yet to be concretely confirmed) origin in immanent alter-ation, characterized in itself, at the same time, as the opposite of itself, as the suspension of the alienness of the Other—and for the reason that I myself posit the I of the Other (through which I am alter-ed) in alter-ation, qua empathy, as *my* I. Insofar as the immanent Other in a similar manner is, beyond its general immanence, in accord with the most immanent immanence, the present immanent alter-ation must also, if it wants to justify its right to being such, be a suspension of the alienness of the (immanent) Other, in conformity with the fact that it is alienation. It is this precisely as presentification. Just as I empathically posit the other I, qua transcendent transcendence, as its own, so I make my past and future I, through presentification of recollection and expectation, into the present I. In this way I suspend the alienness that resides in its past or future existence.

In accordance with the "analogy" between immanent and "transcendent" alter-ation, presentification, as well as depresentification, is carried over to empathy. Like recollection and expectation, empathy is presentification, a "presentification of transcendental consciousness" (EP.II 497 B). It is, however, by the same token, a depresentification of a higher order: "The temporalization of the self, so to speak, through depresentification (through recollection), has its analogy in my alienation (empathy as a depresentification of a higher order—that of my originary presence into a purely presentified originary presence)" (K 189:185).[32]

We now have to consider to what an extent alien-ation, as alter-ating empathy, is a depresentification. First of all, however, we need to show that the primary depresentification is in fact really an alien-ation, not simply as the suspension of the present in favor of what is alien to it (the past and future), but also, in the strict sense, as the delivering over of my present I to *the* (immanent) alien. Alter-ation, in this authentic meaning, is the truly original witness of transcendent transcendence. So recollection and expectation can only then count as alter-ation if it can be shown that transcendent transcendence already breaks into real (*reelle*) immanence with the proliferation into the past and future. This is exactly what Husserl has in mind: "The not-now transcends the now," and in this way, that is, in the intentional mod-ification of the present into past and future, "transcendence is originally brought to consciousness."[33] Transcendence of this kind, however, is not immanent (qua ideal immanence), but, so to speak, a prefiguration of transcendent transcendence. This results from the fact that Husserl grasps the authentically transcendent transcendence (of the transcen-dent Other) as an analogue of the temporal "self-transcendence":[34] "Just as my remembered past transcends my living present as its modification, so the appresented alien being transcends one's own" (CM 145:115).

In relation to the transcendent Other, immanent alter-ation reaches as far as the alter-ation of empathy reaches. The analogy with de-presentification, established by Husserl, also only extends to empathy. Naturally, therefore, on the side of real (*reellen*) immanence there is nothing corresponding to the alter-ation borne by empathy, whose two moments, substantialization and personalization, are brought to-gether in the unity of humanization. In the analogy with empathy, the presentifying depresentification is a *putting oneself into* the immanent other I. If I recall an earlier experience, I put myself back into the I that had this experience. Hereby I place myself empathically in the standpoint of this Other. Even the decentering inextricably bound up with transcendent alter-ation is to be found in immanence. Only there it has no spatial, but only a temporal meaning. To the decline of the here into the there, there corresponds the flowing away of the now into the then or the formerly. And since, according to Husserl, the present furnishes the ultimately valid apodicity, the "absolute reality,"[35] depresentification is still also a depotentiation of the I.

In the previous chapter we reached the conclusion that empathy is alter-ation in a yet more radical sense than that of making onself into an Other. In that I put myself in the position of an Other and experience the world in his position, I am enabled, by the Other, to make myself, at the same time, into one among Others. As one among Others, I am, however, a person. Empathy is therefore also *in itself* personalizing alter-ation, even if not also humanizing. In transcendental empathy I am not a *human* person, but I am a person nonetheless.

Does the presentifying depresentification display a trait corresponding to this state of affairs? In other words, is the extension into past and future also a personalizing extension? The question can only be answered by going back to Husserl's concept of the person. Its precise explication would provide sufficient material for a separate investigation, and cannot be undertaken in the framework of the present work. We shall have to be satisfied with some indications. Accordingly, the answer to our question can only point at the phenomenon. The difficulty that any research into the concept of the person in Husserl has to confront is the bewildering multiplicity of applications this concept has. We only have to remember where it arises within the thematic boundaries of our presentation. We came across it first as the title for my primordinal I that, in the central here of my body with which it is "psychophysically constituted as a unity," operates in the outer world. Then it was the intersubjectively objective I, the I as a human being, which counted as the person. Book II of *Ideas* tells us what "person" means in this usage. As a human being, I am a person, first, insofar as I am a subject in a surrounding world and, second, as a member of a community. Finally, my personal being already manifested itself in my being fitted into the transcendental community in which the objective world is constituted. This being fitted into is the personalizing, referred to a moment earlier, at which I arrive with transcendental empathy as such.

It hardly seems possible to reduce these three meanings of the concept of the person to *one* common denominator. Only the relation to the world is common to them all. But, on the one hand, "world" has a quite different meaning in the three positions, and, on the other, the world relation does not define the personal I in particular but the I in general. To be sure, sociality is one of the two moments of human

personal being and the fundamental component of that concept of
the person that represents the immediate condition of the objective
world. Still, the primordinal I to which Husserl explicitly refers (CM
128–129:97–98) is precisely what it is because it lacks sociality. Above
all, is the person to be housed in the transcendental or in the natural
sphere? The primordinal personal I is transcendental, the human personal I, natural; and the I born out of original empathy is again
transcendentally determined. For all that, this gives us a first indication
with respect to the essence of the person. To the essence of the person,
as Husserl understands it, there belongs the vacillation between transcendental and natural being. Even where the person is rooted in the
"transcendental," it takes up a peculiarly intermediate place between
the deepest transcendental origin, the originary I, and the natural I.
Although the primordinal and the transcendentally communalized I
come before the constitution of the objective world, they are, for their
part, already constituted by the originary I. But the transcendentally
communalized I also has in itself a part in the natural I. It is indeed
the phenomenon that lies at the root of the I of the natural attitude.
Conversely, through abstraction from its sociality, the human person
cleared the way into the originally transcendental I. This placement
in the transition from the transcendental to the natural explains why,
in the course of our investigation, we so often, and at such decisive
points, ran up against the person. For the transition is the theme of
our entire interpretation, that is, the alter-ation that is a continual
movement away from the transcendental origin and that in the end
leads to the natural.

There is, however, one principal meaning of Husserl's concept of
the person that we have still not mentioned. Husserl enunciates it in
§57 of *Ideas*, book II. The paragraph begins with a reference to the
ambiguity of the transcendental and the natural in the personal I that
here even takes on the appearance of an identity with the pure I: "If
we take the personal I, just as we have found it in inspection . . . it at
first appears not to be distinguishable from the pure I" (247). Now it
should be noted that Husserl does not equate the pure I straight off
with the transcendental.[36] The pure I is, in accordance with the dominant linguistic usage, exclusively the pole of intentionality, therefore
the transcendental I, in its restriction to the actual now. Only insofar
as the I, given apodictically in the now, is the transcendental I in its
last origin can the concepts of the pure and the transcendental I be

then also used interchangeably again. The appearance of an identity of the personal I with this pure I, as the, so to speak, temporally punctual, is dissolved by Husserl in what follows. My "personal" I is precisely constituted first of all in the course of my ongoing living activity, in the individual history of my consciousness: "The living course of pure consciousness is necessarily a developmental course in which the pure I has to take on the apperceptive form of the personal I" (251). The I is person insofar as, in the span of time, it is continually motivated in a determinate fashion by its surrounding world. In reflecting upon the how of this being motivated through time, I recognize my personal "specificity," or "what kind of a personal subject I am" (248–249).

In the text Husserl clearly situates this personal subject at the mundane empirical level. Still, the subject matter does not oblige him to do so. With regard to my regulated relationship to the world, it is by no means implied that I apprehend myself as a worldly being. In this way, too, neither my reflexively perceived intentionality nor my personal specificity, which made itself known in the regulated "how" of intentionality, needs to have a mundane empirical constitution. They can also be transcendental. Indeed, all this has to have a transcendental correspondence. If the living course of pure consciousness is necessarily a developmental course in which the pure I has to take on the apperceptive form of the personal I, then even transcendental consciousness itself, in its temporal extension, has to be personal. Even as a title for the historical I, the concept "person" is thereby transcendentally-naturally ambiguous.

This ambiguity betrays itself in the terminological characterization of the personal traits that are disclosed in the "precipitates" that, in the course of time, collect at the base of the I from the world-experiencing acts and attitudes. In the text, Husserl names them the "personal peculiarities" or "character properties" (249) in order to give expression to their mundane-empirical mode of being through these psychological concepts. The precipitates themselves, however, are, from a transcendental point of view, named, as we know, "habitualities." They are the "possessions" that I appropriate for myself, in that I determine myself in all determinate acts and attitudes. As transcendental, the historical I is the "substrate of habitualities" distinguished from the I as empty "identity pole," as continuing "I determinations." In and out of the constitution of the I as substrate of habitualities, a "personal I" is, however, constituted according to the *Cartesian Meditations*: "Since, by its own active genesis, the I constitutes itself as the identical substrate of continuing I properties, it also constitutes itself as a fixed and abiding personal I—in the widest sense, which also allows us to speak of subhuman persons." So Husserl is also able to say here that the I retains a "personal character" in the changing course of its habitual conviction. The person understood "in the broadest possible sense" is, however, together with its character, a transcendental I. For the entire history in which it manifests itself stands under the "lawfulness of the transcendental genesis" (CM 100–102:66–68).[37]

In its transcendental meaning this history is the personalization we are looking for, in which the extension of the self into the past and future has to participate in order that it can be called alter-ation in the correct sense of the word. The immanent-temporal personalization does not overlap with the presentifying depresentification. But, insofar as my transcendental I is personalized in general through its temporalizing self-constitution, even its "self-temporalization"[38] is a personalizing event, in the form of depresentification. More exactly, depresentification and immanent temporal personalization—once again in accordance with the general "analogy"—stand in a similar relation to each other as do the empathic act, as making oneself into a (transcendent) Other, and the personalization that is attached thereto, as becoming one among the (transcendent) Others. In that I make myself into a "transcendent" Other, I give myself over to an isolated there. When, however, I am one among the "transcendent" Others and, at the same time, draw these Others into my world horizon, I am everywhere, that is, at all possible there points. Analogously, making myself into an immanent Other through depresentification, I put myself into a particular then or at that time. Insofar, however, as depresentification is an act on the basis of original personalizing temporalization, I am in it not only then or at that time but always, that is, at all possible "time points." Only due to this personalizing is depresentification really depresentification. For, only to the extent that I, so to speak, distribute myself over all the moments of my conscious life does the actual moment lose the absolute uniqueness that gives the present its presentness. It becomes a now point among now points. This is the first, still purely immanent, form of that "self-objectification" that ends up with the mundanization effected in me by the transcendent Other.

Self-temporalization, whose modes are recollection and expectation, has completely shown itself to be immanent alter-ation. What still has to be shown is simply how the "transcendent" alter-ation of empathy is grounded in the immanent. That it is grounded therein has hitherto been indicated in a purely formal way through the meaning of the "analogue" set up by Husserl, in accordance with which self-temporalization has to be the originary model and empathy the analogon. Even concretely, however, it can be seen straight away that the "transcendent" alter-ation of empathy is presupposed by the immanent alter-ation of self-temporalization and contains the latter as the condition of its possibility. We noticed in the second chapter that in the transition from the analogizing apperception of the alien body to the empathizing of an alter ego, the relationship to the past, which was already in question there, though contained within the relation to the present, is freed for a radical self-relation. The moment, admittedly entitled "reproductive," though, as a matter of fact, distinct from that explicit reproduction that was already required by the analogizing apperception of the alien (organic) body in order to make my own body (as a physical body given outwardly) capable of furnishing the basis for an analogy at all, becomes—we are now able to say— through empathy, an autonomous act of actual re-production, of actual *re*-collection. While Husserl assigns the perception of the alien (organic) body to the "sphere of experience and not of simple reproduction, as with memories" (Id.I 347–348:343–344), I can only empathically attribute an ego to the Other insofar as I feel myself into his world. I can only place myself empathically in his world in that I adopt his standpoint and presentify the world, which is present to me from here, in those appearances in which it presents itself from there. *This* presentification, however, is parasitic upon that other one that I carry out in recollection. My putting myself into the there lives off the strength of my putting myself back into the then. I could not represent something concrete with respect to the Other if I had not already experienced the world itself from the most diverse standpoints and if I were not able to reproduce these experiences at will.[39]

Furthermore, it is characteristic of the transcendental thesis (developed by Heidegger and Sartre) and its difference from "dialogicalism" that empathic depresentification is a lapse into the past, not an anticipation of the future. Of the two modes of self-temporalization, only recollection goes over into empathy, not expectation. This finding corresponds to the circumstance that even in the "analogy" set up by Husserl between empathy and immanent alter-ation, recollection alone actually goes over to the side of immanent alter-ation. However, the lapse into the past empowers an overcoming of transcendent transcendence through immanence. For not only am *I* depresentified in empathy; the Other is also. In that I can only transpose myself over into the Other by transposing myself back into my past I, the I that I transpose over into the Other is not only my I in general but, in particular, my past I. In this way, immanence is enhanced because the experience laid up in my past experience prescribes the boundaries within which alone the Other can be there for me. What I have not already myself experienced, I am unable to encounter in the Other. So Husserl quite correctly calls transcendental empathy an "analogizing that does not yield anything new over against the I" (Id.II 168). Nothing new—that is to say, in a temporal perspective. The Other can never surprise me and change me in the course of an encounter. He can never come at me out of the dim future. This cutting off of the future already makes itself known at the very first level of the experience of the alien, at the essential stage of the appresentation of the alien (organic) body. For, with the possibility of the discharge of this appresentation in fulfilling presentations, there also disappears the expectation of a fulfilment presented and related to me. However, that which is related to me and does not emanate from me is transcendent to me. The overcoming of transcendent transcendence through immanence is temporally concretized in the destruction of the future through the unrestricted mastery of the past.

10 The Constitution of the Other and the Absence of an Equiprimordial Partner

Doubtless, a prefiguration of transcendent transcendence through me and my immanence is already to be found in the most original and, for Husserl, the most self-evident presupposition of the theory of intersubjectivity, that I, the absolutely unique ego, constitute the Other just as well as everything else.[40] Just as Husserl calls attention to the pregiven life-worldly "facts" whenever he brings into play the last principles of the transcendental theory, so he here also draws our attention to the fact that the "appropriation of the meaning of the Other, within me and from me . . . is to be found in advance as a fact" (FTL 214:242). From this fact he draws the right to ground not only the alien "object in the world" but also the alien "subject for the world" in my transcendental subjectivity: "Every alter ego as such receives its meaning and value" in my ego (FTL 210:237). To be sure, the Other is "itself a transcendental subjectivity . . . which, however, necessarily gets posited in me as the ego that, from the first, already exists for itself" (FTL 241:273). In conjunction with the transcendental Other, I even constitute myself—as we saw at the end of the preceding chapter—as one among Others, as also the entire sphere of inter-subjectivity as the monadic community whose members are the Others among whom I am included: "Transcendental intersubjectivity" is only what it is because it "is constituted in me, therefore relative to me, as a multiplicity of 'egos' " (FTL 241:273). Naturally, the "world for everyone" is also correlative—a world that is constituted (immediately) in me and only by me, a "world for me": "First, and before every conceivable thing, *I* am. This 'I am' is for me, who says it, and says it with understanding, the originary intentional ground for my world, whereby I must not overlook the fact that even the 'objective world,' the 'world for us all' as valid for me in this sense, is 'my world' " (FTL 209:236; see also 214:242).

It is well known that there is a dispute among interpreters of Husserl whether Husserl's concept of constitution is subjectivistic, in the tra-ditional sense of that word. Opinions vary widely. Some say, constitution is creation,[41] others that it is receptive understanding.[42] This dispute cannot be decided in favor of one or the other party because Husserl's concept of constitution is intrinsically ambiguous. Constitution looks like receptive understanding insofar as it is only a matter of constituting the objectivity "itself" "in" me, in that it is validated for me in its being-sense. To constitute then only means: to understand the meaning of the objectivity in its being. Constitution takes on an air of creation as soon as Husserl characterizes it as a production or performance of consciousness and says of it that "I" constitute the objectivity. This ambiguity has to be allowed to stand as such.

In the meantime, the doctrine of the constitution of the *Other* in my self would still remain problematic if it could be unequivocally established that the constitution described by Husserl bore no traces of creativity. Even if I can only constitute the Other insofar as his being-sense can only be demonstrated in me, still, I am the one who essentially precedes the Other. Husserl himself stresses this emphatically. Alien transcendental subjectivity necessarily gets posited *"in me as the ego that already and in advance exists for itself."* For, "First and before everything conceivable I am." This is, however, not at all self-evident. The alternative possibility is admittedly not to be found in that, conversely, the Other precedes me. Rather, this is included in Husserl's account. That I precede the Other means that I, as the all-constituting originary I, also constitute the Other, which is itself all-constituting. The constitution of the Other is a constituting of the constituting. So the identification, described in the "Fifth Cartesian Meditation," of a nature constituted in me with that "constituted by the Other" is—"stated with the necessary exactness"—the identification of the nature constituted in me "with a nature constituted in me as one constituted by the Other" (CM 155:126). Just as I constitute what is constituted by the Other, so I constitute the Other itself as constituting, therefore as the one that is equally, for itself, the originary I that among other things constitutes me and, indeed, constitutes me as constituting. In this sense, according to Husserl, the Other also precedes me entirely.

The genuinely alternative possibility, which, however, Husserl excludes from the outset, is that of *equiprimordiality*. To be sure, one can glimpse a recognition of such an equiprimordiality in this, that, in exactly the same way that the Other is *for me* a constituted-constituting, so I am supposed to be for the Other a constituted-constituting. This does not mean, however, according to Husserl's account, that I, in my original I-ness, might be, for myself, a constituted-constituting, that is, constituted as constituted by the Other. I, who *constitute* the Other as constituting, understand myself simply as constituting and not as constituted by the Other, even though the fact that the Other also constitutes me is to be found in the fact that I constitute the Other *as constituting*.[43] While the power of my constitution reaches right up to the originary I that the Other finally is, as constituting, the impotence of my being constituted by the Other is limited to my transcendentally communalized I, from which I, as originary I, am set apart. I actually constitute my transcendentally communalized I as an I constituted by the Other, but not my originary I. This self-withdrawal of my originary I out of the transcendental communalization first makes possible my victory over the "transcendent alter-ation" and the overcoming of transcendent transcendence through immanence. I have indeed already degraded the Other in that I degrade that I that is constituted by him to a derivative mode of myself and affirm him over against myself as an originary I. In this way, however, I remove myself from the equiprimordiality in which I stand as a member of the transcendental monadic community along with the other members.

This state of affairs brings to light the undeniable limitations of Husserl's attempt to overcome "transcendental solipsism," the "transcendental solipsism" of "pure egology," through the theory of intersubjectivity (CM 12:12).[44] The ego that thematizes the pure egology is the absolutely unique and, to that extent, solipsistic ego that I discover myself to be in the phenomenological *epoché*: "The phenomenological *epoché* reduces me to my transcendentally pure I, and, in the first instance at least, I am therefore, in a certain sense, *solus ipse*" (CM 12:11). We know why I am this way only "in a certain sense." I am not this way in the "usual" sense of a human being who, for example, through some catastrophe, is left alone in the world (CM 12:11; see also K 188:185). Such an isolation would not be the result of a reduction but a fact on the basis of the naively assumed world. The human being who is alone in the world or who thinks he is alone in the world is a solipsist "in the ridiculously common sense whose roots are to be sought in the natural attitude" (EP.II 174). Insofar as the usual solipsism—what one commonly understands by "solipsism"—is naive, Husserl is also able, on occasion, to apostrophize the solipsism of egology. He then characterizes egology as, "so to speak," solipsistic phenomenology (EP.II 176). Insofar, however, as one understands solipsism "in the good sense" (EP.II 66), that is, in the transcendental sense, egology is "really" transcendentally solipsistic (FTL 238:270). It is the more radical, the more transcendental solipsism.

Still, in Husserl's opinion, only egology is solipsistic, not phenomenology as a whole, to which the theory of intersubjectivity belongs along with, or rather after, egology (CM 38:38, 181:155). Transcendental solipsism is supposed to be "only a philosophical substratum" (CM 69:30), which is overcome through the theory of intersubjectivity. While Husserl purifies egology only from the appearance of *natural* solipsism, the theory of intersubjectivity is supposed to free the "whole" (CM 12:12) of phenomenology from the appearance of transcendental solipsism, that is, destroy the illusion (*Schein*) that phenomenology *remains* transcendental solipsism. Accordingly, the title of the introductory paragraphs of the "Fifth Cartesian Meditation" runs: "Exposition of the Problem of Alien Experience in Opposition to the Objection of Solipsism" (121:89). At the end of the "Fifth Cartesian Meditation," however, Husserl feels entitled to say that "the illusion of solipsism is dissolved, even though the proposition that everything existing for me must derive its existential sense exclusively from me myself, from my sphere of consciousness, retains its fundamental validity" (176:150).

For Husserl, the second part of the proposition beginning with "even though" does not contradict the first. Indeed, in his eyes, the second does not even limit the first. The illusion of transcendental solipsism really is dissolved,[45] when even Others derive their existential sense exclusively from me, without my deriving my *original* existential sense from the Other, that is, "expressed with the necessary exactness": without my constituting my originary I as constituted by the Other. Certainly the "loneliness" into which I am, in the first instance, driven by the Cartesian-phenomenological *epoché* is broken through, to the extent that the Others are no longer merely phenomena of my universal world phenomenon, but "transcendental realities" (FTL 238:269). It still does not disappear, however, so long as I also do not find an original partner through the "discovery" of transcendental intersubjectivity. This absence of a partner is, however, what primarily determines the "good" sense of transcendental solipsism. This is what Husserl has in mind when he says in *Crisis*, "The *epoché* engenders a peculiar kind of philosophical loneliness that furnishes the methodological basis for a really radical philosophy" (187–188:184). The "really radical philosophy" is transcendental philosophy. However, in that transcendental philosophy finds its completion in the transcendental theory of intersubjectivity, the latter also confirms and reinforces the loneliness on whose basis transcendental philosophy rests.

II

Development and
Transformation of the
Transcendental Project:
The Social Ontologies of
Heidegger and Sartre

5

The Modified Repetition of Husserl's Theory in Heidegger's Social Ontology

1 The Analytic of *Dasein* and Transcendental Phenomenology

The theme of this chapter is narrowly circumscribed. We are going to concern ourselves solely with the analysis of being-with in Heidegger's *Sein und Zeit* [*Being and Time*] (SuZ)[1] and even this we only want to consider with respect to its relationship to the principle of transcendental phenomenology.[2] The general familiarity with Heidegger's early work spares us the duty of offering a detailed presentation of the fundamental ontology set out there. To begin with, however, we do need to examine the way in which Heidegger himself envisages the relation between fundamental ontology and transcendental phenomenology.

This intention is rendered methodologically all the more difficult in that Heidegger hardly comes to terms with Husserl *explicitly* in *Being and Time*.[3] In the chapter in which the social ontological problematic is most exhaustively handled (113–130:149–168), Husserl's name does not crop up at all. Still, the polemical relation to Husserl is, for all that, especially evident here, not least in the concepts with which Heidegger characterizes his own distinctive position. Above all, the introductory paragraph on the "approach to the existential question of the 'who' of *Dasein*" is a unique dialogue with Husserl. A comparison of this paragraph with that of §64 reveals the deeper reason for the anonymity with which Heidegger surrounds his interlocutor. Heidegger deals with Husserl anonymously not only because respect for his teacher forbids any direct approach but also because he regards Husserl simply as a representative of the contemporary position in general. In such a perspective, transcendental philosophy appears primarily as the philosophy of the *I*. §25 disposes of Husserl's I, §64 disposes of Kant's I. The characteristics, however, that are attributed to the latter and to the former are in essence the same. So, with the removal of the specificity of the I, as thematized by Husserl, Husserl's own individuality is removed, that individuality that alone would have given him the right to his name.

In his presentation of Kant, alongside simplicity, Heidegger also adopts, as characteristics of the I, personality and substantiality (318:366). The essential trait that the concept of "personality" brings out is also imprinted upon Husserl's I: This is "that which holds out as identical through the change of behavior and experience" (114:150; see also 47–48:73). Further, it is similarly thought out in line with substantiality, to the extent that it presents what truly lies at the root of it, namely, the "subject" (114:150). Heidegger now lays out the being, which is distinguished in this way through personality and substantiality with his own concept, as "presence-at-hand" (114:150). That, in this way, he also means to cover Husserl's transcendental I can be inferred from his remark that the being-sense of the present-at-hand is implied everywhere where the being of the I is left "undetermined" (114–115:150). Indeed, he reproaches Husserl precisely for this,[4] in *Being and Time* (47–48:73) and also in other works.[5]

In this way he opens up a gap between the object of transcendental phenomenology and the (immediate) object of his fundamental ontology, *Dasein*, as being-in-the-world. For, as present-at-hand, Husserl's I has "the mode of being of an entity whose character is not that of *Dasein*" (115:150). How problematic, nevertheless, both the implicit interpretation of Husserl and also the distancing from the latter turn out to be is evident from the substantive determination of the presence-at-hand of the I. As present-at-hand, the I is a "simple subject without world" (116:152). By worldlessness, however, Heidegger also means the absence of the projective world relation in the constitution of the subject. In this sense the I envisaged by Kant is also exposed to the objection of worldlessness because it exists only as "I think" and not as "I think something." However, even Husserl's transcendental I does not escape this objection, although, in Heidegger's eyes, it is precisely the "I of intentionality," and so is comprehended in the full structure of the "I think something." For, according to Heidegger, the approach through intentionality still leaves the projectively constructed world out of account, a world that is presupposed by the intentional something insofar as it is an inner worldly entity (320–321:367).[6]

We only need to remind ourselves of the first chapter of our investigation to see that here Heidegger misses Husserl's innermost intention. The "subject" that makes itself the theme of transcendental phenomenology is the *subjectivity* that is only what it is in the projection of world.[7] Inasmuch as we, for our part, are directed toward Heidegger's orientation toward the I, we can also say that Heidegger abstracts from what is, phenomenologically speaking, the truly fundamental I, the "concrete" ego or the "monad." His interpretation of the being of the I, however, attests to the fact that he is as little concerned with the I as "substrate of habitualities" as he is with the "historical" ego, transcendentally understood. For the concept "presence-at-hand" means, on the one hand, static occurrence, and, on the other, an emptily abstract being. In accordance with the first interpretation, he denies the performative character that belongs to the I as historical. In accordance with the second interpretation, he withholds from the I that fullness that arises out of its habitual world relatedness. Consequently, of the three forms that the original I assumes, according to Husserl, only one remains over: that in which the I functions as "identical pole." Heidegger's description is only pertinent to *this* I, in accordance with which the I is, in general, what "holds out as identical through the change of behavior and experience." Admittedly, Heidegger never does justice to it. Inasmuch as he interprets the being of the identical pole of lived experience as presence-at-hand, he charges it with inner worldliness and, in the final analysis, with pure thingliness. So he fails to see that Husserl already attributes to the identical I pole an individuality and a facticity that Husserl, at least in name, separates off from the individuality of individual things and from the facticity of inner-worldly matters of fact.

To be sure, this is also the very point at which Heidegger actually goes beyond Husserl in a quite decisive way. Certainly, Husserl proclaims the individual facticity of the transcendental ego and insists upon its difference from mundane factualness. But it is Heidegger who first discovers the *dimension* in which this facticity is rooted, as the facticity of *Dasein*, which is quite distinct from the "factualness of the *factum brutum* of something present at hand" (135:174). The dimension of facticity appropriate to *Dasein* is that very worldliness that Heidegger quite rightly misses in the I when he calls it a "worldless subject." It is neither that of world projection, as which *Dasein*, as well as transcendental subjectivity, are in fact revealed to be, nor that inner-worldly being among inner-worldly beings that Heidegger, just as vigorously as Husserl, separates off from world projection. Nevertheless, it has, in a certain sense, more to do with inner-worldly beings than with the projected world. For the most part, Heidegger distinguishes the latter from the world, which he interprets as the whole of inner-worldly beings, in that he puts it in inverted commas. Thus, in alluding to the phenomenological reduction, he brings together the initial statement about the "givenness of the I" and the methodological reference to disregard "everything else that is 'given,'" and so also the "given 'world'" (115:150). The worldliness that the abstraction from the ontic "world" confers upon the I is, according to Heidegger, not only an occurrence within the "world," the defense of which is justified from a fundamental ontological standpoint, but also the "directedness toward . . . the world" (139:178) or the "being in the midst of . . . ,"[8] namely, of inner-worldly beings. With its suspension, however, the specific facticity of *Dasein* is lost.

Heidegger takes account of the facticity of being in the midst of beings through a peculiarly *anthropological shift*. This anthropological shift, which is carried out in the transition from transcendental phenomenology to an existential analytic of *Dasein*, is of the highest significance—in spite of Heidegger's assurance that the analytic of *Dasein* is not anthropological. On the one hand, Heidegger distances himself from anthropology because he wants to clarify the dependence of his question about *Dasein* upon the question about Being, and, on the other hand, because he only considers as anthropological that doctrine that interprets human being with the categories of entities that do not have the mode of being of *Dasein*, that is, more or less as animal rationale. Regardless of the foregoing, the shift toward human being is the positive characteristic of his shift away from Husserl. This is clearly apparent from his remark on Husserl's article in the *Encyclopaedia Britannica*. There, *Dasein* emerges unscathed as "concrete human being," and the whole reversal from transcendental phenomenology to fundamental ontology appears as the movement away from what is, at bottom, a dehumanizing interpretation of human being as a "real-worldly fact" to the clarification of the true human worldliness and facticity.[9] The nomination of human being as the cornerstone of fundamental ontology, however, is the condition of the reinterpretation of mineness, a reinterpretation discussed in the first chapter of our work and whose characteristics, according to Husserl, are extramundane individuality and facticity. Mineness, insofar as it is transformed into the mineness of *Dasein*, becomes personal because *Dasein* is the being of human being, while human being is a person in communion with persons.

Just as important as the recognition of what is new in the analysis of the specifically human worldliness and facticity of *Dasein*, however, is the insight into Heidegger's express determination to set out the intention of Husserl's phenomenology as a *transcendental philosophy*.[10] As a result of this "observation," the central problem of *Being and Time* is the question, "What is the mode of being of that entity in which the world is constituted?" In Heidegger's opinion, this question should be called a new one because Husserl fails to bear in mind that the constituting is an "entity" just as is the constituted, an entity that has to be investigated with respect to its "mode of being." To this extent, however, it coincides at the same time with that question that first makes Husserl's phenomenology transcendental when it is directed in general toward the "constituting" and the transcendental constitution of the world. Hence Heidegger proceeds in the conviction that it is the clarification of the mode of being of *Dasein*, as the specifically human "existence of the factical self," that first makes possible the right answer to the question concerning the transcendental constitution of the world: "It is important to show that the mode of being of human *Dasein* is totally different from that of all other entities and that, as the very entity that it is, it bears within itself the possibility of transcendental constitution." The place of transcendental constitution in the constitution of the being of *Dasein* is the "project." This is a "projection of the world," that is, "throwing the projected world over what exists" (WG 36). Project is, however, thrown projection, and the "thrownness" without which it cannot exist is the facticity of finding oneself in the midst of beings.

In the final analysis, the discovery of this facticity is also responsible for the progress that Heidegger makes over Husserl in the field of social ontology. That the analysis of being-with nevertheless only reproduces and does not overcome the theory of intersubjectivity has

its basis in its transcendental conception, in the point of departure
from the project as the transcendental constitution of the world.

With the project, however, Heidegger also brings the "I" within
the sphere of *Dasein*. While with respect to the formal division of being-
in-the-world into the three moments "self," "being-in," and "world,"
being-in corresponds to the "there," indicated by projection and
thrownness, and the world (as the totality of inner-worldly entities) is
aligned with thrownness (as the directedness toward it), the self is
consolidated around the project. Together with the world (as the transcendental world horizon),[11] my very own *Dasein* projects "itself"; more
correctly, in projecting "itself," it projects a world. The self, however,
is "the original phenomenal basis for the question concerning the being
of the 'I' " (323:370). The initially instituted relation of exclusion between *Dasein* and I therefore gets transformed on the way over the
self into a grounding relation: The I has its ground in *Dasein* as self.[12]
Indeed, I and self occasionally approach one another so closely that
Heidegger can speak of the "selfhood of the I as self" (320:367).[13] To
be sure, the I upheld by *Dasein* is quite different from that which is
entirely alien to *Dasein*. The latter is the "subject" into which the theory
of concealment converts the I and that is, according to Heidegger,
rooted in the "inauthenticity" of *Dasein* (116:152, 321–322:367–368).
The former is the genuine phenomenon that is revealed in "saying
I." But, in Heidegger's view, Husserl's philosophy itself participates
in the ambiguity of its object. It is not only a metaphysics of the
present-at-hand subject but also the actual Logos of the phenomenon
I. Such a positive evaluation manifests itself when Heidegger, in connection with the implicit characterization of the phenomenological
reduction, says that the "mere, formal, reflective awareness of the
'I' " affords "access to a phenomenological problematic in its own
right that has, in principle, the signification of providing a framework
as a 'formal phenomenology of consciousness' " (115:151).

With this we have not only achieved a preliminary conception of
the general relation between the analytic of *Dasein* and transcendental
phenomenology but, over and beyond that, also already become familiar with a part of the analysis of being-with itself. In the paragraph
from which the sentence cited above was taken, a question is posed
concerning the "who of *Dasein*," more exactly, concerning the "who
of everyday *Dasein*." And the analysis of being-with is supposed to
give the answer to this question. That transcendental phenomenology

at its best, namely, insofar as it is the Logos of the genuine phenomenon of the I, should only have "the signification of providing a framework" means, therefore, in the context of the problem that has arisen, that on the question concerning the who of *Dasein* it can only offer a *formal* answer, the formal statement that *Dasein* "is an I" (114:150). If, however, it predelineates the formal framework, it must be the task of the *analytic of Dasein* to *fill out* this framework concretely. The relation of the truly phenomenological phenomenology of Husserl to fundamental ontology is that of an empty indication to its concrete fulfillment. According to Heidegger, this fulfillment is now secured through the approach by way of "factical" existence (115:150). It is not the formal-ontological mineness that should provide the clue to answering the question posed but the existentiality of this existence (117:152). The concrete fulfillment that Heidegger believes he has reached thereby is, more exactly, to be located in the fact that *Dasein*, as existing factically, always already exists in certain *basic and determinate modes.* Factical existence or the original, that is, existentially comprehended self cannot be grasped in general as a substantial substrate of *Dasein* but " 'only' as a *mode* of being of this entity" (117:153—italics are mine). The *basic* modes of existing are those of "authenticity" and "inauthenticity," with which "everydayness"is here identified. However, if one poses the question concerning the who of *Dasein* in such a way that one becomes aware of its factical division into the modes of being of authenticity and everyday inauthenticity, it is apparent, as Heidegger indicates, that the only answer possible on the basis of transcendental phenomenology is actually misleading, on account of its formality. For "I precisely am *not*" the who of *everyday Dasein* (115:150). To be sure, from a formal-ontic standpoint, *Dasein* also has in its everydayness the character of "I-hood," but it only has it in the modus of "self-forgetfulness" (116:152), and one does not then become aware of this self-forgetfulness if, with respect to the question concerning the who of *Dasein*, one already allows oneself to be satisfied, like Husserl, with the formal answer, that *Dasein* is an I.

So, at the end of Heidegger's implicit confrontation with Husserl and at the beginning of the genuine explanation, one finds, once again, a distancing, even from transcendental phenomenology as Logos of the actual I phenomenon. In the meantime, this result lapses into an immediate contradiction, in that Heidegger draws the *positive* answer to the question concerning the who of everyday *Dasein* out of the reservoir of those insights that Husserl's theory of intersubjectivity furnished him. This will be substantiated in what follows. First, however, we want to enumerate the points in which Heidegger, in his analysis of being-with—guided by a more appropriate understanding of the matter—really moves beyond his teacher in a decisive manner. Only then will it be possible to disclose the analogy that obtains between Heidegger's analysis of being-with and Husserl's theory of intersubjectivity, an analogy grounded, above all, on their common orientation toward the idea of transcendental philosophy.[14]

2 The Most Fruitful "New Approaches" to the Analysis of Being-with

1. Following Heidegger's intention, being with and toward the Other is more deeply rooted in *Dasein* than it is in the ego with Husserl. *Dasein* is "essentially in itself being-with" (*Mitsein*) (120:156). Being-with, as which being with the Other is terminologically determined, as well as *Dasein*-with, the being of the Other itself, are supposed to be already given with the being-in-the-world of *Dasein*. The chapter in which Heidegger, for the first time, explicitly enquires into being with one another "leads to structures of *Dasein* that are equiprimordial with Being-in-the-world: Being-with and *Dasein*-with (*Mitdasein*) (114:149). With respect to being-with, this does not mean that it arises with equal originality *alongside* being-in-the-world,[15] but, much more, "that the being-in-the-world of *Dasein* is essentially constituted through being-with" (120:156).[15] Being-in-the-world is just as original, since it is being-in-the-world and, as such, also being-with, or, put otherwise, being-with is a constitutive moment of what is in itself "with-like (*mithaften*) being-in-the-world" (118:154), and in such a way that without it *Dasein* could not be what it is. The same holds for "caring for" (*Fürsorge*), as which Heidegger interprets the being-with of being with Others, as holds of "taking care of" (*Besorgen*), with respect to the being of entities present-to-hand that do not have the mode of being of *Dasein*: "As essential structures of the constitution of *Dasein*, they belong to the condition of the possibility of existence in general" (263:308). At the same time, it is for this reason that "Being alongside the ready-to-hand belongs just as primordially to Being-in-the-world as does Being-with-Others" (181:225).

In accordance with this approach, the three formal elements into which Being-in-the-world falls apart, the "world," Being-in as such, and the Self, are together colored by Being-with-one-another. The world, "just as originally" as the "surrounding world," that is, the world of concernfully deployed "equipment" (*Zeug*), is also a "with-world" (118:155, 65:93). Being-in is "being-with along with Others" (118:154). Taking care of and caring for are its "possible fundamental modes" (176:220). The tendency to admit being-with-one-another into the foundation of *Dasein* is most extreme where Heidegger—in a unique attempt, admittedly—binds the formal structure of the self together with that of being toward the Other. "Formal" means here: undisturbed by the actual modifications that the self suffers through the modes of effectuation made possible for it by authenticity and inauthenticity. With respect to what concerns the inauthentic self, there can be no doubt that as "one-self," it is preoccupied with the Other. However, whether authentic or inauthentic, the self is *always* the "for-the-sake-of-which" on which the "referential totality of significance" is hung. *Dasein* is "for the sake of itself" (118:225). To the extent, however, that being with the Other belongs to it, it is then implied that, in its being, it is concerned with its "self" and is, at the same time," for the sake of the Other (123:160).

Just as the confrontation with Husserl is carried on without being expressly stated in all those passages in *Being and Time* devoted to the problematic of being-with, so Heidegger in the end also brings out the difference that, in our first point, is manifest between the analysis of being-with and the theory of intersubjectivity: "An isolated I is never given, in the first instance, with the Others" (116:152). According to Heidegger, only those who cut the I off from the Other must latch onto "empathy" as that act that is supposed to instate the initially absent bond between the I and the Other (124:16).[16] In contrast, the original entanglement of being-with and being-in-the-world guarantees that the being-there-too of the Other is already implied and so always already understood in the primary world projection (123:160).

2. Closely bound up with the first difference is the second. It follows directly out of the originality of being-with and out of the prior inclusion of *Dasein*-with that is contained therein. When Heidegger says, "The Being-with and the facticity of Being-with-one-another is not grounded . . . in a coming together of several 'subjects' " he thereby

holds out against the opinion, represented by Husserl too, that Others are originally encountered as a "plurality" of subjects that, thanks to their incarnation, arise "as person-things present-at-hand" among other things. In accordance with his interpretation, the conception of being-with as an existential-ontological determinant wards off such a digression of the "facticity of being-with-one-another," appropriate to *Dasein*, into the mundane factualness of thingly coexistence and characterizes the mode of being of *Dasein*, regardless of whether Others are actually to be met with in its surrounding world: "The phenomenological expression '*Dasein* is essentially being-with' has an existential-ontological sense. It is not intended to establish ontically that, as a matter of fact, I am not alone but that others of my kind are to be found." In Heidegger's opinion, even when no Others are actually found in my field of vision, I still exist as being-with, namely, in the deficient mode of being alone. Indeed, being-with has so little to do with the coming together of subjects that I can even be alone in being "among" Others. This being-alone-among-many, as the deficient mode of being-with, demonstrates, in turn, to what an extent the "indifference and alienness" in which the Others encounter me there has to be distinguished from the ontological unrelatedness of a bare coming together (120–121:156–157).

3. The divergence of fundamental ontology and transcendental phenomenology in their kind of primarily disclosive access to the truth of inner-worldly beings is not purely methodological. Husserl stands in the great and long tradition of those for whom truth manifests itself in the intuition of perception and in the view of theoretical knowledge.[17] Heidegger, on the contrary, proceeds from the truth of observation back to the disclosure of inner-worldly beings in the course of practical interaction with them. So too the understanding of the Other that resides in the being-understanding of *Dasein* as such is no "knowledge developed out of thought" (124:161), but a "caring for" that is qualitatively different from the "taking care of" of equipment, which latter, however, coincides with the former in that it stands for a mode of practical interaction (121–122:157–158).

If one looks back at the three above-mentioned points, one is, first of all, forced to the conclusion that, in both of the last two, the "new approaches" of the analysis of being-with really only consist in a radicalization of positions that we also already found in Husserl. In particular, the powerful influence that Husserl's description of the "personalistic attitude" exercised in *Being and Time* is evident here. Not only the understanding of the Other out of its practical interaction with beings finds its equivalent in the personalistic alien experience. The *Dasein*-related facticity of being-with-one-another is also familiar to us from *Ideas*, book II. There we found an experience of the alien that does not presuppose the "coming together of several subjects" but takes place in the factical absence of Others, solely on the basis of the fact that the natural life-world is always already communalized. Heidegger's placing on a par of world and coworld, in accordance with which the world "is always already the one which I share with Others" (118:154), itself only springs from Husserl's insight into the prior intersubjectivity of the natural world. Insofar, however, as the separation of the facticity of being-with-one-another from the mundane factuality of coming together is motivated by the fundamental conception that the mode of being of *Dasein*-with is to be ontologically distinguished from that of the ready-to-hand and present-at-hand (118:154, 121:157, 124:161), its anticipation, through Husserl, is played out in the transcendental sphere. Indeed, Husserl's transcendental theory of alien experience already follows the goal of securing the independence of the being of the Other over against all thingly beings. Thereby this goal shares with Heidegger's recognition of the difference of the modes of being the character of a simple intention, which, as such, does not signify realization. However, with respect to Heidegger's thesis on the originality of being-with, developed under the first point, it is also a matter of a simple intention and no more. The statement "Insofar as *Dasein is* at all it has the mode of being of being-with-one-another" (125:163) remains a pure supposition so long as it has not been demonstrated.

This result gives birth to the presumption that the analysis of being-with repeats the theory of intersubjectivity exclusively upon another plane, the existential. For if Heidegger frequently responds to the secret admonition of his teacher precisely where he carried the problem of being-with-one-another beyond Husserl's general conception, it is to be expected that he clings much more closely to transcendental phenomenology in those points in which his transcendental approach shines through.

3 The Interpretation of Being-with-One-Another within the Horizon of the World

Like Husserl, Heidegger thinks being-with-one-another completely within the horizon of the world: "Being-with means . . . always being with one another in the same world" (238:282). In the context of this statement, Heidegger attempts to render intelligible why it is possible for being-with to be given not only with the living but also with the dead. This is possible, in his view, because the deceased is, for all that, still present in a world that once was ours, even if he is himself "no longer actually 'there' ": "The deceased has departed our world and left it behind. From out of it the surviving can still be with him" (238:282). The condition of the possibility of being-with with a dead person consequently lies in the worldliness of being with one another. I, the survivor, however, could just as well say, and with more right, that my being with the Other was not simply worldly. Rather, the other encountered me as a self that is beyond the world, and this makes it possible for me to live with him even after the Other has left our world.

With Husserl the mastery of the world over being-with-one-another is conveyed in the continual orientation toward the supposedly natural understanding of the being of the Other as an object in the world, which is, at the same time, subject for the world. Correspondingly, we find with Heidegger the interpretation of the Other as that very entity that "is 'in' the world in which it is encountered as a worldly being in the manner of Being-in-the-world" (118:154). Just as the Husserlian Other participates, as an object in the world, in the mode of being of thingly objects from which he is still wholly distinguished, as subject for the world, so the Other, described in *Being and Time*, still shares with equipment the property of being an entity encountered within the world, even though, as being-in-the-world, it is in no way present-at-hand or ready-to-hand:[18] "The being-character of concern (*Besorgen*) cannot belong to Being-with, even though Being-with, like concern, is a Being toward entities encountered within the world" (121:157).

As an entity encountered within the world, the Other is subject to *Dasein*'s own world projection. For he can only be encountered within the world "because *Dasein*, as Being-with, *lets* the *Dasein* of Others be encountered in his world" (121:157 — italics are mine). In order to be able to be encountered in my world, Being-with has *to be set free*. It is precisely that Being "for which the Others who are (*die seienden Anderen*) are freed within the world" (120:156).

Under this head, one that has already been criticized by Löwith,[19] Husserl's thoughts on the transcendental constitution of the alter ego keep recurring in modified form. The modification consists in this, that that which frees in *Being and Time*, that is, the constituting, is the world and thereby (or so it appears) not the "subject." *Dasein*-with characterizes *Dasein*'s Other, insofar as it is freed for a being-with through its world (121:157). Nevertheless, this difference precisely points to the inner connection between the Husserlian and the Heideggerian ideas of constitution. For the world, in the ontological meaning in which it is taken here, is organized by the self in the total structure of *Dasein* as the for-the-sake-of-which (*worumwillen*) of a referential totality. The self is, however, the existential place in which the I is preserved. So, with Heidegger, even the Other, in the transcendental sense, has to be aligned with "me": he is the projected of my project and is not to be distinguished, in this respect, from the ready-to-hand. Accordingly, being-with-one-another is essentially, and indeed more exclusively than with Husserl, represented by the model of my relation to the Other and not by the model of the relation of the Other to me. So it is for the most part thought in that very direction that is also determinative for being with the ready-to-hand and the present-at-hand and hardly at all in the opposite direction that distinguishes the relation between human beings prior to the relationship to "things."

In that the Other, like the remaining inner-worldly entities, is caught up in my world project, Heidegger, just as much as Husserl, robs it of its alienness and its contrariness. With Heidegger, however, this follows precisely from the originality that he attributes to *Dasein*-with. For only because *Dasein* is originally being-with can it release *Dasein*-with. Only because the worldliness of the world is from the outset structured upon "withness" can Being-there-too also be encountered together with the ready-to-hand in its horizon (123:160). The originality of being-with displaces, in this fashion, the originality of *Dasein*-with. For, whereas the former consists in the fact that Being-with belongs to the structure of *Dasein*, the latter means that the *Dasein*-with of the Other is *not* a structure of my *Dasein*. His orientation toward the idea of constitution, however, compels Heidegger to account not only for Being-with but also indirectly for *Dasein*-with as a structure of *Dasein*.

Being-with and *Dasein*-with are for him both, as we have already heard, "structures of *Dasein*" (114:149).[20]

4 Appresence and Coencounter

In the methodological construction of transcendental phenomenology, the constitution of the alter ego and of the intersubjective-objective world rests on the ground of the constitution of the thing-world. Similarly, in *Being and Time*, the analysis of the ready-to-hand and the present-at-hand methodologically precedes the analysis of *Dasein*-with and the with-world: "In the previous analysis," says Heidegger, at the beginning of the paragraph on *Dasein*-with, "the circuit of what is encountered within the world was limited, in the first instance, to equipment ready-to-hand (for example, Nature present-at-hand), and so to entities not possessing the character of *Dasein*" (118:154). The methodological priority of the ready-to-hand should be just as compatible with the intended equiprimordiality of surrounding world and with-world as is, with Husserl, the point of departure from the thing-world with the fact that the natural world, as objective, is always already the "world for us all." All the same, with Husserl, the methodological primacy also betrays a substantive precedence of thingly being. In what follows, we shall advance the opinion that the same holds for Heidegger.

Of the two moments that together make up the being of the Other for Husserl, the first, that the Other is a subject for the world, is more original than the second, that is, objective being within the world. Similarly, in *Being and Time*, the main weight of the duality of Being-in-the-world and inner-worldly beings constitutive for *Dasein*-with rests upon Being-in-the-world (123:160). Indeed, this gives *Dasein*-with its name. The freely given (*freigegeben*) Being of the Other is "*Dasein*-with" because the Other is in the world with me in a humanly characteristic manner. But how does the encounter with the Other let itself be regarded as Being-in-the-world? Heidegger regards it in the same way as Husserl already regarded it in the framework of his transcendental philosophy—as the *co*encounter of inner-worldly beings that do not have the character of *Dasein*. In the social-ontological sphere, the concept "coencounter" (117:153),[21] in its relationship to encounter, corresponds to the Husserlian concepts "appresence" and "cogivenness" in their relationships to "originary presence" and "absolutely originary givenness." The difference is simply that, with Heidegger, "equipment" takes the place of the originally present physical-organic body: "The *Dasein*-with of the Others is multiply encountered (that is, in multiple ways) out of the inner-worldly ready-to-hand" (120:156). Still, in this modification, only the radicalization of the world-oriented tendency is documented, a tendency that, as with Husserl, owes its disclosive function to the physical body (of the Other to be). Heidegger singles out the fact that Others are encountered out of the world, in their connection with equipment, as the essence of his phenomenological approach. Others "are encountered from out of the *world* in which concernfully circumspective *Dasein* essentially dwells. Theoretically concocted 'explanations' of the being present-at-hand of Others urge themselves upon us all too easily; but over against such explanations we must hold fast to the phenomenal facts of the case that we have pointed out, namely, that Others are encountered *environmentally*."

The merely coencountered presupposes that which is "itself" encountered, in just the same way as appresentation is supported by presentation. In accordance with its intention, this foundational relationship prevails in the Husserlian theory of intersubjectivity without prejudice to the regional independence of appresented beings by contrast with presented beings, and the same obtains in Heidegger, regardless of the declared fact that *Dasein*-with cannot be traced back to the ready-to-hand. Alongside being with the ready-to-hand, being-with is an "autonomous, irreducible relation of being" (125:162). It is not a matter here of the dependence of one kind of being upon another but of the inner order of the *event of encountering*. However, for Heidegger, in this order (and this must be firmly grasped) equipment is the first to be encountered. Heidegger's entire concept of encounter is tailored to this requirement. "Encounter" in *Being and Time* hardly means: *We* encounter *each other*, but almost entirely: Inner-worldly beings encounter a *Dasein* that lets itself be encountered. Even when the being of the entity so encountered is a *Dasein*-with, still, the *specific* sense of *interhuman* encounter, as we shall see more exactly with the interpretation of Buber, is eliminated, from the start, in this presentation of the concept.[22]

If one wants to do justice to Heidegger, it certainly will not do to limit the dependence of the coencountered alien being-in-the-world on the originally encountered equipment to the inner order of the event of encountering, and so to cut it off from the question concerning the equiprimordiality, or nonequiprimordiality, of the types of being. Furthermore, one must take into consideration that, even in the event of encountering, being-founded does not imply a subsequent introduction of something whereby that which emerges first has to be linked up in thought: "The Others who are thus 'encountered' in a ready-to-hand, environmental context of equipment are not somehow added on in thought to some thing that is proximally just present-at-hand. These things are encountered from out of the world in which they are ready-to-hand for Others, which world is also always already mine from the outset" (118:154). The environmental kind of encounter of *Dasein*-with does not suspend the circumstance that the surrounding world is itself already a with-world and that thereby all equipment carries "with-like" traits from the outset. The *Dasein*-with of the Others is encountered "out of the with-world with which we are environmentally concerned" (125:163). Heidegger only protects himself here from the same misunderstanding that Husserl had already confronted in the description of the relationship between presence and appresence. Even the appresent is not thought into the originally present but is already present in the latter.

For all that, the I (for example, *Dasein*), with Husserl, as also with Heidegger, first arrives at the alien being-in-the-world by way of the "reference" (understood without further ado) that lies in the bodily present "thing." Only there still obtains between the two thinkers, even on this point, the general distinction that that which is, with Husserl, played out in the dimension of "viewing" is translated, by Heidegger, into the sphere of practical interaction and the goal directedness that prevails in it: "The 'description' of the proximate surrounding world, for example, the work world of the artisan, showed that, together with the equipment disclosed in the work, the Others for whom the work is determined are encountered. In the type of being of this ready-to-hand item, that is to say, in its involvement, there resides an essential reference to possible bearers for whose bodies it is 'supposed to be tailored' " (117:153). As the for which (*Woraufhin*) of the reference residing in equipment, however, the Other is essentially (not temporally) that which is *mediated* by equipment. This is the most significant of all the points in common: that, in the theory of intersubjectivity and in the analysis of being-with, the *immediacy* of the encounter with the Other is discounted in a similar manner because the *medium* of the "*world*" is interposed between "me" and Others.

This mediatedness is expressed in the state of affairs that is also characteristic of the presence-appresence relation, that the determinateness of *Dasein*-with only actually reaches as far as it can be read off the ready-to-hand. Just as the one for whose body the equipment disclosed in work is supposed to be tailored appears as its bearer and only as this, so the Other is similarly determined, from the determination of the equipment, simply as "producer" or "supplier" of the materials that are made use of (117:153).

Last and principally, the alien being-in-the-world, insofar as it is mediated by the "world"—and here there is no difference between Heidegger and Husserl—is narrowed down to the point that is in itself empty and receives its determinateness only out of "with-like" (*mithaften*) traces in the "world," traces that refer back to it. The fullness that comes out of the *self*, a fullness with respect to which each *Dasein* does at least have precedence over the I of intentional lived experience, is hardly carried over to *Dasein*-with. While I live through my own for-the-sake-of-which concretely as impulse and goal of my comportment, the Other, since I do not actualize it as a self, remains in the same functional abstractness into which the alien I is dissolved.

5 The Natural I and the Inauthentic Self

The alien I is the analogue of the I. It is like the "i" (*ich*) as well as "I" (*Ich*). *Dasein*-with is similarly related to *Dasein*: it is also *Dasein*, and, when it is encountered as *Dasein*-with, is precisely experienced as Being-there-too (*Auch-Dasein*). *Dasein*-with "is just like the self that has been freed for being-there—it is *also there with*" (118:154). The proximity of *Dasein*-with and the analogically apperceived alien I certainly entitles Heidegger to reject, as a misinterpretation, the opinion that he too, like Husserl, makes something like an isolated I the point of departure for the experience of Others: "To avoid this misunderstanding we must notice in what sense we are talking about 'the Others.' By 'Others' we do not mean everyone else but me—those over against whom the 'I' stands out. They are rather those from whom, for the most part, one does *not* distinguish oneself—those among whom one is too" (118:154). Still, instead of refuting the objection that the characteristic of the encounter of *Dasein*-with is oriented about each very own *Dasein*, this conclusion only strengthens what is surprising about it, namely, that such an orientation should, in fact, guide the determination of

Dasein-with. The Others "among whom one also is" are the "they" and therewith "the subject," the who of everyday *Dasein* (126:164). Insofar as the whole problematic of being-with-one-another is only developed by Heidegger with a view to answering the question concerning the who of everyday *Dasein*, Others, as the They, from the outset, form the horizon in which the Others, as *Dasein*-with, are thematized. *Dasein*-with is encountered methodologically only on the way to the They: "The researches toward the phenomenon by means of which the question concerning the who is to be answered leads to structures of *Dasein* that are equiprimordial with Being-in-the-world, that is, Being-with and *Dasein*-with" (114:149). However, there is a snag in the intended alignment of *Dasein*-with with the They. The interpretation of the Others as the They forbids any orientation toward own *Dasein*, which is implied in the interpretation of Others as *Dasein*-with. The snag lies in the relationship between the two passages that have just been introduced. The first deals with *Dasein*-with; the second introduces the They, though not at first under that title. In both instances, Heidegger speaks of being-there-too and being-there-with. In the one instance, where it is a question of the *Dasein*-with included under the rubric of own *Dasein*, he understands the being-there-too and being-there-with of the *Others* as being with me; in the other instance, however, and from the standpoint of the They, it is *my* quite differently structured being-there-too with the Others that is taken into consideration.

To the extent that *Dasein*-with is the existential transformation of the Husserlian alien I, the They is the existential form of the We, which Husserl considers as the basic form of human community.[23] Even that state of affairs that is characteristic of the They, that "I" am not the one who stands over against Others, but one among Others, also pertains to the central truth of the We. Above all, that which already gives its characteristic stamp to Husserl's man, set in the community of the We, is carried over to the They as "subject" of everyday *Dasein*, namely, that, as one among Others, he is *himself an Other*, an "alter-ed" I: "The They itself belongs to the Others," and, indeed, in the strong sense, that being-with-one-another "completely resolves one's *Dasein* into the mode of being of 'the Others' " (126:164).

In accordance with the picture of the alter-ed I that we encountered with Husserl, one's *Dasein* appears on *one* plane with the Others, in order to be merged in with them in leveled-down modes of behavior and, like them, to be absorbed in inner-worldly beings. Even here only the field of concretion has changed. In place of "communalization" in perception, practical interaction with beings, now entirely directed by the They, makes its appearance: "In utilizing public means of transport and in making use of information such as the newspaper, every Other is like the next" (126:164). However, the parity of the They and the We is as such not disturbed by this change. What "the They" does there, "we"[24] do—all of us who live in the same world. Insofar as it is understood as with-world and not interpreted from the standpoint of immediately available equipment as surrounding world, this world is itself "the 'public' we-world" (65:93).[25]

We come now to the most decisive point, for the outline statement of the whole: relating back fundamental ontology to transcendental phenomenology. The "They self" is the "self of everyday *Dasein*" (129:167), or the *inauthentic self.* The splitting up of *Dasein* into the two "types of being," authentic and inauthentic, reproduces, at an existential-ontological level, the transcendental-egological division of original and natural I. The inauthentic self, like the natural I—to speak with Husserl—exists in the "absence of the world" (*Weltverlorenheit*).[26] For, while authentic *Dasein* grasps its "own" self, Heidegger calls the self of everyday *Dasein* "inauthentic" for this reason, that everyday *Dasein* precisely does not understand itself from itself but out of the "world" (146:186). It is "fascinated by its world" and has the "kind of being of being absorbed in the world" (113:149), a kind of being that, in the sharpened analysis of inauthenticity, is interpreted as "fallen": "*Dasein* has, in the first instance, fallen away from itself as an authentic potentiality for Being its self, and has fallen into the 'world' " (175:219).

Inauthentic understanding also has this in common with the natural attitude, that it also reaches out beyond concernful interaction with equipment—Husserl would say: the atheoretical praxis of the "lived world"—to "theory," that is, to all positive sciences and to that philosophy that has still not attained "self-clarification." Husserl's statement, "Positive science is science in the absence of the world" (CM 183:157), retains its complete validity in *Being and Time.* Indeed, we meet again here the thesis that the positive sciences are, by comparison with everyday life, "naiveties of a higher order" (CM 179:153). With Husserl the absence of the world finds its culmination in the scientific-natural attitude to the extent that there the relativity of the worldly relation, in the consciousness of which the life-worldly natural I still feels something of its original operation, sinks into total anonymity. Similarly with Heidegger: theory has fallen even further than the fallen "praxis" because it—a tendency already present in the fallen "praxis" and pushed to the extreme—entirely abstracts from the relativity to *Dasein* of the equipmental totality and—in "just looking at"—changes the ready-to-hand into a present-at-hand that has at the same time been entirely freed from *Dasein*.[27]

Above all however, Heidegger, in his *Dasein* analysis, takes over Husserl's interpretation of the natural I as the I that has been altered and has, *for this reason*, fallen into the world.[28] The inauthentic self is, as the They-self, the one that is "completely fascinated by the 'world' and by the *Dasein*-with of Others in the they" (176:220). However, this should not be understood as though the move from being fascinated by the Others to being fascinated by the "world" entered in as a second factor. Rather, fallenness in the "world" is itself nothing other than being fascinated by the Others: "The fallenness into the 'world' means absorption in being-with-Others, insofar as the latter is guided by idle talk, curiosity, and ambiguity" (175:220).

The identity of "fallenness in the 'world' " and "absorption in being with one another" point to the fact, furthermore, that Heidegger, in a manner similar to Husserl, locates the latter in the *past*. For, in accordance with his conception, fallenness in the "world" is grounded ontologically in thrownness, which, for its part, is a relatedness to the "world" (139:178 and §38). However, just as in the complete structure of being-in-the-world as "being-already-in advance-in-a-world," the project corresponds to "being-in-advance," so thrownness is aligned with "being-already-in" (191–192:236), that is, the "has been" as the existentially understood past.

Heidegger holds consistently to this formal statement in the phenomenal description of being-with-one-another. Accordingly, being-with-one-another is, in the first instance, determined by the has been (*Gewesenheit*) to the extent that, as the *Dasein* that has fallen under the mastery of the They, it draws its experience of being-with from the reservoir of its already made experience: "The Other is, in the first instance, there in terms of what they have heard about him, and what they know about him" (174:218). But even then, when the Other is coencountered in equipment, he is present to *Dasein* only in the presentification of the past. In connection with his exposition of co-encountering, Heidegger says, "The field, for example, . . . appears as belonging to this or that person, as kept in order by him, the used book is bought at . . . sent from . . . and so on" (177–178:222). This means that the presently used book was *first* bought at . . . *previously* once sent from . . . and so on. The "reference" from equipment to being-with is continually the back reference of an is to a has been. In this way, the belonging together of "world" and the has been, a belonging together that is included in the formal conception, is concretely confirmed. Insofar as the Other is encountered out of and on the "world," he necessarily sinks into the "already been."

The supposition that the experience of Others is at bottom a recollection of the has been agrees well with the Husserlian limitation of the possibility of experiencing the alien I by the measure of those lived experiences that I have already had and must reproduce in empathy. Indeed, according to Heidegger, not only does *Dasein* include *Dasein*-with within the boundaries of its beenness; but conversely, as a result, the Others displace the *Dasein* that belongs to them in the past—and he articulates this inverse trait even more sharply than Husserl. They do this insofar as they, as the They, take over the self's own being. For in this way they take away from *Dasein* the project of the future: "With *Dasein*'s lostness in the They, that factical potentiality for-Being that is closest to it . . . has already been decided upon. The They has always kept *Dasein* from taking hold of these possibilities of being" (268:313; see also 126:164), and in such a way that it "preempts all judgment and decision" (127:165). The future in which the They lives, however, is laid out by means of that publicity that takes everything as "known" (127:165). It is itself, therefore, ruled by the past, that is, by that in which "at bottom nothing happens" (174:218), because everything has already happened. It is the illusory future in which the "already" is continued exclusively into the "not-yet."

6 The Transcendental Community of Monads and Authentic Being-with-One-Another

Because being inauthentic arises in the They, *Dasein* is only able to become authentic by freeing itself from the domination of the Others or by "individualization" (187–188:232, 276–277:231–232). We have seen that the phenomenological reduction, in Husserl's sense, is an individualization. Inasmuch as I become aware of my absolutely unique ego, a peculiar "aloneness" is engendered. But, conversely, the "individualization" of becoming authentic is, in a certain respect, a transcendental reduction. Note that we say "in a certain respect." Obviously, it *is* not a reduction. The principal distinction consists in this, that it is itself an existentiel performance, though the reduction is a method administered by the "nonparticipating spectator." However, in the first place, this distinction only corresponds to the difference (generally taken for granted by us) that sets in with the transformation of egology into autology, and, in the second place, upon closer inspection, it is considerably relativized. For, on the one hand, in the course of the development of Husserl's work, the transcendental reduction receives an ever more pronounced "existentiel" function: From the standpoint of *Crisis* (140:179) it is, as universal self-investigation, called upon to "effect a complete personal change," a change that, for mankind too, has the "meaning of the foremost existentiel change." On the other hand, for Heidegger, that "existentiel" element that individualization contains in itself is to be thought of in no way, in a rough-and-ready opposition to the "existential," as material to be existentially analyzed, but as the methodological presupposition of the existential analysis itself. For, "the ontological 'truth' of existential analysis is developed on the basis of the original existentiel truth" (316:364). In this way Heidegger takes aim especially at the methodological role of individualization, namely, that a determinate "conception of authentic existence" leads the ontological interpretation from the outset as the "factical ideal of *Dasein*" (310:358).

From a substantive standpoint too, however, individualization appears as the analogon of the transcendental reduction. As the uncovering of my constituting ego, the latter is the disclosure of the world as a sense constituted by me, in conjunction with the fact that it brackets the world that is unquestionably accepted by all of us. Similarly, individualization, as seizure of the ownmost self, from a negative viewpoint, sets the status of the "public we-world" out of action, in order, from a positive viewpoint, to lay out the transcendental world horizon. The seizure of the ownmost self is already the laying out of this horizon; for each own self functions as the for-the-sake-of-which, upon which the worldly referential totality is fixed. In becoming authentic, I am led back from the "world" to its for-the-sake-of-which, and this regression is necessarily individualization because the for-the-sake-of-which, in opposition to the world, which is hung up on it and which I share with the Others, is exclusively my own.

This correspondence of reduction and individualization includes within itself a further analogy: that between my absolute, unique ego and my authentic self. However, instead of staying with this, we would like to continue by taking account of the modifying repetition of Husserl's thought about the "transcendental community of monads" into Heidegger's idea of "authentic being-with-one-another." What gets repeated on an existentiel-existential level is the initially paradoxical matter of fact that my transcendental ego, which is certainly supposed to be absolutely *unique*, "lives," as transcendental, in community with that of (equally transcendental) Others. Analogously, according to Heidegger, individualization is supposed to make being-with-one-another possible, a being-with-one-another that, by comparison with the absorption in the They, is presented as authentic (298:344). That that *Dasein* which is individualized down to itself has equally to be with Others is derived, purely formally, by Heidegger, from the circumstance that authentic being-self remains being-in-the-world and that this latter is still being-with. "As concernful being alongside and solicitous being with," it has to be authentic (263:307). Out of the same state of affairs Heidegger formally derives the authenticity of being-with-one-another in authentic being-self. Since being-in-the-world becomes authentic together with the self, being with Others must also participate in authenticity (298:344). The question is, however, how individualization and authentic communalization can be thought together *concretely*.

With a view to answering this question and thereby throwing light on the relationship between authentic being-with-one-another and the transcendental community of monads, it would be helpful to consider the resolution of the contradiction that Heidegger, regardless of his recognition of authentic being-with-one-another, very often simply equates the inauthentic everyday[29] with being-with-one-another. This is how the *unworldly* encounter of the Other in *everyday* being-with-one-another is supposed to take place. Accordingly Heidegger says, "The *Dasein*-with of Others is encountered *first and foremost* out of the with-world with which we are environmentally concerned" (125:163 — italics are mine). Generally speaking, however, Heidegger does not bring in the supplementary clause "first and foremost"; that is, he takes the environmental encounter as the essential trait of being-with-one-another purely and simply. We have taken account of this in section 4 of this chapter. We were entitled to do this because, from a particular standpoint, inauthentic everyday being-with-one-another actually does make up being-with-one-another in general, namely, insofar as the authentic is only carried out in a remarkable intermittence or *indirectness*. Indeed, its authenticity lies in such an indirectness because, in another sense, it enjoys no authentic, that is, direct, being-with-one-another.

The indirectness of authentic being-with-one-another is only intelligible out of the existentiel performance of individualization. Each own *Dasein* individualizes itself by running ahead to its death. It is death, its own death, that throws *Dasein* back entirely upon itself. For in death the *Dasein* that in everyday being-with-one-another represents the Other and is represented by the Other is absolutely unrepresentable (239–240:283–284). Insofar as death is, in a quite exceptional sense, "essentially my own" (240:284), it not only cannot be experienced by the Other (237–239:281–282) but, as the "ownmost," is also the most nonrelational possibility, that in which "every relation to another *Dasein* is undone" (250:294, 263–264:307–308). The aloneness that arises in view of this nonrelatedness is the prime fact of the authentic being of the self. Since, in the authentic being of the self, this running ahead toward death has to happen continually, it cannot be suspended, so long as the being of the self is authentic. This means, however, that should authentically existing *Dasein* also exist formally as being-with-Others, this latter can still never work its way into its ownmost being: "The nonrelational character of death, as understood in anticipation, individualizes *Dasein* down to itself. This individualizing . . . makes manifest that all Being-alongside the things with which we are concerned and all Being-with Others will fail us when our ownmost potentiality for Being is at issue" (263:307).[30]

Accordingly, its nonrelational character also determines the sense of "authentic being-with-one-another" that springs from individualization. It gives it the character of unboundedness. The concrete connection of individualization and authentic communalization lies in this, that the seizure of the ownmost first frees one for an awareness of the most alien aspect of the alien—as the ownmost of the Other. Heidegger has this in mind when he says, "As the nonrelational possibility, death individualizes, but only in such a manner that, as the possibility that is not to be outstripped, it makes *Dasein*, as Being-with, have some understanding of the potentiality for Being of Others"

(264:309). Potentiality for Being of Others is here in conformity with "its ownmost potentiality for being itself" (298:344). The understanding of the ownmost potentiality for being itself of Others, aroused by death, has the form of letting be (298:344). Letting be, however, which, from a positive standpoint, stands for the recognition of the ownmost being of Others, is, from a negative standpoint, the dissolution of all direct connection between Others and me. Others can only be freed *for themselves* inasmuch as they are freed *from me*.[31] That Heidegger thinks of the most authentic being-with-one-another as just such a freeing of Others from me becomes clear from the opposition to everyday being-with-one-another. Because inauthentically existing *Dasein* hides from itself its ownmost possibilities and is, for this reason, just as little capable of making the possibilities stored up in this possibility (its death) its own, it is also not capable of respecting, as belonging to it, those possibilities of the Other that are accessible to him within the world. It lives in the possibilities of the Other as if they were its own. Inasmuch, however, as *Dasein*, in the course of laying hold of what is its own, takes possession of what is really its own, it, in a certain respect, dispossesses the possibilities of the Other; that is, it disconnects them from him (264:308). In this way, authentic being-with-one-another that is due to individualization or the releasing of my self from the Others, is, in fact, and in accordance with its origin, only the releasing of the Others from me.

The distinction outlined above between the everyday inauthentic and the authentic being-with-one-another is fixed conceptually by Heidegger through the differentiation of solicitude (*Fürsorge*) into the "leaping-in and dominating" and the "leaping-ahead and freeing" (122:159).[32] In the leaping-in solicitude *Dasein* takes away from the Other its "care" and therefore its being-in-the-world, in order, *on its behalf*, to take care of whatever exists to be taken care of in the "world." The representation of the everyday is carried out in it. This leaping-in can only be a domination insofar as it is at the same time a being dominated. In everyday inauthentic being-with-one-another, Others exercise a domination over me in that they dissolve me in their kind of being. I am dominated by the Others in everyday solicitude in that I act in place of the Other or as an Other. To leap in for an Other means: "to put oneself concernfully in his place" (122:158). On the basis of the dialectic of self-displacement, this is, however, just as originally a domination. By putting myself in his place, I make his possibilities my own. The Other is "thrown out of his place" (122:158). Heidegger, who seeks to overcome the theory of empathy by the approach through solicitude, in reality reproduces the Husserlian conception even here. It is precisely this, the making of the own into the Other and, by the same token, the Other into the own, that characterizes empathy. To be sure, according to Heidegger, the leaping-ahead and freeing solicitude presents itself, in opposition to the appropriation of the Other, as the letting be that is attentive to the ownmost being of the Other: "*Dasein*'s resoluteness toward itself is what first makes it possible to let the Others who are with it 'be' in their ownmost potentiality for Being and to codisclose this potentiality in the solicitude that leaps ahead and liberates" (298:344). Leaping-ahead is the solicitude of authentic being-with-one-another because it holds before it its ownmost being its self as an aim. It is liberating because in this way it frees the Other for himself: "This kind of solicitude pertains essentially to authentic care—that is, to the existence of the Other, not to a '*what*' with which he is concerned; it helps the Other to become transparent to himself *in* his care and to become *free* for it" (122:158). Insofar, however, as I cannot take away existence from the Other, my resolute solicitude only "impinges upon" this existence *indirectly*. Its help must be as indirect as the "Socratic midwife service" that Kierkegaard's "indirect communication" is supposed to provide.[33] This, in its turn, can only mean that it can only consist in this, that I free the Other *from me*.[34]

The indirectness and the negativity of authentic being-with-one-another that resides in it also points to the analogy between the relationship of my absolute, unique ego to the transcendental community of monads as well as to itself as member of this community, and the reference of my authentic self to the self-sustaining Others as well as to itself as one of these Others. In its ownmost being, the authentic self is no less alone than the transcendental ego.[35] The unrelatedness of death casts its shadow upon every communication and, in the voice of conscience, gives the listening *Dasein* to understand that, in the final analysis, it is alone. For this reason the authentic self can no more be *originally and unreservedly* in the equiprimordiality of reciprocal belonging, the one of Others reduced to what is peculiarly their own, than can the transcendental ego. The absence of a partner on the part of the originary I becomes evident in that it also constitutes onesidedly the constituting Other, the alien I in its transcendental reality.

Along similar lines, in *Being and Time* the Other sustains my "freeing" not only as that inner-worldly being that is encountered within the horizon of my world but also as its ownmost existence, as freedom. What holds of authentic being-with-one-another in general holds of that which Heidegger ascribes to the objectivity grounded therein: that it "frees the Other in his freedom for himself" (122:159).

7 The Connection between the Analysis of Being-with and the Theory of Intersubjectivity

With this reference to the—admittedly limited—correspondence of the transcendental community of monads and authentic being-with-one-another, we are going to break off the investigation into the individual connections between Heidegger's analysis of being-with and Husserl's theory of intersubjectivity, even though it could be carried much further. Supported by the externally determined circumstance that it was not possible to expound Heidegger's social ontology as extensively as Husserl's, the impression might very well have arisen that, with all the points of connection indicated, we were simply concerned with a peripheral, and, for the substantive problematic of *Being and Time*, meaningless, configuration. For this reason, instead of discovering still further analogies, we want, at the conclusion of this chapter, to point out, at least in an exemplary manner, that this configuration also helps us better to understand the total conception of fundamental ontology.

Undoubtedly, the murkiest point in *Being and Time* has to do with the meaning of "inauthenticity." We shall only take account of two difficulties. First, the relationship of inauthenticity to "everydayness" is extremely problematic. Projected originally and to all appearances as indifferent with respect to authenticity and inauthenticity—whereby it remains undecided whether such "averageness" is itself existent or not—in the further course of the investigation, everydayness melts more and more into inauthenticity. In most places, Heidegger uses the concepts "everyday" and "inauthentic" as meaning the same. Second, it appears as ungrounded that Heidegger should, on the one hand, characterize inauthenticity as "fallenness into the world," that is, as "absorption in the world," and then again as "fallenness in the They," that is, as "absorption in the They," doubtless with the idea that it is a matter here of one and the same phenomenon.

The attempt has been made to eliminate these difficulties by radically separating fallenness in the "world" and fallenness in the They and treating them as two completely distinct phenomena[36] in explicit opposition to Heidegger's own conception. In this way the relationship of inauthenticity and everydayness is also supposed to be clarified. Inauthenticity would then comprise absorption in the They alone, while absorption in the "world" would belong to everydayness, originally envisaged by Heidegger in the sense of modal indifference, as a being with inner-worldly beings that also makes possible a relation to the "thing," a relation arising out of authenticity. Heidegger's confusion of inauthenticity and everydayness springs, however, out of his erroneous equation of fallenness in the They with the absorption in the "world."

If one takes account of the fact that the analysis of being-with reproduces Husserl's theory of intersubjectivity upon an existential plane, this interpretation can be opposed by another, one that (or so it seems to me) is more adequate to Heidegger's intention. For what, above all, has been made clear through the correspondence worked out above is precisely the substantive belonging together of "fallenness in the They" and "absorption in the world." The unity of this phenomenon is rooted in the derivation, envisaged by Husserl, of my mundanization from my being together with the Others. That Heidegger equally grasps the They as the origin of "lostness in the world" (the Husserlian absence of the world) is noted by the critic referred to above.[37] However, on the basis of his thesis that the identification of absorption in the "world" and fallenness in the They, grounded for its part in this foundational connection, is substantively unjustified, he cannot see that that which lies at the root of Heidegger's identification forbids the identification carried out by *him* of absorption *in* the "world" and concernful being *alongside* the "world." Of course there follows just such an equation of Heidegger's own praxis. Indeed it is *this* equation that is phenomenally unjustified and that is responsible for all disconsonance in the conception of inauthenticity. That being alongside the world that is distinct from absorption in the "world" falls into everyday indifference. For, next to being with Others, a moment of being-in-the-world is present that remains contained in authenticity. So it is *its* equation with *absorption in the "world"* that is the real ground of the confusion of inauthenticity with everydayness. Heidegger keeps inauthenticity and everydayness apart so far and so long as he distinguishes absorption in the "world" and being alongside the "world." And he throws them together as soon as he levels down the distinction between absorption in and being alongside the "world." The unnaturalness of this leveling down betrays itself in the bastardized and linguistically incorrect expression "absorption alongside. . . ." (175 et passim:220). Substantively, however, this leveling down must be seen as unnatural because in being alongside the world, nothing like understanding-oneself-out-of-this-"world" is to be found, which latter is constitutive for falling into or absorption in the "world," and because this understanding-oneself-out-of-the-world is not to be found in it if it is also supposed to function as a moment of authentic being-in-the-world. The same thing is being said in a different way when one says, Being alongside . . . is entirely compatible with being-with-oneself, in line with which it can also become being-with-the-thing-itself. However, as clear as it is that being alongside . . . prepares the possibility for authentic being-with-the-thing-itself, so the correspondence of the analysis of being-with and the theory of intersubjectivity makes it obvious that fallenness into the "world" *excludes* being-alongside the thing that is the primary relation to the thing. As the fruit of alteration, it exists in the first instance as the inseparable unity of world loss in the sense of lostness in the world, and self-loss in the sense of the lostness of the self. In such self-loss, however, it is then also the lostness *of the* "world," namely, of the universe of those things that confront me in my transcendental world horizon.

With Husserl, world loss is lostness in that world that gets set up in the loss of the original world insofar as the apparently unrelated world, in which precisely the natural I loses itself, proceeds out of the derelativization of the world that exists for me and can only exist as being-for-me. We now want to suggest that in *Being and Time* something analogous obtains. First, it can be proved that Heidegger thinks of fallenness into the world on a basis of unity with fallenness into the They, as loss of the initial relation to this thing. Second, it can be shown that he gives this loss prominence as loss of that original *Dasein*-related world, that is, the world of the ready-to-hand. And, third, it can be added that the They, inasmuch as it takes *Dasein* away from the ready-to-hand, has lastly and authentically fallen into *the* world that emerges with the sinking away of original relativity, that is, the present-at-hand.

Having uncovered the "existential structures of the disclosure of Being-in-the-world" (166:210)—mood, understanding and discourse— he goes on to investigate in what way these structures get modified insofar as *Dasein* "as everyday (that is, inauthentic) holds itself in the mode of being of the They" (167:210). He characterizes idle talk, curiosity, and ambiguity as phenomena of that specific disclosure of the They that falls together with "publicity" (167–175:210–219).[38] These three phenomena are supposed to characterize that "authentic" in- authenticity in which fallenness in the They and fallenness in the "world" form an original unity. Accordingly, it should have been Heidegger's task to follow up its constitution in being-with-one-another. In fact, however, this is only carried out in part. Heidegger does not enquire into the constitution of ambiguity at all. Admittedly, this can be justified on the grounds that he envisages ambiguity simply as the general composition of the public world of fallen *Dasein*, one that is already constituted through curiosity and idle talk. This certainly saves Heidegger, but in such a way that, in name at least, only the constitution of idle talk can be grasped, as such, out of being-with-one-another.

According to Heidegger, idle talk is ontologically grounded in the communicative character of spoken discourse. As communication, dis- course shares with the Other the relation to the thing that the discourse is about (162:205). Therein, at the same time, lies the possibility that the Other, instead of being directed with the interlocutor upon that which is talked about, stays exclusively on the plane of the talking about. Thus he does not arrive exactly at an "originally understanding being-relation to the 'about-which' of discourse." Inasmuch as he now talks about the talking and continues to do so without any genuine understanding for the thing in question, "the initially already defective basis is accentuated to complete baselessness." And "idle talk is con- stituted therein" (168:212). Hence inauthenticity rests upon the covering over of the initial uncoveredness of beings through the seeming in- telligibility of that which the They discusses. Heidegger's demonstration of the constitution of idle talk reveals it to be both the loss of the primarily discovered and also a lostness *in* a world whose unoriginality is underscored by the essential trait of ambiguity.

That the loss of the primary relation to the thing does, however, bring the springing-out of the initially ready-to-hand world and the fallenness into the degenerate world down to the absorption in the present-at-hand is indicated by the constitution of curiosity, despite the verbal concealment of its "social" descent. Heidegger explains this as the reversal of concern from the initially ready-to-hand into a looking at the outward appearance of the remote present-at-hand. In curiosity, we find the discretionary tendency that guides concern, namely, to turn away "from the immediately ready-to-hand into a remote and alien world," in order to create for *Dasein* the possibility "of seeing the 'world' in a tranquil tarrying only in its *outward appearance.*" Moreover, once again we are able to appreciate here the threefold nature of the signification that is appropriate to the "absence of a world" appended to Husserl's thought, as also to that thematized by Heidegger. As the lostness of losing-oneself, or "being-left over to-the-world," the world loss of curiosity is at the same time the loss of the self and the immediately encountered world: "*Dasein* lets itself be carried along solely by the outward appearance of the world. In this kind of being, it concerns itself with getting rid of itself as being-in-the-world and getting rid of its being alongside that which, in the closest everyday manner, is ready-to-hand" (172:216).

It has to be admitted that elsewhere Heidegger also characterizes fallenness exclusively as fallenness into the ready-to-hand. Only too often, however, this characteristic documents the unjustified confusion of fallenness into . . . with being alongside. . . . Where this does not hold, it can lay claim to validity simply insofar as it distinguishes the *first* account of the movement that enables *Dasein* to understand itself out of the world. The movement of falling *comes to an end*, in any case, in the present-at-hand. Its end comes with the theory that covers up the original understanding of being. The theory, however, whose constitution bears traits that are not accidentally similar to those of curiosity, is an "only-just-looking" at the present-at-hand. In the ontological interpretation of being developed out of it, therefore, "the being of what is proximally ready-to-hand gets passed over, and entities are first conceived as a configuration of things (*res*) that are present-at-hand" (201:245). Given that fallenness is essentially understanding oneself out of the "world," this means, above all, that, in the end, *Dasein* interprets itself as something present-at-hand (201:245). The ontology of the present-at-hand subject gets constituted. Thereby, however, the event of alter-ation is brought to a close in that most radical mundanization, which is arrived at even with Husserl. With the present-at-hand there arises in *Dasein* that factuality that is not characteristic of *Dasein* and to which the ego succumbed, in that it grasped itself from the standpoint of the Others as an object appearing in the world.

As an indication not against but for the correspondence of the analysis of being-with and the theory of intersubjectivity, we may count the far-reaching failure to articulate, in *Being and Time*, that state of affairs disclosed here. Precisely the unquestioned manner in which Heidegger identifies "fallenness into the They" and "fallenness in the world," without adequately grounding the identity, points to presuppositions that he no longer reflects upon because he already brings them in with his starting point in Husserl. In Sartre, however, we shall now encounter a thinker who—in connection with Heidegger *and* Husserl—once again, and on Heidegger's existential plane, thematizes the alter-ation discovered by Husserl and places it at the center of his social ontology.

6

The Destructive Repetition of Husserl's Theory in Sartre's Social Ontology

1 The New Clue: The Immediacy of the Originally Encountered Other

In comparison with Husserl's theory of intersubjectivity and with Heidegger's analysis of being-with, Sartre's social ontology, set out in *L'Être et le néant* [*Being and Nothingness*] (En),[1] comes a good bit nearer to the essence and reality of interhuman encounter. Sartre is himself perfectly well aware of this progress. He introduces his reflections, in the third part of *Being and Nothingness*, with a critique of the doctrine of alien experience offered by "realism" and "idealism" (277–288:303–315), as well as by Husserl, Hegel, and Heidegger (288–310:315–339), no doubt with a view to carrying through his contribution as a way out of the confusion brought about by his predecessors.

If, with respect to the problem of the interhuman relation, I place Sartre above Husserl and Heidegger, still I am not in any way following Sartre's own self-understanding. Sartre does not really move beyond the positions of Husserl and Heidegger on all those points on which he thinks he has superseded them. Conversely, the direction in which he really does move beyond them does not altogether fall in line with that which, in his own eyes, marks the progressive development from Husserl to himself. For this reason we want to refuse the invitation to be brought to the new through the destruction of the old and to take account of Sartre's positive statement from the outset. In this way the most important objections to Husserl and Heidegger will be articulated from time to time in their proper places.[2]

The *intention* that Sartre pursues in his description of the presence of the Other seems to undermine Husserl's and Heidegger's central thesis so radically that, at first, one asks whether one can even talk about a common character here at all. Sartre strives for nothing less than to break through the transcendental philosophical conception of a duality of world and "world," of a horizon given in advance and beings appearing therein, in the field of the interhuman relation. In this way he circumvents the fundamental alternatives into which the being and the mode of encounter of the Other are forced in transcendental-phenomenological and existential-ontological philosophy. Originally the Other is *neither* an "object in the world" or "inner-worldly being" *nor*, "like myself," a "subject for the world," oriented toward things, or an alien "being-in-the-world" who, like myself, is open to inner-worldly beings.

Being an inner-worldly being caught up in my world project already, according to Sartre, contradicts the most general concept of the Other. For what stands under my world project can be prescribed by me from the mode of its presence. The Other, however, in that meaning which is constitutive for Sartre's theory of the alienating-alien, is the one who is "not I" and for this reason declines any patronage on my part (285:312; see also Crd 183:102, 186:105). In proportion to the extent to which he evades me and my apprehension, however, he transcends the world. So with the same stress with which he proclaims the being of the Other as the negation of my own being, he also emphasizes the *extramundane* character of the Other, the "extramundane being" (290:318), the extramundane existence (291:319), the "transmundane presence of the Other" (318:363). This extramundane character belongs to the Other not accidentally or externally but out of the necessity of its essence: "The Other is *by nature* out of the world" (290:317 — italics are mine). Indeed, the initial experience of the Other is not only an experience of something essentially extramundane but, in general, the experience that the world possesses an extramundane dimension (329:364).

By means of these expressions the concept of the extramundane is now aimed at the state of affairs that has already been grounded in detail, namely, that the Other who is originally present is not an inner-worldly being or, in Husserl's language, is not a "mundane" object. Because, in this sense, the Other does "not belong to the world," he cannot—as Sartre brings out critically against Husserl— ever fall a prey to the phenomenological reduction. Over and above this, however, the characterization of the Other as the purely and simply extramundane being likewise removes it from that world re- latedness that still also attaches to the transcendental and, to that extent, for *Husserl*, extramundane, alter ego. As constitutive of the objective world, the pure alter ego is still of this world, not to be found in it, to be sure, but directed *toward* it (289–290:316). In contrast, the primarily present Other is, according to Sartre, supposed to be "a real being existing beyond this world" (289–290:316–317—italics are mine), that is, an entity that does not first achieve its fullness of being for me out of its world relation. And once again the Other is this of necessity. For his self-sustaining unworldly "reality" is the condition of the possibility of his extramundanity in the most radical sense of his not needing the world. The pursuit of this insight separates Sartre from Husserl and equally from Heidegger. The originary ex- perience of the Other is not the experience of an alien being-in-the- world, but that of a "being-beyond-the-world" (337:370).[3]

As a presence that is not first mediated through the world, the "extramundane presence" of the Other is an *immediate* presence: "présence immédiate" (316:348, 328:362). The Other is "immediately present" to me (308:338; see also 347:380). This concept of immediacy, only occasionally employed by Husserl and as soon withdrawn is one we shall encounter again in the analysis of the philosophy of dialogue. It plays a dominant role for Sartre in its close connection with the concept of extramundanity. At least two positive shades of meaning especially deserve emphasis. On the one hand, the immediate encounter with the Other has the character of *suddenness* (318:349, 324:353, 326:355); on the other, an essence is given in it *wholly* and *completely*: "From the first encounter, in fact, the Other is given "entirely and immediately without concealment or mystery" (417:447). Both are only possible on the basis of a circumstance that, in the first instance, is only negatively characterized, that the Other is present to me *without mediation* (329:358). The middle term that is excluded here, however, is the world. Because I do not first reach the Other in the course of going through the world, I am able to grasp him without mediation, that is, suddenly and undisguisedly, which means wholly.

In accordance with the double meaning of the extramundane, the world, whose intermediary status is rejected by the thesis about the immediacy of alien personal experience, is also envisaged in a twofold manner. As a non-inner-worldly entity, the Other cannot be mediated by the world that I project. Between him and myself there does not lie the medium of my world horizon. As not-being-in-the-world, however, the Other can just as little be mediated by inner-worldly beings. Following transcendental phenomenology, alien subjectivity is mediated by the organic body that is laid out in a worldly-thingly manner and, indeed, just as much through that of the Other itself as through my own. In this respect, therefore, Husserl—and others as well—represents the position that Sartre ascribes to realism: "Between the consciousness of the Other and my own, my body, as a worldly thing, and the body of the Other, are the necessary intermediaries" (277:303). According to Heidegger, it is in its most worldly form as equipment that inner worldly beings mediate the alien being-in-the-world. Against both viewpoints, Sartre advances the same argument, namely, that the Other must already be experienced in some other manner than as Other in order that the reference of inner-worldly beings to him can be understood at all. The medition of the "world" comes too late. Without it I am already immediately aware of the Other.

That the knowledge of Others precedes all encounters with inner-worldly beings does not mean anything like saying that it is integrated in my world project and is for this reason "always already" present. This is the second alternative that Sartre rejects. Just as one leaves out of account the essential core of the Other when one specifies the extremes of his being as object in the world and as subject for the world, so the same holds when, out of the legitimate fear that he could lose what is characteristic of him through inner-worldly isolation, one delivers him over to the a priori worldliness of my world horizon. Sartre's criticism of this procedure is directed most particularly at the form that it took with Heidegger. On account of this we should go into the matter a little more fully.

Sartre begins his Heidegger interpretation (301–307:330–337) with a commendation. That Heidegger thinks of the interhuman relation as a "relation of being" that makes its members dependent upon one another in the depths of their being raises him above Husserl and Hegel. Still, a condemnation follows closely on the heels of the commendation. To start off with, Sartre condemns the gap between intention and execution. It amounts, or so he thinks, to little more than suppositions. In the second place, however, a grave mistake is already to be found, according to Sartre, in the composition of the thesis about the fundamentality of the social relation, namely, insofar as "being-with" is explained as an "essential structure" of my being. In this way—and this is the general objection against Heidegger—the Other is dissolved into an abstract and dependent element that permits no transition to *this concrete* Other. Ontological being-with cannot ground the concrete encounter with this determinate Other; indeed, it even makes it impossible. What is problematic about the "problem of alien existence" is, however, precisely the "concrete presence of this or that concrete Other" (308:438). So Heidegger skirts by the genuine problem.

It is not very easy to estimate the truth and untruth of this criticism. What is clear and unambiguous is simply the relevance of all this for Sartre, its relevance for the above-mentioned shift in the difference between world and "world," which is the sign of modern trancendental philosophy, or, as Sartre would say, of "Idealism." In that Heidegger fits *Dasein*-with, as an inner-worldly entity that is "at the same time" obscurely fitted into being-in-the-world, into that world horizon of mine that is colored by being-with, he falls back into precisely that "Idealism," according to *Being and Nothingness*, that he believes he has overcome. That in this criticism Sartre equates the ontological dimension of being-with with the "a priori" can, within certain limits, be substantiated from the text. It is nothing to the contrary that Heidegger hits upon a power that Sartre attributes to being-with and that precisely extends far beyond that of an a priori. And so, in being-with, it is not a matter of taking up the Other right away (as Sartre does throughout), an abstract Other that then has to be played out against the concrete. Naturally, for Heidegger, the Other is solely *Dasein*-with, and being-with is exclusively the *space* of the encounter with the Other.[4] Sartre, who, *expressis verbis*, only talks of being-with and not of *Dasein*-with, actually brings *Dasein*-with into being-with and also, conversely, being-with into *Dasein*-with.

Heidegger is completely disfigured where Sartre wants to demonstrate the incapacity of the "ontological and consequently a priori being-with" for the "grounding of an ontic being-with." Sartre writes, "If, in fact, in the ex-static upsurge of its being-in-the-world, human reality makes a world exist, one is not entitled to say nevertheless of its being-with, that it brings about another human reality" (305:334).

Sartre himself assumes that the *realité humaine*—identified with Heidegger's *Dasein*—lets a world be. This thesis keeps on coming back—in a formulation similar to the one offered here—in the course of his own thoughts. In relation to the "things," the transcendental philosopher of *Being and Nothingness* remains perhaps the most decisive that there has ever been. He only stands opposed to the opinion that the being-with of *Dasein* effects "the emergence of an other human reality." But does *Heidegger* really believe this? That the "with-like" structured world of one's own *Dasein* also releases, alongside the ready-to-hand, beings of the character of being of *Dasein*-with is in no way supposed to mean that being-with as such already brings about the factical appearance of the Other—just as little as this, that, due to being-in-the-world, "a world exists" can mean that due to *Dasein*'s claim to power, things are in reality brought forth. According to Sartre, I am the one through whom there is being, but not the one through whom—as Heidegger contends—there is an *other Dasein*. Questioning into the meaning of this "there is," Sartre formulates an alternative: it means that through me either the Other exists *for me* or the Other exists in general. The first would be a truism, which Sartre clearly would not believe his teacher capable of. The second supposition would amount to a relapse into the most crass solipsism. However, since Sartre reproaches fundamental ontology with precisely this relapse, he appears, in fact, to want to hold Heidegger to the second supposition.[5]

Only, we are not concerned with Sartre's Heidegger criticism as such, but with the standpoint that Sartre gains for himself in opposition to Heidegger. According to Sartre, Heidegger shuts off access to the fundamental state of affairs "that the 'being-with-Peter' or 'being-with-Annie' is a constitutive structure of my being-concrete" (304:334). Sartre wants to demonstrate precisely this. What is peculiar to such an attempt is to be sought in the overcoming of the alternative of the ontologically abstract (the "constitutive structure") and the ontically concrete (the "being-with-Peter") through the reconciliation of the transcendentally opposed members. We must see this attempt against the background of the general intention to run together the transcendental difference between world and "world" and all the differences posited in it. The beyond of world and its ontological horizon structure, as well as of "world" and its ontic empirical concreteness, can, for conceptual thought, only be revealed in the first instance as the sublated falling together of transcended antitheses. Sartre knows perfectly well that it is a matter here of "two irreconcilable levels." When he nevertheless treats being with the Other and, in the final analysis, the Other itself as the unity of the ontologically constitutive and the ontically concrete, this can only make sense on the basis of the presupposition that this being, as the beyond of world and "world," is in itself neither an ontologically a priori *constituens* nor an ontically empirical *concretum*. Nevertheless, it still turns out to be concrete and constitutive at the same time. The Other is a "concrete and individual condition" (327:359), a "concrete and transcendent condition" (333:366).

One finds in *Being and Nothingness* countless expressions of just such a *coincidentia oppositorum* in the being and the being present of the Other: for example, the metaphysical event that reveals the "contingence of being" (253:260) and the "antihistorical historicalization" (324–325:350). Reference should be made above all to the—certainly not in this sense paradoxical but for the same tendency distinctively fundamental—thesis that the present of the Other represents "an irreducible fact" (314:345; see also 334), to which, nevertheless, an absolute evidence pertains. With this thesis, Sartre frees the Other from the mundane facticity of transcendent things of the world that can always only exist with a degree of probability, in order to raise it to the level of that quite different facticity that also belongs to consciousness itself. The Other is supposed to be just as originally and absolutely evident as the *cogito* that forms the *fundamentum inconcussum* (307–308:337, 340:373). Even though also only transcendent, he is still supposed to be a matter of fact "evident from itself" and to that extent "absolute" (419:464, 430:477), a matter of fact whose contingence is coupled with necessity. Alien existence has a "contingent," a *"factical necessity"* (307:337). A social ontology that remains true to the facts should not take away either its extramundane facticity or its necessity or absolute evidence. Its task has much rather to be, or so Sartre thinks, that of leaving the encounter with the Other its factical character and still exhibiting its indubitability (307:337).

We shall have to clarify the point at which Sartre breaks through to this goal. Thereby, in particular, a clarification of the fundamental premises of his theory will have to be provided. Still, beforehand we must briefly orient ourselves with regard to the basic position that covers the total conception laid down in *Being and Nothingness* in contrast with the philosophy of Husserl and Heidegger.

2 The Old Point of Departure: World-Constituting Subjectivity

Our research has uncovered the duality that adheres to *Being and Nothingness* through the fact that Sartre binds together the method of an "objective" ontology of totality and a "subject-oriented" transcendental philosophy.[6] The claim to that ontology seems to be conveyed already in the construction of the work. Sartre begins, or so it appears, with an analysis of "being-in-itself," in order, first, from that point, to accomplish a leap into "being-for-itself." This most universal distinction is, as it were, the framework on which Sartre hangs his theory of "being-for Others." For being-for-Others is—as we shall see—supposed to mediate the in-itself and the for-itself. Out of the corner of the eye of the theory of being-for-Others, it is also, however, easy to see that the objective ontology and the transcendental subjectivism have not contracted a happy partnership because one of the partners, transcendental subjectivism, exercises genuine mastery while the other on occasion refuses obedience. The basis of this unequal relationship lies in the character of Sartre's "phenomenological ontology" as an—as K. Hartmann rightly calls it[7]—"ontology of intentionality." The question concerning the being constitution of intentionality is the real beginning of *Being and Nothingness*. Within its horizon, being-in-itself, as well as being-for-itself, is first encountered. With being-in-itself, the question concerning the transphenomenal being of the intended object gets answered, and with being-for-itself, the question concerning the original being of the intending subject. Insofar, however, as being-for-itself is also intentionality itself, it acquires an essential precedence over being-in-itself, while transcendental subjectivism acquires a superiority over "objective" ontology.

Accordingly, at the beginning of the theory of being-for-Others, too, we find the thesis "that the only possible point of departure is the Cartesian *cogito*" (308:338). And not only at the beginning: the *cogito*, the intentionality of the intending subject, remains the foundation of the entire theory. At the end of his concrete description of the primary presence of the Other, Sartre emphasizes that this description "operated exclusively on the plane of the *cogito*" (326:358)—to which there corresponds the methodological orientation toward the "interiority" of being-for-itself or of "consciousness." In it, mineness is already presupposed. It is for Sartre entirely self-evident that a genuine experience of freedom always has in mind only *my* freedom, a genuine experience of consciousness always only *my* consciousness (330:362). However, in his view, the following stipulation falls to the phenomenologist: to recognize as a phenomenal finding solely that which is revealed to him out of his own inner perspective. Therewith the very procedure of "objective" ontology is rejected. Thus Sartre thinks that one misses the phenomenon of being-with-one-another from the start if one represents the one and the Other externally and places oneself above both in order to consider their relationship from the outer perspective of the neutral observer. Instead of this, the phenomenologist has to describe how he himself, as the only I accessible to him, experiences the Other, the not-I. For the Other *is* in general only (namely, as Other) for "me." Where "I" have to do with the Other, however, there we find not "two or several" individuals (344:377) but only the Other and what he does to me. There is no "reverse side" (*d'envers*) to our relation: situated in it, I cannot bring the relation before me as an external totality (363:399).[8] This impossibility is rooted, however, in the still more fundamental incapacity to step out of my own being, that is, in the insurmountability of the *intériorité* of the *cogito* (300:329).

The fundamental meaning of *intériorité* for Sartre's doctrine of alien existence attests, above all else, to the circumstance that it first brings to light the sense of that negation mentioned in the previous paragraphs, a negation that characterizes the Other from the ground up as "not being I." For this *négation* is a "négation d'intériorité." It stands in opposition to the "négation d'extériorité," to the purely external or spatial negation, as which, according to Sartre, realism and idealism interpret the relation between me and the Other (285–286:313; see also Crd 132:36, 182:100, 185–186:104, 248:201, 331–333:284–286). For realists, the relation of exclusion of I and alien I is grounded in the impenetrability of bodies. In this way the fact that the Other is not I and I am not the Other is equated with the distinctness of things appearing next to one another. The nothingness that separates me from the Other and the Other from me is denatured to a passively suffered distance given in advance to me and to him, a distance of purely mundane origin. According to Sartre, such a view does not even get to the level of the relation proceeding from me to things, which is likewise an *inner* negation. The "négation d'intériorité," however, which distinguishes the social relationship, is to be distinguished from the external negation in that it is, first, immediate, second, active, and third, reciprocal (243:321, 309:339, 344:377). It does not first come into being through the separation of bodies (290:318), but already lies in the original being-phenomenon, that I am only myself in that I *project* myself as not being the Other and that the Other is only the Other in that he *projects* himself as not being I (292:320).

By means of this approach, guided by the thought of *intériorité*, Sartre first of all runs up against a separatedness of the personal partner that is much more radical than that established by the realist. Not an ontic but an ontological separatedness shuts off the Other from me and me from the Other (299:328). Because it is anchored in the depths of my consciousness and that of the alien, it cannot be circumvented like the mundane division of bodies, through an identity in consciousness or in the I. Nevertheless, it does imply a connection, far removed from identity, which, starting out from the external negation, remains just as inaccessible. For when the Other and I posit each other as not being the Other, we are, in the originary project of our being, "determined" through one another (288:315; see also Crd 183:101, 191:110). It will be the task of the subsequent investigation to analyze separation and connection more exactly in their belonging together. For the moment it is sufficient to hold on to the fact that the unity of both is already demanded by the interpretation of the social relationship as *négation d'intériorité*.[9]

With the reference to inner negation we have already pushed through to the region of the Sartrian theory of intersubjectivity. As important as the matter is in itself, still, it should only interest us here insofar as it documents the methodologically crucial position of *intériorité* in general and therewith the preeminence of the transcendental approach as opposed to the tendency toward "objective" ontology. However, how this tendency and the schema corresponding to it, of being-in-itself, being-for-itself, and being-for Other (as metamorphoses of being-in-and-for-itself), reflect the influence of *Hegel* is indicated by the transcendental constitution of Sartre's phenomenological ontology, whose sources are *Husserl's* transcendental phenomenology and *Heidegger's* fundamental ontology. It is, indeed, these three that, according to Sartre, have made progress over realism and idealism in the solution of the problem of alien existence. All of them stand out from the tradition, in that they, first, have at least attempted to overcome the approach through external negation and, second, in relation thereto, have envisaged the connection to the Other as a constitutive moment of my consciousness (288:315). That on the second point Hegel goes deeper than Husserl appears to Sartre as the most significant ground on which his procedure can be legitimized, a procedure that consists on the whole in preferring Hegel to Husserl and in creating a place for his social ontology, in the substantive history of the problem, *between* the transcendental theory of intersubjectivity and the analysis of being-with. Still, as can be seen from its grounding, the precedence is not accorded to the representative of the "objective" ontology of totality. Rather, the latter merits the reproach of "ontological optimism," which is supposed to consist in this, that Hegel develops the dialectic of master and slave from without, from the standpoint of a nonparticipating third party, instead of situating himself in one of the individuals and experiencing the Other, as Other, from his point of view (299–300:219). It is also the representative of "objective" ontology who remains behind Heidegger. For Hegel does that, according to Sartre, insofar as he grasps the social relationship as an epistemological relation and so carries over to it the point of view of the nonparticipating third party. In this way, he too slips again into the sphere of external negation. However, in that Heidegger discloses being-with as a relation of being, he is—in spite of all his criticism, Sartre places the greatest weight upon this conclusion—the only one who is genuinely true to the claim of "négation d'intériorité" (300–301:330). His fundamental ontology presents itself accordingly as the purest embodiment of that transcendental philosophy assumed as the model.

So Sartre's determination of being-for-itself reminds one, above all, of Heidegger. At bottom, Sartre carries over to the latter the whole conception of *Dasein* thematized in *Being and Time*. Being-for-itself is essentially being-in-the-world (*être dans le monde*)—and, indeed, precisely in the sense that Heidegger has given to this concept. In the first instance, it does not arise as such in the "world," but is that entity through which, in general, there is world, as the horizon of the appearance of worldly entities. Instead of first going out to the "world" as an "isolated subject," it always maintains itself already along with it. Just as with Heidegger, however, the world relation is carried by the self relation. Even being-for-itself is an "entity that is concerned about this self in its being" (29:24). For it has *to be* what it is (33:28). The being constituted in this way is articulated in the same two moments that are constitutive of *Dasein*: in the transcendence of the project (*projet*) and the facticity of being-in-the-midst-of-the-world (*être au milieu du monde*) (45:89). In this way, being-in-the-midst-of-the-world is, in the original worldliness of consciousness, distinguished from the appearing-in-the-world of objects, just as the facticity of *Dasein* is distinguished from the factuality of the present-at-hand. As a moment of being-in-the-world, it is taken up in the project and already transcended toward possibilities.[10]

The determination of the for-itself, in which Heidegger's characterization of *Dasein* is taken up directly and verbatim, provides, at the same time, a clue to the understanding of those principal concepts of Sartre's that are not already prefigured by Heidegger. The foundation upon which the whole "phenomenological ontology" of *Being and Nothingness*, and so also Sartre's theory of the Other, rests is the thesis that the for-itself (in opposition to the identity of the in-itself with itself) *is* what it *is not*, and *is not* what it *is*. In this thesis, however, the whole of the being-constitution of *Dasein* is played out. In the first instance, it is simply the formula for being-in-the-world, thanks to which *Dasein* already maintains itself alongside those entities that it is not itself, and is with itself only in such being-beyond-itself. The for-itself is what it is not because it is essentially transcendence, that is, outside itself, with that entity that forms it for the world. It *is* this entity insofar as it lives in it and has not itself but only it before itself. In accord therewith, it is not what it is because, in order to be able to be alongside the world, it must always already have abandoned itself as this factical entity. How, therefore, the transcendence of the for-itself consists in this, that it is what it is not, is formulated in the sentence to the effect that it is not what it is, the specifically human-related facticity stamped by that transcendence that, in distinction to the facticity enclosed within itself, only exists as transgressed.

No less questionable than his attachment to Heidegger, and just as openly conceded by Sartre,[11] is his dependence upon Husserl. In the fundamental positions of *Being and Nothingness* it emerges still more strongly. In common with Husserl, Sartre latches onto the Cartesian *cogito* as the point of departure from which, according to his own remarks (301:330), Heidegger does not start out. Sartre repeats yet again Husserl's repetition of the Cartesian account. One would, therefore, misunderstand the entirely self-sufficient character of his transcendental philosophy were one to consider it as a mixture that is put together in equal proportions, so to speak, out of Husserlian phenomenology and Heideggerian fundamental ontology, and that only conveys the appearance of an original vision through the addition of Hegelian dialectic. Rather, Sartre immediately carries forward Husserl's transcendental conception of philosophy. Being-for-itself is *consciousness*. But he carries Husserl's conception forward in this way, that he himself cultivated for the philosophy of consciousness those insights that led Heidegger to the concept of *Dasein* in reaction to the philosophy of consciousness.[12] With a view to repeating Husserl's repetition of the Cartesian account in a more original manner, he therefore, at the same time, repeats Heidegger's step back into the ontological ground of the "I"[13] and the intentionality centered in the "I," but in such a way that he draws back into the sphere of consciousness that ontological ground that Heidegger called "Dasein." In this way, the for-itself is at the root of consciousness and being in one, namely, in being *the* being that is its own Nothingness. In distinction to mere consciousness, the consciousness that posits its object (*conscience positionelle d'objet*), it is itself the nonpositional consciousness of this consciousness (*conscience non positionelle d'elle-même*) or consciousness of itself, that is, *conscience (de) soi* (19–20:13). As this, it is still not a self-consciousness, for it neither has already the structure of intentionality nor yet makes its own I into an object. Precisely for this reason, Sartre brackets the "de" ("of"). Nevertheless, it is, exactly like Heidegger's *Dasein*, the ground of intentionality as well as of the I (20:13, 23–24:17). In other words, it is the original being of intentionality toward which *Being and Nothingness*, fundamentally and as a whole, is directed.

3 The Transformation of the Transcendental Approach at the Level of the Being-for-Me of Others

In the first paragraphs of this chapter we paid attention to the intention underlying Sartre's theory of alien existence. In the second, we sketched out the point of departure for the "ontological phenomenology" developed in *Being and Nothingness* in terms of positions that were immediately relevant to this theory and, in part, already included in it. While the former intention points beyond Husserl's and Heidegger's transcendental account, the latter positions rest wholly and entirely upon this basis. We now have to outline Sartre's theory of alien existence and thereby raise the question, by means of what modifications of the transcendental model Sartre frees himself from the terrain occupied by his predecessors, and whether these modifications suffice for the realization of that intention that can no longer be grasped transcendentally.

In answering this question one has to bear in mind that Sartre only wants to disengage the transcendental duality of worldly objectivity and world-constituting subjectivity from the originally encountered Other and not from the Other in general. So Sartre distinguishes an originally and a nonoriginally encountered Other. Only the former is supposed to be neither an object in the world nor a subject for the world, while, in contrast, the latter is, in his view, both.

According to *Being and Nothingness*, as we all know, the Other encounters me only in my being-for-him or my "being looked at," while the being-for-me of the Other looked at by me affords simply a derivative alien experience. However, in that Sartre calls the one looking at me the "subject-Other" and the one looked at by me the "object-Other," he runs into the misunderstanding that even he remains in the framework of transcendental duality. The impression could be given that he divides objectness in the world and subjectness for the world, which, with Husserl and Heidegger, belong to *one* experience, exclusively into two different experiences. Nevertheless, this is by no means the case. For the subject-Other is, according to Sartre, certainly the only real alien subjectivity (314:344), but he is not a subject for the world. The world is not his object, but I am. If this does not present a genuine alternative for Husserl, it is only because for him, the fact that the Other perceives me is only a special case of the all-encompassing situation in which the Other perceives the things of the world. By contrast, it is precisely Sartre's greatest service to social philosophy that he should have made it clear that the experience of the Other who is directed toward me is essentially to be distinguished from the lived experience of that cohuman being who is preoccupied with things.

This essential distinction is that between my being-for-the-Other and the being-for-me of the Other. For the latter reveals the Other to me continually as the one who is concerned about it and about the things surrounding me. The object-Other and he alone is therefore a subject for the world. Only, on the plane of the being-for-me of the Other—this is Sartre's thesis—alien subjecthood is interwoven with alien objecthood (313:343). To this extent one may say that, on this plane, on which the difference between the alien object in the world and the alien subject for the world really belongs, Sartre does not do justice to this difference. The difference is leveled down in that the subject for the world is at bottom only an object in the world.

We next want to see how Sartre establishes the objectness of the alien subject that is oriented toward things. He does not arrive at this thesis through an intellectual operation, but through one that precedes all intellectual operations, one that consists in a modification (hardly thematized by him at all) of that spatial schema that, with Husserl, lies at the root of the initial relation of ego and alter ego. With Husserl, my primordial ego and the alien primordial ego stand, so to speak, at an equal height. In this equality of level, the world whose middle point I am and the world whose middle point the alter ego is form two circles, which only partly overlap. Sartre, on the contrary, represents the alien world as one circle that lies within the compass of my world circle. This means that, along with the things that we see in common, even if not in the same way, entities that I alone see make their appearance, but not entities that the Other alone sees. Certainly this last possibility is also taken for granted by Sartre, as by everyone else, but for all that it is excluded by the basic premises of the theory. Indeed, the validity of the thesis defended by Sartre hangs upon the exclusion of this possibility. For only because, over and beyond what the Other also sees, I see still more without the Other, who, for his part, is able to fall back on something not seen by me, the equality of level collapses into my superiority vis-à-vis the Other. And only because the world of the alien I is included within the limits of my world can it become for me, in a certain respect, as much an object as the purely objective alien (physical) body that is anchored at a particular point in space. Insofar as the Other, as well as the thing looked at by him, lies in my field of vision, the relationship to the thing that the Other unfolds is also given to me in its entirety and therefore as an object (312:342). The subjectness of those cohuman beings that arise as objects in my world is for Sartre, however, and in accordance with his account, nothing else but the alien being-in-the-world that is concretized in that relationship. Thus the alien subjectivity has itself become an object.

To be sure, the objective givenness is only *one* side of the being-for-me of the relation obtaining between the objectively given Other and the things of my world. The other side is that in my being-in-the-world, which comprehends the being-in-the-world of that Other whose subjectness is still present, the object-Other stands for a subject-object and not for a pure subject. Insofar, namely, as the world relation of that Other looked at by me is carried by its subjectness, it escapes me (312:342, see also 183–184:210). With this expression, Sartre aims at the same state of affairs—as his explicit description indicates (311–314:341–344)—as that which also with Husserl guarantees the alienness of the alien I, or the other subject in its subjectness. The relationship of the Other appearing before me to its object escapes me because I certainly also see this object, but not in the same way that the Other sees it. The difference between my and the alien system of appearances is grounded, however, in the difference of the standpoints that I and the Other take up. From the standpoint of the Other, the world is put together differently than from my own point of view. Even here Sartre agrees with Husserl. However, the paths of the two thinkers diverge as soon as it is a question of the interpretation of the phenomenon. With Husserl, the distinctiveness of the worlds underlines the worldliness of the world. By means of the empathically executed identification of the systems of appearances, my still subjective world takes on the character of the objective, now for the first time genuinely worldly, world. Sartre, in his debate with Husserl, places a special emphasis upon this (288:315). He himself, however, draws the opposite consequence, that, thanks to his own world relation, the Other takes my world away from me. He, the Other, has "stolen the world from me," and this already because the very same objects that I arrange around myself are, on his side, oriented toward him. So he decenters the world centered on me. For this reason, Sartre can liken the object-Other to a hole that is bored somewhere in my world and through which this world gradually and irregularly runs away.

On Husserl's basis the flowing away of the world could be picked up in such a way that in empathy I make the world relation of the Other into my own. For Sartre, however, that is no longer possible. In his opinion, I cannot place myself at the center of the alien world. The basis of this possibility lies in his holding consistently to *intériorité*, which does not permit a circumvention of the separateness of individuals through the insinuation of my ego into the Other. What remains is simply the radical and reciprocal exclusion. As *négation d'intériorité*, the relationship to the lawn of the man going for a walk over there excludes right away my similarly interior relationship to this lawn. So it also negates the relation that I establish as a *négation externe* between the man-object and the lawn-object. Absolutely irreconcilable (namely, with the objective distance that I measure out between the exchangeable members of this external relation), the Other exists in a distantless relationship with the lawn, which at the same time unfolds its own distance from the Other to the lawn.

While, with Husserl, the removal of the alien system of appearances is overcome through the identification of the ego in the Other with my own ego, according to Sartre, only the ensnarement of the other subject in the object puts a stop to the running away of my world. So he can say that the running away of my world is "entirely hemmed in and localized" because "the dissolution of my universe is itself contained within the boundaries of this universe." Still, according to Sartre's own interpretation, and in the spirit of other statements, this expression is subject to correction by him. Namely, it fails to attain the full truth, for the reason that it hardly does justice to the contradictory character of the object-Other as a subject-object. In the object-Other, subjectness is certainly interwoven with objectness, and, insofar as that is the case, the alien being-in-the-world that is responsible for the running away of my world is, in fact, at the same time included in this world of mine, which is my universal object. Insofar, however, as the alien subjectness is the ownmost being of the Other as a nothing, it cannot be interwoven with objectness, which means that the running away of my world cannot, in the final analysis, be limited. The limitation is a mere appearance, which I can only maintain so long as I confine the effectiveness of the alien subject to its purely momentary actuality. Correspondingly, Sartre remarks in the passage given above that the alien world relationship appears to me only "*like* a *partial* structure of the world*," although, *as a matter of fact*, it is a question of "a *total* dissolution of the universe" (italics are mine). Still, the Other is in no way tied down by the relationship to the lawn that is precisely now— or so it seems—looked at by him. Already in this relationship, and in a way that is not transparent to me, the entire surrounding world is brought into play as an unthematic background. Suddenly, and in a way that cannot be foreseen by me, the alien can, however, also turn to other things and so alienate me even more from my world, bit by bit. The dissolution of my world proceeds continually forward. Only thanks to an unconscious disregard for the potentiality of the alien world can the representation of its limitedness and objective givenness therefore be maintained. In this way, there does not transpire, in reality, the latent totality of the shattering of my world.

The questionableness that attaches to the limiting localization of the running out of my world shows that the alien subject cannot really be brought into the object-world. Again, this proves that the experience of the subjectness of the object-Other is by no means contained originally in the experience of the object-Other, but only instates the memory (brought over into the object-world) of a quite different experience, that of the subject-Other (357). By this is meant: I must already have had the experience of the subject-Other in order to be able to have the experience of the object-Other. I must have been seen by the Other in order to be able to see him as Other. Although the understanding for the subjectness of the object-Other, supplied by the experience of the subject-Other, is at bottom incompatible with the object experience, still the experience of the object-Other owes to it its peculiarity precisely by contrast with all experience of things that are nothing but objects. The result: "Being seen by the Other" is the *truth* of "seeing the Other" (315:345). What makes the Other who is seen by me into an Other lies not on the plane on which I see him but, more precisely, in the deeper and more original dimension in which I am seen by him.

4 The Undermining of the Transcendental Approach through the Regression to My Being-for-Others

In this way we are referred back from the being-for-me of the Other itself to my being-for-the-Other. Something of the essence of this original alien experience dawns on us when we enquire a little more exactly into the mode of this reference. In accordance with what was said before, the dependent, not self-sufficient, object-Other, due to just such a dependence, points to the subject-Other as its truth and as that which sustains it. But does not Sartre say exactly the opposite? Both kinds of presence of the Other, so he thinks, are self-sufficing and also only refer to themselves (357:389). The contradiction is apparent. However, it obtains not between one of Sartre's statements and the interpretation just carried through, but between Sartre's own expressions. Sartre explicitly confirms "that my apprehension of the Other as an object . . . refers back essentially to a fundamental grasp of the Other, where the Other no longer manifests himself to me as an object but as a 'presence in person' " (310:340). Certainly he turns against the "classical theory" (310:340) and Husserl's theory (314:344), following which the body of the Other that is seen by me refers to a separate consciousness situated behind it. However, what he criticizes there are only the terms of the reference, not the reference itself. So little does he attack the latter that he appears to be much more of the opinion that in the reference from the object-Other to the subject-Other he has found that which the tradition, misled by the duality of present body and absent consciousness, pursued in the wrong direction.

When, in spite of this, Sartre emphasizes the self-sufficiency of both modes of presence of the Other, he does so primarily on two grounds. In the first place, with regard to their supposedly radical distinction. He draws attention to this precisely there where he follows up the questionable reference. The object-Other refers "to a fundamental link, where the Other manifests himself otherwise than by the knowledge which I have of him" (310:340). Correspondingly, the sudden change from the object to the subject-Other is "a radical conversion of the Other" (314:344). The subject-Other only appears on the basis of a total destruction of the object-Other (358:391). So the reference of the object- to the subject-Other cannot in any case have the meaning of an analogy that leads from a given to a cogiven that is similar to it. If one understands reference in this way, then one must, of course, say that the object-Other refers only to itself and not to the subject-Other. The very reference that can alone be at issue here is, however, in no way excluded thereby: the reference back of the object-Other to the subject-Other (essentially pregiven to him) whose alien consciousness is not, as with Husserl, merely indirectly experienced from the alien body, but was present before any indicative relation with a directness that infinitely surpasses that of the object-Other. But if one asks how the radical difference between object- and subject-Other can be affirmed over against the transposition of subjectness from the latter to the former, Sartre, without any satisfactory ground, can only reply that subjectness itself undergoes a complete metamorphosis in this transposition: "The Other could not look at me as he looks at the lawn" (314:343). This answer seems unsatisfactory above all else because it glosses over the fact that the use of the subject concept on both planes of the alien personal present presupposes a common character lying at the root of all difference. Insofar as the object-Other has borrowed its suppressed subjectivity from the subject-Other, it cannot be as autarchic as the latter, which can be so because, in accordance with Sartre's intention, it has no objectness about it.

The second reason that clearly impels Sartre to affirm the self-sufficiency of both modes of presence in reality only bears upon the thesis about the autarchy of the subject-Other with respect to the object-Other. It lies in the specific alien personal facticity of being-seen, the facticity that, according to the introductory paragraph of this chapter, is supposed, at the same time, to attest to the originality of the encounter with the subject-Other. The subject-Other cannot be derived from the object-Other because "being-seen-by-the-Other" stands for an "irreducible fact" (314–315:345). For, that the Other, whose look—to stay with Sartre's example—still rests upon the lawn, now suddenly looks at me is a matter of the alien freedom and thereby precisely not of one's own. I cannot circumvent the being-seen-by-the-Other. It takes me over without my consent.

It is this total passivity that separates the experience of the subject-Other from that of the object-Other. That being-seen-by-the-Other is related to the seeing of the Other as passion to action seems to be self-evident, to be sure, and to require no explanation. Still, for all theoreticians of alien existence oriented toward empathy, this is not at all self-evident. Even Husserl changes the being-seen-by-the-Other by means of empathy into an indirect act of the I. Blind to the qualitative difference between the act of the Other directed toward things and that directed toward me, he believes it to be possible to carry through the latter in an empathic transposition of the self into the standpoint of the Other, just as fundamentally as the former. Admittedly what, in that case, is merely mediately experienced is not really this, that I am seen by the Other, but that the Other sees me. With Sartre, on the contrary, and once again strictly in line with the methodological principle of *intériorité*, it is really only a question of being seen. Following his conception, I do not go out of myself in order then, with the Other, to accede to myself. Rather, I simply suffer the coming-to-me of the Other. With the experience of the subject-Other, therefore, it is at bottom not at all a matter of an experience of the alien subject but of my objectness, in which alone the subjectness of the Other will be perceptible to me (314).

Everything that will be said in what follows on the Sartrian approach to social ontology can, in the final analysis, only be an interpretation of the meaning of my objectness. In the securing and clarification of the simple fact that I am an object for the Other without the Other being my object, two things are accomplished by Sartre: the partial realization of the goal set out at the beginning, that of overcoming the world-"world" difference constitutive for transcendental philosophy, and the falling away from this goal, as the falling back upon the fundamental position of the transcendental theory of intersubjectivity.

I would like to elucidate, with a few examples, to what an extent Sartre, starting out from my being-for-the-Other, is at all permitted to hope to be able to realize his leading intention. This will be done with the help of the analysis of shame, in which Sartre, at the beginning of his investigation into the for-Other, whose basic theme sounds and is played through for the first time as in an overture (275–277:301–303), sketches out the connection between my objective being and the envisaged immediacy. Sartre pins down the two terms of this connection as sharply as one could ever wish for. The first thing that, in his opinion, has to be said about shame is that in it I am an object for the Other: "It is as an object that I appear to the Other." The second is that, as a feeling, shame discloses an immediate affectedness: "Shame is an immediate shudder that runs through me from head to foot without any discursive preparation."

To be sure, the connection itself is still not explained by this. Its explanation first requires proof of one still unverified thesis in accordance with which the Other whose object I am is not my object. Testimony on behalf of immediacy is provided by the complete passivity of my objectness. That by which Husserl makes my being-seen into a sheerly mediate experience is the weakening of the passivity of my being-seen through the action of empathy in the alien act. When, on the contrary, I endure my being-seen inactively, without breaking out into the alien action center in a quasi activity, I then feel immediately, that is, stripped of the medium of the practical project, the presence of the Other resting on me. Only, such a passivity—as is evident— presupposes the nonobjectivity of the Other who looks at me. Sartre has to clear this up if he wants to uncover the immediacy of the encounter with the subject-Other. He then, for the first time, touches upon immediacy in the specific meaning of the nonmediatedness of the world. That which does not appear as an inner-worldly entity in the horizon of my world project, that which therefore is not my object, is, namely, not mediated by the world.

Likewise, Sartre can only subscribe to the immediacy of the experience of the subject-Other in that, in conjunction therewith, he verifies everything that, in accordance with the introductory paragraphs of this chapter, he still strives for. Including therein above all is the "absolute evidence" that is supposed to adhere to my being-for-the-Other, even though it is only an "irreducible fact." This has also to be clarified because I can only say that I feel the presence of the subject-Other immediately when I experience it immediately as that of the Other and am able to become fully aware of the Other in it—regardless of the fact that I do not posit him objectively as Other. On the basis of *Being and Nothingness*, however, the project of the original certainty of alien existence can, for its part, only be secured through the confirmation of the thesis just announced at the start, following which the factically encountered Other is turned into a transcendent *constituens*, a "concrete and individual condition" of my being. For, thanks to experience alone, my being an object, as the undeniable presence of the *Other*, informs me that therein I myself become *something other* without becoming this through myself, or at least only with my assistance.

The proof of immediacy therefore demands from Sartre at the same time that of the nonobjectness of the subject-Other as well as that of the absolute evidence of the alien-personal presence. This demand is met by demonstrating that the subject-Other constitutes me in my being. Sartre fulfills this requirement, at least in part, by investigating the formal structure of shame. In its formal structure, shame is—or so he determines with unquestionable propriety—a becoming-ashamed-of-oneself-before-the-Other. Therein we find, to start off with, the nonobjectness of the Other before whom I am ashamed. For I am myself the necessary object of shame, and, indeed, in such a way that my objectness prohibits that of the Other. The Other cannot be my object because he is, so to speak, the forum before which I become aware of myself, or the tribunal before which I feel myself to be called. He is the light in which I see myself. But for that very reason he is not someone that I see myself.

In the second place, the formal structure of shame attests to the Other as the concrete and individual condition of my being. For the I that I am ashamed of is, first of all, posited by the Other before whom I am ashamed. As long as I remain alone, shame cannot arise in me because not only is the one before whom I am ashamed lacking but also the one I can be ashamed of. I must be seen by the Other in order to experience shame, that is, be ashamed of the one whom the Other sees. This is the peculiarity of the phenomenon: that the object of my shame is not I as existing for myself but I insofar as I am *for the Other*, and therefore am constituted by him. The Other "constitutes me in a new type of being"; he conditions me in the very being that he brings to light. In that he, in contrast with my earlier being, makes me into an Other in this way, the experience of shame serves, in the third place, as a guarantor for the absolute evidence of the alien personal presence.

Finally, insight into the alien constitutive operation strengthens the thesis of immediacy that is already supported by the knowledge of the nonobjectness of the subject-Other. Sartre says in our text that, in its originality, shame is not a reflexive phenomenon and cannot be such because the presence of the Other, expressed in the determination "before," cannot be reconciled with the reflexive attitude. He acquires the right to this affirmation through the above-mentioned state of affairs, in accordance with which the I that I am ashamed of is not that which exists for me, but that which appears to the Other. The exclusion of reflection follows from the exclusion of being-for-me. The negation of reflection is, however, the establishment of immediacy. We shall see in a moment, at the beginning of the next section, how immediacy as unreflectedness is imprinted upon the character of shame.

However, alongside this negative signification, and alongside the equally negative signification that it shares with the nonobjectness of the subject-Other, immediacy also receives a positive signification from the justification of it that has been given here. In our investigation, the concept of "immediacy" has a negative meaning in that the Other is mediated neither by the world nor by me. The nonmediatedness of the world lies in its nonobjectness. The Husserlian doctrine of the mediation of the Other through myself, however, is turned into its opposite by Sartre in the theory that the *Other* mediates *me with myself.* As the concrete and individual condition of my being, the Other is—this is what the description of shame means—the indispensable medium between me, the one who is ashamed, and myself, as the one who is first brought to light by him as the object of my shame.

5 My Objectification through the Other as a Fall into the Present-at-Hand

The Other "constitutes me in a new type of being," in that he makes me into his object. This type of being, however, is not new because

I am the object of the Other but because I am now, for the first time, an object at all. For, in being-for-me, I cannot, according to Sartre, be brought before myself as an object, not even through reflection, which never attains the plane of real objectness. In order to be able to observe myself as an object, I must receive myself, so to speak, out of the hands of the Other. Sartre characterizes the act of this acceptance as "*recognition.*" In it I recognize that, as the object of the Other, I am not *only* for the Other, that is, that I actually am just as the Other sees me: "I recognize that I am as the Other sees me" (276:302).[14]

How far Sartre distances himself from Husserl through his insistence upon immediacy will become particularly clear here. For, while that self-objectification made possible by the Other that concerns Husserl is the most mediated act in which I carry over to myself the alien "representation of myself," Sartre, with the reference to the recognitive character of shame, wants to avert just such a transposition. In recognition I do not compare the subjective picture that the Other makes of me with my factical being as it presents itself for me (276:302).

This is at the same time the very point on which Sartre, in spite of everything, falls in with the line of thought leading from Husserl: in the thought that I first become a *genuine object* through the Other, an object, namely, in the sense of something *present-at-hand*. The genuineness of this object consists in this, that it is something that actually makes its appearance, that is present-at-hand. In that I am the object that I am for the Other not only for the Other but purely and simply in itself, I am, for Sartre as well as for Husserl, present-at-hand as an object through the Other. With the objectification undergone in being-seen, I lapse at the same time into facticity as presence-at-hand.

The addition "as presence-at-hand" is necessary in order to distinguish the facticity that first comes over me in the presence of the Other from the facticity that my consciousness always already possesses. These two kinds of facticity, the original facticity of the for-itself and that which is introduced by being-for-Other, have to be kept strictly apart. In a certain respect, the enormous change that takes place in me through my objectification stands for nothing other than the lapse of the facticity of being-for-itself into the facticity of the present-at-hand.

The former—as already indicated in the sketch of the Sartrian account—is wholly and entirely determined in the following manner:

that, as consciousness, I am not what I am and am what I am not. Because I am what I am not, that is, given over as transcendence to worldly beings, I am not what I am, that is, I do not abide with myself as a factical entity or within the limits of my being-present-at-hand. As caught up in transcendence, the facticity of the for-itself manifests itself in a continual "self-sundering" (359:395) of consciousness from its facticity qua presence-at-hand. In being-for-myself I exist at all times beyond my factical being and am precisely in this way saturated by my facticity.

The facticity of being-for-Other is quite different. Seen by the Other, I am, according to Sartre's analysis of shame, ashamed of the commonness of my behavior. The latter did not appear to me before as common because I was not confronted with it at all. I was not confronted with it because I existed in the mode of having to be it, therefore in such a way that, at the same time, I was not it. Under the look of the Other, however, I become aware of the commonness of my behavior because I am now suddenly confronted with myself and, indeed, in the same way that the Other is confronted with me. The Other is confronted with me, however, as that which I am, as an entity that has sunk down into an identity with itself. I am for him only the one who behaves commonly and nothing over and beyond that. Since, however, I am not simply what I am not, but also really am what I am, in that I am not it, I have to recognize myself as being identical with myself and as having become, for this reason, an objective entity. I, who am not what I am, am now what I am: "In order to be what I am, it is sufficient that the Other look at me"(320:351). When Sartre says, "I recognize that I am how Others see me," the "am" has the being-sense of a present-at-hand that is identical with itself. For the Other, and on the basis of him for myself also, I am "anyone" (322:354), any something. The Other drives me back to factical being-there and compels me to tear myself away from it or to "negate"—in Sartre's terminology—what makes up the "first ex-stasy" of the for-itself or the self-constitution of consciousness (359:395). The Other seizes the for-itself in its "flight" (428–430:502–504) from that which it is factically and posits it as imprisoned in its facticity—the flight itself, which is one with the original movement of consciousness, is "congealed through and through by facticity" (429:504).

Now, that entity that is what it is is an "in-itself," Sartre is not even afraid of the conclusion that the event of being-seen should be interpreted as the "solidification" (502:574)[15] of the for-itself into an in-itself. Already with the paradigmatic analysis of shame, he speaks of the "in-itself that I am for the Other" (276:302). Where he then posits the recognition of shame in conjunction with the acceptance of the fact that I am what I am, he takes up this expression once again in a sharper and more emphatic form: I am the being that the Other makes me over into, not "in the mode of the was or of 'having to be' but in-itself" (320:351).[16] I am what I am, I am factically present-at-hand, I am an in-itself—all these are articulations of the meaning of my objectivity. Being an object means being-in-itself (446:491).[17] This equation becomes clear when one notes that the Other makes me into an object in that he bestows properties—predicative and adequate to judgment or prepredicative—upon me. In this way he grasps me as that substance that underlies properties, that is, as an in-itself; "The qualification wicked . . . characterizes me as an in-itself" (322:353).

The thesis in accordance with which being-for-Other changes being-for-itself into being-in-itself provides, in Sartre's own words, the key to the entire investigation into the Other (322:353). Indeed, in the final analysis, it even answers the fundamental question underlying the entire ontology projected in *Being and Nothingness*. For its most pressing problem is the possibility of establishing an original relation of the for-itself to the quite differently constituted in-itself. So toward the end of the section on the *for-Other*, Sartre can say, "So we have made progress in our investigation: we wanted to determine the original relation of the for-itself to the in-itself. We learned first that the for-itself was the annihilation and radical negation of the in-itself; at present we affirm that, solely on account of the competition of the Other and without any contradiction, it is totally in-itself, present in the midst of the in-itself" (502:555).

To be sure, the rendering intelligible of the thesis brought to the fore in this way must bring with it certain difficulties. Sartre characterizes the for-itself, the in-itself, and the for-Other quite generally as three irreducible "modes of being" whose reciprocal independence also pre-supposes the ultimate goal to be attained, that is, the "metaphysical theory of being in general." In particular, however, Sartre also expressly brings to light the separateness of my being-for-Others from being-in-itself. He says of my objectivity, "This being is not in-itself, for it does not manifest itself in the pure exteriority of indifference; but it is not for-itself either, for it is not the being that I have to be in annihilating myself. It is precisely my being-for-Others" (347:381). Being-for-Others therefore is, and is not, being-in-itself. The formal, abstract dissolution of this contradiction lies in the simple fact that the in-itself, qua being-for-Other, is the in-itself of a for-itself. Being-for-Others is the specific way in which the for-itself participates in the in-itself. To this extent, it is being-in-itself and yet not a *pure* being-In-itself. Rather, according to Sartre, it is the desired bond of the for-itself and the in-itself (428:502).

This conclusion, in its abstractness, simply points to a "task"; it still does not contain the concrete solution of the problem. It remains to ask how the complete, heterogeneous modes of being of the for-itself and the in-itself can be bound together in being-for-Other. The question is all the more pressing as being-for-Other does not simply stand for the neutral middle between both remaining modes of being, but leans decisively to the side of being-in-itself, Sartre emphasizes its difference from being-for-itself frequently (322:363, 342:375, 367–368:403), but its difference from the in-itself, on the contrary—so far as I can see— is only indicated in the place referred to above.

If being-for-Others were not in itself a being-for-itself, it would only be affected by the latter inasmuch as it is *my* being: "a being who is *my* being without being-for-me" (275:301). In contrast, being-in-itself is, as we know, the transphenomenal being of the *things* that appear in the *outer world*. The question concerning the concrete unification of the for-itself and the in-itself in being-for-Others therefore reads, How can being-for-Others be the being of a worldly thing and still be my being? The answer thereto lies in Sartre's determination of that very worldliness brought over to me from the Other.

6 My Objectification through the Other as Mundanization and Humanization

At first glance, the sudden transformation of the facticity of the for-itself into the facticity of the present-at-hand, a change that enters into my being-for-Others, appears as the loss of my transcendence. Only the loss of my transcendence can, or so it appears, nail me down to my factical being, that being over and beyond which I existed in my being-for-myself, precisely on account of my transcendence. Numerous formulations in *Being and Nothingness* agree therewith. The possibility of the Other "negates my transcendence" (326:358). "The Other is the secret death of my possibilities" (323:354). Through the look of the Other, my own look is "stripped of its transcendence" (324:355). It is, however, the loss of transcendence that equates me with things in the world. For precisely this distinguishes the being-in-itself of things from the being-for-itself of consciousness: that, instead of being present to the Other, it remains in itself void of transcendence: "For the Other, I am seated like this inkwell is on the table; for the Other, I am leaning over the hole in the lock, like this tree is bent by the wind. So, for the Other, I am stripped of my transcendence" (320–321:352).

But these expressions still do not touch the real issues. Certainly, with my being-seen it is a matter of a peculiar depotentiation of transcendence, but not of its loss. Were my transcendence to be entirely lost, then certainly my physicalization would be demonstrated, but so equally would be the dissolution of my being. However, that, in the presence of the Other, transcendence does not simply fall away from me is proved by the phenomenon of fear thematized by Sartre in this connection. Fear is, for Sartre, alongside shame, which is still aligned with pride, one of the basic modes in which I experience myself as an object for the Other. If shame and pride are determined as the feeling of "being in the end what I am but elsewhere and for the Other," then fear appears as the "feeling of being in danger with respect to the freedom of the Other" (326:358).

In what does the danger consist? According to Sartre, it already consists in my being looked at. My entire being-in-the-world is offered up to the Other and not only my bodily concretized facticity is turned into an object, but equally my transcendence or freedom. Freedom itself becomes a "given object" (319:350, see also 429:350). It becomes this in that my transcendence is transcended by the Other. The subject-Other is nothing other than "my transcendence transcended" (321:352). As transcended, however, my transcendence is not simply abolished but, so to speak, only crippled. In the pursuit situation from which Sartre reads off the structure of fear and, over and beyond that, being-for-Others in general, the Other who pursues me transcends my transcendence, in that he foresees the possibilities that I could project for myself and takes them over for his own. In this way, however, my possible actions are nipped in the bud even before they are realized. So I may arrive at the idea of fleeing from the look of the Other in some dark corner of the corridor. But this idea is already crippled by the representation of those possibilities of the Other directed toward my capture, for example, to light up the corner with his table lamp in order then to be able to seize me more securely (321–323:352–353). This all takes place in the suddenness and simplicity of the immediate. Not that I first think out possibilities from which I later withdraw, due to empathy into the possibilities of the Other. Rather, everything is already to be found in the awareness of that presence of the Other that bears down upon me: the thought of flight, the presentiment of the alien reaction, and the sinking down of the thought of flight in anticipation of this reaction.

Ontologically, the crippling or coagulation of my possibilities is to be interpreted as the encroachment of my facticity upon my transcendence.[18] Transcendence (in the for-itself the surpassing and therefore the overpowering of facticity) occurs as for its part surpassed by the power of facticity: it "is congealed through and through by facticity." But being-for-Others remains *my being* in spite of all physicalization. Even though the looked-at transcendence also shares with things the fate of being taken over, its facticity is to be distinguished from the facticity of a fact lacking transcendence in that it is surpassed *surpassing*. On the one hand, to be sure, being surpassed destroys the surpassing. On the other hand, however, the surpassing remains in the being surpassed as a *living death*. For this reason, Sartre calls the death of my possibilities a "subtle death": "Subtle death, for my possibility of hiding still remains *my* possibility; inasmuch as I am it, it still lives" (322:354).

In order to illustrate this and the consequences drawn from it, it is helpful to bear in mind the spatial model on which Sartre orients his theory of being-for-Others. I have already pointed out[19] the schema that lies at the root of Sartre's representation of the *being-for-me of the Other*. If I, as subject, look at the Other, as object, then, according to this schema, I am the superordinate and the Other is the subordinate. This follows from the inclusion of the alien in my world. The Other who stands *beneath* me at the same time stands before me. Insofar as he is an object, I have him *before* me. On the contrary, the subject-Other is to be found neither before me, like an object, nor alongside me, like my companions in the community of the we, nor opposite me, as my peer partners. Rather, he is behind me: more exactly, coming *from behind me*. And in this position he is at the same time *superior* to me. He is no longer, like the object-Other, sub-, but super-ordinate, that is, he deals with me *from above.*[20]

This model also makes it easier to understand the Sartrian statements on the transformation of my worldliness brought about by the subject-Other. Insofar as I project the world in transcendence, there lies in the depotentiation of my transcendence a peculiar *demundanization*: "But the presence of the Other in his looking look cannot contribute to a reinforcement of the world. On the contrary, it demundanizes it, for it is responsible for the fact that the world eludes me" (331:363–364). In the look of the object-Other I already had to experience the fact that the world eludes me. While here, however, I could still believe that the flowing away of my world was localizable, and for this reason only relative, my being-for-the Other forced me to the view that the Other takes the world away from me *altogether.* I can no longer conceal from myself the fact that the flowing away of my world is limitless and cannot be brought to a halt (331:364). This becomes immediately clear from a comparison of the spatial situation of the being-for-me of the Other and my being-for-the-Other. Even through the object-Other my world flowed away because the things to which this Other was directed turned toward him a side that was turned away from me. The metaphor "flowing away" has the meaning of being-turned-away-from-me just as much here where what is in question is my being looked at (319). Still, two significant distinctions should be taken account of. First, already here in the actual moment it is no longer only a small circle of objects that is affected by my *entire* world. The Other who hounds me down from behind and follows me from above with his look overlooks, thanks to his higher standpoint, my entire world and even looks over and beyond it. He has a wider horizon than I. Second, my entire world is so radically affected, however, by its being surpassed that its *meaning* goes over from me to the Other. The same things that display an inaccessible side to the *object*-Other nevertheless are still offered to my eyes from another side. They are in a similar manner objects for me and for the Other. Things offer themselves to the *subject*-Other, however, wholly and unreservedly, even though they also only turn a particular side toward him, to the extent that they leave no other side over for me. The objectivity that the Other confers upon things necessarily brings with it, since he also confers it upon me, the destruction of every objectivity that exists for me: "The look of the Other, as the necessary condition of my objectivity, is the destruction of all objectivity for me" (328:361). For objects can only be things for me thanks to my world project, which is the very thing that has sunk into impotence with the objectification of my transcendence.

What now, however, appears as demundanization, in the light of impotent transcendence, shows itself to be mundanization in another sense of "world" under the aspect of sinking into facticity. Precisely for this reason that the world that I am able to project freely gradually disappears, I myself am turned into something worldly. Therefore Sartre determines my being-for-the-Other more closely as "being-in-the-midst-of-the-world-for-Others" (224:356) This title says more than simply this, that the Other comes upon me in the world. It is supposed to bring to expression the fact that, first and foremost, the Other runs up against me in the world. My lapse into the universe of inner-worldly beings, a lapse incited by the alien subject, is, according to Sartre, the genuine "fall from grace." The guilt feeling of shame is related to it and not to any other particular failing, and extends just as well to my objectivity as to the fact that "I have fallen into the world, into the midst of things" (349:384; see also 509).

This being-in-the-midst-of-the-world (être-au-milieu-du-monde), this "being-a-piece-of-the-world" (as Alexa Wagner sensitively translates it[21]), that is first forced upon me by the Other is distinguished from the original worldliness of consciousness in exactly the same way as the facticity identical with my objectivity is distinguished from the facticity of the for-itself. It is therefore not only distinct from the being-in-the-midst-of-the-world that is a world-projecting transcendence (348) but also from that being-in-the-midst-of-the-world that Heidegger names "thrownness." For thrownness does not exist without the project. The project, however, is crippled precisely by that being-in-the-midst-of-the-world founded in the alien personal. Hence the original being-in-the-midst-of-the-world is also altered. Above all, it loses the centrality that came to it in connection with the project that posits deseverance. So the world in which I find myself on account of the Other is the alien world, which can only be mine in the mode of alienation (319:350; see also 322). In it, however, I am not the midpoint, but something or other at some point on the periphery. For this reason, in the experience of being seen, I become aware "that I am located at a particular point" (316:348). Instead of orienting the surrounding things—table, chair, and walls—with regard to myself and being with them in the mode of approach or withdrawal, I now stand "near" the table in the same way that the table stands near the chair, and indeed solely and exclusively on the basis of the fact that the Other looks at me among these things. I, the "spatializer," am now "spatialized." This is what is meant by the sentence, "The look of the Other confers spatiality upon me" (325:357). In this purely mundane sense the Other equally bestows temporality upon me. He orders me in world time in that he provides me with the lived experience of "simultaneity" (326:357). In the way that Sartre grasps this concept,[22] the for-itself alone cannot experience "simultaneity." There it is not beings in time that are simultaneous but the times themselves, that is, my and the alien temporality. In the experience of simultaneity, understood in this way, my own temporality is, however, alienated from me into a "universal present in which I take up my place." For, in my temporalizing, the Other arises as the one who temporalizes me. Through his presence alongside me, I, the temporalizing, become, by the same token, the temporalized—temporalized, however, in a system that is not grounded in my subjectivity and, to that extent, refers to an objective time. Temporalized and spatialized, I am then the world object that the Other sees me as being, a "spatiotemporal object of the world" (326:358).

Objectivation, mundanization, physicalization, integration in space and time—it is clear that Sartre herewith describes the same movement to which, with Husserl, my absolute, unique ego succumbs through the alter ego. This agreement is underscored by the fact that, with both thinkers, the path, marked out by these concepts, also has the same goal: the intersubjective constitution of human being. Human being, according to *Being and Nothingness*, is the for-itself that is also for-Others and was made into a spatiotemporally localizing object in the world by the Other. Since being-for-Others does not, according to Sartre, stand for an "ontological structure of the for-itself," even without being-for-Others the latter would be for-itself, but it would not be human. It is, however, as a matter of fact, human being. As "factical," the necessity of being-for-Others is therefore grounded not in the essence of the for-itself, but solely in the fact that "our human reality demands that it be simultaneously for-itself and for-Others" (342:376). It is only the complete grasping of being human that, in *Being and Nothingness*, demands in general the progression from the for-itself to the for-Others. (275:301). So we have before us the peculiar state of affairs that Sartre already confers upon the for-itself the original facticity of being-in-the-midst-of-beings that constitutes the humanness of "*Dasein*" in Heidegger's sense and that he nevertheless turns back to Husserl's formulation, in accordance with which consciousness first then becomes human when the Other forces upon it the facticity of the inner-worldly present-at-hand.

7 My Objectification through the Other as Alter-ation

The agreement between Husserl's theory of intersubjectivity and the guiding idea of the Sartrian theory of being-for-Others goes deeper still. Sartre grasps the objectification of consciousness, just as explicitly as Husserl, as a depotentiation that is disclosed in its positive form as alter-ation. The I bestowed upon me by the Other is a "degraded consciousness," and my being-for-the-Other is exhibited as "my being-Other" (322:353). Alter-ation itself Sartre grasps in a concept of "alienation" (*Entfremdung*) already related to Husserl, that of "alienation" (*aliénation*) (321:352, 334:367). The reality of the Other is "alienating reality" purely and simply (441:506).

To be sure, it is in modified form that Husserl's alter-ation idea returns in Sartre. On the one hand, it is abbreviated. So, on the basis of the Sartrian ontology, there is no room for the alter-ation that persists in the transcendental sphere, for the transformation of my absolute, unique ego into myself as member of the community of monads. Sartre only acknowledges the mundanizing alter-ation, and even this appears more impoverished with him than with Husserl because—in conformity with the general conception of his social ontology—it can only be in its origin a substantializing, and still not a personalizing, alter-ation. (We shall soon see where, in accordance with his project, the personalizing alter-ation is to be located.) On the other hand, Sartre's doctrine of alien existence first brings the Husserlian alter-ation idea to an awareness of itself. In particular, the orientation toward the immediacy of my being-for-Others frees it from the ambiguity in which it is caught up with Husserl on account of the fact that the one who makes me into an Other is the one who is essentially supposed to be made into an Other by me. Perhaps Sartre is playing upon this, at bottom unclarified, dialectic when he says, in a supplement to the formulation whereby I receive my properties from the Other, "Doubtless this is taken to be settled: it has already been said for some time that the Other teaches me what I am. But the same people who represented this thesis affirmed that I derive the concept of the Other from myself, through reflection upon my own capacities and by means of projection or analogy. So they got stuck in a vicious circle, which they could not get out of" (333:366). Sartre breaks through the circle in that he situates the alter-ation of the own and the appropriation of the Other at two different levels, and indeed in such a way that, at the same time, the level of alter-ation receives priority over the level of appropriation. This radicalization of the idea of alter-ation is, as has already been shown, connected with the effort to arrive at a more exact answer to the question how far, and to what extent, "I" can be an "Other," or how that which is externalized by me into a "world" can nonetheless be "my" consciousness.

Over and beyond this configuration Sartre acknowledges two forms of alter-ation in a heightened sense: love (l'amour) and the experience of the we, in particular of the "we-object" (le nous-objet). Since both will be thematized at an advanced stage of the theory, which is here only set out in rudimentary form, I am only going to go into it in outline.[23] Erotic love already belongs to that "behavior" that I assume vis-à-vis the Other in reaction to the original situation of my being-for-Other. It is the attempt, as object, to be at the same time the subject for which I am an object. This, however, means nothing other than that in love I myself want to become the Other: "In fact, it is a matter, for me, of making myself be by acquiring the possibility of adopting toward myself the point of view of the Other" (432:476). In any case, according to Sartre, this undertaking has to fail. For since existing is carried out as inner negation, and since inner negation leaves me to be the one who is not the Other, and the Other, the one who is not I, our separation remains an insurpassable fact. Nevertheless, the lover's desire to be the Other for itself is no subjective wish, for "to be Other to oneself—an ideal that is always concretely aimed at under the auspices of being to oneself this Other—is the primary value of relations with the Other" (432:476). The alter-ation that I experience in being-for-the Other is henceforth driven into a striving after a complete transformation of the loved one, and its impossibility is only the revelation of the inconsistency that already resides in alter-ation as such.

In a quite distinct sense alter-ation is heightened in the experience of the "we-object." Like love, language, and masochism, on the one hand, and indifference, desire, hate, and sadism, on the other, the "we-object" and the "we-subject" also stand on the foundation of the original situation of being-for-Others (484–503:537–556). But it does so differently. The former behavior reaches beyond the basic situation to the extent that it seeks to weaken the alternative that either I am an object and the Other a subject or the Other is an object and I am a subject, or at least to take away the tension inherent in it. At the same time, it still persists—and, indeed, not only insofar as this alternative cannot be weakened as a matter of fact but also because there I remain *alone* just as well in the positing of the subject as in that of the object. I remain in the singular even when the subjective or objective counterpart can also consist of several Others. It is in the subject- and object-we that the I is first extended into the plural. Therefore the we exceeds the basic situation in that very point in which it remains true to the former behavior. Conversely, however, the we remains true to the basic situation wherever the reactional behavior seeks to remove itself from it. The we accepts without further ado, so to speak, the subject-object tension and only repeats it in a pluralistic modification.[24]

The we-object, which Sartre is genuinely concerned about, first arises when, in the situation of my original being-for-Other or of the being-for-me of the Other, a *"third"* emerges as subject.[25] I may previously have looked at the Other or have been looked at by him—in that moment in which the third looks at both of us we withdraw together into a community in which neither has any priority over the Other. For both of our possibilities are now alienated from us (489:545). And, by comparison with that which befalls me alone, this alienation is an "alienation of the for-itself that is still more radical" (490–546). The "being-outside" that is here conferred upon me (489:545) is more radical because the third not only sees me as worldly object but sees the whole situation in which I am stuck together with the Other. I must consequently recognize myself as someone who is fundamentally like the Other. This means, however, that, under the look of the Other, I first experience myself in a distinctive sense as "one among Others" (493:549). Personalizing alter-ation first occurs to me in the we-object, which, according to Husserl, is in play from the very beginning because I am already, in transcendental originality, a member of a we (understood as a community of subjects), and so can only be human insofar as I am a human being among human beings. For Sartre, however, who strikes out the presupposition of the transcendental we, I still cannot personalize myself in the original encounter with the Other that makes me into a human being because the conflict situation of this encounter excludes that solidarity that would contribute to the constitution of the we community.

8 The Dialectic of Alter-ation and Being-Myself

I have touched upon the theme of the "we" (which is in no way exhausted herewith) only out of interest in the problem of alter-ation. With regard to this problem, that side now still has to be more closely considered whose thematization represents a particular service rendered by Sartre. Certainly, I can only be an Other in that I am at the same time myself, in that my alienated being is still my own and not simply alien being. The obscurity of the thought process in which Sartre takes this state of affairs into account once again throws an illuminating light upon the genuinely two-sided transitional position of his social ontology lying between the transcendental theory of intersubjectivity and that dialogical thought that is situated beyond the transcendental alternatives. To be sure, the thought process exists from the very outset in the service of the explication of the idea of alter-ation and therewith of the repetition of a transcendental approach. But, at the same time, something comes to light in it which refers to a completely different constitutive relation, namely, to a *positive* one between the Other and my ownmost self.

That in being-for-Others I am an Other or alienated from myself means, according to Sartre's sharpest formulation, that I am taken away from myself. I no longer dispose of that dimension of my being that is bestowed upon me by the Other, and that consciousness that I have of myself as I-object is "consciousness of myself inasmuch as I escape myself" (318:349). I am already torn away from myself simply through the emergence of the alien freedom (334:367). For, because there exists in the freedom of the Other something that happens to me, I am in its presence no longer "master of the situation" (323:355). The situation is not, as Sartre usually puts it, circumscribed by my possibilities, but by those of the Other. In this sense, my being-for-Other is my "being-outside-myself" (332:365), and indeed for precisely this reason, that I, who in my being-for-myself stand to a certain extent above the situation, am, through the look of the Other, dragged into the situation, that is, welded in together with my surroundings. In this way my—previously quite unnoticed—bond with the people investigated by me is, as one that is itself subject to investigation, "suddenly given outside of me" (324:356). Simply posited and delivered over to the looks of the Others, I am "out of my reach, outside my action, outside my knowledge" (327:359). I am inaccessible to myself.

This situation, however, first becomes really provocative through the fact that the dimension of my being taken away from me is supposed to make up its innermost substance: "The profound meaning of my being is outside of me" (430:474). If my externalization were external to me, I could then realize "myself," so to speak, behind the being "stolen" from me by the Other (431). But it is precisely my self that is stolen from me. Freedom itself is taken away from the sovereign power of freedom. It is this that, in being-for-Other, is "given outside of me" (321:352). In freedom, however, everything that I am is grounded. Therefore, in being-for-Other, my basis is located "outside of myself" (318:349).

Positively this means "that the freedom of the Other is the basis of my self" (433:477). I am possessed by the Other, entirely and right to the root of my being. The Other possesses the "secret of my being" (430:474; see also 431). So the paradox arises that the freedom of the Other has taken up residence in the innermost region of my being, where my freedom is at home: "The very material of my being is the unpredictable liberty of an Other" (320:351). I am directed not by myself but by the freedom of the Other. But this freedom has got a footing in my self, in the depths of my being (326:358). It is not mine because I cannot dispose of it. However, the condition of my being penetrates deeper into my self than that which is under my control because it is the uncontrollable basis of what sustains my control. And the Other is this. In conjunction with the conclusion that the immediate presence of the subject-Other is the necessary condition of any thought that I generate about my self, Sartre is, for this reason, able to say, "The Other is that myself from which nothing separates me, absolutely nothing unless it be his pure and complete liberty" (330:363; see also 331).

The Other is my I-self. The statement sounds similar to Husserl's thesis that the ego in the alter ego is I myself. In accordance with its meaning, however, he stands in complete opposition to this thesis. Husserl seeks immanence in transcendence. Sartre, however, seeks absolute transcendence in absolute immanence. Figuratively speaking, he wants to push through the shell of immanence right to the transcendence concealed in it. One must, or so he says with an urgency that can hardly be exaggerated, ask absolute immanence to transpose us into absolute transcendence: "In the deepest depths of my self I must . . . find the Other itself as the one who is not I" (309:339).[26]

This thought, whose linguistic form reminds one of mysticism—and hardly incidentally—we shall find similarly expressed by Buber and Marcel. In it the idea of alter-ation is, so to speak, dialectically reversed at its highest point into its opposite. On the one hand, it expresses the completion of alter-ation: the alter-ed being is not merely *my* being but even my being *itself*; alter-ation affects me radically and totally; the Other not only has something of my being, he has purely and simply stolen my being as a whole. On the other hand, however, the being constituted by the Other as my being itself is also my selfhood. When I am myself in my being-for-the-Other, then I am not alienated from myself. With the totalization of alienation, that tension that is thought along with the concept of alienation must also be suspended.

To be sure, this dialectical reversal is carried out behind Sartre's back. Furthermore, the totalization of alter-ation described above remains, as such, restricted to individual passages from *Being and Nothingness*. In general, Sartre understands my being-for-Others throughout as a being that, on the basis of its mineness, is certainly not alien, but that, for that very reason, is not already my being itself. Following this general characterization, he distances himself as much from the Other as from my self, as something distinct from my ownmost being, if not also from my being in general.

In this connection it is significant that Sartre calls being-for-Others the "outside" (*dehors*) (346:380), "reverse side" (*envers*) (324:356), or even the "representational side" (*dessous*) (320:350) of my consciousness, the last in a metaphorical play upon the representational side of playing cards, concealed from me by the coplayer, which symbolize my being in the hand of the Other. A representative meaning attaches to these concepts because in them the guiding idea that Sartre pursues in the explication of the idea of alter-ation is suppressed, the idea, namely, that being-for-Other should be envisaged as a middle term between the for-itself and the in-itself, between mundane externality and an internality appropriate to consciousness. Through it the basic question — how being-for-Other, as the being of a worldly object, can still be mine — is supposed to find its conclusive answer. On the one hand, I am, as an entity endowed with an outside, "a piece of nature" (321:352). On the other hand, being-for-Other is *my* outside, something that is not outside of my being but falls entirely within it, precisely as the reverse side of internality itself: "It is my *being outside*, assumed and recognized as *my* outside" (346:380).

At the same time, however, being for-Others, insofar as it is regarded as my outside, is pushed from the midpoint, at which it is localized by Sartre in the words given again above, to the periphery of my being. I do not in any way find the Other who bestows an outside upon me, "in the very depths of myself." Rather, I find him at my "limit." As the "representational side," my being-for-Others is at the same time "the limit of my liberty" (320:351). It is the limit of my freedom in the twofold sense of that which is inaccessible to my freedom and which, nevertheless, goes to make up its being: "limit that I cannot attain and that I am nevertheless" (334:367; see also 346).

The self, as the innermost region of my being, now has to withdraw from being-for-Others, which is located at the periphery of my being instead of at the center. It is constituted not in and out of it, but over against it. In this way, Sartre's social ontology renews the Heideggerian theory of the connection of authentic being-self and being-with-one-another: Even in accordance with *its* basic tendency, the self results from the *rebound* from the Other. Even in accordance with *its* average judgment, the intersubjective constitution of being-self is not a positive but only a negative one: constitution out of a *release* from the Other.

Accordingly, Sartre erects his doctrine of the self-becoming of the for-itself on the foundation of his general theory of internal negation (343–345:377–379). In the rejection of the Other I grasp myself as the not-Other. Still, the Other who I myself decline to be only exists for his part in such way that he himself declines to be me. In contrast to the internal negation of things, that between human beings is — as we know — reciprocal. Since, however, the encounter with the subject-Other is more original than that with the object-Other, my rejection through the Other comes essentially before that of the Other through me. Only as the one who rejects me can the Other be rejected by me.

That the Other rejects me means: he makes me into his object. Insofar, however, as I experience the alien subjectivity in my objectness alone, I can only reject the Other who rejects me in that I reject that object-I of mine that is rejected by him. Self-becoming is, as liberation from the Other, nothing other than this refusal of the object-I. Still, the refusal is not allowed to contradict the affirmation of the object-I. For the recognition that I really am the object-I is irreversible. This recognition is also furthered just as much by the dialectic of self-becoming. Because I want to be I myself and so not the Other, I must reject my object-I and, at the same time, take it upon myself. I must reject it insofar as it is grounded in the Other and is the locus of his present; I have to take it up, however, insofar as it is for the Other precisely what he does not have to be. Such a rejecting acceptance or accepting rejection takes place in the form of a positing of the object-I as "alienated," as the not completely alien and yet not quite own I. The explicit insight into the alienated character, or the being-external, of my objectness already in itself implies, however, the recovery of the self, which gets set up in its interiority behind the external side.

9 The Reversal of My Objectification by the Other into the Objectification of the Other by Me and Sartre's Return to the Transcendental Approach

The price that, according to Sartre, I have to pay for the recovery of my self is the loss of the original presence of the Other. For, in that, with my self the transcendence of my project is also awakened out of impotence, my objectification through the Other is converted into the "objectification of the Other, as a second moment of my relation to him" (347–349:381–383).

Insofar as this is now the end of the story that runs through "my relation to the Other," Sartre's social ontology falls completely into that transcendentalism from whose destruction it took its start. If a further proof of this were required, it would be found in the fact that the liberation from the Other (343) means also, for Sartre, the "restitution" of the Other in Heidegger's sense. For the withdrawal from the Other "results in there being an Other" (343:377; see also 349).

To be sure, Sartre carefully limits the meaning of this thesis: "This does not mean that it (the for-itself) gives being to the Other, but simply that it gives it being-Other or the essential condition of the 'there is' " (343–344:378). But Heidegger also understands his concepts of restitution in the same way. In contrast with Sartre's interpretation, whose unfoundedness I have attempted to lay bare, in *Being and Time* it is a question of the ontological priority of that space in which the Other can be present and not at all of conferring ontic being upon the Other. Instead, therefore, of the interpretative appendix marking off the preceding theory from that of Heidegger, it brings to light precisely the community of level. It is the transcendental level upon which the Other appears as a given object in the horizon of the world and, in the breakdown of his own transcendence, first receives sense and being-status from my project: "it is I who by the very affirmation of my free spontaneity make there be an Other. . . . The Other is therefore placed out of account as that which depends on me for not being, and, in this way, his transcendence is no longer a transcendence that transcends me toward itself; it is a purely contemplated transcendence, a circuit of selfhood that is simply given" (348:382–383).

From the end, however, the *entire* theory now betrays itself, in accordance with its basic characteristic, as transcendental philosophy. Certainly, the end envisaged is, in Sartre's opinion, not the completion and apogee, but, on the contrary, the lapse of original being-with-one-another. To this extent one cannot infer directly from this to the beginning and development of the whole. Indirectly, however, one can. The reversal of the relation that, in striving toward an overcoming of transcendental philosophy, Sartre construed as fundamental shows, in the transcendental schema, that that striving is not radical enough. It does not attain its goal because it simply inverts the transcendental schema. To be sure, it is not the Other but the I that is object in being-for-Other; to be sure, a world project takes hold not of it but of myself and assigns to me a particular place in space and time; to be sure, not the alien but my being becomes a quasi thing present-at-hand. What remains in this inversion is the transcendental duality itself, the bipolar unity of world and "world," of the a priori project overthrow and the factically given, of the horizon and the horizonally appearing. Only that now the members of this synthesis are distributed by Sartre between me and the Others in inverted fashion, somewhat as with Heidegger. To what extent Husserl's approach is also preserved in such an inversion is demonstrated by the circumstance that Sartre certainly substitutes a being-seen for the seeing in which the encounter of ego and alter ego is grounded for Husserl, but does not really abandon the latter therewith. Seeing, as my action overcome, returns again as the passively suffered indication of the alien consciousness.[27] On the whole, the alternative of action and passion is subjected to the domination of the subject-object split, from which, according to Sartre — this is the upshot of his observation — there is for me and the Others no escape: "It is therefore useless for human reality to seek to get out of this dilemma: either to transcend the Other or to allow oneself to be transcended by him. The essence of relations between consciousnesses is not *Mitsein*, it is conflict" (502:555; see also 484).

With the failure of the attempt to overcome transcendental philosophy, the fully valid realization of the intention sketched out at the beginning miscarries also, the intention, namely, to suspend the world-"world" difference through the paradoxical positing in one another of their extremes. Remember that the originally encountered Other is, as a constituent of my being, supposed to be concrete and individual, as a transcendent fact, and at the same time absolutely evident. Herewith Sartre takes aim at a facticity that is supposed to have as little to do with the empirical, mundane facticity as with the generality and universality of the horizon in which the empirical fact appears. Falling back into the duality of a worldly pregiven and a world that has been given up, even he in the end displays this specific facticity of alien existence over the two sides of an ontologically irrelevant empiricism and a super individual a priori.

Proof of this is the line of argument with which Sartre seeks to defuse a more directly pertinent objection to his thesis about the absolute evidence of alien existence (334–342:376–384). In accord with this objection, the Other who looks at me stands on the same level of mere probability with the one looked at by me because the feeling of being looked at can be sustained by a deception just as well as by the act of sensible seeing. Sartre's retort is that the experience of the look reaching me can only turn out to be deceptive to the extent that it becomes clear that the particular Other by whom I believe myself to be observed is not really there at that very moment. However, the being-looked-at in general thereby remains indubitable. Sartre feels that he is justified in drawing such a distinction on the basis of an entirely everyday phenomenon. Anyone who has looked inquisitively through a keyhole and suddenly thinks he hears footsteps behind him might breathe more easily when he searches the corridor with his eyes and establishes that there is no one there. But, were he to bend down once again to the keyhole, the feeling of being-for-Others would not leave him. Indeed, this feeling of fear would grow in strength. For the Other who could see him is "now everywhere" (336:369). Far from it being the case that that individual whose presence proved to be a deception has disappeared, he is now, for the first time, universally threatening. According to Sartre, however, this means that it is not the subject-Other and therewith not the "Other himself" who has turned out to be an illusion, but solely the "*being-there* of the Other" as "a historical and concrete event" or his "*facticity*" as the "accidental connection of the Other with an object-being in *my* world" (337:370).

In the present context we should concern ourselves not so much with the phenomenon as, rather, with its ontological interpretation. The reality of the phenomenon is not in doubt, even though its ontological interpretation is. So one has to ask, Why should the particular individual who, as a matter of fact, either is or is not in the room, be in every instance the object-Other? Why does Sartre only address this facticity and not the subject-Other? How can the indubitability of the "Other itself" be saved when the "historical and concrete event" of being looked at sinks into mere probability?

It is clear that Sartre here contradicts his own directive. At the beginning stood this thesis: The originally encountered alien existence, and thus the subject-Other," has the nature of a contingent and irreducible fact" (307:337). The maxim that was derived therefrom was that the theory that sought to establish the "indubitability" of the Other must at the same time leave to "the encounter its character of facticity." Now, on the contrary, Sartre defends the indubitability of the subject-Other at the expense of its facticity. In that the latter, however, falls continually on the side of the object-Other, it appears to be self-evidently a *mundane* facticity, which is precisely what it cannot be in connection with the transmundane subject-Other. Facticity, pure and simple, is mundane facticity; the historicality of the concrete encounter—in accordance with its intention as "absolute event," removed from the course of the world—is the historicity of an occurrence in the world. This supposition already lies at the root of the interpretation of the concrete Other as an object-Other. The facticity of the Other presents itself as its accidental directedness toward "an object-being in my world" because the very facticity that I catch sight of when I turn toward the Other is its bodily (physical and organic) existence in the midst of things. But this is not the facticity of the subject-Other that is experienced in being looked at. The inner-worldly factuality of the object-Other can be attributed to the sphere of mere probability (of merely "presumptive" evidence in Husserl's sense), but not the world-transcending facticity of the subject-Other, when besides it is a matter of disclosing its absolute evidence in the signification of "the concrete and indubitable present of *this* or *that* Other" (308:338).

In the passages presently under discussion, we are not actually concerned with this initial objective of Sartre. To be sure, following it, my being-for-Others *in general* is absolutely evident, but this should not extend to the fact that I am an object "precisely at this moment and for one single Other." However, that with this the subject-Other to whom alone one can still ascribe absolute evidence is turned into something general and nonindividual is indicative of a corresponding reinterpretation of his presence. What was previously meant by "presence"—the factical presence of the alien momentarily observing me—now becomes, alongside a factical *ab*sence, the futural modus of a "fundamental presence" that in comparison with the presence of the object-Other, looks like a mere "empirical presence." Accordingly, each is for everyone "present or absent on the basis of an original presence." In its opposition to the fleeting being-there of individual fellows, the original and foundational present is, so to speak, the universal present of the Other raised to universality, an Other who is precisely "always" and "everywhere" present. This universal present remains "undifferentiated"; it is a "prenumerical" present, a present of "infinite undifferentiatedness" or the "presence of a reality that cannot be enumerated" (339–341:372–374).

As a nonnotational, prenumerical, undifferentiated, and leveled-down reality, the always and everywhere present subject is, however, nothing other than the "they." According to Sartre, this name is more suitable than that which is characterized by Heidegger as "state of inauthenticity of human reality" (342:376). To a certain extent, this is entirely correct. For the ontological character of the "they," namely, indeterminacy, never becomes more pressingly apparent than when "they" look at me continually and from everywhere. So the sudden apparent association with fundamental ontology only confirms the failure of the attempt to overcome the transcendental approach in the theory of alien existence. With the return of the duality of mundane fact and a priori world project, the secret of the world-transcending and yet factically present, of the constitutive and yet individual, co-human being is removed. In its place there arises, on the one side, the mundane fact of cohuman objects whose individuality only has empirical significance and, on the other, the "undifferentiated transcendence" of the they, the world project of the alien subject whose universality is purchased at the cost of his individuality and whose continuing presence is bought with the surrender of his momentary being-there.

In this way the circuit of Sartre's interpretation is closed. Sartre does not get to—this has at least been shown with respect to one example—that goal that was fixed at the outset and could only be reached through a radical overcoming of transcendental philosophy, and for the following reason, namely, because he approaches it on the way to a simple reversal of the transcendental conception, which reversal is itself, however, again converted into its opposite. So the transformation of the subject-Other into the object-Other is the reversal of a reversal and thereby the restoration of the transcendental model. In it, however, it is quite clear to what extent the original reversal also already stands under the sway of Husserl's and Heidegger's transcendental philosophy.

10 Excursus on Sartre's *Critique of Dialectical Reason*

In the introductory remarks to the present investigation the methodological principle was explained whereby the interpretation of the "secondary positions" should, as far as possible, be directed toward one single writing. In Sartre's case I have selected as just such a "model text" the book *Being and Nothingness*. This choice, however, still requires a special justification to the extent that one can legitimately ask why, instead of the earlier work, *Critique de la raison dialectique* [*Critique of Dialectical Reason*] (Crd)[28] was not adopted as basic, a work that possesses an entirely social philosophical content and enjoys, besides, the advantage of contemporary value.

The choice of a model text for the interpretation of Sartre's social ontology did not turn out against the *Critique of Dialectical Reason* simply because this text is still not completed. More significant are two other reasons each of which would in itself, in my opinion, suffice for the legitimation of the procedure entered upon. The first reason is that the genuine social philosophical themes of the *Critique* are the groups and collectives that are certainly rooted in the "bilateral bond" but that reach out beyond it, and that are excluded from the scope of the work. The second consists in the fact that the *Critique*, to the extent that it makes Marxism serviceable, is no longer as indebted to the modern transcendental philosophy of Husserlian origin as is *Being and Nothingness*. For this reason, a significance attaches to this circumstance because Sartre's social ontology—as also that of Heidegger—should, in the final analysis, not be considered for its own sake but with regard to the subsequent history of Husserl's transcendental theory of intersubjectivity.

To be sure, in his later work, Sartre does not depart entirely from Husserlian phenomenology. He expressly emphasizes that his epistemological point of departure is still consciousness (30n). Nevertheless, he does at the same time point to a departure from his earlier approach, which shows, by means of examples, that the *Critique*, despite any resemblance that may also persist in the social-ontological area, can no longer be envisaged, like *Being and Nothingness*, within the horizon of that transcendentalism set up by Husserl. Consciousness should not be interrogated with respect to itself, but with respect to that life in the world of the Other that is opened up by him (142:51). It is a point of departure that is immediately abandoned. It throws the Marxist dialectician back upon that which precisely is not consciousness. To this extent, Sartre is able to oppose rigorously Husserl's theme, formal consiousness, to his own theme, the concrete world of history (131:35). On the noetic side, this opposition is one between a transcendental philosophy of consciousness and a "structural and historical anthropology." Precisely through the laying of the foundation of such an anthropology, Sartre would like to release dialectical materialism from its present stagnation and give it a new lease on life. Insofar, however, as he pursues anthropology, he removes himself even further from Husserl than in his earlier main work. In this he still follows—as we have seen—the Husserlian conception, in accordance with which my consciousness (which is thematized from the beginning on) first becomes human through the mediation of the Others. Now, on the contrary, that original reality whose status he establishes with his attempt at an existential reformation of Marxism is human from the very outset. In spite of this change, there still is, of course, a certain analogy between the construction of the *Critique* and the specific method of Husserl's former work. For the conviction remains that it is the relation to Others that first engenders for me, the actual, individual, concrete reality (181:94). The question, how the former work grasps that human reality of consciousness from which it started out, on the way over the Other, is answered by the latter with the abstract "praxis" of the individual, which is introduced in order to investigate from this standpoint the relation to Others and, on the basis of this relation, eventually to uncover the individual in its absolute concretion, that is, in the reality of historical human being (143:53). This method obeys what Sartre called "dialectical circularity," that is, the fact that the individual is the constitutive source of every social grouping and the group, in its turn, is the creator of the individual as an absolute, concrete, historical reality (155:67). It undoubtedly provides proof of the continuity not only of Sartre's inner development but also of the connection between Sartre's present thought and Husserl's transcendental philosophy. On this matter, it should be noted that Sartre, with his anthropological approach, only goes in the same direction as that already entered upon by Heidegger in contrast to Husserl. Indeed, in many respects, the intention of his *Critique* can be understood as a radicalization of the tendencies of fundamental ontology. So Sartre carries out that restructuring of intersubjectivity out of the medium of theory and into the element of praxis, a restructuring undertaken by Heidegger and also required by him (182:100), more consequentially than is the case in *Being and Time*. An example will serve to elucidate this. In a polemical reference to Husserl, Heidegger says that Others encounter us not in simple intuition as person-things present-at-hand, but "in the course of work," therefore in their practical involvement with beings (SuZ 120:156). Sartre, however, even unmasks the looking on of Others at work as a knowing that is still abstract and theoretical, that is deprived of the concrete reality of praxis, and precisely to the extent that work is also an interhuman relation and never only a relationship to things (174:91, 252:186). Only, Sartre handles praxis with reference to Marx, and so, when he connects with Heidegger on this point, he does so only because Heidegger, for his part, already stands in the Marxist, neo-Hegelian tradition. In that Sartre integrates his own existentialism with Marxism, he also thereby suspends the presuppositions that he brings with him as a pupil of Husserl and Heidegger.

This is not the place to decide the question whether such a suspension can succeed[29] or, rather, runs into a self-contradiction. It seems to me as though the fluctuation between Hegelian ontology and modern transcendental philosophy from *Being and Nothingness* is renewed in the *Critique* on the plane of a contradiction between the latter and Marxist ontology, only that now it is not transcendentalism but its opponent that is victorious. However that may be, it is certain that already the attempt at a suspension of transcendentalism in favor of historical materialism has to alter decisively Sartre's social ontology, an ontology originally developed in the confrontation with the former. In what follows, I would like to point out at least four such alterations—the four most important. In doing so I still do not overstep those limits to the investigation marked out in the introduction. In comparing both theories of intersubjectivity from the earlier work, I only draw on those passages, therefore, that Sartre devotes to the elementary and not yet collectivized and organized relations (178–279:95–120). These relations, the object of social philosophy in *Being and Nothingness*, are not—as we said—Sartre's immediate theme in the *Critique*, but they do nevertheless play a significant role. For the *Critique* stands in the succession to Simmel's *Soziologie* [*Sociology*] to this extent, that it also raises the bi- and trilateral relationships into a *constituens* (182:100, 191:111)—indeed, even into a genuine reality of the groups and collectives, which latter therefore only possess a "parasitic" reality. Sartre does not believe it possible in the end to carry the reform of the presently atrophied Marxism through such a regression to elementary, interhuman relations (179:95).

1. Nothing has been altered in the *Critique* with respect to the leading thesis of *Being and Nothingness*, in accordance with which the interhuman relation is primarily a subject-object relationship. Correspondingly, Sartre further affirms that the original intersubjective situation is "conflict" (206:130), which can turn into acute "warfare," and that the original comportment of all human beings toward one another is "power" (225n:152), which can break out into open, warlike "force" (211:136). The "danger" that thereby each objectively presents for the other makes the Other for me, just as well as me for the Other, into an "inhuman human being" or into an "alien race" (206:130, 208:132). To be sure, it is not seen against the background of the conditioning of human being by matter. The Other is a danger for me insofar as

he embodies, through the material destruction of an urgently needed object, the possibility of my own destruction (204–205:128–129). His dangerousness rests, therefore, upon "scarcity" (*rareté*) as the (in spite of its contingency) universal and radical basic trait of our historical world.

But it is not this materialistic grounding of the negativity of the Other that shakes the foundations of Sartre's social ontology as laid down in *Being and Nothingness*, but the concession of the reciprocity (*réciprocité*) of the subject-object relationship. In contrast with the earlier work, the *Critique* teaches that I discover myself as the object of the Other in the same act as that in which the Other is constituted as my object (192:113). At the very same time, I am supposed to "transcend" the Other as means to my ends and "be transcended" (193:114, 198:120) by him as his instrument. Sartre also carries over this law of "reciprocal integration" to the relationship of groups to one another: each group treats the others as an instrumental object, and each of their members knows that he is treated in the same way by the other group (210:135). Thereby, however, Sartre suspends the sharp opposition of my being-for-Others and the being-for-me of Others, which opposition serves as the systematic platform of the social ontology of *Being and Nothingness*.

Indeed, in the final analysis, even the monopoly of the war-and-conflict model is thereby broken. To be sure, even in the *Critique* Sartre envisages war as the most adequate realization of the interhuman relation, but he still concedes that reciprocity can likewise be expressed in a positive manner (192:113).[30] In the latter case, it either takes the form of exchange and the mutual performance of services or that of a common work directed to the same goal. The consideration of positive forms of reciprocity is, however, only a consequence of a basic affirmation of reciprocity in general, which in itself is something positive.

This should by no means be taken to mean that, wherever he talks about reciprocity, Sartre has in view the personal mutuality that belongs to the essence of the dialogical I-Thou relation and not to the subject-object relationship. Even with exchange and with common undertakings, each, according to the *Critique*, makes himself the instrument of the Other without respecting the latter as an end in itself—which, subsequently, just as previously, Sartre takes to be impossible (192:112). For all that, a transcending of the subject-object relationship goes hand in hand with the relativizing of struggle—though only occasionally, to be sure. Symptomatic of this is the change in the concept of recognition. In *Being and Nothingness* there is a recognition of the Other only as the recognition of the fact that I am the object that the alien subject sees me as. In contrast, on the basis of the supposition of a fundamental reciprocity, the meaning of the concept of recognition approaches the sense of that respect before the autonomy of the person that was disavowed in *Being and Nothingness* (194:115). This is supported by a few remarks in which Sartre attributes to the dialogical personality— for instance, in the relation between doctor and patient—precisely the reality that he calls in question in *Being and Nothingness* (349n1:306).

2. In comparison with the earlier work, in the *Critique* even the relationship of the "binary" and "trinary" relations, of the bilateral and trilateral bonds, has been altered. To be sure, "duality" still counts as the basis of the "trinity." What is new, however, is that Sartre, in reverse, regards the latter as the basis of the former (189:109, 195:116). To be sure, according to the *Critique* the trinity grounds the duality in a manner other than that in which the duality grounds the trinity. The bilateral bond provides the basis for the trilateral bond insofar as it is an element of the community that comes into being through the "third" (189:109). In contrast, it presupposes the trilateral bond insofar as the latter first makes it what it is (188:108). In order to find out what is genuinely new in this approach of the *Critique*, we must determine more exactly what Sartre means thereby. What is not meant thereby is the fact, forcefully brought out in the *Critique* as well as in *Being and Nothingness*, that the third of the "dyad" provides unity and totality (194:115, 197:119, 398:366). For the dyad dispenses with unity and totality—in this the earlier publication is entirely in agreement with the later (191:111, 193–194:114). In that the third confers this characteristic upon it, he does not make it into that which, in the depth of its being, it is. That he does, only in that he realizes the reciprocity essentially belonging to the dyad (187:107). Thanks to this function, the trinary relation can be evaluated as the basis of the binary.

What reveals itself here is the methodological connection between the renewal, noted in the first point above, and that noted here. Sartre comes to see reciprocity because he thematizes the dyad from the standpoint of the third. The analysis of the dyad is supposed to stand at the beginning of his social philosophical explanations (189:109). As a matter of fact, however, it is the description of the trinary relation that stands at the beginning, a relation in which he himself is the third who observes two separately working individuals without being seen by them (182:100). This is a striking departure from *Being and Nothingness*, where Sartre plays the role of one of the two human beings who are encountered in the duality. The inner, living reality of the relation between the two discloses itself all the more immediately because Sartre has before himself, not two, but only the one who is for him the Other. On the other hand, the fact that the first object of the *Critique* consists in the bilateral bond as such (that is, in the reciprocal interaction of its members) attests to the methodological precedence of the trilateral bond. This precedence, however, refers, in the end, to the conviction that that duality is conditioned by the social "plurality," by societal relationships. For the societal plurality is, for its part, supposed to be the presupposition of the trinity presupposed by the duality (188:108). Accordingly, it forms the horizon of the elements in which the two- and threefold relations appear in advance. In the role of the third, Sartre experiences both individuals, whom he observes not abstractly, as human beings in general, but as belonging to a particular class, and their look also classifies him conversely as a "petit bourgeois intellectual" (183–184:101–102).

3. The *Critique*, unlike *Being and Nothingness*, no longer aims at the "immediacy" of the encounter with the Other in the sense of the nonmediatedness of the world. We have to establish the fact that, even in *Being and Nothingness*, Sartre is not capable of fully realizing this intention. However, in the *Critique* the intention itself is missing. The earlier work conceives the thesis about the immediacy of the interhuman relation in a striving to overcome the transcendental project of social ontology. And it falls away from the height of this thesis because it itself sinks back again into transcendentalism. In that the Sartre of the *Critique* has shaken off the domination of modern transcendental philosophy and exchanged it for another, he has also lost sight of the goal that was once made available to him out of the opposition to Husserl and Heidegger.

To be sure, even in the *Critique* he still calls the interhuman relation, principally the relation between two, "immediate." But this word can no longer have the meaning of the nonmediatedness of the world. For such a meaning would prohibit the commitment to dialectical materialism. In accordance with Sartre's new approach, the intersubjective relationship must be mediate in principle because it requires mediation through the materiality that it conditions (198:120). According to the *Critique*, matter mediates between me and the Other just as the Other mediates between me and matter (132:36, 154n:66n). In this way, the universe of material objects is the world, either as present-at-hand nature or as the totality of instrumentally employed things.

That mediation of the Other through the world that particularly interests us with regard to *Being and Nothingness* is, for the Sartre of the *Critique*, the most essential feature of sociality. It takes place in many ways. First, inasmuch as the material, surrounding world "totalizes" (199:121) human relations, by simultaneously uniting (184:104, 200:122, 211:138, 234–235:164, 250:183) and separating (246:179, 252–253:186) its members. Even the dyad receives from the material employed a quasi totality (191:111). With better means at its disposal, matter here takes over the function of the third, which Sartre regards as the mediator between the partners of the dyad (184:102, 197:119). In addition, however, it also has a gnostic mediating function; not only does the comportment of the Other open up for me the practical field of instrumental things, but, conversely, the equipmental totality opens up the alien praxis. Everyone is cognizant of the Other starting out from the use object or product (205:129). This is particularly the case insofar as every product mirrors the Other who produced it (231:161). Just as the material employed, however, as "materialized praxis" is made into the medium between myself and the Other, so it is also made into the mediator between the Other and me. It mediates the demands that the Other makes upon me: "All imperative forms come to Man through the material employed" (254:189). For example, the Others by whose means a tool has been engendered have from the start addressed the latter to me, in that they have, so to speak, stamped into the matter the movement that I have to carry out in order to be able to use it (250–251:184–185, 254:189).

To be sure, as the one to whom they turn by means of material, I am myself like every Other, only one arbitrarily drawn from the totality of those who are all addressees of the earlier work (252:186). Sartre here, therefore, falls back upon the ideas brought forward in *Being and Nothingness* under the title of the "we-subject," ideas about the "undifferentiated transcendence" with which I, as they, follow those references to Others that are imprinted in the world. However, this positive connection at the same time brings to light the difference between the earlier and the more recent work. The difference between the positions becomes noticeable in that the same thoughts now occupy a completely different position in the systematic construction of social ontology. Whereas, in *Being and Nothingness*, they are located at the conclusion of the section on Being-for-Others (*Pour-Autrui*), they are now to be found in the originary dimension of social ontology. This is grounded, however, in the abandonment of the thesis in accordance with which the Other originally encounters me without the mediation of the world and in accordance with which I must already have experienced him in order to be able to discover him among the things of the world.

4. With what has been said above, I have touched upon the general theme of the first part of the investigation, which now lies behind us: "alter-ation." It is also the overarching theme of the *Critique*. Sartre thinks of it in terms of the concept (developed out of Marx) of alienation (*aliénation*), a concept that Husserl also occasionally adopts for the characterization of the phenomenon of alter-ation. On the one hand, with the *Critique*, the movement of ideas reproduced in the first part of the investigation returns to its genuine starting point, a starting point that is no longer really present to its modern locus of origination. Alter-ation in Husserl's sense, or in that of Heidegger, or even that of the earlier Sartre, is rethought along the lines of the problematic of alienation worked out by Marx, or it is modified in accordance with the fundamental position of materialism. On the other hand, however, Sartre draws the phenomenological idea of alter-ation into the Marxist concept of alienation. The starting point, which appears once again at the provisional end of the movement, is—to speak Hegelian language—no longer simple immediacy, but the mediated immediacy that has taken up the entire process within itself.

We have to take note of the moments that run from the transcendental idea of alter-ation into the concept of alienation belonging to dialectical materialism, just as well as the transformation of the former idea in accordance with the latter concept. With respect to the matter at hand, the general enrichment of Marxist thought through the contribution of phenomenological ontology consists in a regression from capitalistic exploitation (to which the traditional Marxist concept of alienation is limited) to a more original alienation that first makes possible the exploitation of the worker by the capitalist (154n1:66n27, 224:152, 234:164). As an a priori possibility of being human, this primarily constitutive alienation should, in comparison with that absolutized by Marxism, even be the more universal, first, insofar as it also arises in the precapitalistic time of human history (225n:153n), second, insofar as it traces the life history of the individual all the way back to his youth rather than to his start as a wage earner, and third, because it is not limited to the public world of society but threatens intimate familial and friendship relations as well (225n:153n). Sartre intentionally emphasizes that even dual reciprocity does not protect human beings from alienation (191:111).

From the standpoint of its concrete content, the so-formed fundamental and universal alienation is, in his view, most deeply grounded upon that very phenomenon that was called "alter-ation" in the present work: I myself become an Other through the Other (202:124, 208:132, 224:152, 252:186, 314:263). Such an alter-ation happens to each and every one especially in the above-indicated manner, that is, in such a way that the anticipation of the Other, read off the means and objects of work, constitutes him as one who is other than himself ("comme autre que lui-meme") (253–254:187–188, 224:152, 256:190). Beyond this, however, Sartre acknowledges many other forms, of which I can only treat a few by way of illustration. The individual worker in a factory perceives the latter, insofar as it stands for the appropriation of his "social field" by the Other, as an alien and, at the same time, own power that not only relates him to the Other but also to himself as Other; it presents him with "his work as the work of the Others and of all Others to whom he also belongs" (254:186). "Interest" alter-ates the employer (261–279:197–219), and competition changes the boss of an economic enterprise into an "Autre que soi" because it compels him to direct his business with regard to Others (254:188). Alienation in this sense is not only to be found in the modern world of the division of labor. The passive unity necessitated by the deforestation of the Chinese farmer, over centuries, is, "for praxis, his unity as Other and in the domain of the Other" (233:163). So, according to the *Critique*, one's own praxis is alter-ed by every common action. The whole of history makes us into something "other than we want to be and to become" because not only each, but likewise the Other who confers upon it the lineaments of an alien power, makes it for himself.[31]

As in *Being and Nothingness*, Sartre again envisages the alter-ation of myself through the Other as reification (*réification*). What remains, however, is what is also so characteristic of *Being and Nothingness*, namely, the separation of this reification from the complete transformation into a thing (243:175) and the conception of that existence brought forth by it as the perverted state (one which needs to be overcome) of an essence that in itself is not thingly, of my free action (190:110, 248:181). In the properly adjusted dialectic of these opposed tendencies there lies the point of coincidence of the originally Marxist and the modern transcendental tradition. Not only Husserl but also Marx interprets alienation as reification, and accordingly, it is also for him a matter of the freedom of human being. As a commodity, the latter does not lose the possibility of taking upon itself the battle against his alienation. This is the humanistic pathos that links existentialism to Marxism.

The agreement between the two traditions is converted into the appropriation of the phenomenological idea of alter-ation by a radically materialistic concept of alienation, in that Sartre finally substitutes things themselves for the Others who reify me. The "basis of every possible alienation" is accounted for by the "relationship of the agent to the Other through the mediation of the thing and to the thing through the mediation of the Other" (154n1:66n27). According to that relationship, the material employed leads my alienation (effected by the Other) on further. In contrast, following this relationship, Others are simply the bearers of the alienation that stems from matter. Doubtless we are dealing here with two quite distinct alienations. That Sartre sometimes means the one and then again the other gives his new concept of alienation an ambiguity that cannot be overlooked. One is also entitled to presume, however, that the alienation grounded in the mediation of the thing through the Others is for him the decisive one. The fundamental alienation, on whose basis the capitalist exploitation is constituted, is "the domination of human beings through matter . . . and by means of the praxis of the Others . . . as the necessary result of the domination of matter through human beings" (224:152). Insofar as man becomes herein the product of his product, Sartre characterizes the condition of its possibility as "materialization of regressivity" (234:164) In the backlash of his praxis, that human being who humanizes the thing is reified by the thing. Here, therefore, matter, and not the Other, is, in the final instance, the alienating factor: "Matter alienates the very act that works upon it" (224:152).

How far Sartre hereby removes himself from *Being and Nothingness* is also indicated by the change in the concept of objectivation. The earlier and the later works agree in equating this concept with that of alienation. However, whereas earlier Sartre took the line that I was only objectified through Others, and could not really objectify myself, the *Critique* teaches that each one is "constituted in his objectivity through himself and through everyone" (206:130). Self-objectivation is still only modified by the objectivation of Others (244:176). The basis of this divergence lies in this, that in the *Critique*, and in *Being and Nothingness*, "objectivation" means completely different things; in the former, it means materialization: "The human being objectifies himself through work with matter" (238:169; see also, inter alia, 262–263:198–199, 270:210, 284:226, 285n:227n68). Otherwise expressed: matter objectifies him. For the craftsman, for instance, the machine to which his productivity is geared is precisely "the object whose object he is" (254:188). This in turn means that it is matter that alienates me. It takes over the task that transcendental social ontology entrusted to the Other. The dialectical inversion of the materialization of the alter-ator, however, is the alter-ation of matter. As the alter-ator, matter in the end becomes the genuine Other (224:152, 241:173).

III

The Philosophy of Dialogue as the Counterproject to Transcendental Philosophy: The Dialogic of Martin Buber

7
The Ontology of the "Between"

1 The Opposition of the Philosophy of Dialogue to Transcendental Philosophy

In this third part of our investigation we shall follow the lead provided by Buber's thought, which Buber himself calls "dialogical," in order to work out the fundamental approach that characterizes this intellectual current as a whole. As I already indicated in the introductory exposition of the method to be employed, I shall proceed in such a way that, in the course of the Buber interpretation, I shall refer from time to time — either in the notes or in the main body of the text — to parallel thoughts of other representatives of the philosophy of dialogue, and at the end sketch out their positions for their own sake, to the extent that they either seek to make up the essential failings of Buber's dialogic in another way or essentially fall short of the Buberian approach.[1]

That the thinkers who are to be presented agree with each other on one positive point, namely, the orientation to the "dialogical principle," and thus, despite all their divergences and disregarding their very different rank, can be brought under the common title of "dialogicalism" will have to be established through the interpretation itself. At this point, only their negative agreement will be established, that is, that they find themselves aligned in battle against the same opponent. This oppositional side does not enter expressly into dialogicalism. Rather, dialogicalism is at root, and as such, a movement of opposition. This is most evidently attested to by its self-conception. It describes

itself as the "new thought." "The new thought" is not only the title
of a book by Herrigel from the year 1928; it is also the title of an
article by Rosenzweig (KS 373–398), in which, three years previously,
dialogicalism took stock of itself and reproduced its own history.[2]
Where Buber himself makes such an attempt, he also speaks of the
"new thought."[3] H. Ehrenberg opposes the "I-Thou logic" as the
"new" to the "old" subject-object logic (Disp. I 167–169), and
Rosenstock-Huessy proclaims dialogicalism, as does Husserl his transcendentalism, to be the "new science" (AG section 1). In all this the
word "new" is supposed to refer to that "turnaround in thought"
that, according to Steinbüchel, also takes place in the philosophy of
Ebner.[4]

But who is now the opponent of the philosophy of dialogue? What
is the old thought in comparison with which the "new" is perceived
as new? If we ask its representatives themselves, they answer, "Idealism" or "Metaphysics." However, if we analyze the issue that lies
hidden behind these cliché-ridden concepts, we find two answers to
our question, the second of which, in my opinion, first grasps the
oppositional character of the philosophy of dialogue in that depth in
which the opposition is the position itself.

The tradition, criticized by dialogical thought, is first idealism as
the philosophy of the "universal" subject or of "consciousness in general." As a countermove to this philosophy, the "new thought" takes
its start from my factical I, which, in its view, is always at the same
time also a human I. The distinction between the I-Thou and the
I-it that we shall encounter with Buber already marks a difference
within my factical human I that counts as *the* I pure and simple. The
supposition of this identity leads H. Ehrenberg to his thesis that the
"epistemological subject" is the "we." Because from this standpoint
H. Ehrenberg has to reject the idealistic theory of a superindividual
consciousness, though, on the other hand, he shies away from carrying
over the epistemological function that, according to idealism, the
superindividual consciousness exercises to my factical human I, he
replaces the universal consciousness with the we, which is itself the
outcome of the community of the factical I with its Thou (Disp.I
171–173). Even more vociferously than he, Ebner polemicizes against
the theory of the universal subject, which, in his language, is the
"ideal" or "abstract I." The latter is for him a pure contrivance of
idealism, a "soap bubble of speculative intellect" (WR 17). The I is in

reality only the "concrete I" or, what should be the same thing, the "real Man" (WR 17, 40, 110, 113, 138). Even Ebner's distinction between the Thou-related I and the I shut up inside itself (though never becoming truly autarchic) disjoins two possibilities, which are both connected with the concrete I and encompassed by it (WR 41, 115).

As a withdrawal from the philosophy of the universal subject and as a turning toward my factical human I, dialogicalism belongs entirely to the same movement of thought as modern transcendentalism, in particular, that of Heidegger and Sartre. Two examples will suffice to show the awareness of this proximity. Husserl's regress to transcendental facticity lies outside its field of vision. Heidegger's regress to the facticity of human *Dasein*, however, enables Rosenzweig, whom Löwith calls Heidegger's true "contemporary,"[5] to subsume fundamental ontology under the generation of "new thought" (KS 355–356). In this way Rosenzweig regards the analytic of *Dasein*, undertaken in *Being and Time*, as the antithesis of neo-Kantianism, which, for him as for most dialogicians, embodies the philosophy of the universal subject in its purest form. Heim takes the concept of "consciousness in general" from the work of Rickerts (GD 148). However, even he places in a line with Heidegger's *Dasein* the humanly factical I that he enthrones with the dethroning of consciousness in general. And even he sees what is common to the starting point in the facticity of being-in-the-midst-of-beings. This is what he has in mind in an article composed three years before the appearance of *Being and Time* in which we read, "The I is precisely never, as the idealists thought, simply there as a nonobjective reality; it is always at the same time anchored as a point of view at a fixed place in the objective world. . . . The real I (in distinction to the abstracted I-hood of idealism) for this reason never recognizes itself as something absolute, but suffers under the enigmatic arbitrariness of its spatial and temporal bondage" (GL 480–481). It may very well be that even the theologian when he wrote this had not yet clarified in his own mind the distinction between the specific facticity of *Dasein*, thrownness, and the facticity of the present-at-hand. In any case, after the reception of *Being and Time*, he explicitly takes hold of Heidegger's concepts of "thrownness" and "state of mind" (GD 115, 138–139, 186) in order to be able to say yet again where he himself was already at before.

Transcendental philosophy, as the doctrine of the constitution of the world out of subjectivity, is, however, in the second place, and more importantly, the object of dialogicalistic criticism. To it should also be attributed those systems that grasp world-constituting subjectivity as my factical or even my human subjectivity. Looked at in this way, the philosophy of dialogue also stands in opposition to the transcendentalism that is carried on from Husserl to Heidegger and Sartre. The following presentation will demonstrate this, above all with respect to the example of Buber's dialogic. It will be shown that Buber conceives the I-it, against which he musters the I-Thou, as a world-constituting subject. However, even Ebner understands the "relatively thou-less I that remains enclosed within itself" precisely not just as a worldless soul driven back into its interiority, but as "the I of an individual in its relationship to the world whose being-given-to-be-an-individual presupposes its being lived by the latter" (WR 96; see also 154). As lived and constituted in living, the world belongs to the sphere of the "I solitude" that is seen in contemporary humanity by Ebner, and that consists exclusively in this, that the I to which the world is counterposed as its *constitutum* is confronted with nothing of equal primordiality. Even the "external world," and by no means only the psychic "internal world," is likewise that "interiority" or "immanence" with which Grisebach underpins his criticism and that he nevertheless differentiates from "transcendence" as the "external." The external world also falls within the immanence of the "self," that is, of the positing subject, because as "remembered world . . . it is posited by the self" (GW 69; see also 53). So, in Grisebach's sense, only that factualness counts as really external that precedes all constitution, that "reality" that is set over against the "essence" or the "truth" of the interior.

Nothing could illuminate this negative unity of dialogical thought better than the correspondence between this formal conception of Grisebach and Rosenzweig's approach, which is quite differently set up. Even Rosenzweig distinguishes reality from essence, that is, from truth (KS 360, 377, 380), and even he determines the reality toward which the "new thought" is directed as the "pure factualness that precedes all objectivity" (KS 335, 369–371). Just as the former distinction is taken from Schelling's later philosophy, so Rosenzweig's concept of pure factualness also admittedly receives its specific meaning from Schelling.[6] He certainly does not mean that totality of facts present in the experience of the world that is elevated by positivism into the sole reality. Rather, he has in mind the being of the facts present in experience that itself is present prior to such an experience: "In a cognition from which something is obtained, something has also to be put in, just as with a cake. In Rosenzweig's *Der Stern der Erlösung* [*Star of Redemption*] (SE), what is put in at the start is the experience of factualness prior to all facts of actual experience" (KS 395). In *Star* itself, Rosenzweig calls this "factualness outside of the vast, consciousness-dominated, wealth of facts of the knowable world" (SE I 17), the "infinite" (SE I 37, 39) or "absolute factualness" (SE I 33; see also I 42, 67, 83, 89, 112–114) on the basis of which, in his own interpretation of the *Star*, he can then give the name "absolute empiricism" to the philosophy developed there (KS 398).[7] As "the factualness of being" (SE I 112), it is, in immediate agreement with Schelling's "nonintellectualized being," a "being before thought" (SE I 29).

Rosenzweig confronts its philosophical experience, one that guides "new thought," with that *constitution* brought to light by idealism, a constitution that first makes available the "facts of real experience," that is, the "thinkable" world, the "knowable" whole (SE I 16). It is in this manner that, in the introduction to the Jewish writings of Cohen, he interprets his development from idealism to dialogicalism as a path from the transcendental philosophy of constitution, in which all the fundamental concepts are generative, originary concepts, to the philosophy of pure factualness (KS 334–335). The idealistic concept of generation has its correlate, according to Rosenzweig, in the concept of reduction. In the opinion of "new thought," all past philosophies have been oriented toward the principle of "tracing back"; contemporary philosophy, in particular, is a "tracing back to the I as the ground of the world, and the experience of God requires a tracing back to the I that has this experience" (KS 377–378). Insofar as it thereby subscribes to the belief that every entity is something other (KS 377), it necessarily follows an "alter-ating" method (KS 378, 380).

From the standpoint of "experiencing philosophy," on the contrary, which begins where the constituting philosophy comes to an end, each entity is "only to be traced back to itself" (KS 379), "in its own reality" (KS 383). Its basic concept is that of "correlation." Cohen's path to the dialogical "reciprocal relationship of I and Thou" (KS 296) leads from constitution to correlation (KS 334–335, 296–297, 338). In Rosenzweig's eyes, Cohen's late work has the "philosophical significance of the emergence of correlation as the basic concept" (KS 336). With correlation, however, Cohen—in Rosenzweig's opinion—sets out on a search for pure factualness. This correlation is the only mode of behavior toward beings that lets factualness be in the factuality of its being: "For what is reciprocally related does not stand in any danger of engendering a conflicting reality for both parties, as is almost necessarily the case with the generative concepts with respect to what it generates. . . . In the reciprocity of this relation it is projected against a dissolution of its own being by the 'still more authentic' being of the other. So for both members of the correlative relation, factualness is saved" (KS 335).

For Griesbach, just as much as for Rosenzweig, it can be shown that the positive objective of the philosophy of dialogue is, through its criticism of transcendental philosophy, disclosed still more immediately than through the polemic against the theory of consciousness in general. In the so-called "original germ" of the *Star of Redemption*, a letter to his fellow combatant Rudolf Ehrenberg dated 18 November 1917, Rosenzweig constructs the "philosophical Archimedean point" (KS 357), which he thinks he has at last discovered and upon which, in fact, the entirety of the thought construction developed later rests. He develops his idea along two lines, of which, in his opinion, the first does not really reach the goal in view.

In the first line of approach, Rosenzweig sets out how "philosophical reason," which in its occidental history has, "in the end," assimilated every object within itself, namely, in Hegel's dialectic, comes to terms with itself and grounds itself. Thereby it has become "self-sufficient," that is, absolute. What has still been left out of account is the one who philosophizes, who does not stand objectively before it, but, so to speak, behind its back: "After it has taken everything into itself and proclaimed its solitary existence, mankind suddenly discovers that he . . . is still there" (KS 359). *Star* attributes this discovery to Kierkegaard (SE I 12–13). It is the discovery of the facticity of my factical I: "I, the entirely insignificant private subject, I with first and last name, the I of dust and ashes, I am still there" (KS 359). For new thought, a thought that distances itself from the philosophy of the universal subject, the horizon has been opened up.

So Rosenzweig regards it as necessary, in a second line of approach, "to think through the same thing" once again. In this second line of approach, instead of going in Kierkegaard's direction, he goes in the direction of Schelling and beyond Hegel. The thesis now runs, "Reason is not simply the basis of reality; it also yields a reality of reason itself"

(KS 359). Reason itself discovers its "contingency" (SE I 21; see also 19); that is, that it, the one who posits everything, is, without its compliance, always already instated in a positing. In this way it discovers the illusion of its self-foundation (KS 360). It is not able to found itself because its own reality takes it away from itself as that "something that in reasoning is beyond reason" (KS 360). The regression to the facticity of the constituter, imposed by Rosenzweig upon "new thought," appears, at first glance in any case, more like the repetition than the countermovement to modern transcendental philosophy. This impression is strengthened if one follows Rosenzweig's second line of approach to the place where it leads in to the first. The reality of reason—this is Rosenzweig's final explanation—is nothing other than human "freedom" (KS 362); it is human being itself insofar as the latter is not simply a fact in the sense of a present entity, but in that of the facticity of a comportment of the self toward itself (KS 362–363). Indeed, this is also the very approach of *Being and Time*, which grounds the transcendental constitution of the world upon the facticity of the human "self." Only, Rosenzweig is to be distinguished from Heidegger, and from all transcendental philosophers, in that he does not go back to the facticity of the constituting with a view to grounding transcendental constitution. He does not go back to it like Heidegger and, even more so, Husserl, in order from that foundation to be able to mount once again to the relation of *constituens* to *constitutum*. In his view, this would be the attempt, now unmasked as an illusion, to effect a self-grounding of reason, an attempt that, according to Rosenzweig, is continually undertaken "in order to render being intelligible" (KS 360). Instead of proceeding from the facticity of the constituter to thematize its relation to the constituted, he, by sinking into facticity, comes to terms with the "correlation" that is ontologically presupposed by the former relation and that also brings about the reality of freedom (KS 363–365). So the very facticity that he envisages is different from the one that Heidegger brings to light. It will be an essential task of the following interpretation to determine this specifically dialogical facticity. Just as its proximity to the facticity of thrownness makes it understandable why Rosenzweig finds in Heidegger a confederate, so its remoteness provides the most profound reason for the autonomy of "new thought" in comparison with fundamental ontology.

It is Grisebach who deliberately draws attention to this difference between the philosophy of dialogue and Heidegger's philosophy. According to his assessment, the difference obtains regardless of the common front established against all systems that are developed "from the standpoint of universal consciousness (Gw 88–89). Grisebach's *Gegenwart* [*Present*] (Gw) appreciates the change of method brought about by the "phenomenological school," which has brought with it a turning away from "universal consciousness" and a turning to the "existence and givenness" of *Dasein*'s mineness, as a "remarkable deepening of the self" (Gw 51)—but precisely of the self, therefore of transcendental subjectivity. And for Grisebach, the irremovable boundary between his own thought and that of Heidegger is hereby drawn. Whether, namely, it is a question of the "universal logical self" or of the "ontologicoexistentially interpreted self" (Gw 94), in each case the system of thought aims at the constitution of the world. For this reason, Grisebach proceeds further: "But at bottom, and in spite of the change of method, everything remains as it was. The self stands at the midpoint of its world, which is related to it and formed in accordance with its essence" (Gw 51). In *Being and Time*, too, the world is "only discovered and projected by the self" (Gw 111). To be sure, Grisebach is perfectly well aware that in addressing the "problem of being," Heidegger reaches beyond constituting *Dasein* and "back to a structure of being given in advance" (Gw 88) and, from this point, "investigates the *mode of being* of the self, of the I" (Gw 131—italics are mine). But insofar as even this takes place with regard to the question concerning the transcendental constitution of the world, Heidegger's being problem still—in Grisebach's opinion—lies "within a world dominated by the self and its principles" (Gw 131).

The circular structure of fundamental ontology is taken to be symptomatic of this. In that the latter believes it to be possible to master "reality within the infinite circle of pure essence" (Gw 77), it demonstrates that in reality it is not concerned with reality, with that which is really not anticipated. The circularity of its method is then also the basis on which it finds common ground with the idealism criticized by it (Gw 188). Indeed, insofar as Heidegger explicitly affirms the ontological circle, he drives the "immanental system" to its uttermost possibility. *Being and Time* forms "perhaps for some time the high point of humanistic-technical thought" (Gw 511n). Even the question concerning the meaning of being is posited in it "on the basis of an explicit, prior commitment to the immanence of the system, to a self that thinks itself, to humanistic man" (Gw 512n; see also 524n).[8]

In contrast, Grisebach considers as the goal of his own thought not only the discovery of the dogmatic "metaphysics" of *Being and Time* (Gw 512n) but also, and before all else, the radical "overcoming" (Gw 88) of the entire transcendental philosophy that culminates in *Being and Time*. He thus takes upon himself the task of breaking through the circle in which understanding lies. Only in this way, according to him, can human being attain the true reality of transcendence or the external. It all comes down to "overcoming and avoiding the circle, that is, establishing a boundary from without" (Gw 7–8, 79). The circle cannot, however, be broken through by means of cognition. Rather, it only breaks down in the breakthrough of transcendence (Gw 137). This is the reversal on which everything depends in the final analysis. The task that neofundamental ontological thought has to take over is no longer a genuine doing but a desisting and a "quiet listening" (Gw 578; see also 577, 588), grounded in the comportment of "attunement" (Gw 507), a listening to the voice of a reality that manifests itself from itself.

This is not the place to show how this listening thought is unfolded by Grisebach. At this point, the philosophy of dialogue will simply be presented with regard to the example of Grisebach and others as the counterproject of transcendental philosophy. The following interpretation will have to establish that it is this in its deepest roots, that is, that the position that it holds is determined by its opposition to transcendental philosophy. The dependence upon transcendental philosophy, as the counterproject to transcendental philosophy, a dependence in which it naturally finds itself involved, will, in the course of the investigation, come to light in such a way that it discloses the negativity that attaches to the ontology of dialogical reality. Already at this point, however, we should point to another kind of dependence. In it dialogicalism—with the exception of those thinkers, like H. Ehrenberg (Disp. I 174–175, 183) and Rosenstock-Huessy,[9] who integrate the It in the I-Thou relationship—already comes about in that it posits the dialogical reality that is in question exclusively alongside the transcendentally constituted world, instead of replacing the latter with the former. So it not only distances itself from transcendental philosophy but at the same time—in opposition to the idealistic theory of consciousness in general—takes it up into itself when it relativizes it from the standpoint of the newly discovered reality.

2 Historical Connections

Before we take account of the "positive" approach of the philosophy of dialogue in line with Buber's dialogic, we want to cast an eye on the historical connection between Buber's *Ich und Du* [*I and Thou*], 1923, the model text for the following interpretation,[10] and the other publications that were introduced at the beginning of the previous section, as well as the historical connections among these publications themselves.

What attracts attention immediately, and is thought to be extremely significant by the contributors themselves in retrospect, is that any such connection is really not to be found. Independent of each other, and of the other documents from the early period of dialogicalism, are Cohen's later work composed in the winter of 1917/1918, Ebner's "pneumatological fragments," written in the winter of 1918/1919, Marcel's indications in *Journal métaphysique* [*Metaphysical Diary*] (JM), which, more or less, from July 1918 on turn on the dialogical principle,[11] and finally, in essence, also *I and Thou* itself. For, although the conclusive conception of this book, whose preliminary writing falls in the fall of 1919, was first completed in the spring of 1922, Buber, according to his own statement (DP 294–295), knew of none of the other first fruits of dialogicalism, at least during the work on parts I and II. To be sure, he adds, "When I wrote the third and last part, I broke my reading fast and began with Ebner's fragments." This remark must obviously be understood to mean that Buber, beginning with Ebner's fragments, read others too before finishing his book. For Rosenzweig, who already in August 1919 had asked Buber for a recommendation for the publication of *Star* in a Jewish edition (1935 371), informed his wife on 4 January 1922 that Buber had now read *Star* and had spoken with him about it (1935 414). Admittedly, everything that Buber might have taken up at so advanced a stage in his preoccupation with the dialogical life could still have worked on him like a confirmation of the thought that had arisen in him of its own accord. It is also pertinent to note that Buber had already wrestled with the dialogical principle many years earlier, namely, at the beginning of his Hasidic studies about 1905, even if he was not to think it through philosophically for the first time until *I and Thou*.[12] The reference to the introduction to the *Legend of Baal*,[13] stemming from the autumn of 1907, which he gives as evidence of this fact (DP 293), can be supplemented with a reference to the essay written even before the summer of 1906, an essay called *Rabbi Nachman and the Jewish Mysticism* (CB 6–38),[14] in which already constitutive moments in the essential conception of discourse are discovered. So in 1925 Rosenzweig concludes (KS 388) that Buber pushed through to what, in the central book of *Star*, was envisaged as the "focus of new thought" independently of him and the other representatives of dialogicalism, such as Ebner.[15]

No less characteristic than the absence of any connection, however, is on the other side, the close alliance that, especially in the circle around Rosenzweig, made possible a συμφιλοσοφεῖν, the like of which has rarely occurred in the history of philosophy. Rosenzweig regards himself as a pupil of Cohen. Cohen, of whom he had read nothing outside of a "few incidental Jewish theological works," he got to know personally in November 1913, at the Berlin Academy for Jewish Science to which Cohen had moved from Marburg one year previously (KS 291). There he took part in Cohen's seminar on the "concept of religion in the system of philosophy," which immediately preceded and anticipated his posthumous work (1935 83).[16] In February 1918 he had already read with great enthusiasm the proofs of Cohen's *Religion der Vernunft* [*Religion of Reason*] (RV). On 5 March 1918 he wrote to R. Ehrenberg that "it *would be difficult* on the Christian side to find anything to set over against the *Religion of Reason* as being of equal worth . . . since Hegel and Schelling" (1935 281).

Later he expressed the opinion that the decisive effect upon *Star* proceeded not from Cohen but from Rosenstock-Huessy (KS 388; see also 1935 475). This undoubtedly corresponds to the facts. In 1913 his study visit to Leipzig gave him the opportunity to converse with Rosenstock-Huessy (1935 65, 71–73), who very strongly influenced his religious development. And in 1916 he began a friendly exchange of letters on Judaism and Christianity (1935 641–720). Indeed, already in 1910, the two of them together with Viktor von Weizsäcker[17] and Hans and Rudolf Ehrenberg, met in Baden-Baden on the occasion of a conference of historians and philosophers. Above all, however, already in 1916, Rosenzweig became acquainted with Rosenstock-Huessy's first outline of *Doctrine of Language*, which was written for him and sent over to him immediately; this work was printed in 1924 under the title *Angewandte Seelenkunde* [*Applied Soul Science*] (AS) (KS 388; AG 8,265).[18]

The traces of this outline in *Star* are indiscernible. *Star*, for its part, which Rosenzweig began to write in August 1918 in the trenches of the Macedonian front, and which he completed in February of the following year (1935 724; DP 291), enriched H. Ehrenberg's *Disputation* (volume I written 1921/1922), which is dedicated to *Star* and its author. To be sure, in many respects H. Ehrenberg seems, conversely, to have had an influence upon his cousin Rosenzweig. The exchange of letters between them reaches back to the year 1906. In the "germinal cell" to *Star*, Rosenzweig remarks that he is using the concept "reality of reason" in Ehrenberg's sense (KS 362) and, in *Star* itself, he operates "with a term propagated by Ehrenberg—"metalogical" (SE I 21).[19] So he had occasion to say that he recognized himself to be with Ehrenberg in "a common philosophical cause" (1935 475). And yet the philosophy of dialogue as a whole is characterized by what, in spite of their mutual connection, also holds of the members of this community: that here the unitary is in the final analysis arrived at by divergent paths—a fact that Rosenzweig himself affirms when, in a letter to H. Ehrenberg, he emphasizes the "striking affinity of our thought that has come to be without any contact with one another" (1935 310.)[20]

Nevertheless, one must of course bear in mind that "new thought" was prepared by philosophers such as Hamann, Wilhelm von Humboldt, Fichte, and Feuerbach, and that its unity is due to them before all inner connections. Ebner traces his dialogical thought primarily back to Hamann and Humboldt but also to Jakob Grimm. H. Ehrenberg, whose *Disputation*, book I, deals with Fichte's theory of intersubjectivity, is also at the same time concerned therein with Feuerbach's "basic principles" (165–167).[21] Of Feuerbach, Buber, who also occasionally refers to Hamann, Fichte, and Jacobi, says that Yes and No had become for him, since his student days, a part of his existence (DP 295).[22] Over and above this, several representatives of the philosophy of dialogue—the earlier and the later, those set apart and those in communication—stand in succession to Kierkegaard. Rosenzweig, however, who clearly came of age in the course of his encounter with German idealism, also surpasses them in this, that he is aware of his dependence—as is also H. Ehrenberg in another way—not only upon the postidealistic thought of Kierkegaard and upon the late idealistic philosophy of Schelling, but also upon the philosophy of Hegel. In particular, he has Hegel in mind when, in the "germinal cell" to *Star*, he says that the "unrest" in his timely thought is "1800" (KS

358). Hegel's philosophy represents for him—as was said—the completion of ancient thought, with respect to which the new thought has to distance itself. But he foresees that the "new" thought, precisely because it is the counterproject to the ancient, will remain within its jurisdiction.

3 The Meaning and Limits of a Philosophical Interpretation of Buber

We turn to Buber.[23] The great caesura in phenomenological philosophy from Husserl to Sartre and his thought is grounded internally not only in the difference in content of their principles and goals but just as much in the formal distinction of the place that the theme "the Other" takes in the totality of their respective works as well as in the methods with which it is approached.

With Sartre, reflection upon being-for-Others presupposes the description of the for-itself and the in-itself. Husserl is interested in intersubjectivity simply in connection with the question concerning subjectivity and the world constituted in it. In *Being and Time*, the problematic of being-with only lies at the border of the analytic of *Dasein*, which itself is simply supposed to prepare the way for a genuine clarification of the meaning of being. For Buber, on the contrary, the problem of "dialogical life" is the problem pure and simple, and indeed not only inasmuch as the entire philosophical production of the mature man is dedicated, directly or indirectly, to the "Thou" but also, and before all else, because, in the ontology projected by Buber, there is no other problem that might take precedence over that of the dialogical life, or might surpass it in scope. The explication of dialogical life is supposed to lay the foundation of ontology.

In crass opposition to the fundamental meaning of being-with-one-another, we now find, however, a lack of differentiation in the argumentative operations and an inadequacy in the concepts with which Buber seeks to dominate his theme. It can hardly be a matter of doubt that, from a methodological point of view, Buber, and with him all dialogicians, remains far behind Sartre, but also behind Husserl and Heidegger. For all that, this lack has a positive foundation with Buber: the thought about the "dialogical principle" springs not from a metaphysical experience but from an "experience of faith"[24] and must, for this reason, first be translated into philosophical concepts. Such a translation is necessarily inadequate. Therefore, instead of reproaching Buber for the irrelevance of his philosophical nomenclature, interpreters are far more interested in the question concerning the justification for his venture, one that attempts to bring a religiously founded thought form before the seat of judgment of philosophical criticism. The justification consists in this, that Buber himself translates his thought into philosophical language (1962 1111–1113). But this kind of legitimacy limits at the same time the worth of the interpretation that follows. On the one hand, the philosophical interpretation remains, in a certain respect, external to Buber's intention. For, in place of the regression to the experience of faith as the source of the thought to be interpreted, its legitimation must bring it to a specifically philosophical experience. To this extent, Buber is judged by foreign standards here. To be sure, it is not implied therewith that the issue should be judged by other standards. For the issue of the second part of the investigation is precisely the question whether a philosophical experience also lies at the root of the primarily religiously experienced "Thou," as opposed to a creative presentation of the Buberian work. Alongside the testimony of other authors, Buber's work alone provides the material by means of which this question can be answered. On the other hand, however, the philosophical analysis is subjected to a restriction to the extent that its field may only range as far as Buber's translation of the experience of faith into philosophical language reaches. Where Buber expresses his beliefs immediately or chooses languages other than that of philosophy as his means of expression, he removes himself from our purview.

In the field of the philosophical word, however, the "critique" bound up with the interpretation is directed against the inadequacy of the concept with respect to a *philosophical* and not a *religious* experience. Even this is not, therefore, a genuine criticism of Buber. For it "distinguishes" neither Buber's innermost intention from the (supposed) truth of the matter nor Buber's innermost intention from its actual execution. Rather, it distinguishes the actual execution from the idea that is displayed before a philosophical experience of the matter, therefore one that is not explicitly carried out by Buber. To the extent, therefore, that the religiously experienced reality can also be experienced philosophically—something that in any case can provisionally only be hypothetically assumed—the idea that functions as a criterion is also mirrored in Buber's own intentions. So the distinction between execution and intention once again mediates the critique to be brought forth, as was in part already the case in the first part of the investigation.

4 The Negative Delimitation of the Sphere of the Between from the Sphere of Subjectivity

As is well known, the text *I and Thou* has for its main content the description of two "basic words," the "basic word I-It" and that which gives the writing its name: the "basic word I-Thou." The two basic words are reciprocally related. One, the basic word I-It, gives expression to what in the tradition is the already explicated relationship of human being to world; the other, the basic word I-Thou, is the conceptual sign of the experience that Buber would like to introduce into the game. What is at issue with it, and what Buber wants to do with it, will become clear through a reflection upon the concept "between."

The concept between is the key word that opens the way to Buber's intention—indeed, to the whole of dialogicalism.[25] In the postscript to the "writings on the dialogical principle," Buber sketches—as already mentioned—the historical position that *I and Thou* assumes in connection with the previous, contemporary, and later efforts directed toward the same problem. Even in comparison with his own earlier attempts, like *Daniel* (1913), there appears, as the authentically new in *I and Thou*, the discovery of a relation that is "no longer grounded in the sphere of subjectivity, but in that of the between." And with regard to the contemporary dialogical movement, Buber proceeds, "This is, however, the decisive change that took place in a group of thinkers in the time of World War I" (DP 259).

In accord with the commanding position that is granted to the little word "between," the "path" pursued by *I and Thou* comes to an end in the "sphere *between the essence*," in the "realm that is concealed in our midst, in the between" (DP 121). This realm, in which the original facts like "spirit" and "love" are situated (DP 18–19, 41),[26] is programmatically presented in the "problem of human being" in the following manner: "This sphere that is posited with the existence of human being as human being, but that is still not conceptually fixed, I name the sphere of the between. It is an originary category of human reality." At this point, just as in the little treatise *The Elements of the Interhuman*, the meaning of the concept between is, in opposition to *I and Thou*, restricted to the anthropological realm. So the ontology that Buber wants to work out there is called the "ontology of the innerhuman" (DP 276). If one abstracts from the anthropological restriction, then, in support thereof, one can characterize Buber's goal, insofar as it lies within the field of philosophical conceptuality, as an *ontology of the between*.[27]

It would be pertinent to prepare for the positive determination of the between through an elucidation of that against which it is set off. The "sphere of subjectivity" is above all the living, "noetic"[28] interiority of the I: "Spirit is not in the I but between the I and the Thou" (DP 41:89). This interiority manifests itself, from a psychological standpoint, as soul: "Feelings accompany only the metaphysical and the metaphysical fact of the relation, which is carried out not in the soul but between I and Thou" (DP 82:129). The sphere of subjectivity reaches out over the inner psychic transactions or "noeses" to encompass also the "noemata." Since the relation that is realized in the between is not an intentional *act* of the subject, that to which it is related can also not be an intentional *object*: "This is not a metaphor but the reality: love does not get attached to the I so that it only has the Thou as a 'content,' as an object; it is *between* I and Thou" (DP 18–19:66).

Accordingly, the sphere of subjectivity is not coextensive with the realm of the subject in distinction to the realm of the object. Indeed, its full weight, following Buber's understanding, lies on the side of noematic objectivity. So, for Buber, it is not a question of overcoming the I, which positively, would be equivalent to a "turning toward the object," but of the relativization of the I that envisages beings as "It," by means of the I that confronts beings as a Thou. The Thou therefore stands out in relief against the It and not the I. The It is, however, an object and, indeed, precisely an object in the sense of the correlate of an act. The I-It relations are "activities . . . that have a something for object. I perceive something. I sense something. I feel something. I think something. . . . All this and the like together ground the realm of the It" (DP 8:54).

Accordingly, the realm of the It or the sphere of subjectivity includes the acting subject together with the world intentionally dominated by him. Therefore stepping over the sphere of subjectivity striven for in the ontology of the between is nothing other than a leap down from the transcendental level, which Husserl opened up, and onto the level on which, in spite of all corrections and modifications, Heidegger and Sartre operate. This is confirmed by a look at the three formal features of the I-It relation and the corresponding moments of the I-Thou relation.

First, the realm of the It, or what corresponds to it in the other dialogicians, is, like Husserl's world, *perspectivally ordered*. All entities in it are oriented toward the I as the midpoint of the world. The It-I perceives the world "around itself" (DP 35:82). It is "surrounded by a multiplicity of contents" (DP 16:63). Grisebach emphasizes this even more energetically than Buber. According to him, there necessarily belongs to the I that constitutes the world as its "interiority" the "assumption of a determinate standpoint" (Gw 52). From this standpoint, it orders the world in accordance with a "principle" adopted by it (Gw 48). The relatedness of the world to the principle posited by the I makes the I into the "midpoint of its world" (Gw 48, 51; see also 63, 515, 519). As internal, the world is "always centered from there" (Gw 515), perspectivally centered around the subject that constitutes it (Gw 65). Similarly for Marcel. He apprehends the sphere of what is called by Buber "realm of the It" as that sphere of "having" that is distinguished from the dialogical sphere of being. The sphere of having, however, is that of intentionality and, as such, is centered upon the having and intentionally directed subject. According to Marcel, one can only talk about having where "a certain what is related to a certain who regarded as a center of inherence and of apprehension that is to some extent transcendent" (Ea 219; see also 194).

In the perspectival orientedness of the It to the I that corresponds to it, we already find the second moment of the I-It relation: the It is the determined; the I that posits itself as "subject" (DP 65:112), the determining. Or, as H. Ehrenberg says in the terminology of Rosenzweig, the subject is the "producer"; the object or the It, the "product" (Disp.I 174–175, 183). Those entities that are lodged around the I have to be ordered in accordance with the latter. The I-It relationship is therefore a relationship of mastery and slavery, of *sub*-and *super*-ordination. Cohen speaks of "subordination," "submission" (RV 148), Grisebach principally of "mastery" (Gw 51, 94–95, 150, 552). In this case the concept of mastery does not mean an external domination, but solely the constituting capacity of subjectivity. Mastery in this sense is any kind of objectification. Modern science, which carries the objectification of beings to its furthest extreme, also possesses, for this reason, according to Grisebach, the most radical will to mastery. In its critique, Grisebach's *Present* anticipates, in a characteristic manner, certain essential traits of late Heidegger's critique of science. On the basis of its extraordinary relation to objectivity, Grisebach regards modern science, just as does late Heidegger, as an affair already in itself disposed to the technical, carried out for the sake of the technical (Gw 17, 170, 482), which, for this reason, Grisebach can call the "absolutizing of the human essence" (Gw 54) because it—like the systematic philosophy in which it is unfolded—secures "for the human being the mastery of his essence" (Gw IX).

However, the I exercises its universal mastery over beings by means of the *world project* in which it ensnares things. So the intentionality that holds the realm of the It together is, in the third place, as with Husserl, Heidegger, and Sartre, a sense and horizon intentionality, that is, a directedness that in the self-direction toward objects at the same time makes way for the opposition of the latter.

In sharp contrast with the mediation of the It through the world project, however typified, the I-Thou relation is now above all characterized by "immediacy."[29] We already came across this concept in the first part of the investigation, and, indeed, wherever the incalculable encounter with personal being obliged us to recognize its difference from the horizon-bound knowledge of things. What was there illuminated, and then again covered over, is retained by Buber from beginning to end as the sustaining ground of his social ontology. The talk about immediacy is the tenor of his entire work. It has—as, in the end, has everything that Buber says—the character of an appeal: "Be immediate!"—that is the answer to the question posed by him in 1919: "What should be done?"[30] The necessity of the appeal, however, results from the distress of the historical situation, whose danger is essentially the loss of immediacy (H 315). This demand concerns, above all, that immediacy "between man and man" (H 112, 291, 325), which is alone under discussion in Husserl and Sartre. Already in 1914 Buber had elevated it to the "criterion" of human efficacy (H 12–13). But the present endangering of immediacy reaches right over and beyond the interhuman relationship: "Immediacy has been damaged not only between man and man but between the essence man and the originary ground of being" (H 325).[31] Immediacy in the relation to all beings, therefore, has also to be reinstated from out of the originary ground of being.

Buber has this universal immediacy in view when, in *I and Thou*, he says, "The relation to the Thou is immediate. Between I and Thou there is no conceptuality, no foreknowledge, and no fantasy. . . . Between I and Thou there is no end, no greed, and no anticipation. . . . Every means is an impediment. Only where all means have fallen away can the meeting come about" (DP 15–16:62). As with Husserl and Sartre, here too "immediacy" is, in the end, a negative concept. What is negated is the "means." "Means," however, means two things. It is, first of all, a "means to an end." As the nonobjective "toward which" of the immediate relation, the Thou is not a means that I can use for my ends. In the second place, the means is a medium. The medium is, however, nothing other than the horizonal space with which I surround beings in their objectification. In theoretical comportment, such a medium is that conceptuality that fixes beings with a determinate sense and orders them into the system of unified signs. Or that foreknowledge (anticipation in the practical sphere) that reckons with proceedings in the world in advance and protects itself from the suddenness of their occurrence. Or even that fantasy that, in spite of the freedom that it allows itself, detains its object within the boundaries of that which has been thought out. The meaning of "means" as medium is, however, the more comprehensive and even includes within itself the meaning of means as the correlate of an end. For even the means-ends connection is a mode of the medial project. Along with greed, which only appears as the counterpart of an instinctual drive, and along with anticipation, the end is also a practical impediment that obstructs the immediate relation of I and Thou. The relation to the Thou is, however, immediate because in it the I is separated from its partner, but not through the barrier of the meaning-instituting project. In it there is, as Grisebach says, "no fore-having and no fore-statement" (Gw 508)—indeed, "no kind of a priori whatsoever . . . because it runs counter to all a priori thought" (Gw 481).

The I-It relationship is, as we said, essentially a relationship of dependence of the object on the subject. Even in this respect, the I-Thou relationship turns out to be its antithesis: "To want to understand the pure relation as one of dependence means to want to derealize the one bearer of the relation and thereby the relation itself" (DP 84:131). Here Buber not only refers to my prior mastery over the Other but also to that superordination of the Other over me that Sartre declares to be the original situation. As a community of equally primordial and equally legitimate essences, of which no one disposes of the other, the I-Thou relationship, to which alone Buber ascribes the name "relation" (DP 8:55, 10:57),[32] is a relationship of *mutuality*: "Relation is mutuality" (DP 12:58).[33] Without the latter there is no "dialogical" relationship. To the "minimal condition of the dialogical" there belongs inseparably "the mutuality of the inner behavior" (DP 135). Like immediacy, mutuality is, in the first instance, a concern of interhuman intercourse.[34] It is realized among human beings more or less as the "mutuality of presentification" or as the "mutuality of acceptation, of affirmation and confirmation" (UB 43). But, like immediacy, "the complete fullness of actual mutuality" (DP 111:167) does not get exhausted in the relation of human beings to one another. The "value of values" is the "mutuality of the relation between the human and the divine."[35] On the basis of this relation, there also arises mutuality as a being character of the all. It becomes the "flowing mutuality of the universe" (DP 20:67): A "mutuality of giving" rules between me and the whole world addressed as Thou (DP 36:84).[36]

We now have to look for the dialogical counterpart to the perspectival centering of the It-world upon the I. We find it, as also the more precise sense of immediacy and mutuality, in the concept of the *between* itself.[37] From it we want to obtain information about Buber's fundamental approach. Hitherto, the between has been delimited exclusively against the "sphere of subjectivity" as the point of departure for Husserl, Heidegger, and Sartre. Accordingly, the between is not to be found "in the I," that is, neither in the (psychic) interiority of the subjective pole of intentionality nor in the noematic objectivity of a horizontally comprehended world, oriented upon the I, and dependent upon it. If we follow Buber's own negative characterization of the between a step farther, we find that what already follows from the mutuality has still to be added in, namely, that the between is just as little to be found in the Other, neither in his act-center nor in me nor in the remaining entities as his objects. So Buber sets out—we find here, in a negative way, what is peculiar to his approach—neither from the I nor from the Other. He does not replace the centering of the world upon the I, as does Sartre in the social realm, with the orientation of all things, and even of my given being, upon the Other.

Buber, however, does not take his point of departure from a third who comprehends the partners. To be sure, a few expressions and locutions might lead to such a misunderstanding. That spiritual activity is not in the I but between the I and the Thou signifies, for Buber, as for Rosenstock-Huessy (AS 68), not that the I embraces the spirit, but the spirit the I (DP 41:89). This "reversal" accentuates the over-coming of subjectivity aimed at in the ontology of the between. It determines, in a similar way, the essence of love (DP 18–19:66) and of language (DP 41:89). But the basic ontological phenomena are comprehensive only in the relationship to the I, not in relation to the I and the Thou together. It is just as important to emphasize this as to indicate that Buber sets out neither from the I nor from the Other. The renunciation of egology and its conversion in no way implies a return to that "objective" conception of the totality that Sartre criticizes in Hegel. I and Thou are not imbedded in a totality and, so to speak, neutralized with respect to it. No "third," neither the "world of ideas" (DP 17:65) nor the world of realities, spans and supervises the "two-foldness" that lies in the "opposition to one another" (DP 262) of the partners, as also in the antithesis of the "basic words": "A real con-versation . . . is carried out not in one or the other participant, or in a neutral world that encompasses both and all other things, but in the most precise sense between both, in a dimension, so to speak, that is only accessible to them both" (PM 167).

Now one might suppose that the between was to be located, if not in one of the partners, or in an encompassing third, then in both partners together. But Buber even denies this. The meaning of the conversation is to be met with "neither in one of the two partners nor in both together" (DP 262). According to Buber, beginning with a unity consisting of me and the Other is no more appropriate than the point of departure from me as an isolated subject. He would then have offended against that law of ontological difference posited by Sartre, which, in a certain manner, even Buber recognizes as valid. The between really rules between the partners and so prevents their being taken up in each other. Admittedly, it cannot be found like a thing between the partners. It is certainly a fact, but a metaphysical fact, a fact beyond all physical being (DP 18:66). It most certainly does not exist in such a way between I and Thou that it separates them ontically and sets up something different from themselves among them. For then it would once again be a third thing, and, indeed, in distinction from that which encompassed I and Thou, it would be one that was encompassed by them. Above all, however, it would in this case be an "impediment," which, in exactly the same way as the encompassing third, would destroy the immediacy of the relation and therewith the relation itself.

5 The Positive Determination of the Between as "Meeting"

What now remains for the positive determination of the between after all this demarcating? Simply and solely the explication of the "metaphysical and metapsychic fact." This fact is the meeting: "The other side of the subjective, this side of the objective, on the narrow ridge at which I and Thou meet one another, is the realm of the between" (PM 169—italics are mine; see also Marcel in MB 38–39). For this reason Buber can say, "All real life is a meeting" (DP 15:62). We shall first be able to estimate the range of this statement at the end of *I and Thou*, when we know how fundamental and universal a significance Buber accords to the concept of reality and of the real life. In a preliminary way, we must get closer to the meeting character of the between in a further abstraction from the subject-object relationship.

The subject is as such necessarily in action, the object in passion; the subject is the one who acts, the object the one that is acted upon. This difference is straightforwardly posited in the concept of the subject. For, in accordance with the concept, the *subjectum* is what it is (that is, what underlies) because it does not simply lie there but lets the *objectum* lie there, which latter thereby becomes the passively given, the static counterpart. The I-It or subject-object relationship is therefore, to this extent, a union of unequals, since the activity of the one presupposes the passivity of the other.

Ex negativo, this circumstance throws light upon the I-Thou relation, that is, the community of partners of equal rank. An equality of level and of origin can only be reached in this way, that both partners meet either in action or in passion. A relationship of two passive members would be a pure, inner-worldly relation of things indifferently present alongside each other. So I and Thou must be together in action (GD 162–163; RV 103). Thereby they, admittedly, still will not be subjects. The proximity to the subject is only greater than that to the object because both partners are "I" 's in a quite broad sense. Even the Other who exists over against me as a Thou is, "for himself," an I. The I is, however, the, so to speak, neutral point of exchange for the subject (the It-I) and that being of mine that corresponds to the Thou. On the basis of the indirect connection to the subject produced by this, Buber is also able to call my Thou-being "subjectivity," though, of course, in a completely different sense from that sphere that underlies the ontology of the between (DP 65:111). The Thou-I is, in a certain respect, the "true" subject. In the same manner, it first brings its action, the action of the subject, back to itself. For where action runs its "for which" into passivity, it itself remains ensnared in its opposite. It first fulfills itself there where it responds to its equal. This, however, only happens in a dialogical manner when the acts of the partners make contact with one another *reciprocally*. To the extent that they run parallel to one another, it is not a matter of an I-Thou community, but (according to Buber) of a we-community grounded in it (PM 115–117, W 17). In contrast with the latter, the I-Thou relationship is to the very highest degree—to use Sartre's expression—a relation between "frontally" opposed counterparts. The behavior of the Thou confronts me, the agent, from the other side. The assembly of partners who make contact with each other is "the meeting."

Buber's "phenomenology" of the meeting is characterized by the unity of two moments, which, at first glance, seem to exclude one another. That Buber, as we already saw, does not envisage "the real connection of the real duality I and Thou" (DP 62:111) from the standpoint of an encompassing totality means, positively: regardless of his intention to overcome the supremacy of the I, he remains, in thinking of the fact "we meet each other," true to that inner perspective prescribed by the "mineness" of the I. Only those who see both sides, the displacement of egology and the orientation toward "interiority," will do justice to Buber's account. As in *Being and Nothingness*, so also in *I and Thou*, the action of the Other is experienced as *coming* to me and not as *going* to me.

Buber himself formulates as a methodological maxim, "What we have to be concerned with, what we have to care about, is not the other, but our side" (DP 77:124). It is not a matter, therefore, of empathic insight into the activity of the Other, but of the elucidation of our own action. This requirement follows from what is really experienced: "When we go a certain way and meet a human being who comes up to us and who also went a certain way, we only know our stretch, not his. We only experience his stretch in the meeting" (DP 77:124). With this renunciation of empathic insight into the alien way, I am not deprived, in any way, of the participation of the Other. His deed contributes to the meeting as it is really experienced. The experience of the meeting is therefore, at the same time, and even if it can only be had from my side and in the execution of my own act, the counterexperience of the alien deed. In the meeting, however, the alien deed encounters me, in the twofold meaning of the word, as a "cooperation" of the Other and as an encounter in the sense of a reception of kindness and generosity. Buber speaks here of "grace." That a meeting can never be brought about through my deed but requires a cooperation from the other side presents itself out of the inner perspective of the meeting, in such a way that when it happens, it happens "out of will and grace in one" (DP 11:57). Grace is the gift of what is not at my disposal. The freedom of the Other manifests itself to the experience of the meeting out of the basic root of one's own freedom as that which can no longer be willed but only conceded. But precisely as the nondisposable, the alien contribution remains the nonknowable. Its characterization as grace by no means reduces it to a "something beyond the meeting" (DP 77:124), but consists in the reception of its grace: "What we deal with . . . is not grace, but the will. Grace concerns us to the extent that we go out to it and await its presence. It is not our object" (DP 77:124). A real meeting can just as well "never happen through me" as "without me" (DP 15:62). However, what is required from me is the act; and not what is not at my disposal, to which I can only open myself expectantly.

The second essential trait of the meeting worked out by Buber is clearly difficult to reconcile with the methodological orientation toward "my" experience. If the activity of the participants necessarily belongs to the latter, it can itself not be a "fact," in the sense of a present and completed matter of fact. Its factical character must rather be grounded in the mode of its being as a pure occurrence. By the sphere of the between, Buber means "exclusively actual events" (DP 261). So he is able to say, "Feelings are 'had'; love happens" (DP 18:66); see also Rosenzweig (SE II 98). The meeting is, however, the occurrence of an event that discloses the between in all its concretion and in such a way that it is itself the event and not simply something that takes place. For precisely this reason, I call it a pure occurrence. The occurrence could not be *pure*, however, if it was put together out of the acts of those who meet each other. That would suit the "simple, original fact of the meeting" (DP 78:125) very poorly. The purity or the original simplicity requires much more that the fact of the meeting essentially presupposes the fact of those who meet. Instead of the I and the Thou, as already finished beings, bringing the meeting into being, they must, according to the dialogical approach, themselves first spring out of the occurrence of the meeting. Only so can the between be affirmed as more original in contrast to the "sphere of subjectivity," my own as well as that of the alien.

In fact, Buber has drawn these consequences. The opposition between the I-It and the I-Thou relationships ranges not only over the "for which" (here the Thou, there the It) and the I corresponding to it, but also over the relationship itself. To be sure, as an intentional object, the It is what it is only in relation to the subject that intends it, just as the I of the I-It relationship only exists as subject in relation to the It. In connection with this, however, it lies in the essence of the intentional object that, in the I-It relationship, the *relata* precede the *relatio*, even if only potentially. That toward which the act of the subject is directed must already, in some way, be given prior to the act—H. Ehrenberg (Disp.I 175)—and, in the same way, the subject, in order to be able to function as the pole of intentionality, must previously be present. To the extent, therefore, that here the relationship does not permit the being of the members of the relationship to proceed forth from itself in the complete and authentic sense, it remains external to the latter. This means at the same time that in it as an "experiencing" and a "using"—Buber applies these terms in *I and Thou* exclusively to the characterization of the I-It relationship—neither the I is decisively involved with the world nor the world with the I (DP 9:56). The mutual lack of participation is grounded in the fact that I and It do not stand in need of the relationship in order to be able to exist at all. Conversely, however, the dialogical relationship joins the relating terms together in a fateful manner because it first calls them into being. Buber has this difference in mind when he characterizes the basic word I-It as the spiritual form of the "natural suspension," and the basic word I-Thou as the spiritual form of the "natural connection" (DP 28:76, 33:81, 65:112).

Not until the concrete analysis of the opposition of Thou and It in the next chapter will we be able to confirm that Buber seeks the ontological condition of the suspension itself (what concerns its intent) in the dialectic of the noematic object as I related and still also somehow pregiven. For the moment, it must suffice to show that he has seen the corresponding dialectic of the subject and has, on the basis of it, explained the suspension of the members of the I-It relationship from the side of the I.

"The I of the basic word I-It appears as an own being (*Eigenwesen*) and is conscious of itself as a subject (of experiencing and utilizing).

The I of the basic word I-Thou appears as a person and is conscious of itself as subjectivity (without a dependent genitive). Own being appears in that it sets itself off against other own beings. A person appears in that it stands in relation to other persons" (DP 65:112). The subject is, on the one hand, simply the functional and punctual pole of the intentionality that *Dasein* only possesses in the accomplishment of the objectifying act. On the other hand, it is something continually present and even present outside of its intentional function. This is its essential dialectic. In this passage, the one side of it is given expression in the locution "subject (of experiencing and utilizing)." The subject is precisely nothing more than the center of those acts that direct it to an object. As such it receives its determinateness solely from its objects. From out of itself it is without fullness and substance. For this reason, it has no genuine continuity. Present only in its acts, it is dissolved in disparate points: "The subject . . . remains punctual, functional, the one who experiences and utilizes, nothing more" (DP 67:114). The other side of the dialectic is articulated in the concept "own being." As own being, the It-I precisely has something to make own. It is something entirely determinate. Only because it is determined in this way and not in another can it "set itself off" against other own beings. It is something for itself and for this reason against others. For itself, however, it exists as something continually present, as an entity that maintains itself in being, so to speak, behind its acts and uninfluenced by the relationships that it enters into in the change of objects.

The two sides of the dialectic do not fall apart in absolute incompatibility. Rather, they agree in the *emptiness* of the being-present-at-hand that is attributed to the subject as its own being. In spite of its individual determinateness, the being-present-at-hand of the subject does not contradict its punctual functionality because it is itself completely substanceless: "No matter how much the subject may make its own, there does not emerge therefrom any substance. . . . All his extended and multifarious being, all his eager 'individuality' cannot help him to any substance" (DP 67:114). From the standpoint of the actual act, it looks as though the subject did not exist outside of this act precisely because it only exists in the abstract pallor of a potentiality that gains fullness only in its actualization, that is, the worldly fullness of objectivity. In reality, however, it is in the moment of acting that it stands out of the background of its empty being-present-at-hand.

It stands out in order to take hold of the It that is already previously abstracted and present "for itself," and to become actual together with it. In a passage in which he tries to display the origin of the I-It relation from out of the I-Thou relationship, Buber proceeds with the description of the "relational event," constitutive of the I and the Thou in the first instance: "Now, however, the disconnected I arises, transformed: reduced from substantial fullness to the functional punctuality of an experiencing and utilizing subject, it is empowered by all this 'It for itself' and situates itself, together with it, in the other basic word" (DP 33:80). The subject could not take hold of the It if it itself, just as well as the It, were not already present-at-hand before their relationship. In taking hold and positing together, however, the externality of the I-It relationship, and the disconnectedness of its members from one another, is evident. So the ontological condition of disconnectedness is the preexistence of the *relata* before the *relatio*.

Even the Thou-I has its dialectic. Its sides are precisely the opposite of those of the dialectic of the subject. In the sense of own being, the Thou-I is nothing existing for itself. So it only appears as a "person" in the relation to other persons. And yet, in contrast with the subject, it is conscious of itself as "subjectivity (without dependent genitive)." From this side, the It-I manifests itself precisely as the essentially related, the Thou-I, however, as that very I that is not relationally directed. While the It-I is only the subjective correlate of the experienced and utilized object, the Thou-I, precisely because it does not make anything dependent upon itself, remains independent in itself.

But even this contradiction can be reconciled. The Thou-I is nothing simply in accordance with its present composition, which, in the one determines it in one way, in the Other, in another. This determinateness is that of the individual, which Buber sharply distinguishes from the person (DP 155, 233). Each thing can also be an individual (PM 169). Only the I can be a person. In that the Thou-I is not suited to individual determinateness—as Cohen also emphasizes (RV 192)—it is also not to be distinguished, in this respect, from other persons. But the failure of individual determinateness in no way means total undeterminateness. On the contrary, the autarchy of the person presupposes the participation in one being, which, in contrast with the emptiness of the present-at-hand, is absolute fullness itself: "The person is conscious of itself as someone who takes part in being, as a being-with and therefore as an entity. Own being is conscious of itself as an entity that exists in this way rather than another. In that own being sets itself off against others, it distances itself from being" (DP 66:113–114). The dialectic of the subject and its inversion reflected in the dialectic of the person are rooted accordingly in the duality of being itself. In the horizon of being as present-at-hand, the subject manifests itself as determinate and the person as nothing. In contrast, in the light of being, the subject that holds sway in the reality of the between reveals itself as empty and the person as fulfilled being. In this its fullness, the person, according to Buber, is a "self" (DP 67; see also GF 118). The self-sufficiency of the self is the positive aspect of the independence from the object, which develops in subjectivity out of the independence of the object from it.

The difference between the It-I and the Thou-I exhibits, accordingly, a certain similarity to the distinction between the I, attributed by Heidegger to Husserl in *Being and Time*, and the self, which Heidegger substitutes for it. The grounding of the basic word I-It through the basic world I-Thou, four years before the appearance of *Being and Time*, anticipates, at least in what concerns the I, Heidegger's modified correction of egology through autology. Buber's personal subjectivity is, like Heidegger's self, a dynamic performance, a mode of being (DP 66:113), and even in this respect represents a correction of the subject whose activity is raised above that of a static basis. While, according to Heidegger, the self can only come to itself in a voluntary separation of itself from the other self, according to Buber, it has its being solely in the relation. This is valid of both directions, that "a genuine relation only obtains between genuine persons" (PM 164) and that genuine persons only exist in a genuine relation, in other words, that the relation, as encounter, first brings forth those who meet each other as persons (DP 155). Therefore personal subjectivity does not possess its substantial fullness beyond the relationship to the Other in the same sense as the subject its being present-at-hand. Rather, its fullness is entirely encompassed by the relation. Precisely for this reason, the person is also, however, a subjectivity without dependent genitive. For its fullness protects it from losing itself as an empty pole in a dependence upon its counterpart. It is not directed toward the relation simply insofar as it reposes in its own fullness. But since its being is not the being of a separated entity, but the reality of the between, this, its fullness, is only lived in and out of the relation.

Let us look back: In accordance with the fundamental clarification of the concept "meeting," we have, in this section, concerned ourselves with two things in particular: first, with the access to the meeting on the part of my I; and second, with the origination of my I and that of the Other out of the meeting. The difficulty that stands in the way of a unification of both points is easy to see: The I and the between seem to compete with each other over the legitimacy of the point of departure. The I wants to be the point of departure because the event of meeting can only be experienced with respect to that which takes place in it. The between, however, grounds its claim to being logically first on this, that, even ontologically, it constitutes the beginning. In accordance with everything that has been said hitherto, it should be clear that in this conflict, Buber is primarily committed to the between. In any case, he is just as plainly of this persuasion in order that the conflict should be settled and the I also retain its right. Starting out from the between only stands in contradiction to starting out from the I, as individual—not, however, from the I as person. Buber is completely aware of this. He knows that the true alternatives are not starting out from the between and from an I opposed to the former, but beginning with the individual I, on the one hand, and with the between, and so also with the personal I, on the other. Above all, one finds the insight that for the "philosophical science of human being," "the point of departure is given" in the reality of the between and nowhere else (PM 169). For this reason, Buber can also say, "I take the individual to be neither the starting point nor even the end point of the human world. But I take the human person to be the irremovable central location of the battle between the movement of the world away from God and its movement toward God" (DP 233). To the extent that the philosophical science of human being has to set out from the between, it is therefore the "real person" from which the "genuine philosophical anthropology has to set out in all earnestness" (PM 44). For the beginning of the person is the beginning, pure and simple: the reality of the between.

6 The Reciprocal Constitution of the Partners as a Symbol for the Origination of I and Thou out of the Between

Buber thinks the birth of the partner out of the event of meeting as the reciprocal constitution of I and Thou, as the generation of the

I out of the Thou and of the Thou out of the I: "I-effecting-Thou and Thou-effecting-I" (DP 25:73) is supposed to be the originary genesis that precedes the institution of all subjectivity, as well as of all objectivity. But thought about the reciprocal constitution only has a conceptual meaning as a cipher for the source of the I and the Thou out of the between. If one takes him at his word, it is not possible to make out how the I constitutes the Thou and, in conjunction therewith, how the I is supposed to be constituted by it. In order to be able to constitute the Thou, it, for its part, would already have to be there. According to the theory of reciprocal constitution, however, it cannot be there without the Thou, which it has first to constitute. One escapes this vicious circle only when one understands the "I-effecting-Thou and Thou-effecting-I" as the expression of a common interaction in the meeting. Then equiprimordiality discloses itself as what is genuinely intended in the thought about reciprocal constitution, an equi-primordiality that, admittedly, has nothing to do with the indifference with which things exist in isolation from one another. The equi-primodiality that is envisaged here means, rather, the same primor-diality on the basis of the origination from the same—or, to put it better, the same origin. The "Thou-effecting-I" accordingly describes the "grace" that confronts me in the experience of the meeting, and "I-effecting-Thou" the same grace as it manifests itself to the Other. "I-effecting-Thou and Thou-effecting-I" then means: in its self-occurrence, the meeting happens at the same time to I and Thou.

Since we, however, have to see reciprocal constitution in the horizon of equiprimordiality, we have to consider Buber's thesis on the con-stitution of the I in the Thou as the specification of a partial aspect of reciprocal constitution. This thesis is intrinsically ambiguous. The claim that "human being becomes an I on account of the Thou" (DP 32:80) refers to the Other, insofar as he is a cohuman being, just as much as it does to "me." We are both an I, and we become such as the statement expresses it, "on account of the Thou," therefore on account of the Other. Therefore, at bottom, the statement only for-mulates the thought of reciprocal constitution. The locution "on account of the Thou" means, however, in more exact language: in the rela-tionship to the Thou qua Other: "The I first exists out of the *relationship* to the Thou" (PM 170).[38] So, in the final analysis, the statement for-mulates the thought of the origination of the partners out of the between.

That we, the other and "I," first become an I on account of the Thou can nevertheless be apprehended in a different way. As will be shown in what follows, what is characterized as "Thou" is coposited in common with the Other, coposited in the strict sense of the word in which I mean the Other when I address him and in which the Other means me when he addresses me. Even the I, therefore, is nominally related to "me" as to the Other. In this way the statement that "human being becomes an I on account of the Thou" once again invites a twofold interpretation in the relation to me as well as in the relation to the Other. For the other the statement means either that he, the Other, becomes an I, in that he is addressed by me, or that he becomes an I, in that he addresses me. In exactly the same way, in its application to me, the statement leaves it open whether "I" become an I in being addressed or in addressing.[39] However that may be, in one way or the other, and even when one locates the Thou in addressing or being addressed, therefore in the intersphere of the relation, the statement proceeds upon an assertion about the origination of the partners out of their meeting.

Those very places in which the I is identified with "me" contribute most readily to the erroneous opinion that it is a matter here of a one-sided constitution in which the Other is the constituting and I am the constituted. This occurs, for instance, in the statement, "I am on account of the Thou; becoming an I, I say Thou" (DP 15:62). The statement seems to mean that "I" first arise in being addressed and, as the one addressed, first become capable, for my part, of addressing the Other. With this, however, Buber does not exclude the possibility that the Other is first constituted as a person when he is addressed by me and that he too is only first able to address me as the one addressed. In the meantime, "reciprocal constitution," itself only a cipher, appears in "my" talk about it necessarily in the shortened perspective of a precedence of the Thou over the I, that is, of the "thou" over "me," because I, in accordance with the methodological orientation toward mineness, am only in a position to speak about it from my side and not from the other. So the precedence of the Thou over the I in all those significations that it can have following the different senses of "I" and "Thou" is still only the clothing in which the precedence of the between over the I and the Thou manifests itself to me, the one who is met in the meeting.

The interpretation of the dialogical theorem of the "I-Thou succession" (AS 35) as a cipher for the origination of the partner out of the between admittedly makes no claim to reproducing the factically intended sense of all those kinds of expressions that were made in dialogicalism. It does, however, claim to bear upon the content of these expressions insofar as it possesses a dialogical character in general and is, as such, phenomenologically provable. Accordingly, the doctrine of the "I-Thou succession" can have a different meaning from the one set out when, for instance, it is theologically-dogmatically motivated—therefore, for example, wants to bring to expression that God is the creator and human being the creation, or that, in accordance with the precepts of love, I have to respond to the claims of my "nearest." Even in the field of Christian theology, however, when this doctrine is directed toward the phenomenon, and restricts its claims to validity to the interhuman sphere, it is exclusively concerned with the state of affairs explicated here. In Karl Barth's typically phenomenological analyses of cohuman being, the thesis of the primacy of the Thou is, more explicitly than anywhere else, restricted to the significance of an assertion about the origin of the I and the Thou from the between. Gogarten's shorter, and, in its brevity, misleading, statement, "I am through you" (GW 57), appears in Barth in the most careful of all interpretations: "I am in that Thou art" (KD III/2 292–297)—whereby the being of both of us is supposed to be characterized as "being in the meeting." In a similar manner, Gogarten necessarily goes back to the phenomenon described above when he specifies more exactly, and without recourse to dogma, his thesis, in accordance with which "the I first becomes a real I on account of the Thou and through the Thou" (GW 29). What he then means is that "only out of the meeting with the *Thou* does the I become real" (GW 31—italics are mine), and in such a way that "I" first really become an I in being addressed (1926) and "that my reality is given solely in my *relatedness* to the temporal, transient Thou" (1926 37—italics are mine). This phenomenologically verifiable but, so to speak, ethically neutral claim has, admittedly, to be distinguished from the other claim, following which there is "no being-I . . . in the unconditioned, responsible bond with the Thou" (1926 59). The latter Gogarten is only able to ground theologically. We are, so he says, indissolubly bound to the Thou, for the reason that God speaks to us through the latter (1926 60).

The theologically grounded discussion of the "Thou-I-succession" has a dialogical character even if it cannot be phenomenologically demonstrated. In the writings of the dialogicians, the "Thou-I-succession" is also discussed in one sense that can be followed up phenomenologically, but that still does not have a specifically dialogical stamp. In Rosenzweig, for instance. In the *Star of Redemption* we read, "The I constantly bears witness to a No. With 'I' an opposite is always posited, it is continually underlined; it is always an 'I but' " (SE II 110; see also KS 382). Of this I, Rosenzweig says that it consists first in the "discovery of the Thou" (SE II 112; see also RV 17). So the genesis of the I as "I but" is nothing other than that happening, similarly described by Husserl, in which the "originary *I*" becomes "an" I, an I among Others in "the discovery of the Thou," that is, of the Other. This is confirmed by a letter from Rosenzweig from the year 1917 (!) that takes issue indirectly with the same "where art Thou?" (Genesis 3,9), in connection with the interpretation of which *Star* develops the thesis of the "I but" (see also KS 364): "The real marvel, my I, does not consist at all in the I. For the I, as the substance (*ante festum*) is not at all my I, but precisely I in general. . . . But my I consists in the Thou. In Thou-saying I understand that the other is not a thing that is 'like I.' However, because in consequence an Other can be like I, the I ceases to be the single, 'transcendental' *ante omnia festa*, and becomes an I, my I" (1935 254). Rosenzweig here only diverges from Husserl insofar as he does not have in mind the thought of transcendental mineness and, for this reason, is able to think the transcendental I solely as "I in general." He loses sight of mineness, as also of personal mineness, but the latter is constituted for him, as for Husserl, by means of the Other. In that the I has become *an* I, it has become—so he continues—"a person on account of the Thou," a person once again in Husserl's sense. It goes without saying that such becoming-a-person is essentially to be distinguished from what, in Buber's dialogic, is also conceived as becoming-a-person, namely, the birth of the partner out of the meeting.

After having specified the basic antithetical character of the modern philosophy of dialogue in general, the task of this chapter was essentially the preparatory determination of the goal of Buber's ontology. We now have to take the measure of the path along which Buber strove to attain his goal. This path should be the path of the realization of the intention laid down in the concept of the between. It will now be shown that, to a considerable extent, the ontology of the between remains, in its execution, a purely negative ontology. This means, above all, that Buber grasps the "sphere of the between" only in abstraction from the "sphere of subjectivity." To be sure, he explains that the categories of the I-It relationship, in which traditional metaphysics interpreted the world, are not applicable to the I-Thou relationship. But he himself only actually pursues his quest for a positive categorial elucidation of the I-thou relationship (DP 34:82) in a piecemeal fashion. Accordingly, he thinks of the I-It and the I-Thou relationships in a similar manner, after a model whose ontological basis can only be sustained by the I-It and not by the I-Thou relationship. Buber only becomes aware of the inappropriateness of this model in relation to the reality of the between, which has to be formed in it, in that he presents the event of the meeting as the breakdown of the position that is really at issue in the model. This is the path that he takes. As *via negationis* he presupposes—even if only unclearly—a knowledge of the inadequacy of the model maintained, so to speak, only as a supporting structure. He only uses the latter like a ladder that is supposed to make possible the ascent from the conceptually unclarified sphere of the between to its conceptual clarification, a ladder that he takes away again as soon as he has succeeded in "climbing up."

The Destruction of the Transcendental Model of Intentionality

1 The Insertion of the I-It and the I-Thou Relationships in the Schema of World-Projecting Intentionality

The model toward which Buber is principally oriented is barely to be distinguished from the schema of the transcendental interpretation of the world. Although in its particulars it stands nearer to Husserl than to Heidegger, it especially reminds one of the approach of fundamental ontology to the extent that, in it too, it is not a uniformly composed I but the being of human being that forms the foundation upon which the proposed ontology is to be constructed. Human being stands there in the midst of beings whose totality Buber entitles "the world." The world is disclosed, however, in two different ways, depending on whether human being speaks the basic word I-Thou or the basic I-It: "For human being the world is twofold according to his twofold comportment. The comportment of human being is twofold according to the duality of the basic words that he is able to speak" (DP 7:53).

In these statements, it is the concept of "comportment" that is most illuminating. It says the same as the concept "attitude" in Husserl. That I adopt this or that comportment vis-à-vis this or that means that I have this or that attitude toward it. Both concepts name the horizonal intentionality. The I-It and the I-Thou relationships are comportments in which I am intentionally directed toward something. Everything antithetical about it rests on the basis of this commonness. As already noted, the difference between the basic words extends not only to the It and the Thou but also to the relationship itself and to the functioning I. But the components into which Buber dissolves the basic words are here, just as well as there, the three elements of intentionality: alongside the intention, the intending and the intended. It is certainly true that "the I of the basic word I-Thou is different from that of the basic word I-It" (DP 7:53). Still, it is apprehended, no less than the latter, as the subjective pole of intentionality. It is certainly true that "there is no I in itself but only the I of the basic word I-Thou and the I of the basic word I-It" (DP 8:54). But the necessity with which the neutral locus "human being" is taken over, according to the comportment, from I-Thou or from I-It, itself lies in the mechanism of intentionality, which therewith unites the divided I beings behind the scenes.

Likewise Buber formally conceives the Thou in the same way as the It: as what is intended, as the noematic object, now, admittedly, not of the I-It, but of the I-Thou. The connection with the intentional act first permits the freedom from the particular, the universality that consciously distinguishes the Buberian "Thou" and separates it from the anthropologically restricted "Other" of Husserl, Heidegger, and Sartre.[1] Thou and It are not separated realms in the totality of what is. They are, rather, the totality of what is or the world itself, according to the attitude in which I exist in the world. They are not to be distinguished, therefore, on the basis of the objective composition of what actually exists that is intended therewith. *Anything* can be an It: not only a Thing but also an idea (DP 17:65) and even a human being: "Without any alteration of the basic word, one of the words he and you can be introduced for It" (DP 7:53).[2] *Anything*, however, can also be Thou: not only the other human beings but also "spiritual beings" and natural things (DP 10:56). Therefore it comes down to the same thing when we say that nothing is really and actually already in itself Thou or It. It first becomes such in that moment in which I adopt toward it either the Thou or the It comportment: "Basic words do not express something that would exist without them, but inasmuch as they are spoken, they institute a state of affairs" (DP 7:53). This is precisely what is peculiar to the noematic object: that it certainly is related to something that arises outside of the intentional act, but is not itself this thing existing for itself. Thou and It are nothing other than the intentional "for which" of the comportment corresponding to them, in which beings in general are constituted *as* Thou or *as* It.[3]

I, this human being behaving in such and such a way, am therefore the one who makes something into a Thou or an It. According to the change of my attitudes, I change what still was an It into a Thou and what was a Thou into an It. Thou and It are, to be sure, modes of the presence of beings, but modes that I prescribe to beings. In other words, it depends upon my *project* whether entities confront me as Thou or as It. The intentionality upon which Buber set up his model is really therefore horizonal intentionality, like Husserl's life of consciousness and Heidegger's being-in-the-world. In this way, however, the Thou loses what Buber explicitly attributes to it: immediacy. The Thou is encountered not at all immediately, but exactly like the It, in a horizon that is continually a means in the sense of a mediating medium. The Thou itself is split into the "encountered" and the "native" Thou (DP 72–73), that is, into the one that appears in the horizon and the horizon in which it appears. The native Thou is an a priori structure of my being constitution and, as such, the condition of the possibility of the meeting: "In the beginning is the relation: as a category of being, as readiness, forming form, model of the soul; the a priori of the relation; *the innate Thou*" (DP 31). In contrast, the encountered Thou is simply the a posteriori fulfillment of the a priori, simply the actualization of a potentiality always already laid up in me: "Lived relations are realizations of the innate Thou with regard to the encounter. That the latter, apprehended as over against, taken up in exclusiveness, can in the end be addressed with the basic word is grounded in the a priori of the relation" (DP 31:79). The grounding of the encountered through the native Thou takes from the latter, however, the suddenness that is just as essential to the immediacy of the meeting as the independence from the sense-instituting project. Thou is not encountered unexpectedly, but beforehand in the constantly extended expectation of the "relational striving" that, with respect to the subsequent "relation," is "the first" (DP 31:79).

Immediacy, the reciprocity of the partners, and their common origination out of the between are the three fundamental characteristics of the I-Thou relationship, which, in the previous section, I compared with the projectedness, subordination, and I-centeredness of the It sphere. The understanding of the basic word I-Thou, in accord with the model of intentionality, also, along with immediacy, delivers the other two moments of the I-Thou relationship over to the I-It relationship. Just as the domination of the I follows from its objectivity, so reciprocity is the positive determination of the nonobjectivity of the Thou to which Buber refers with repeated emphasis. While the It appears as "object among objects" (DP 21:69), the Thou is "not an object" (H 223): "This is what is decisive: not being an object" (DP 260). The objectivity that Buber refuses to accord to the Thou is not, however, simply the massive thingliness of the externally appearing body. It is also and specifically the noematic objectivity that belongs to entities as the correlate of intentional acts: "Whoever says Thou does not have something as an object" (DP 8:54). What else is the Thou when it pays attention to my behavior and behaves as it does only in relation to my behavior?

Intentionality also compels the Thou to adopt a perspectival orientation to the I as the midpoint of the world. The human being engaged by the Thou-I or the It-I occupies the central position to the extent that he is the place at which the destiny of the world is decided. The world, however, no matter whether It-world or Thou-world, surrounds the actual I in concentric circles. Thereby, however, the I—despite all Buber's assurances to the contrary—assumes precedence over the Thou. The disempowering of the between, whose primacy finds its shortened expression in the thesis on the precedence of the Thou over the I, is due to it. One can just as well say that the origination of the I out of the between founds my own addressing in my being addressed. Accordingly, the disempowering of the between is conveyed in this, that Buber, despite occasional indications that lead one to believe in the originality of being addressed (DP 41), does, as a matter of fact, demonstrate the I-Thou relationship almost entirely with respect to the model of that relation in which I turn to the Other. With respect to this model, however, the constitution of the I is only incompletely exhibited. The I, and just as well the human being who is appropriated by it, must, in the end, be presupposed as "absolute here" and "absolute now."

2 Language as the Basis of the Departure from Intentionality

According to the thesis developed earlier, Buber's ontology of the between can arrive at its theme only through the destruction of the model of intentionality. We now want to pursue the path of this destruction, which is accomplished in two steps. First of all, we need a presentification of the regions through which the path leads. It is a completely different region from the one in which Husserl, Heidegger, and Sartre locate "the Other." With Husserl and the Sartre of *Being and Nothingness*, the Other moves principally in the medium of sense perception, with Heidegger in the work world of concernful trans-actions. In contrast, *language* is the home of the Thou.[4] The I-Thou and the I-It relationships are precisely "basic *words*," and basic words are spoken (DP 7:53). Whoever relates to something as a Thou or an It *says* "Thou" or "It," and he himself is only an "I" insofar as he says "I," the I of the basic word I-Thou or the basic word I-It: "I am and I speak are one and the same. Saying I and saying one of the basic words are one and the same. Whoever says a basic word enters into the word and stays there" (DP 8:54).

He "stays there." Or, as Buber says in later places, "In truth, language is not stuck into human being but human being stays in language" (DP 41:89; see also Soz. II 559). Language therefore moves beneath that "sphere of subjectivity" with which the model of intentionality stands or falls. Certainly, in the course of his behavior, the human being posits beings as Thou or It, but it is language that first sets up the human being in his behavior: "The comportment of the human being is twofold according to the duality of the basic words that he can speak" (DP 7:53). Certainly, the human being is that place in the world at which the world itself is revealed in its essentially twofold character. But it is this only inasmuch as language is transferred to it. So, from far off, language already promises to show us the way that is supposed to lead us from the worldly surface of subjectivity into the depths of the between.[5]

First, we must obviously come to an understanding about the mean-ing of the concept "language" in Buber. Above all, what has to be clarified is this question: Is language, in Buber's sense, to be equated with articulate discourse, or does it include the manifold ways of communication beyond the vocally articulated word? If, however, the latter is supposed to be the case, how, then, are the I-Thou and the I-It relationships related to articulate language and to nonarticulate language? We shall prepare an answer to these questions inasmuch as we make articulate language phenomenally clear in its dialogicality, as well as in its intentionality.[6]

Since both of the entirely antithetically determined basic words are, nevertheless, "spoken," language itself, whether articulated or not, must be twofold. The speaking of the basic word I-Thou is a speaking to; that of the basic word I-It, a speaking about. Accordingly, in the sphere of talk, it is a matter of the duality of talking to and talking about. The Thou is always and essentially the one spoken to or talked to, whether this is now the Other (in the case of my speaking to) or I myself (in the case of my being spoken to). This is understood to be the case not only with Buber but explicitly or implicitly throughout the entire philosophy of dialogue. Where this is not so understood, we are also not dealing with dialogical thought, no matter how frequently the word "Thou" appears, a word that is then, for the most part, only a synonymous expression for the "Other" or even for the "alien I," pure and simple. Marcel explicitly defines the Thou as "that which can be invoked by me" (Jm 196), and even Ebner, although, as a matter of fact, he refuses the identification of the Thou with the Other and myself, determines it formally as the person "spoken to" (WR 78; see also 111, 161–162), as the "one speaking to" and the "one spoken to" (WR 87) or—still more sharply restricted—as the other's "addressability" (WR 18; see also 96). That, in a similar fashion, Wilhelm von Humboldt already distinguished the Thou precisely as the "one talked to" from all other Others (*Gesammelte Schriften* VI/1 17, 161) makes him more directly a pathfinder of the modern philosophy of dialogue than, for instance, Fichte or Feuerbach, who, in spite of his transformation of the monological dialectic into the "dialogue between I and Thou," in the end still only regards the latter as the true "object."[7]

Talking to and talking about are the two original dimensions of discourse, which correspond to the duality of the basic words. In full agreement with Buber's comportmental schema, Rosenzweig says that the personal pronoun designates "in its three persons nothing other . . . than the three dimensions of being-present-to-me, that is, the capacity for speaking to, the capacity for understanding, the capacity for being spoken about" (1935 602). Discourse differentiated in this way appears, above all, as the original image in accordance with which the intentional model of behavior is projected. Talking to and talking about are attitudes that bring the being of beings to language in different ways. One and the same entity can be talked to and about (Jm 157), but, as talked to, it exists otherwise than as talked about. Occasionally, the I also exists differently according to whether it is talked to or about. The spoken to and the spoken about live, writes Rosenstock-Huessy, "on opposite planets," and I turn through "all of

180 degrees when, instead of speaking to Fritz, I speak of him" (AG 54; see also 87; Soz. I 155).[8] In this way the determinateness of talking to and being talked to, on the one side, and of talking about and being talked about, on the other, results from the determinateness of those intentions of talking to and talking about, which codetermine the correlated subject pole and the intentional "for which."

However, it belongs to the ambiguous essence of discourse, which is wholly and fundamentally imprisoned by intentionality, that, as talking to, it stands equally opposed to the intentional schema. So, regardless of its intentional constitution, talking to hands over the basis for the resistance of the I-Thou relation to the structure of intentionality. Only talking about gets integrated effortlessly into the intentional schema. That which is talked about (whether masculine, feminine, or neuter) is first of all the wherefore or the noematic object of discourse. Because I make the Other into an object, to the extent that I talk about him in the third person (being an object conflicting with being a person), talking about someone means, according to Ebner, to "depersonalize" him. For this reason, or so Ebner thinks, it makes ever less sense for me to talk about a human being "substantively and therefore quite authentically in the 'third person,' " the more I am tied to him personally (WR 169–170). As an object, however, what is talked about is, in the second place, subordinated to the one doing the talking, is dependent upon him. This is crassly expressed in the pejorative use of the expression "talk about." Whoever is talked about in gossip is delivered over to the gossip, and the spokesmen of the discussion are raised above him merely in that they talk about him. In the meantime, even in a talking about that is not devaluing or valueless, the dependence of the one talked about betrays itself through its passivity. The one talked about can do nothing either for or against his being talked about. The talking about takes place in his absence. The one talked about is not even questioned. He is made into an object whether he wants it or not. For this reason, I can talk about anything and everything. For this reason, too, talking about does not need the actual presence of the one talked about. Indeed, this would annoy the one doing the talking just as much as the one talked about.[9] This becomes particularly evident in gossip. I am only talked about where I am not present. But even where I am in my presence quite neutrally referred with the title "he," I feel myself to be painfully disturbed. (Jm 160; AG 54). This uneasiness is further aggravated by the fact that, as a passively pregiven object, I am dependent upon the horizon in which I am talked about. What is talked about (whether masculine, feminine, or neuter) is, in the third place, as the wherefore of discourse, continually determined by those respects in which he is the object of discourse.

On the other hand, the one (masculine, feminine, or neuter) talked about is not really an object. Positively, the Thou is—as Reinach calls it[10]—much rather the "addressee" or—as Rosenstock-Huessy puts it[11]—the "recipient." The "dative" addressing is, however, separated from the objectifying by a chasm. Above all, in place of a subordination that is fixating and that condemns to passivity, we find the call to reciprocity and to a partnership of equality. Speaking to, as "turning oneself toward" (Reinach), calls on the activity of the counterpart. This trait emerges all the more strongly in discourse, the more it becomes a matter of talking to. In communication, for instance, the moment of talking about predominates in general. In the middle of the field of interest there stands the "about which" of discourse, for the most part a neutral state of affairs that is distinguished from me, the one who communicates, just as much as it is from the one about whom I make the communication. The same holds of presentations and lectures in writing. Accordingly, the activity of the partner in all this is relatively small. It is limited to taking in (for example, reading). Even taking in is never merely passive. In listening I have to attend to what is said and work on it internally. So Humboldt says quite rightly "that even understanding depends upon an inner activity, and that speaking with one another is only a reciprocal awakening of the capacity for listening" (*Gesammelte Schriften* VI/1 176). However, complete reciprocity is still missing here, insofar as the one who understands, so long as he is only that, is not to be equated with the speaker. This happens first, when, in his orientation to what is communicated, or even in discussion, he himself searches for words. It happens in just the same way when he answers a question. But even there we find multiple distinctions in the grades of active participation. It advances in proportion as the matter, as a neutral "about which," retreats. To the extent that "it" is no more in question, then "you" are not only the addressee but also the sole theme of discourse without being its object. You are no longer placed in relation to objects. With non-objectivity and reciprocal equality, the third essential determination of being talked to is, however, also brought to completion: *immediacy.*

Unveiled and unmediated by material relations, the Thou stands here before me. As independence from my project, this immediacy belongs within determinate limits to that being talked to. Still, the action of the partner, as the accomplishment of *his* freedom, cannot be projected by me. The more questionable my question is, the more decisively the answer brings me something new, something abrupt, something unforseen. If I knew already what the Other was going to say to me, I would not ask. But the intention to immediacy, which dwells in talking to, is related not only to the encounter of the partner but also to its essence and presence. For this reason, the Thou is most present in that completely immediate summons in which I only say "Thou" and nothing else. What is "meant" thereby is not this or that aspect of the Other, but the Other itself in the immediacy of its being.[12]

The nonobjectivity, partnership, and immediacy of talking to prove that the I-Thou relation, which is realized as discourse, fulfills the essential requirements that Buber imposes for a community grounded in the between and lying beyond intentional correlation. Of the characteristics of the fully valid I-Thou relation, only one is not to be found again in talking to: the collapse of the perspectival order as the displacement of the origin from my I into the between. In this respect, talking to is not to be distinguished from talking about. Even as the one talking to, I am the midpoint from which the initiative goes out. With regard to the goal of undermining the subject and elevating the between, this appears admittedly as a particularly weighty lack. How far talking to remains behind the demands of the ontology of the between is indicated by the fact that the central position of the one who does the talking also impairs the immediacy and the equiprimordiality (negatively: nonobjectivity) of the Thou talked to. Because, in talking to, the initiative goes out from me, I have to know beforehand how I have to talk to the Other. It is necessary, therefore, to that "anticipation" that belongs to the medium-projecting orientation toward. Above all, however, the primacy of talking to over talking back prevents the full equality of status of the partner. To be sure, talking to proceeds continually from reply or, at least, from reception, but where the reaction of the Other is of equal rank to my action, it is never already actual in the moment of talking to. Understanding is simultaneous with discourse, but it is also only an incomplete correspondence. However, the answer that links the question with dialogical reciprocity still has to be waited for. Even when it is immediately given, it is still only joined to the question. Articulated assertion and articulated response fit together in a successive sequence, but not simultaneously. Whoever talks to me at the same time precisely forgoes the rules of audibly articulate communication. However, true partnership is first fulfilled in simultaneity. And so the following results from the phenomenological analysis of talking to, namely, that the basic word I-Thou certainly finds its home in discourse, but still cannot be completed in it. Which means positively that it must be completed in that form of language that no longer needs expression and the articulated word.

Buber emphasizes this—in opposition to most other "philosophers of language," in particular, to Ebner and Rosenstock-Huessy—so strongly that, at first glance, it almost looks as though he wanted to contest the claim of discourse in general to any right to the I-Thou relationship. In his opinion, the "linguistic form" is, in the final analysis, not decisive for the basic word I-Thou (DP 64:111). Even and precisely the mute communion in the "magical fullness of being with one another" (H 13) is, in Buber's eyes, a "conversation," while, conversely, that discourse in which I do not turn to my partner with my complete being is lacking in what is most important to conversation (DP 127–128). Consequently, the opposition of the basic words is not settled in the field of discourse—so little, in fact, that discourse is capable of concealing the behavior that a human being adopts vis-à-vis the world. Someone can say Thou and nevertheless mean It or say It and thereby have a Thou in mind (DP 64; GF 37). What is at issue, and only at issue in such affirmations, still has to be investigated more precisely. Buber's notion that the Thou is developed to its highest completion not in discourse but in silence is, however, something we may at least take to be already phenomenally demonstrated (DP 42).[13]

In apparent contradiction to this, we find that, in accordance with other statements by Buber, it is precisely discourse in which the I-Thou relationship not only participates but in which it is actually fulfilled. To start with, let us attend to these sentences: "From among the three spheres, one stands out: life with human beings. Here language is, as a result, consummated in discourse and response. Here alone does the linguistically formed word meet its answer. Only here does the basic word go back and forth in the same form; that of address and that of response live in One tongue; I and Thou do not simply exist in the relation but also in forthright 'communicability.'

Here and only here the relational moments are linked through the element of language in which they are immersed. Here the counterpart has blossomed into the complete reality of the Thou" (DP 104:151).

In the present passage, Buber is, of course, concerned not with the fulfillment of the basic word I-Thou in discourse, but with its completion in the interhuman realm. The genuine, the completely realized, relation is supposed to be present only in life with human beings, and not in life with nature and with spiritual beings. Even this thesis, as banal as it may sound, is significant with respect to the fundamental problem of the relationship of the I-Thou relation and intentionality. For in it there is already to be found a modification of the initially posited schema. In accordance with this schema, the three "spheres" are equally justified. But their equal justification springs, as was said, from the character of the Thou and the It as intentional correlates whose distinction is not grounded in the ontic difference of the actually intended entities, but simply upon the ontological difference of the comportment that the *being* of the entity lets itself display in such and such a way. The suspension of this equality given with the precedence of the partner therefore also suppresses, to a certain extent, the mastery of intentionality over the basic word I-Thou. The basic word I-It, however, remains under this domination. For the partner enjoys a privileged position vis-à-vis sub- and superhuman beings in the world simply as Thou and not as It.

Buber makes discourse an issue simply in order to ground the primacy of the interhuman sphere. Nevertheless, even this only takes place in a highly mediated manner. Buber does not say, Because the relation is consummated in discourse, and because only human beings can discourse, the relation is consummated in the interhuman sphere. Rather, with a view to justifying his claim, he relies upon a particular moment of discourse as address, that is, upon reciprocity. In this way, he admittedly arouses the impression that reciprocity is to be found exclusively in address. That it is only in life with human beings that the basic word goes "back and forth in a similar fashion" and that only in it do the partners stand in "forthright 'communicability'" appear to be one and the same thing. The completion of language as response, that is, reciprocity, and its completion in discourse and debate also appear to be one and the same. If we review these statements, however, it can be clearly seen that, according to Buber, it is not really the "discursive" reciprocity as such, but the possibility of full reciprocity in general that grounds the distinctiveness of the interhuman sphere. Buber regards the possibility of full reciprocity in general as the specific trait of life with human beings. Only in this life, or so he thinks, does receiving stand over against giving as of equal rank (DP 10:57). To be sure, "life with nature" is not supposed to stand out in contrast with the former through the total passivity of the partner. That the natural thing may also react actively is the condition of the possibility of its being-Thou. Finally, it is not the recognition of the capacity for action on the part of the thing, which is only passively present as a thing and not as an It, that distinguishes Buber's ontology from transcendental philosophies such as those of Husserl or Sartre, where the passivity of the thing also remains the unquestioned presupposition of all attempts to mark off a space (independent of my world project) for the freedom of fellowship.[14] But the sensitive and attentive self-activation of natural beings is still not a "response" like the answer of one's fellow human being: "Creatures react to us, but they are not capable of responding to us" (DP 10:57). In a certain way, "life with spiritual beings" behaves in reverse. There the first thing is not our call but our inarticulate being called, which we follow up just as inarticulately without our response being able to do justice to the claim (DP 10; see also 14). "Life with human beings" also stands out in contrast through the equiprimordiality of claim and response or through full reciprocity. This reciprocity is, for Buber, however, the basis of the primacy of the interhuman sphere as one that does not get realized in talking to. As stated in conjunction with the passages cited above, it is also this reciprocity of "looking at and being looked at, knowing and being known, loving and being loved" (DP 104:151).

However, since the interhuman sphere now also owes its precedence over the natural and ideal to that full reciprocity alone possible in it and not to the fulfillment of the basic word I-Thou in discourse, there must then be a motive that permits Buber to say that language fulfills itself "in discourse and debate" and that the interhuman relation is distinguished in this, that in it the partners stand in forthright "discursiveness." If language is fulfilled in discourse and debate, then so is the basic word I-Thou. For its language is in turn the genuine language. The following remark lets it be known how such a fulfillment is to be thought: "Human dialogue can . . . exist without signs . . . no matter how much it has its genuine life . . . in signs, therefore in sound and gesture—admittedly, not in a form that can be really apprehended"

(DP 129–130). Consequently, human dialogue, that is, the basic word I-Thou spoken between human beings, has its genuine life in signs, and so also in articulate discourse, because only here can it exist in a form that can be really apprehended. The real apprehensibility of discursive dialogue rests upon the articulateness of discourse in the particularity of its overt-expression, in the object relatedness as well as in the determinateness of the verbal significance that arises therefrom and in the division of its syntactic formations. This articulateness preserves the highest degree of real apprehensibility. Accordingly, the basic word I-Thou is fulfilled in discourse to the extent that it is really apprehended in the most genuine way in the latter.

Because Buber assumes that language is fulfilled in discourse and debate, he is able elsewhere to equate the concepts of "discourse" and "language," in contrast with the previously presented passages, in accordance with which language occasionally oversteps the realm of what can be expressed and comes down to "community" pure and simple. He alternates between the broad and the narrow concepts of language there, where he describes life with nature, life with human beings, and life with spiritual beings in their characteristic features (DP 10:57). On the one hand, he says that in life with spiritual beings, we would be addressed without a sound being uttered and we would speak without discourse. On the other hand, however, he names this sphere the "extralinguistic." In accordance with the same meaning of language, the relation to nature is "sublinguistic." Our Thou-saying to creatures only clings to the "threshold of language." The relation to nature is sublinguistic because it is played out beneath the possibility of discourse. So when Buber acknowledges that it stands on the threshold of language, his attention is directed to the fact that we frequently talk, in particular, to animals, as distinct from "lifeless" things, in a mode of discourse that is certainly deficient, simply because we expect a response even if not a reply—see the postscript to the new edition of *I and Thou* in Buber (1960 466–467). Because in all this he equates language with discourse, in the end he saves up the former for the interhuman sphere. Only here is the "relation evident and linguistic in character." The synonymous nature of the concepts "linguistic" and "linguistic in character" also refers, however, to the basic justification for the identification of "language" and "discourse"; that is, it confirms the above-mentioned motive for the assumption that in reality language fulfills itself in discourse. Language fulfills itself in discourse because only in the latter does it achieve a fully developed form. In turn, discourse can only confer form on account of its articulateness.

Up to now Buber has said three things: first, that the basic word I-Thou is fulfilled in nonarticulate language, in silence; second, that it is fulfilled in articulate language, in discourse; and third, that it is fulfilled in discourse, to the extent that its articulateness preserves for it the highest substantive comprehensibility. In order that Buber's thought should not run into a contradiction, the basic word I-Thou must be fulfilled in silence in another respect than in discourse. In what respect becomes clear when we bear in mind what the discursive fulfillment of the basic word I-Thou cannot be. It cannot be a completion, in the sense that discourse posits the end in which the essence of the basic word I-Thou is fully unfolded. Such a completion specifically *contradicts* the real comprehensibility that the basic word I-Thou retains through discourse. We have seen that, in discourse, too, the Thou comes that much more clearly to prominence, the more the "matter" in hand retreats into the background. The matter in hand, however, is not merely the "about which" of discourse but also the verbal material that contributes more than anything else to the relation to real comprehensibility. The Thou addressed is most present, as was noticed, at that moment when nothing is discussed and the discourse itself disappears into the one word "Thou." In that the Thou transcends the matter in hand, it also abandons discourse. It reaches out from itself beyond discourse. This means that it reaches into silence. Silence is, therefore, the finalizing end that discourse is not, although, for its part, it is not what discourse is. In making possible real apprehensibility, the essence of the Thou is completed in it. In it this essence is realized without being externalized, as in that discourse in which it is also realized (through structuration). In this way something decisive is said at the same time about specifically dialogical silence. Essentially it lies not before but after discourse and is itself, for this reason, "articulate" silence. Essentially this means that discourse is the ontological presupposition, but not the ontic condition for the factical occurrence of silence. Only someone who can speak can keep silent. And only vis-à-vis that with which I can enter into a conversation, can I remain silent. However, I do not have to have conversed previously with anyone whom I encounter in silence.[15]

In distinction from the completion of the basic word I-Thou in silence, its discursive fulfillment, formally considered, lies in this, that discourse, thanks to its articulateness, is the beginning, and therewith also the continuously effective principle, of the basic word I-Thou. This will be abundantly demonstrated in what follows. At this point we only need to note that whatever can be bound up with talking to, as, for instance, seeing the Other, still cannot reach the Thou, because it remains in the realm of intentional objectivity. Another thing: on account of the precedence of the basic word I-Thou over the basic word I-It, the Other, in order that he can be seen as Other, already has to be experienced as susceptible to being addressed. Discourse, as talking to, is the beginning of the Thou. But because the Thou is ontologically prior to the It, it is the beginning pure and simple. Indeed, this holds merely in the sense of ontological constitution. As a matter of fact, I always first catch sight of the Other again in order to talk to him thereafter. Here the ontological priority of the Thou over the It is only noticeable in that even the perceived Other is known latently as someone who is potentially a speaker and someone who can be spoken to. However, this does not alter the fact that, in being perceived, he is himself an object and not a partner.

The essence of address, as the beginning of the Thou, also explains that nonentity that I pursue in talking to when I say Thou and mean It. One should not draw the conclusion from the possibility of such comportment that what is genuine about the behavior toward the Thou is enacted in meaning. Rather, one must conclude, on the contrary, that the comportment toward the Thou is localized in address and over and above that in the higher regions of speaking to. For this reason, the nonentity consists in this, that the meaning is subordinated to the address. Then in Thou-saying, I already mean It, when I mean something before and outside of Thou-saying. For I then make talking to into what talking about is—into the subsequent expression of a prior meaning. Then talking to is no longer itself the act that reveals the Thou, and so no longer talking to.

To be sure, this interpretation cannot immediately be supported literally by the text of *I and Thou*, though it can by a thought-provoking passage in the lecture *The word That Is Spoken*. We find there, "The relationship between meaning and saying refers us to the relationship between the intended unity of meaning and saying on the one hand, and that between meaning and saying and the personable being, on the other" (1962 451–452). What Buber has in view is talking to, as the undivided unity of meaning and saying, as a unity that is itself again one with the personal being of the one doing the talking. Rosenstock-Huessy performed a special service in emphasizing this unity more urgently than anyone else. Rosenstock-Huessy also saw that, insofar as it is not the subsequent expression of a meaning, talking to can at bottom no longer be understood as "articulation." It is not the making articulate of an act carried out inwardly, but, in its purest form, that of the "pledge," a happening whose originality is conveyed above all in this, that it changes the speaker himself (AG 68–72, 65, 83–84; Soz. I 142, 145–147, 168, 312–314).

At quite another level, we find the reverse case, where the stated It at bottom means a Thou. This is possible due to the latency of the Thou in the It. The latent presence of the factically absent Thou is always, then, stronger than the objectivity (spoken in the It) of the Other (meant with the Thou) when, in that moment in which I talk *about* the Other, I speak *with* him, speak in the language that binds those who are even in separate places, as, for example, the language that links lovers who have once given each other their word. It is this super-, not subarticulate, language that meaning means here.

Now, just as talking to is the beginning of the Thou, so talking about is the end of the It. When I talk about something, I simply bring to expression what I have already "perceived, seen, heard, felt externally"—see Humboldt (*Gesammelte Schriften* VI/1 164). The object of discourse is only the logicized form of that object that I also already have before me in representation, perception, and so forth. For this reason, Buber can call the comportment toward the It an "experience and utilization" and, so to speak, a speaking. This speaking is, however, exclusively discourse. The comportment toward the It is not also discourse among other things, but, as experience and utilization, it is at most talking about. For expression in judgment completes the objectivity of the object. Therefore discourse is, so to speak, the null point on the line of human life, the null point that, for the plus side of the basic word I-Thou, means the beginning and, for the minus side of the basic word I-It, means the conclusion.

If one compares Buber's statements on the connection of the basic word I-Thou to discourse with its phenomenal givenness, as was described above, one has to acknowledge their appropriateness, seen as a whole. The twofold placement of talking, which, on the one side, is subjected to intentionality, and, on the other, breaks out of it, is mirrored in the dialectical tension of the statements involved, which, taken together, reach both—both the root of the Thou in talking to and its completion, the other side of talking to. However, Buber's theory of the connection of the relation to articulated language and to nonarticulated language is one thing. The roles that articulated language and nonarticulated language play, as the clue to the general project of "I and Thou," is quite another. Here it is discourse that sets the tone. Not that the text deals only or preponderantly with it. Buber offers enough examples of silent being with one another. All the same, his descriptions of the structures of the I-Thou relationship in general are oriented toward the grammatical laws of discourse. Its methodologically leading position is certainly justified within specific limits on the basis of the concrete comprehensibility of what is fixed in discourse. But that Buber attributes the highest degree of concrete comprehensibility to the latter itself attests to the precedence that he accords to discourse. And insofar as the concrete comprehensibility of what is fixed in discourse results primarily from the object relatedness of the words, this precedence at the same time confirms the critical supplement to the thesis presented at the end of the previous chapter, a thesis in accordance with which Buber certainly breaks down the schema of intentionality, but still remains entrapped by it in the negativity of the breakdown. The breakdown of the intentional schema succeeds in the departure from language in general. But the methodological orientation toward the language form that is still most deeply marked by intentionality indicates that Buber remains entrapped by intentionality.

3 The Present of the Thou and the Past of the It

It is the task of the following analyses to demonstrate Buber's destruction of the transcendental model of intentionality. In pursuit of this goal we shall move through the concrete determinations of the antithesis of the basic words. Concretely, I call them determinations because they fill out the general frame formed by the formal characteristics that we have already handled. With their elucidation, the description of the phenomenon of discourse given above will be confirmed retrospectively as true to the text. Such a confirmation is provided, above all, by the first antithetical pair, the *present* and the *past*.[16]

The concept "past" characterizes the concrete ways in which I live objectivity intentionally. Correspondingly, the nonobjectivity of the Thou confers upon the concept "present" a concretely positive sense. What, however, does Buber mean by "present"? "The present, not the punctual present, which only confers the appearance of a running off upon the end point of the expired time actually posited in thought, but the really fulfilled present, only exists insofar as presentness, meeting, and relation exist. Only inasmuch as the Thou is present does the present exist. The I of the basic word I-It . . . only has a past, not a present." It has "nothing as objects; for objects only exist in having been. The present is not the fleeting and transitory but the presenting and preserving" (DP 16–17:64).

From the preliminary concept that we derived from talking about it, it should be easy to set out what Buber has in view when he refers the It to the past. The concept "past" interprets the being constitution of talking about as an expression of what has been preconceived. What is talked about is, as such, the past because, already before its being talked about, it is the object of my knowledge. This does not mean that even that givenness that is at issue must fall into the past. Even if it is present right now or has yet to make its appearance, it is, as what is talked about, experienced in the mode of the past. Just as objectivity is intentional objectivity and not objectivity pure and simple, so, in a similar way, its past is an essential trait of the noematic correlate and not of being "in itself." The now point belongs just as well to this past, a now point that encapsulates the past in itself through its explicit affirmation in the articulate word. The encapsulation that belongs to the past of the It is not so much the exhaustion of what lies more or less far behind—in distinction to the past that still lays claim to the now, that Heidegger calls "having been" (*Gewesenheit*)—as, rather, the completion in the now, beyond which the act of talking about does not reach out. On the basis of this encapsulation, as Sartre clearly sees, any judgment on an Other is a condemnation, even when it is not a negative evaluation. It pins the Other down to that which he has shown himself to be *hitherto*, and in this way makes his past definitive.[17] It is not only talking about that fixates in this way, but also any intentional objectification that is given to him in advance. Just as, in the change of the noematic correlate of perception, representation, and so forth into the "about which" of discourse, objectivity is only increased and does not first come into being, so we also find something similar with respect to the intentional past. It too already belongs implicitly to those objects that have not been brought to expression in discourse. It follows from this that I stop at those objects without expecting from them anything over and beyond their objectivity. The object of the intentional act is its goal and end point, that in which it shuts itself up and comes to rest. So it is, in fact, true that not only the one who recalls what is given lives in the past, but even the one who at this very moment is surrounded by objects does so.

On closer inspection, the distinction drawn by Buber between past and present, therefore, turns out to be a tension within the present. The present is itself "twofold" in itself, and this twofoldness corresponds to that of the basic words. In this way, both modes of the present are as little equivalent to one another as the basic words. The present of the Thou is the original, the "real" present. This affirmation on Buber's part can be phenomenally demonstrated, to the extent that the present of the Thou is extended in its own fullness and affirms itself to be the new, pure and simple, by contrast to everything past, while the present of the It precisely only presents the "conclusion of the time elapsed" and, therefore, not being self-sufficient, at bottom itself only belongs to the past. Hence this conclusion is only posited "in thought" and is therefore unreal because it disappears on account of its punctuality. This present is the now, and the now is only a boundary between the no longer and the not yet existing, a boundary that, outside of its function of being a point of intersection, possesses no reality of its own.

The interpretation of the temporal difference between the basic words as a distinction between present and past points toward the inner constitution of the dialogical present. In distinction to the past, it is the futural present. This is also confirmed by a glance at the phenomenon of the performance of discourse. The one talked to is present to me because he stands before me. He stands before me because I exist in the meeting or in the confrontation. Any speaking to—this is one of the basic insights of the philosophy of dialogue—is a claim to correspondence. The "word that is to be spoken"—as Buber says in his lecture of the same name—is not supposed "to remain with the speaker. . . . It reaches out toward a hearer, it grasps him; indeed, it makes the hearer into a speaker, even if only perhaps an inaudible one" (1962 443). In this way, the act of speaking to swings out beyond itself and its immediate correlate. It maintains itself in the future, as it were, without already anticipating this future itself. For the one doing the speaking precisely awaits the decision about the future from the answer of the one spoken to. On the basis of such an expectation, Buber can call the dialogical present "the presenting and preserving." It is the dimension of the future that gives to the dialogical present the tension of a present dimension and that separates it from the fleeting now. Because I am present to the one spoken to, he is present to me. Because he comes to me out of the future, I really have something to do with him at this point in time.

Admittedly, the present dimension of the future in view here needs emphasizing no less than the future dimension of the genuine present.[18] The futural dimension of the one who owes me an answer or to whose question I have to assume a stand is contained in the present of the dialogical occurrence. What stands before me from the Thou does not fall into the far future of a not yet operative anytime. To be sure, as opposed to the always already decided being of the It, it is the essentially undecided. But, as the latter, it is, at the same time, what has to be decided today. The dialogical future is only undetermined and open to the extent that I cannot determine it in advance. The anticipated and planned for future belongs to the sphere of the It, to the means and mediations of objective experience. Accordingly, it is nothing other than the extension of the past. In reckoning out in advance, I draw out the line of the past, in that I determine the not yet existing out of the determinateness of the already existing. This is what happens in experiments with the givens of the natural world and in predictions of the natural course of events. This is also what happens when I reckon with a particular behavior of a human being because I think I know this human being from his earlier behavior. In all this, the future is, in the final analysis, a project of the subject, a project that the object fits or does not fit. In contrast, the preserving future, however my being may also be decided in it, is originally a matter of the Thou, to whom, in the very act of speaking to, I hand over the initiative. In swinging out beyond myself in speaking to, I deliver myself over to the Other, place my future destiny in his hands. I "let myself"—to use a vulgar expression to characterize a nonvulgar reality—be "taken by surprise" by the Other. For Buber, "Otherness" itself is, "concretely" apprehended, "the moment of surprise" (1962 445), just as, for him, human being pure and simple, from God's standpoint, represents the "surprise center of creation."[19] To deal with the Other as Other and to let oneself be surprised by him is therefore the same thing. The uncertainty about what is to come, an uncertainty that springs from letting oneself be surprised, the openness to all possibilities, brings the specific sense of the future much more radically to mind than the relative certainty that the predetermining project is only able to accord because it takes from the future the sharp edge of surprise. Such a genuine future is, however, one with the genuine present, even though the latter, just like the former, is differently linked with the immediacy of the abrupt.[20]

Buber's interpretation of the temporality of the Thou and the It is representative for the philosophy of dialogue in general. Indeed, there is hardly another respect in which the unitary character of this philosophical current comes to prominence so clearly. This is no accident. According to the dialogicians, "new thought," to the extent that it thinks of language as conversation,[21] must, at the same time, be the philosophy of the time. Rosenzweig states this insight (KS 383–387) in words similar to those employed by Rosenstock-Huessy (AG 26, 97, 99, 234; Soz. I 287), and even Grisebach says, in his main work, that the problem of real time is "the most important problem in the entire book" (Gw 552; see also 555). The identity of thought about language and thought about time is based, in the minds of the dialogicians, upon the circumstance, appreciated by Rosenstock-Huessy, in particular (AG 100, 102-103, 153; Soz. I 258), that time pure and simple is first constituted in the inner temporality of the dialogue. It follows therefrom that—as Augustine's dialogue *De Magistro* showed, according to Rosenstock-Huessy's interpretation—the "presentification of secret time," just like the "bringing to speech of one's fellow human being" (AG 99: see also Soz. I 310), and—in Rosenzweig's formulation—the "need of the other" and the "taking seriously of time" (KS 387) are identical.

Rosenzweig and Rosenstock-Huessy also agree in this, that the most original time is the present, the dialogical present in which I and Thou are found together (KS 386; Soz. I 313). This present is named in the title of Grisebach's main work. As with Buber, it is also more or less implicit already with Rosenzweig and Rosenstock-Huessy (see, for instance, AG 140); explicitly, however, with Grisebach (Gw 130–131, 147–148) and Heim (GD 116, 162–163), it is the opponent of the object. With Grisebach, its distinction from the inauthentic present of the abstract now point comes back again (Gw 128, 147, 570–571). Following

Buber, however, Grisebach relegates the object to the past (Gw 15, 109, 146, 175, 179, 362). In this he at the same time follows Rosenstock-Huessy, who describes the past of the It not first in his late *Sociology* (Soz. I 105, 300) but already in the *Applied Soul Science* (AS 29–31, 33). Further, in common with Rosenstock-Huessy, he has a particular understanding of this past; for both, the It is past, in the sense that it is exhausted (Soz. I 300; Gw 146, 518, 520). In contrast, Heim sees in the past or the having been, as he also characterizes objectivity (GD 106), much more the still present having been (GD 117), which, according to Rosenstock-Huessy, characterizes not the It but the We (related to Heidegger's "They") (AG 198, 234; Soz. I 159, 190–192). For all that, this difference is relativized, in that with Grisebach even Heim ascribes to the object the "form of being decided" (GD 108). The present, on the contrary, is "what is not yet decided" (GD 113–114). It implies, therefore, that toward which Heim explicitly refers (GD 115)—the future. Grisebach has thought about this futural dimension most penetratingly (Gw 180, 575–576, 580, 586, inter alia): "Only what is present has a future" (Gw 594); for it is an "element of the today" (Gw 575), a moment "within the present" (Gw 588). Still more: according to Grisebach, the genuine, dialogical present in the end itself coincides with the future. Whoever says Thou is directed "forward in the present" (Gw 150), into the "foreworld" (Gw 126) as the genuine antithesis to the exhausted, depleted afterworld" (Gw 109). For this reason, Grisebach repeats Buber's interpretation of the present as the pre-sent (Gw 78–79, 114, 148). Contemporaneously with Buber, however, Rosenzweig and Rosenstock-Huessy have also understood the present in the same way. For Rosenzweig, the dialogical present essentially includes a "not yet" in itself: "The word, the letter, etc., are always said and written on the basis of a 'not yet' " (1935 417) and the *Star of Redemption* develops the thesis that, in the fundamental dialogical comportment, in hoping trust, the future is present (SE II 211). Rosenstock-Huessy, who characterizes the present as the "force field in which the future and the past intertwine" (Soz. I 313), emphasizes that the future and not the past has the "preponderance over the present" (Soz. I 213). The pure present means for him, as for the author of *Star*, the "inrush of the coming into the today" (AS 30–31). The language that gets developed in the present dimension of conversation is developed precisely as conversation, as a speaking to out of the future (AG 41, 44), and this future toward which and from out of which the linguistic thought of "new science" wants to interpret time (AG 132; Soz. I 229) is immediately identical with the "Thou": " 'Thou' is future" (Soz. I 157)—an equation that is to be found again in Grisebach's *Present* (Gw 148, 506).

Both the early representatives of dialogicalism—Rosenzweig and Rosenstock-Huessy—and Grisebach, who already belongs to the later stage of dialogicalism, now come together with Buber in the effort to delimit the dialogical future as the true one against that future that, in reality, is not at all futural, namely, that of subjectivity. For all three, the principal characteristic of the genuine future is openness, in the sense elucidated above in our interpretation of Buber.[22] According to Rosenzweig, it is grounded in this, that I "do not know in advance what the other will say to me" and cannot determine "in advance" where the conversation "will come out" (KS 387). As Rosenstock-Huessy says, this makes up "the absolutely surprising character of the genuine future" (Soz. I 98; see also Gw 149). The reckoning, foreseeing, or foreplanning forbidden thereby precisely distinguishes the future, which stays in the power of subjectivity. This too all the authors named emphasize. According to Rosenstock-Huessy, the double character of the future as openness and as fixedness finds its grammatical expression in the distinction of the future tense, which the future predetermines, and of the imperative, which is committed to the "true, that means the new, future" (AS 30–31; AG 195–196, 234; Soz. I 159). To the twofoldness of the future there corresponds similarly a positive-negative double evaluation of the concept "expectation" that is most prominent in Grisebach. Expectation is, on the one hand, the nonanticipatory preparedness for the correspondence of the partner and, on the other, it is precisely reckoning anticipation. Grisebach means the former when he talks of the "expectation of an experience" (Gw 136), the "expectation of one's own calling in question" (Gw 70), or the "readiness and expectation of a future (of a speaking to)" (Gw 506). Expectation is then always the openness for what is not at one's disposal: "The self thus remains in the expectation of something external, which it itself cannot give itself" (Gw 70), "in the expectation of a situation in which I shall no longer furnish the norm" (Gw 150). From such "expectation as holding back," Grisebach separates off expectation as "the calculation of tomorrow's future" (Gw 576). This pejorative meaning of the concept even wins the upper hand with him. Because, according to him, even the dialogically justified expectation, properly understood, results in a prehension, there remains, in the end, as an ethical requirement, in his view, only the "complete liberation from all expectation" (Gw 578), a requirement that leaves preparedness quite simply as the paradoxical "expectation of the unexpected" (Gw 576; see also 134, 579). In this way, Grisebach refuses anticipating expectation, for the same reason as does Rosenzweig in *Star* (SE II 164–165): because it judges the future from the past and so makes itself into something past. The represented future is, in the broadest sense, simply the "continuation of the past" (Gw 148; see also 180, 187, 417, 428–429, 568, 588). One should frankly consider this to be a topic of dialogicalism. According to Rosenstock-Huessy, even the future "figured out in advance," like any future generally predicted, anticipated, and programmatically planned, is "nothing other than the past posited in advance, ad infinitum" (AG 213; see also 195). Precisely for this reason, it can be seen as the inauthentic future that has been deprived of its futureness. For this reason, too, the dialogicians have the right to a simplifying opposition of present and past. The future is split into these two modes of time. As dialogical, it is present; as a project of the subject, past.

That the past of the future is dependent upon its transcendentally subjective projectedness is once again brought to expression most clearly in Grisebach's *Present*. The world dominated by subjectivity is called in this book, as we saw, the "inner" or the "essential" world. The inner is, however, according to Grisebach, the world of "remembrance"; the essential, the "has been" (Gw 514). Conversely, therefore, even the has been is what it is, as essential or inner, as that which is projected by world-projecting subjectivity. It is "that remembered world that is related to us" (Gw 52). Worldly beings are already turned into the have been simply in that they appear in the transcendental horizon. For they are only encountered in that essence in which they are already encountered as the fulfillment of an a priori. It is, therefore, "the circle of presupposition and determination, of fore-having and confirmation" (Gw 52), which degrades the future to the past. Grisebach contends that in it there moves not only metaphysical thought and scientific research but also all practical everyday comportment of the subjectivity that extends into its world. Even all "norms" (Gw 307, 338), values, goals, and plans (Gw 255, 260) are modes of the recuperation of the futural in the past. Along with Heidegger, Grisebach calls the universal "system of remembrance" the "care" that is grounded in the being-ahead-of-itself of *Dasein* (Gw 560; see also 140, 275, 568)—whereby he once again conveys his admiration, at the same time as his criticism, of *Being and Time*. Since for him fundamental ontology stands for the high point of transcendental thought about immanence, but for that very reason is farthest removed from true "transcendence," it has also, in his interpretation, brought the past future to ultimate transparency, without still leaving room for the futural future. Out of such a perspective, Grisebach is able to say that "Heidegger, in spite of his emphasis upon the future, fails to see the problem of ethical reality" (Gw 589n). Heidegger certainly questions into death. But, insofar as it only manifests itself as "death thought out beforehand in earnest resoluteness" (Gw 590n), it is, in the end, simply "a phenomenon out of the language of yesterday, even when it seems to stand before us as futural. It is always something remembered and expected but not experienced" (Gw 558). In a similar fashion, *Dasein*-with is something remembered that "we encounter every day in our concern" (Gw 559), the fellow human being who is there in our solicitude. Between him and the Thou, in consequence— Grisebach has seen this very clearly—a radical opposition reigns. The dialogical Thou is futural, a future that really approaches me (Gw 148). The human being, on the other hand, to the extent that he represents a "moment" in the care system, is "something that has been, that we remember, but not someone who limits us in the today" (Gw 559–560).

4 The First Step of the Destruction: Characterization of the Thou as Nothing and of the It as Something

While the difference between a present big with the future and a quasi-present past appears to leave the model of intentionality undisturbed, the second concretely antithetical pair immediately brings this model to the point of an obvious collapse. In contrast with the It as "something," the Thou is here characterized as "nothing": "Whoever speaks Thou does not have something for an object. For where there is something there is another something. Each It borders on another It. It exists only in that It limits another It. Where, however, Thou is spoken, there is no something. Whoever speaks Thou has no something, has nothing. But he stands in relation" (DP 8:55).[23]

The contradiction between these sentences and the comportmental schema laid down initially seems, at first, to consist only in this, that the Thou is released from this schema. In contrast, Buber continues to think of the It, or so it seems at first glance, on the model of intentionality. For the something is certainly the noematic correlate or the intentional object of perception, sensation, representation, willing, feeling, thinking, and, in the end, talking about. Nothing, however, is "not something," and therefore not an intentional object. Whoever speaks Thou has nothing for this very reason, that he has nothing for an intentional object.

Without doubt, Buber's theory of the Thou proceeds along these lines. However, it rests upon the basis of a much more comprehensive destruction of intentionality, a destruction that also wrests the It away from the comportmental schema. For the interpretation of the Thou as "nothing" already presupposes a characteristic transformation of the something. The transformed something is precisely no longer the noematic correlate that what is present can become through the act of objectifying experience, but is *what is present itself*; it is an object, not in the sense of the intentional object, but in that of the noematically unmodified thing. That the Thou once again has to become an It means for Buber that the Thou must become a thing. The thesis, in accordance with which "every Thou in our world must become an It," means the same thing as the statement that "in accordance with its essence, every Thou in the world is condemned to becoming a thing or lapsing repeatedly into thingliness" (DP 20–21:68). However, just as the It, as something, is a thing, so the Thou is a not-something or a nothing because it is not a thing: "If I confront a human being as my Thou, and speak the basic word I-Thou to him, he is not a thing among things and is not made up of things" (DP 12:58).

In order to be able to assess the extent to which the identification of the It and the present something conflicts with the point of departure from the comportmental schema, one only needs to recall the statement, already cited from the beginning of the text: "Basic words do not express something that would exist without them, but, insofar as they are spoken, they generate a state of affairs." This is precisely the characteristic feature of what is present pure and simple, that it also exists outside of the acts directed toward it and is not first generated by them. However, that Buber, in the realization of his thought, does, as a matter of fact, entirely equate the It with what is present will be frequently confirmed by the explanation of the further antithetical pairs. At this point, we only have to ask how we are able to arrive at such an equation. The condition of its possibility lies in the representational character of representing and talking about. To be sure, what is talked about is, as such, not that present thing to which it is related, but it represents the latter as it presents itself. Formally one could say that talking about is the conclusive *letting be present of the already present presencing.* The identity that Buber establishes between the It and what is present is only, therefore, the more incisive expression of the equation that really obtains between them.

The ontological structure of discourse does not, however, only justify, within specific limits, the interpretation of the It as something present; it also makes it evident to what an extent the Thou can appear as "nothing." For, as certain as it is that the It is the representative of what is present, it is just as clear, on the other hand, that talking to has no representational function. The Thou certainly always means something or someone, but it represents nothing of this. What Ebner pointed out can be connected up with this (WR 195), that the second person pronoun (just like the first) moves beyond that difference of gender to which the third person comes back. Between it and the being addressed therein there can be no resemblance. A quite simple, grammatical state of affairs already attests to this. For the "It," I can always substitute the concept or the name of the actually presented being "He" or "She." It is a matter of indifference whether I say that "he has blue eyes" or that "Mr. X has blue eyes." In contrast—Ebner draws our attention to this (WR 167)—grammar militates against the attempt to exchange the personal pronoun of the second person for the "corresponding" name. Where, instead of the Thou, I give the entity a name, talking to has already become talking about. The second person has given way to the third.[24]

Admittedly, this does not mean that the Thou is an empty word that contains no reality. On the contrary, that reality that is simply represented in the It is immediately present in the Thou. The being of the Thou is—to use Ebner's words—"an immediate being, not just a thought or represented being, and so also not a being that is spoken about" (WR 176). Whereas talking about simply repeats what already is, the being of the entity addressed is initially offered to talking to. Because that which it aims at is immediately present to it, it does not need to presentify what has already entered into the system of my representations and is therewith past. In this difference between representation and presentation, we find coming back again in a more original conception that which the alternative of past and present already brought to words.

What is at first only abstractly indicated gets concrete content as soon as one examines more precisely the mode of being of the something present: "One says that the human being experiences his world. What does that mean? The human being travels over the surface of things and experiences them. He draws from them a knowledge concerning their qualities, an experience. He experiences what is on things" (DP 9:55). That human being who speaks the basic word I-It experiences what is "on" things, not the things themselves. He does not penetrate to the inner core of their essence, but, from above, travels over their surface. However, what he discovers in this way are only the qualities of things, that is, their properties. He is confronted with a "quality, experienceable, describable, a loose bundle of named properties" (DP 12:58). He experiences "things as sums of properties" (DP 33:81).[25]

This description agrees with the phenomenal findings of discourse. There are, in fact, always only properties in which the about which of discourse represents what is present. Talking about can only let what is present present itself as it is in the attribution of predicates. It follows from this that the determining assertion never attains the totality of beings. For, on the one hand, beings always have still more qualities than I can predicate, and, on the other, they are not resolved into the totality of their qualities. Therefore, even if I continue to heap up predicates indefinitely, I would still never come into possession of the beings themselves—indeed, perhaps even get farther from them by this route. Admittedly, the predicates are predicates of a subject that relates to them as the whole to its parts. But the subject is really only the *subjectum*, only what lies under, which is simply presupposed and is not grasped otherwise than in its predicates.

In that talking about must presuppose the propositional subject, and the representation the substance, both presuppose the basic word I-Thou: "For it is the core of the substance governing in the Thou, the substance, all of those properties are inclusively manifest" (DP 34:82). Precisely that "essence" that is removed from experience and utilization offers itself to the knowledge of the Thou (DP 42:90). A tree, for instance, that is present to me confronts me as "its very self" (DP 12:58), and even in the interhuman realm, the "essential relation" temporalizes a "disclosedness of essence to essence," a "presentification of the Other not in simple representation, and so not simply in pure feeling, but in substantial depth" (PM 160–161).

Even this can be demonstrated by the phenomenon of discourse. For, as a summons to a response, discourse aims at the freedom of the Other, but of which it realizes its essence: "In treating the Other as Thou I treat him, I grasp him, as a liberty" (Ea 154). In talking to, I turn to the Other "itself." This becomes particularly clear when the conversation with him is preceded by a conversation about him. For the selfhood of the Other, his peculiar essence, then manifests itself so immediately and preponderantly that talking-about-him now takes on the character of a talking over and beyond him. Not because other properties become evident alongside those already discussed, but because it becomes clear that the Other "himself" is something different and something more than everything that can be said about him. The Other reveals himself in a totality that cannot be discussed, but that is illuminated in dialogue.

Just as the substance itself gets hidden in the accumulation of properties, so, conversely, the individual properties disappear in the presence of the essence (DP 12:58).[26] On this basis, the dialogue put together out of discourse and debate has the tendency to renounce the realm of words and to reassemble upon the simply saying and hearing of the Thou. Where two speak about a third (a person or a thing), the immediacy of being over against one another is still not there. The genuine I-Thou community is realized even less where I speak about myself and the Other about itself. For the "bending back," the reflection upon itself, is, as the "fundamental monological movement," the death of the dialogue that only lives in reciprocal turning toward (DP 157). Just as little, however, does the essence of the Other open up to me when I turn toward him in such a way that I dwell upon his properties. Certainly, all this is also necessary between I and Thou from time to time. Again and again, I have to speak with the Other about a third party, before the Other about myself, and to the Other about himself, and when that really happens between I and Thou, the speaking is, in each of these three forms, borne by discourse. For talking about something is only that assertion that brings the partners near to each other, talking about oneself only that speaking out in which, instead of closing myself rigidly up upon myself, I open myself to the Other in order to be entirely taken up by him in the relation (WR 18, 89,

96, 108, 111). For, above all, talking to the Other about himself is not an affirmative communication, but an addressing and a confirmation of that with which he addressed me. The sentence, "You are beautiful, my love," has, even grammatically, a completely different meaning from the judgment about my girl friend expressed by persons unknown to me: "You are beautiful." The latter judgment establishes something that is objectively manifest. The former sentence, however, is an appeal, addressed to my girl friend, and for this reason only meant for her because it brings to expression what she is for me and in relation to me, not what she might be in herself and as manifest to anyone (Jm 155, 156–157).

For every word that says something about the Other is in danger of damaging the self-presence of the Other. Why? Because the entity is not "itself" what it is in terms of its properties. For the properties that are ascribed to it are to be found just as well in other entities. Those very properties that attempt in vain to distinguish what actually belongs to the entity, in reality deliver it over to the general. The self, however, is the inexpressibly individual, not the individual as an instance of the general, but the personal element that withstands general categories. Whoever learns about the Other's properties—"the color of his hair, or the color of his discourse, or the color of his goodness" (DP 12:59)—bypasses the Thou to the extent that he covers over the uniqueness of his opposite number. Whoever possesses this particular color is already subsumed under the general; for he is compared with those who possess this same color as well as with those who possess another color.

The It is something; the Thou, nothing. While in this confrontation being still falls entirely on the side of the It, the ontological relationship concerning the clarification of the concepts "something" and "nothing" has almost reversed itself; what was characterized as nothing now manifests itself as authentic being, and what wanted to be something now reveals its nothingness. Being is ascribed to substance more than to the accidents, to the essence more than to the inessential, to the entity itself more than to that which is simply appended to the entity.

Buber is, of course, familiar with the proximity of being and substance. In the article "Bergson's Concept of Intuition" (1943), he writes, "A fruitful meeting between two human beings results precisely from a breakthrough from image to being. The Thou that I meet in this way is no longer a sum of representations, no longer an object of knowledge, but a substance experienced in giving and taking" (H 223). In *I and Thou*, he presents the transformation himself; nothing changes into being and therewith "nothing" into "everything": "What therefore does one learn about the Thou? Precisely nothing. For one does not experience it. What, therefore, does one know about the Thou? Only everything. For one no longer knows anything individual about him" (OP 15:62). This dialectic of being and nothingness in the relationship of Thou and It proceeds in an exactly parallel way to the dialectic of Being already discussed in the relationship of the Thou-I and the It-I.

Meanwhile, it emerges that it is being and not nothingness that dominates in Buber's theory of the Thou. The almost complete negativity of the determinations of the Thou, which will be discussed in what follows, make this clear enough. However, the ontology of the dialogical life also proves to be negative in this, that the concept of substance that is supposed to articulate the being in nothingness is taken from a tradition oriented toward the It and, consequently, is only significant in relation to accidents. This is something that Marcel has also seen. For he notes in his *Metaphysical Diary* that "perhaps substantialism is only the metaphysics of the it" (Jm 227). In the basic word I-It, an entity is present as that which lies at the root of accidents. The Thou, however, in reality discards all qualitative characteristics together with substantiality. So the being experienced in the Thou is not as itself brought to words but only to images, which, in the end, draw it off into the sphere of the It. Only what the Thou is not, not what it is, remains certain.

5 The Interpretation of "Speaking to" as Transcending the "World" and the Thesis of the Spatiotemporal Discontinuity of the Thou-World

From Buber's standpoint, the persistence in the negative does not really stand for a refusal of language, at least not if one understands thereby the impotence of expression in comparison with the thing intended. For that relation to the Thou that is to be expressed is, according to Buber, itself only the transcending of everything present. This is of decisive significance for the understanding of his thought. What is clearly and unequivocally known in this movement of transcendence is only that from which it arises, but not its goal. Dialogical transcending is not therefore a stepping across from one to the other in such a way that the "toward" crystallizes into the end point in a manner similar to that in which the "from which" is fixed as the point of departure. It is, rather, a *swinging* across from the empirically determined into the empirically undetermined. The swing accommodates such a swinging across simply out of the power of its thrust. However, because the toward does not exist for itself like the "from which," the swinging across can never arrive at it and stay with it. So it necessarily swings back to its point of departure. Accordingly, the Thou is, in Buber's sense, experienced as nothing and not characterized as nothing only for lack of adequate expressions. It is also nothing from the standpoint of experience because I cannot go to it straight away as existing, but can only approach it by suspending that which initially forces itself upon me as existing.

At least this is how Buber sees it. The criticism that the negativity of his ontology registers is, of course, by no means reduced to silence thereby. To be sure, it has to take note of the fact that the negativity of the concept of negativity corresponds to the thing intended, but it may reasonably be doubted whether the thing is as negative as Buber thinks. Of course, if it is correct, it will confirm two things. First, that, as a matter of fact, the I-Thou relationship does largely support the structures described by Buber. What is under discussion is not whether such a negative experience of the Thou obtains, but whether this experience reflects the essence of the Thou in a complete form. In other words, it is the question whether the conception of the relation to the Thou as the transcending of the It does not in the end follow from a transcendental understanding of being and out of an orientation toward intentionality. This understanding seeks out articulate discourse as its field of operation, and discourse also confirms the transcendence of the Thou. But does it confirm it only because, caught up in the schema of intentionality, it is not able to grasp the complete reality of the Thou? It could still be the case that the consummation of the Thou in discourse also disposes of the transcendence that still links it to the It. Second, it also has to be confirmed that even in that I-Thou relationship, which Buber regards as exemplary, nothingness is known as being. The present of nonobjective being, operative out of the future, is, indeed, the impulse to transcend everything objective. I would not remove myself from what is present if I were not driven out by the intimation of a more powerful being beyond it. But this being is concealed behind beings that I find around myself. It draws me and withdraws itself, so much so that it would not draw me if it did not withdraw itself. Because it withdraws, the swinging out exhausts itself and sinks back into the present. For this very reason, however, I am once again attracted by it, helplessly, to establish myself conclusively on firm ground.

The thesis that Buber grasps the relation to the Thou essentially as the transcending of everything present would not be satisfactorily grounded through the interpretation of the concepts "nothing" and "something." It is corroborated, however, in the analysis of the concrete It-Thou difference, to which we should now turn our attention. Above all, we find here the contradiction that Buber formulates elsewhere in almost the same form: "The It-world hangs together in space and time. The Thou-world does not hang together in space and time" (DP 37:84). First, the negativity of the Thou cannot be stated more clearly. To be sure, an isolated passage can be found in which Buber, alongside the specific temporality that is at least indicated in the concept of the futural present, also attributes a spatiality distinct from the objective, and where he expressly emphasizes that the dialogical temporality can only be determined from itself and not from the time of the It-world: "The Thou certanly appears in space, but precisely in that of the exclusively over against, in which everything else can only be the background out of which it emerges, not that by which it is limited and measured. It appears in time, but in that of a fulfilled procedure that is lived, not as a component of a continuous and strictly differentiated succession, but in that of a duration whose purely intensive dimension is only determinable from out of itself" (DP 34:81). However, despite the insight that the time of dialogue is only determinable from out of itself, such a determination is actually omitted (except for the explanation of the dialogical present). Instead of attending to the explication of the inner temporality and spatiality of dialogical community, the attention falls exclusively upon the negative relation of the entity addressed as Thou to the totality of the remaining entities, that is, of the It or of the present in general whose temporality and spatiality Buber, as a rule, sees as *the* temporality and *the* spatiality.

On the basis of the statement about the continuity of the It-world and the discontinuity of the Thou-world wth regard to space and time (see also MB 637–638), this thesis can be grasped in the following formula: The relation to the Thou is the swinging beyond of the world as the universe of what is present in general.[27] This seems to be contradicted by the fact that the world, in the view of this statement, is also apparently a Thou-world and not merely an It-world. For all that, the It-world alone is a world in the sense of the universe of what is present in general. Its index is the thoroughgoing determination of everything through everything else, universal causality in space and time. Whoever experiences and utilizes things, situates them "in a spatiotemporal-causal connection" of such a kind that "each is assigned its place, its course, its measure, its condition" (DP 34:82). Causality is only possible in space and time, but the characteristic of that space and that time in which it is alone possible is that they are only realized in causal relations. In time means for things: in the order of succession; in space: in the order of contiguity. But successive and contiguous beings are, in the final analysis, linked through causality. Thus, in the spatiality and temporality of things, there is already to be found their connection with other things. Insofar as it exists in time and space, it is fitted into the "coordinate system" of causal relations. And this coordinate system is the It-world as the "ordered world": "things inserted into the spatial network, processes inserted into the temporal network, things and processes limited by other things and processes, measured by them, comparable with them, ordered world, separated world" (DP 35:83). The world swinging beyond the universe of what is present means, correspondingly: releasing beings from their connection with other beings, letting them be present, unlimited by other beings: "This belongs to the basic truth of the human world: Only It can be ordered. Things can only first be coordinated in that they are removed from our Thou to our It. The Thou knows no coordinate system" (DP 34:83).[28]

In distinction to the It-world as the "ordered world," the Thou-world is the "world order": "The ordered world is not the world order. There are moments of suppressed reason in which the world order is intuited as present. That tone whose indistinct musical image is the ordered world is then instantly understood" (DP 34:83). Even if the world order lies at the root of the ordered world in a manner that cannot be more precisely characterized, it is of a completely different kind. In any case, it is not the order that holds things together as a coordinate system. For, in the sense of a coordinate system, meetings are not integrated in the world: "Meetings are not integrated into the world, but each is a sign of the world order" (DP 36:85). A "sign" of the world order—that means that the world order does not allow itself to be taken over by meetings like something existing, but simply announces itself in the former without giving itself up. The being that is foreshadowed in the meeting is indicated in that world that I transcend in the meeting. It manifests itself out of the present world in not being present itself. For everything that is present must be present somewhere and at some time, and therefore within the world as the coordinate system of spatial and temporal localization. The world order, however, cannot be present because it cannot be present anywhere and at any time. If it were to present itself anywhere and at any time, it would not be the world order, but something ordered by the world and integrated in it.

6 Articulation of the Spatial Discontinuity of the Thou-World in the Concept of Exclusiveness

The fact that the Thou cannot be fitted into space is grasped by Buber primarily by means of the concept of "exclusiveness"—an equally negative concept. Its negativity emerges with particular clarity when Buber writes about love: "Whoever is situated in it, perceives from within it, to him human beings are released from their entanglements in busyness: good and evil, clever and stupid, beautiful and ugly, one after another become for him really Thou, that is, disengaged, prominent, uniquely and differently present. Exclusiveness arises, wonderfully, again and again" (DP 14:66). In its exclusive presence, the Thou is "disengaged, prominent." The condition of the correct understanding of what is meant thereby is the knowledge that the Thou is not present. If one takes the Thou to be something present at hand, its exclusiveness receives a sense that is only adequate to the It: "Disengaged, prominent," then means: isolated alongside other present things in such a way that, with the disengagement, the delimitation of the Thou through beings remaining over would be given. Even this would be exclusiveness, but that of the It and not that of the Thou. For "each It borders on another It. . . . The Thou does not delimit" (DP 8:55); or, as Marcel says, "Nothing could be more false than to identify the Thou with a delimited, circumscribed content" (Jm 157). That the Thou is disengaged from others, but the It connected up in a spatio-temporal-causal fashion, is an entirely vacuous distinction, so long as one considers the disengagement of the Thou on the plane of what is present. For then one thinks of it as it pertains to the It and as it exists precisely as a correlate and not as an alternative to causal connection. Whatever entertains causal relations with other things is always also disengaged insofar as it is present for itself, as it is limited to itself and thereby delimits other things. For precisely because it is already present for itself, its relations to other things are of a causal nature, that is, such as are only subsequently attributed to its being. The claim that "the Thou does not delimit" follows immediately upon the remark that where the Thou is spoken, there is no something. Because the Thou is not present, it cannot therefore exclude all other beings in such a manner that it allows the latter to exist alongside itself, as its limit.

The legitimate meaning of dialogical exclusiveness is to be found in the claim that the Thou appears in the space of the "exclusively over against, in which everything else can only be the background out of which it emerges and not its limit and its measure." From the standpoint of the exclusiveness of the It, this exclusiveness seems more like inclusiveness. In relation to the "eternal" Thou, ex- and inclusiveness, as we shall see, fall together as a matter of fact. Not so, however, in the relation to that very Thou that I deliver over to itself out of the world. Here exclusiveness is, in a certain respect, a medium between the exclusiveness of the It and inclusiveness. The individual Thou neither excludes all other beings so that the latter exist independently alongside it, nor does it include them in such a way that they exist in it. Rather, the other is, so to speak, attached to it as the court that the Thou gathers around itself. The Thou is not itself the other and is nevertheless everything insofar as everything gathers around it and its presence permeates everything: "Solitary and seamless, he (that is, the fellow human being addressed) is the Thou and fills the heavenly circuit. Not as though nothing else existed except himself: but everything else lives in his light" (DP 12:59).

7 Articulation of the Temporal Discontinuity of the Thou-World in the Thought of Impermanence

The negative concept of the exclusiveness of the Thou negates the presence of the Thou in space. It denies that the Thou manifests itself alongside the other and thereby the other alongside the Thou. The other does not manifest itself alongside the Thou because it does not come forth, but remains in the background. To the extent that it is not at all present, however, the Thou manifests itself just as little in time. The thing that I represent and talk about is "my object, and it has its place and its appointed time, its nature and its qualitative determination" (DP 11:58). The qualitative determination reveals it to be present in one way and not another. As present in this way, however, it has its position in the world, and this position is not only spatially determined, as "place," but also temporally, as "appointed time." Accordingly, "I do not locate the human beings to whom I say Thou at any place and at any time" (DP 13:59). I do not even locate them at any time. To be sure, Buber does not have a concept for the being fitted into time of the Thou that, in terminological rigor, bears comparison with that of exclusiveness. But he has at least described the matter as penetratingly as the spatial not being fitted in. Orienting oneself upon these descriptions (DP 34–35:82), one can name the temporal lack of connection of the Thou—with expressions from *Gottesfinsternis* [*Eclipse of the Gods*] (Gf 44, 53)—"momentary" or "momentariness." Even better we may speak here of "impermanence." The advantage of this concept is that its temporal sense, which makes it a synonym for "momentariness," is carried by its more comprehensive ontological sense, in accordance with which it means "contentlessness," and therefore brings to expression the nonpresence of the encountered Thou.[29]

Corresponding to the double meaning of "impermanence," the permanence of the It-world is, according to Buber, on the one hand, the "density," that is, the compact presence at hand of the continuum of what is present in general, and, on the other, the "duration," which continuity is temporally articulated as being: "This world (that is, the It-world) is in some measure reliable; it has density and duration; its organization can be surveyed; one can always reproduce it. . . ; it stands there. . . ; it is indeed your object, and remains so at your pleasure and remains primordially alien to you, outside and in you" (DP 35:83). Nowhere is it as clear as in these statements that the It has made itself independent of the representing and judging act. The It-world "stands there" as the content that (even if it is signified as an inner event) is present outside of the actual execution of the basic words. For this reason, it is supposed to be able to exist even outside and after the representational talking about. This makes up its reliability. For because it remains what it is, independent of the actual speaking of the basic word, it can "always be reproduced." Indeed, its constancy appears as the condition of the possibility of talking about: "You can make yourself understood with others only over it" (DP 35:82), for it alone—this is how one has to flesh out the rationale—guarantees an identity for the different individual consciousnesses, thanks to that identity that persists through time. In connection with this, Buber takes the permanence presupposed in talking about, which is the topic of discourse, as obviously valid for the continuity of the It, even though the It is originally supposed to be only what is talked about as such and not the matter talked about. What is talked about as such is, however, just as impermanent as what is addressed in its being addressed.

Now, the impermanent Thou-world is the negation of all this. It is "unreliable," "without density," "without duration," "incapable of being surveyed," not a possible object of intersubjective understanding (DP 36:83). In the light of the original thesis, in accordance with which Thou and It are nothing, as noematic correlates of opposed and exclusive attitudes, this thesis may, as a thesis about the temporal impermanence of the Thou, appear at first unproblematic, just as, on the other side, the thesis about the permanence of the It appears inconsequential. If the Thou is primarily the one addressed, as such, and not, for example, simply that human being whom I address, it is then clear that this human being is only present in the moment of address as Thou. I can, indeed, in the very next moment already talk about him, and then he is not Thou but He. That the affirmation of the impermanence of the Thou in no way remains true to the subjective-intentionalistic approach is evident in the reflection upon its general ontological signification, namely, that the Thou is "nothing." Herewith intentionality breaks down in a manner opposed to what takes place in the case of the It through its identification with what is present. In both cases the unity in diversity constitutive for the intentional object, as the noematic modification of the object in general, is lost. As a noematic modification, the intentional object stands in strict correlation to the act and the movement of the acting I. As a modification of the object in general, however, it is just as much related to that present element that is posited in it. The identification of the It with what is present brings about the abandonment of act relatedness. The assignment of the Thou to the not-present is nevertheless contested by the relation to the object in general. Here, too, the sense of a noematic correlate is annulled. The Thou is not only nothing insofar as it is not present, but because it is not present, it is precisely nothing insofar as it is not an intentional object. That means that "whoever says Thou does not have something for an object." This, that the Thou is not something present or nothing, has as a consequence that whoever says Thou does not have an object. Or otherwise put, because the Thou *is* nothing, whoever says Thou also *has* nothing: "Whoever says Thou does not *have* something, *has* nothing." The Thou is nothing even in relation to the act related having. So this is the first major step in the destruction of the intentionality of speaking to: that *the intentum is taken away from* the intentional act.

8 The Idea of the Pure Act

Deprived of its object, however, the intentional act of speaking to— following Buber's conception—seems to be strengthened rather than to sink back into itself. The disconnection from the object clearly frees it for itself. In that it finds no rest or stay in its "for which," in swinging out beyond, it swings back into itself. It becomes pure act, and the Thou becomes that which is illuminated solely in the actuality of the pure act. In a picturesque manner, Buber says that "the It is the eternal chrysalis, the Thou the eternal butterfly" (DP 21:69). Accordingly, the It exists in potentiality, the Thou in act.[30] Beings in potentiality are, however, according to Buber, at the same time, the static, firm, and opaque present at hand, which make the pure act of speaking to fluid and transparent. The "impermeable It-world" (DP 107:154) must from moment to moment "be stirred up and melted down by the action of the Thou" (DP 64). "These moments are immortal; they are the most transient: no content can be secured from them, but their strength enters into the creation and the knowledge of human being; rays of their strength stream into the ordered world and melt it down again and again" (DP 34–35:82).

What remains unspoken in the background is the thought that the melting down leads the It-world back to that origin from which human being has removed itself, in that it solidifies the pure actuality of being into static beings. Against this background, even that melancholy that Buber experiences in connection with the impermanence of the Thou becomes comprehensible: "This is, however, the sublime despondency of our lot, that each Thou in our world must become an It. As exclusively present as it was in the immediate relation, as soon as it has worked itself out, or has been mediated, it becomes an object among objects" (DP 20–21:68). In that the Thou sinks back in the exhaustion of the pure act in the It, that is, in the permanent world, despondency comes over me because the origin is overcome by that which has issued from it. In despondency, however, the origin still calls me repeatedly to itself. Engaged in the permanent world as I am, I can only follow this call in the swinging away of transcending. To transcend and to carry out the pure act are the same thing. Only in the transcendence of swinging beyond am I able to overcome the impenetrability of the thing and raise beings into "transparency" (DP 103:150).

That Buber thinks the relation to the Thou as a pure act can be supported by numerous places in the text. Principally, it is for him "pure efficacy" (DP 44:93), and pure efficacy counts for him as genuine reality (DP 90:137). One title for this reality with Buber is the concept "sense." About sense, however, he says, "It will not be signified by us—that we are not entitled to do—only effected by us" (DP 112:159). Even the form that confronts me as Thou can "only be actualized" by me (DP 14:62). In the relation to the Thou, it is a matter of "the complete actualization of the Thou" (PM 115).[31] In other words, it is a matter of an "essential act" (DP 13:59, 15:61), that is, of an act that I must bring about with the insertion of my whole essence, and for this reason, that it does not proceed from the already present, but in swinging beyond everything present, brings to expression what lies at hand.

All those traditions out of which Buber's thought has arisen may have contributed to the historical genesis of this philosophy of the act.[32] Like the idea of transcending, that of the pure act also belongs as a supreme human possibility to the intellectual estate of those philosophers who were Buber's teachers. Buber himself even finds a highly actual trait in Jewish religiosity.[33] According to his interpretation, the spirit of Israel is the "spirit of actualization" (W 18; see also 23). His own world, the "human world" (W 19), is there, first and foremost, for human beings to actualize. Over and beyond this, however, God charges mankind with the responsibility for consummating the whole of creation through his action. To be sure, even in the Chinese tao and in the Greek concept of justice, "being possesses an aspect directed toward mankind that is an ought" (W 39), but only in old Israel has the sovereign singled out one people for this purpose, "that through the actualization of righteousness the created earth is held in readiness for him as a kingdom" (W 41). This spirit, already aroused to new life in the Cabala, is, according to Buber, fulfilled in Hasidism (W 80). Because in Hasidism the "essential treatment of mankind was bound up with the secret of being" more closely than anywhere else, one can, in Buber's opinion, really talk here of that very "active mysticism" that Buber had in mind (W 81). The Hasidic belief that God "is to be reached through each pure act" (CB 658) can be aligned with this, just as well as with the "old-new principle" of Hasidism: "the principle of the responsibility of mankind for the destiny of God in the world" (CB 343; see also 349).

9 The Second Step of the Destruction: Characterization of the Pure Act as the Unity of Action and Passion

Although I do not regard it as my task to question dialogic with respect to its historical ancestry, I have brought forward these remarks in order to make clear the original connection of the theory of the pure act to the totality of Buber's thought. But the particular form that Buber gave to the thought of the pure act shows itself first in the philosophical interpretation. There, what still looked like a limitless and excessive subjectivism turns into its opposite. The suspension of the intentional act itself proves to be the second major step in the destruction of intentionality, after the negation of the intentional object. This suspension does not, however, suspend that consummation of the act that is implied by the loss of the object. Rather, it is carried out through, and by way of, this consummation. More exactly: the act can only be brought to completion in that it is suspended as act. Therefore, the destruction of the *intentio* proceeds in the same direction as that of the *intentum*. Even the *intentum* falls apart, precisely in that it relates purely to itself, to the exclusion of the relation to something present. We now have to pursue the parallel movement of the act.

It is easy to estimate the direction that this movement has to take. Where the opposition of act and object, unified in intentionality, is dissolved through the negation of the something, the opposition of action and passion, of doing and suffering, can also no longer obtain. Insofar as the intentional object—in actual noematic modification— still also offers what is present, it stands over against the act as the (without its assistance and so as the passively) pregiven. That act, therefore, that swings out beyond its object and, to this extent, is not directed toward it has, accordingly, been withdrawn from the confrontation with the passive. The primary consequence of this is that the act that is rendered objectless in this manner becomes an absolute act. For its activity is no longer limited by passivity. This is entirely correct. Just as evident, however, is the fact that activity can only be meaningfully characterized as activity in a polar relation to passivity. So the act that relinquishes the relation to the passive arises as act and, indeed, in this way, that it is endlessly empowered in its activity. The relation to the Thou disappears into a region that lies on the other side of the difference between action and passion.

If Buber could have named and articulated this region in thought without making use of the concepts of "action" and "passion," he would, in this regard, have pushed through to a positive ontology of the I-Thou relation. However, he was not able to do so. Instead, he contents himself with the attempt to grasp what is neither action nor passion as the *unity* of both: "So the relation is being chosen and choosing, passion and action, in one. For an action of the whole essence, as the suspension of all partial comportments, . . . must be similar to a passion" (DP 15:62).[34] Accordingly, Buber sees quite clearly that the unity of action and passion comes into being in that the act becomes the act of the whole essence or, what comes down to the same thing, act pure and entire.[35] This throws light on the meaning that the talk about "unity" has here. Unity does not mean the belonging together of a diversity. In the sense of belonging together, a unity is formed in the intentionality of the act and its object. But this unity presupposes the diversity of its members. Were the unity of action and passion of such a kind, passion would diminish action. For it would limit the activity as that which is different from it. However, if the unity of action and passion is supposed to be an expression of the consummation of action, it can only be a unity in the sense of an identity. For passion does not impede action only if the latter *itself* is a passion, if doing is *in itself* not doing. After the repetition of the sentence cited above, Buber says that "it is the activity of the human being who has become a whole that has been called nonactivity" (DP 78:125). The identity of doing and not doing is, however, a paradox that, as such, cannot be thought.[36] In its unthinkability, the talk about it is revealed as the cipher of a being that presides over the difference between action and passion. This being can be thought of symbolically as the unity of action and passion because it cannot be taken up either in the concept of action or in that of passion. It is, therefore, neither passion nor action alone and, to this extent, the unthinkable unity of both.

10 Phenomenal Demonstration of the Unity of Action and Passion in Addressing

We tried above to point out the necessity of the breakdown of intentionality, from the side of the *intentum*, with reference to the phenomenon of being addressed. Now the self-suspension of the *intentio* must also be concretized in a conclusive fashion with reference to the model of address. That this model is less adequate for its demonstration than for the illustration of the dissolution of the *intentum* is grounded in the matter in hand. For talking to, as we said, still stands under the domination of intentionality. The ontological process of the breakdown of intentionality, which arises with the dissolution of the *intentum*, is attained, however, with the self-suspension of the *intentio* in its final stage. So the discrepancy between talking to and the self-suspension of the *intentio* is greater than that between talking to and the dissolution of the *intentum*.

To what extent does the *intentio* of address get suspended in its self-completion; why can that which is my action, as address, only come to itself as passion? With a view to answering this question, we would do well to bear in mind that any speaking to, and so also talking to, lays claim to a correspondence. Communication, for instance, is intent upon agreement, question upon answer. We have read off the futural character of address from this state of affairs. However, as was established thereby, the dialogical future is present. This gives us a first clue to the phenomenon in question. The current correspondence does not attach itself to speaking to in such a way that first the act of speaking runs off, and then the act of correspondence follows. Rather, the intention to correspondence already belongs so completely to speaking that the latter would not be what it is without it. It is the expectation of correspondence that, therefore, first constitutes speaking to. To constitute in accordance with being means to give meaning. Accordingly, communication has the being-sense "communication" only in that it is intent upon agreement and question has the being-sense "question" only in that it wants to have an answer. Negatively expressed: Communication without an orientation toward agreement would not be communication. A question without the intention of obtaining an answer would not be a question, but would then be "rhetorical," and therefore an illusory question.[37] This constitution is common not only to communication and question but to all acts of speaking to, to which, in the sphere of articulation, there also belongs something like the interrogative and the imperative.[38] Indeed, the more addressive and plaintive the act of speaking to, the further it swings out into the future. Communication does not seek anything more than agreement; the request, on the contrary, awaits its fulfillment beyond agreement and consent. Admittedly, insofar as the futural character sets in in the moment of expectation of speaking to, and does not consist in the fact that the correspondence first sets in after the running off of the addressive act, it also already approximates to communication. Although agreement is simultaneous with communication, it is, nevertheless, not already given with it, but only intended by it. On the other side is the fact that the answer is not spoken out at the same time as the question and stands in the foreground, in comparison with the present character that it has for the questioner, in that it gives his question meaning. The present character of dialogue, just like its future character, consists solely in the constitution of speaking to through the intention toward correspondence. And only in the conception of this constitution can the unity of both the present and future character be thought.

Now, admittedly, the constitution of speaking to through the *intention* to correspondence is still not a constitution through factical correspondence. Between the intention to correspondence and the factical correspondence there opens up an abyss that cannot be bridged by me, the one who intends. The intention to correspondence is wholly and entirely a matter of my intentionality; the correspondence itself, however, is an affair of the Other. I may want the response to my address as passionately as possible. But whether the Other responds to me remains within his freedom, and not within mine. Nevertheless, even the act of my address is affected by his decision. To be sure, the address is already meaningful solely through the expectation of the response. Even if the response is absent, it is therefore constituted to the extent that it can be what it is according to its being status. However, from this, so to speak, minimal constitution, we must distinguish that complete constitution in which the actual being-sense is fulfilled and consummated. The act of address is first fulfilled, however, in and with the correspondence actually carried out by the Other. Or, as Rosenzweig says in *Star of Redemption*, "The word is simply a beginning until it reaches the ear that intercepts it and the mouth that answers it" (SE II 29).

This becomes phenomenally clearest if one represents to oneself what happens, for example, to a question in the event of an answer not being forthcoming. The proof of the unfulfilledness in which the question then gets stuck is, for the one questioning, a peculiar feeling of dissatisfaction, a feeling that can increase — principally when it is a matter of a question to a fellow human being — right up to a limitless pain. Otherwise put, this pain proves that the permanence to which the denial of the answer condemns the question is the essence of the question as an impermanent address. It proves that the question wants to "come to an end" in the answer, precisely because such an ending is its completion. Whoever questions wants, insofar as he is in earnest, to have an answer. But insofar as he wants an answer, he wants the end of his question, or — as Marcel says — "the question itself, in reality, eliminates itself as a question" (Jm 140). In contrast, admittedly, the question to which no answer is forthcoming continues to exist in a certain respect as a question. But this continuance is its lack. It continues because it has not reached its goal.

Admittedly, the originality of those very questions that must persist for the present should in no way be denied just because they cannot be answered without further ado. Generally speaking, those kinds of questions are more original than ones that are answered in a trice because they question in a more original manner. But they also prove to be real questions only through that unfortunate awareness that results in the impossibility of an answer. That no answer is forthcoming can mean, in addition, that there is no answer to it at all. What is excluded is only this, that, at the moment of putting the question, the one questioning takes an answer to be impossible. Since to question means to want to have an answer, one must, in questioning, believe in the possibility of an answer, which one still does even when one restricts this possibility, whether it be that one expects an exhaustive answer only at a later time, in another historical situation, or at the end of time, which would, at the same time, be the end of all questions.

We have to sketch out the fullness of the ultimate metaphysical problems that the question about the question stirs up on account of the transparency of the one thought whose unfolding is up to us. What had to be made apparent with respect to the phenomenon of address was that the completion of the relation in the unity of action and passion has already been clearly pointed out in the fulfillment of the act of address through actual correspondence. As the doing of the Other, correspondence is my nondoing; as an alien action, for me, the one speaking to, it is passion. But in this passion, my own action comes into its own. It comes into its own in this way, that it gives itself up as intention and becomes a doing that, at the same time, is a not doing, to the extent that it is done to me by the Other: "Utterance is therefore withheld from my free will, although I do it" (Soz. I 181; see also AG 126).

One only has to let fall the bounds within which the thought of the unity of action and passion is constrained through its illustration with reference to the model of discourse to become immediately aware of the significance of this conception. In accordance with its link with intentionality, address is originally still an act carried out by me, an act that is first delivered over to the Other in fulfillment. That conception of the thought according to which only the action that is completed becomes passion bears responsibility for this state of affairs. Besides, address is the act of an already constituted I, to whose being-oriented constitution the act of correspondence can consequently hardly contribute anything. Could these constraints, however, not be thought away if one sought the unity of action and passion on the other side of the boundaries of talking with one another? It then becomes apparent, perhaps, that the origin of my being is a doing, as the origin of being myself, a doing that is not only at the same time but even more primordially a suffering, a doing that can only be my doing for the reason that it was previously enacted by the Other and is ever anew enacted by him.

11 Facticity in *I and Thou* and in *Being and Time*

Before we turn to those statements of Buber's that point in this direction, a comparison with *Being and Time* should suffice to underline the meaning that pertains to the thought of the unity of action and passion. The point of comparison will deliver over the concept of facticity. One is entitled to talk about facticity in the following connection primarily insofar as the correspondence to my claim represents a fact independent of my intention. More significant than this, however, is that the fulfillment of my act of speaking to depends upon this fact. Speaking, taken as a speaking to, referred to correspondence, means, according to Rosenzweig, "the dependence of one's own upon the other" (KS 387). Dependence upon what is, for its part, independent of me, but that nevertheless contributes to my being—this is implied in the concept of a specifically human facticity. So, according to Heidegger, the facticity of *Dasein* is still not given in that inner-worldly beings manifest themselves as a fact independent of own *Dasein*. Rather, what is revealed therein is that my own *Dasein* is dependent upon inner-worldly beings. In its similarity of meaning with "thrownness," facticity says as much as "directedness toward inner-worldly beings." But my own *Dasein* is thrown into the "world" because it is thrown being in general, that is, put into its being without its consent. Therefore its own being is not at the disposal of *Dasein*. Before any dependence upon facts discovered in the world, *Dasein* is dependent upon itself as a ground that is not itself at its disposal and that is, to that extent, independent of all its arrangements.

The most important difference between fundamental ontological facticity and the facticity aimed at by Buber consists in the fact that its unity is, for Heidegger's projection (to the extent that he equates facticity with thrownness), a belonging together. For Buber, on the contrary, as we saw, it is an identity. According to Heidegger, projection and thrownness are one because there is no projection without thrownness and no thrownness without projection. Projection is always thrown projection, and thrownness is always the basis for projection. But projection is not itself thrownness. This very identity is indicative, however, of the thought of the unity of action and passion. Action is itself passion. Or, to put it in Heidegger's terminology, projection is intrinsically, and as such, a being thrown. The thrownness, understood in this way, comes to me, the one who projects, out of that future that projection moves into. To be sure, even the fundamental ontological thrownness does not in any way precede projection like an element of the present at hand, but, in comparison with the futural character of projection, is determined, in an existential sense, as pastness. Behind this temporal difference, there lies concealed a still more radical difference between a facticity that falls within the innermost sphere of the self and one that stands farther away from the self than projection, even though it belongs to *Dasein*. Closely connected with all this, moreover, is the fact that Buber's thesis about the *consummation* of action in passion stands opposed to the Heideggerian doctrine of the *limitation* of projection through thrownness. Because *Dasein* is not only projective but also projected, specific possibilities are "removed" from it from the very outset (WG 43). While, according to Buber, action as passion becomes pure action, according to Heidegger, thrownness hinders projection from being pure projection. In this antithesis, however, the fundamental distinction between unity as simple belonging together and unity as identity is once again made known.

Without doubt, the concept of facticity in Heidegger and in Buber is to be distinguished in many other respects. Simply to mention the most obvious difference, one needs only to reflect that the fundamental ontological conception of thrownness prevents one raising the question concerning the one who projects, while the action of the one doing the speaking can only be considered with regard to the doing of an Other as passion. More illuminating still than the enumeration of such differences is the fact that Buber's theory is, in a certain respect, better adjusted to Heidegger's original intention than Heidegger's own elaboration, to the extent that Heidegger puts down the concept of facticity to the ontic meaning of absorption by inner-worldly beings. The original intention of the existential concept of facticity is bound up with the state of affairs, briefly discussed above, that my own *Dasein* is not its own ground and, to that extent, cannot dispose of itself. It is essentially projection, but it has not projected itself with a view to being projection. For it is already thrown into the projecting or—idealistically formulated—posited in positing. But would not the thrownness of projection be rendered infinitely more powerful if projection itself were thrown instead of *Dasein* simply being thrown *in* projection? The nondoing of thrownness, as the presupposition of projecting doing, is revealed in *Dasein*'s being thrown into projection. Only then, however, when projection itself is thrown, is it thrownness. Only then is doing, in itself, not-doing; is action, passion. In that the belonging together of projection and thrownness is transformed into the identity of action and passion, even facticity, in the sense of not-being-disposable, is, as a matter of fact, more radically established.

12 The Reality of the Between as the Unity of Destiny and Freedom

The falling together of facticity and essential act characterizes the extreme point on the other side of intentionality and the transcendental separation of act and fact, of the pregiven and the overthrow. Never-theless, Buber attains it—as we saw—simply by way of the completion of projection because he can only approach what has to be situated on the other side of intentionality from the standpoint of intentionality, and can only reach it though the suspension that terminates in the completion. Strictly speaking, he is, admittedly, not able to "reach" it. If the goal is to be found on the other side of intentionality, no path that takes its point of departure from intentionality, and only goes as far as its breakdown, can get to it.

That goal was outlined in the previous chapter. It is the "fact of the meeting in its original simplicity." In what relationship does the facticity of meeting, as the goal, stand to that recently described facticity of the essential act, as the end point of the path to this goal?

In the meeting, the active moment cannot be one-sidedly attributed to me or to the Other. Rather, our acts reach into one another in such a way that that which I do is, at the same time, done to me. Therefore the initiative lies neither with me nor with the Other. The meeting is, in other words, originally neither simply my speaking to nor my being spoken to. Consequently, the originality of the between in the concrete experience of meeting manifests itself as the precedence of being spoken to over speaking to. As the facticity of meeting, I, accordingly, experience dialogical facticity primarily in being spoken to. In contrast, and in accordance with the peculiarity of the path that Buber takes to get to it, its conceptual unfolding follows the act of speaking to. Even when this act, which is fulfilled in self-surrender, breaks through the basis of subjectivity through the Other's answer, it still remains qualitatively separated from the fact of being spoken to. Here the Other is precisely the one who comes to me with his claim, while I have to correspond. In accordance with that distance that still separates the end of the path of the destruction of intentionality from the goal that is to be found behind intentionality, speaking to never flows into being spoken to. However, it is certainly clear that that facticity of dialogical life that is exemplified with reference to speaking to, as address, is only possible (in the complete form in which it was compared above with fundamental ontological facticity) in being spoken to. For in this completeness it should not first, as was the case with speaking to, be established in the final stage of an already sensibly constituted act and as an experience undergone by an already con-stituted I. Rather, the fact of the act of the Other should precede my entire being, that being that is consummated as "essential act," and in such a way that I first become myself in it. This can, however, only take place in being spoken to. Only, there the beginning of the occurrence that my essential act is fitted into is not at my disposal. For *that* the Other speaks to me takes place, as Ebner noted (WR 120), without my consent. But the act of the Other is the beginning, not simply in the sense of a disappearing beginning, but more in the sense of a governing ground. To the extent that the response of the Other, in relation to my claim, is exclusively its fulfillment, the claim of the Other is the basis of my correspondence.

If one tests those concepts in which *I and Thou* initiates the problem of facticity developed here, two things force themselves upon our attention. On the one hand, it becomes clear that, as a matter of fact, Buber does regard dialogical facticity from the standpoint of the self-suspension of the act of speaking to. On the other hand, it should not be overlooked that he thinks of it with reference to the original fact of the meeting. The rubric under which he thematizes facticity is that of "reality" or "real life" (DP 13:59). However, what it has to do with reality or the real life is most clearly delineated by Buber when he says, "Whoever stands in relation takes part in a reality, which means, in a being that is not simply in him and not simply outside of him. All reality is an action in which I participate without being able to make it my own. Where there is no participation, there is no reality. Where there is no self-appropriation, there is no reality. Participation is that much more complete, the more immediately the Thou is affected" (DP 65–66:113).

This definition begins with a negative delimitation: The reality aimed at is a being that is not simply in me and not simply outside of me. In this way, all those alternatives that are circumvented by dialogical facticity are rejected: the separation between the own, as the not-Other, and the Other, as the not-own; between that which is immanent to me and that which is transcendent to me; between my action and that which is passively pregiven to me. Buber takes up, once again, the denial of such dualities when he says, "Where there is no participation, there is no reality. Where there is no self-appropriation, there is no reality." In the concept of participation, with whose help that task of a positive determination of reality is supposed to be brought under control, Buber emphasizes, particularly strongly, the "active" moment of self-participation, which, in a certain respect, says much the same thing as self-activation. To participation, however, there belongs, in equal measure, the "passive" moment of taking and receiving. Only the two moments together make up the essence of participation. And it is precisely their unity that befits the concept of participation for the disclosure of reality.

Already the bringing back to prominence of the active meaning of the concept "participation" indicates that Buber achieves access to dialogical facticity from the accomplishment of my act. Regardless of this, he nevertheless, in the end, already conceives participation with reference to the between, as the originally simple fact of meeting. That in which I take part when I stand in relation is a reality that is present neither in nor outside of me. This I experience, above all, as the reality of the Other. The partners of a relation must take part in one another. The relation itself is "an actual participation in one another, not of a psychic, but of an ontic order"(PM 107). Admittedly, not a participation in the Other as an entity, but in the being of the Other: "Only participation in the being of the existing essence discloses the meaning at the root of own being" (PM 146). The being, or the reality of the Other, is neither simply in nor simply outside of me because it is the action of the Other that initially and throughout supports my own action as claim, or that, as response, completes my own action, and in all this remains an action of the Other. Insofar as it regulates my own action, it is not simply outside of me; to the extent that it remains alien to me, it is not simply in me. Positively, it is my ground, a ground that is not at my disposal. As *my* ground, it is that which is closest to me, the innermost part of my interiority. As my *ground*, however, it cannot itself be made my own again. It is that transcendence, foreseen by Sartre, but covered over again, which I come across in the midst of my immanence.[39] Buber says of the Thou-world, "It does not exist outside of you; it touches your very ground. And should you say 'soul of my soul,' you have not said too much. But beware of wanting to transfer it into your soul—for then you destroy it" (DP 36:84). Likewise, I would destroy reality if I were to attribute solely to my efficacy what, in original unity, I do and suffer at the same time. It only opens up to me "when I know 'I am subjected to it' and know at the same time 'It depends on me' " (DP 97:144). This is the "paradox that I have to live" (DP 97:144), paradoxical unity of doing and suffering. It depends upon my action. But my action is an accomplishment of my entire essence simply for this reason, that

I submit myself to the action of the Other. In this way I live out reality, reality as "an operation in which I take part without being able to appropriate it for myself."

As "an" operation, however, reality, no matter whether primarily experienced as the reality of the Other, is originally neither my operation nor that of the Other. It is, rather, the reality of the between, as the pure occurrence of the meeting. The latter, in turn, is reality pure and simple or "being itself" (1962 I 473). So, taking part in the reality of the Other is, in its deepest roots, "participation in being itself" (H 219).

Envisaged on the plane of the between, the unity of action and passion appears as the reality revealed at the same time by destiny and freedom. "Destiny [*Schicksal*] and freedom [*Freiheit*] are entrusted to each other" (DP 55:102; see also Gf 43).[40] Together they institute that "sense" that Buber thinks of as reality (DP 56:102). In what way are they "entrusted to each other," however? Freedom is the dialogical counterpart to an It-like will, destiny the dialogical counterpart to an objectively determined fate. But even will and fate form a unity: "Just as freedom and destiny belong together so do will [*Willkür*] and fate [*Verhängnis*] (DP 61:108). The unity of will and fate is, for all that, simply the polar belonging together of thesis and antithesis, of position and opposition. Just as the subject demands an object and the object a subject, so willfulness [*Willkür*] brings fate with it and fate, willfulness. Willfulness is itself nothing other than the power of the subject, a power that dominates and determines the world of objects. Fate is the correlated "being determined" (DP 62:109) of an object-world solidified into mechanical necessity, an object-world into which the subject is always itself also fitted in. Willfulness is a pure and "awkward" action that brutally invades the world and transforms it according to the subject's representations. Fate is the dull passivity that stands counter to such an action. The unity of willfulness and fate is, therefore, of the same order as the belonging together of activity and passivity in the field of the subject-object schism. It is not a harmony, but the hostile opposition of poles that reciprocally challenge each other to combat.

On the other hand, the unity of freedom and destiny is quite different. There the members are related to one another in a "friendly" manner. There is no freedom without destiny and no destiny without freedom. To be sure, it is equally valid to say that there is no willfulness without fate and no fate without willfulness. But what appears formally as an equal and reciprocal reference has to be taken account of in its difference, as soon as one considers the friendly meaning in the one instance and the hostile meaning in the other. The friendliness of the relationship between freedom and destiny means that destiny not only needs freedom in order to be destiny but that, over and beyond that, it is only destiny as freedom. Likewise, freedom is only freedom as destiny. The unity of willfulness and fate presupposes that willfulness is not fate and that fate is not willfulness. But the unity of destiny and freedom is the unity of destiny, as the unity of destiny and freedom; and of freedom, as the unity of freedom and destiny.

Freedom, as the unity of freedom and destiny: this is the "will" that belongs to meeting or the action that is my "determination." For in determination there comes together what, as free determining and fateful being determined, falls apart.[41] The free human being "believes in determination and believes that he needs it. It does not constrain him: it awaits him; and he must go up to it, and yet does not know where it stands. He has to proceed with his entire essence, that he knows. . . . There he no longer takes hold, and yet does not simply let things happen. He is on the watch for what comes out of it, the path of human being in the world: not in order to be carried by it, but in order to develop it in the same way as it wants to be developed from him, the one who needs it, with the human spirit and human action, with human life and human death. I said, he believes; implied therein, however, is that he encounters" (DP 62:108–109).

Destiny as the unity of destiny and freedom is the other moment that belongs to meeting alongside that of the "will": "grace." That destiny itself already includes freedom in itself means that meeting is not the brute fact of an accident, but a gift. Since, however, for us — as Buber emphasizes — only will, and not grace, can be an object of our preoccupation, the unity of freedom and destiny, which is destiny itself, is no longer susceptible to conceptual comprehension. Buber can only point to it indirectly in such a way that he unfolds the relation of a freedom that, for its part, is already destinal to this destiny, which implies freedom. And certainly, that freedom that stands over against destiny in a friendly manner belongs within destiny itself in a double orientation. In the passage just referred to, Buber takes account of one orientation: I "must proceed with my entire essence," proceed, namely, toward a meeting. Freedom is here the letting be of destiny as readiness for the meeting, as an opening up of oneself to it. Because only meeting is accorded to me when I approach in this fashion, destiny is referred to a freedom that is appropriately determined. It is so, however, in still another respect: insofar as I have to correspond to the claim of the meeting in freedom and this claim is first fulfilled in my correspondence. Buber has this principally in mind when he says, "Destiny and freedom are entrusted to one another. Destiny is encountered only where freedom is realized. That I discovered the action that is aimed at me, in this, in the movement of my freedom, the mystery is revealed to me" (DP 55:102).

Abstractly expressed, freedom as readiness for the meeting is located *ante factum*, while freedom as correspondence to the claim of the meeting is located *post factum*. But in this abstraction it is easy to overlook the fact that not only destiny but also freedom is a unity of destiny and freedom, that, therefore, freedom qua readiness, just as well as freedom qua correspondence, bears destiny within itself. Freedom qua readiness leads to determination and is therewith already determined by the meeting. If it were not this, it would be what it cannot be at any price: an a priori into whose sphere the fact that emerges a posteriori is introduced. However, freedom, as correspondence, is in itself permeated by destiny because it realizes not what it has given up to itself, but what has been given up to it by the meeting. In this way, its doing itself becomes an undergoing. The action that I had in mind becomes the "action that is aimed at me." This means that the challenge of freedom to correspondence is a claim that is made upon me and not a claim that I raise. As a response to the friendly challenge, the "movement of my freedom" is then no longer a self-posited positing, but is simply the discovery of the action that is aimed at me, that is, the apprehension of my determination, which is rooted in a hearing of the claim.

Appendix I
Transcendental Philosophy and the Illusion of Dialogue: Alfred Schütz's Social Ontology

The social ontology of Alfred Schütz[1] is an example of the fact that the orientation toward Husserl's *transcendental* phenomenology does not for one moment accommodate dialogic on the scale of early phenomenology. Admittedly, this claim contradicts the first impression created by *Der sinnhafte Aufbau der sozialen Welt* [*The Phenomenology of the Social World*] (1932). Indeed, the indebtedness to Husserl's transcendental phenomenology is unmistakable. Schütz draws attention to it subsequently (IV 10, 106, 190). What he has in mind is the grounding of Max Weber's interpretative sociology[2] through a constitutive analysis of meaning. When, in the transition to the social world, he leaps out of the transcendental into the natural attitude (41–42:43–44, 106–107:97–98), this only means that he situates his social ontology at a level on which the transcendental constitution of the Other is already presupposed.

The orientation toward the dialogical principle appears to be just as certain as this presupposition. In Schütz's linguistic usage, the Other is simply the "Thou." To the extent that it is original, the relationship to him is evidently set out as a dialogical one. Both of the sections principally devoted to social ontology attest to this, or so it seems. At the root of that "theory of alien understanding" (106–155:97–138) offered in the first, "conversation" [*Gespräch*] is to be found, as the guiding model, and, indeed, primarily, the question-answer dialogue (see, for example, 141–143). The "structural analysis of the social world" given in the second (156–246:139–214) divides up this world (starting out from the supposition of its heterogeneity (5:8, 149:135, 156:139, 168:150) into "surrounding-world" [*Umwelt*], "with-world" [*Mitwelt*], "world of predecessors" [*Vorwelt*], and "world of successors" [*Folgewelt*]. In this respect, the difference between surrounding-world and with-world is the decisive one (12:15). In the social surrounding-world, however, the Thou should be entirely at home. In it the Other is encountered as "fellow human being"; in the social with-world, simply as "contemporaries" [*Nebenmensch*] (160:142, 199:181). Functioning as the original norm for the understanding of the with-predecessor-, and successor-worlds, it (the surrounding world) has its own center in the "environmental social relation," the characteristic of which Schütz takes to be dialogical "reciprocity" (176–177:157–158, 183:163, 186:166). The entire environmental [*umweltliche*] experience of the alien is, however, distinguished from the with-worldly through its "immediacy" (129:204, 181:163, 199:181, 203:185).

It is the task of the following exposition to dissolve the appearance of dialogic that attaches to this conception. The meaninglessness of the expression "Thou" is easy to recognize. Schütz applies the expression in a double sense that obscures the issue. In the first place, every Other is meant thereby. But in the second place, only the Other experienced in the surrounding-world is referred to. Still, in both senses, the word "Thou" is exclusively directed toward the "alter ego" (see, for example, 106–107:97–98, 126:117). With this claim, a judgment has already been passed upon the transcendental-phenomenologically founded "dialogic." But let us take a closer look. Just as easy to demonstrate as the dialogical irrelevance of the Thou concept is that of the concept of "immediacy." "Immediacy of alien experience" means exactly the same thing with Schütz as "mediacy of alien experience" with Husserl (187:164, 203:180). When Schütz denies the mediacy of environmental alien experience, he simply negates that mediacy withdrawn from total alien experience by Husserl but attributed to the with-worldly alien experience by him (5:8, 202–209:180–182, 206:190, 230–232:198–199, 208–209:240) as inferential mediacy. In a similar fashion, he refuses the sort of genuine immediacy that Scheler confers upon alien experience (17:20, 21:23).

It may be a little more difficult to get a clear view of the exemplary thematization of conversation and the abstraction of the environmentally experienced cohuman being from the contemporary disclosed in the with-world, with regard to its undialogical tendency. The relation of the "theory of alien understanding" (in which conversation is chiefly investigated) to the "structural analysis of the social world" (in which the characteristics of the surrounding-world and the with-world are distinguished) is already unclear. Since the environmental, social relation is supposed to provide the "understanding" sociologist with the means of elucidating the social relation in general, it is difficult to understand why Schütz prefaces its description with a "theory of alien understanding" that more or less abstracts from the inner differences of the social world. To this contradiction there corresponds that ambiguity that, on the one hand, is supposed to make the "structural analysis of the social world" the "central core" (11–12:14), but, on the other hand, is supposed to make the "theory of alien understanding" the central locus of the entire book (161:143). Insofar as the latter is the case, the work of Schütz stands in the tradition of Dilthey, Troeltsch, and Spranger's endeavors, which have nothing to do with the philosophy of dialogue. But, looked at more closely, Schütz is only able to demonstrate alien understanding with regard to the example of conversation because he already has a preconception of the environmental, social relation. The question-answer dialogue then first finds its interpretation in the analysis of the surrounding-world, an interpretation that is appropriate to the conception of the author. So it is worth starting with an assessment of this analysis, and, in particular, with the analysis of the environmental phenomenon of relation.

Schütz makes the same presuppositions there as those that separate early phenomenology from radical dialogic. The social relation is also for him secondary in comparison with the "individuals" entering into it (3:6). This cardinal distinction demands, just as well, the orientation toward Max Weber as the point of departure from Husserl. According to Weber (1913), the "individuals" are the basic elements of any social formation. Schütz takes over from Husserl, however, the transcendental-solipsistic approach. Prior to the "theory of alien understanding" and the "structural analysis of the social world," he gets involved with "meaning constitution in the very own experience of the solitary I" (10:13). Further, he shares with early phenomenologists the view that the social relation is constituted in the "intentional acts" of the individuals (7:10; MR 542). With an appearance of self-evidence he speaks of the "instantiation of the social relation" (174:156), whose field of force is "living intentionality" (157:140, 159:143, 181:163).

What, in opposition to early phenomenological dialogic, falls away is the quest for the between. In its place, we find the explanation of the projective character of intentionality. The "lived experiences of consciousness intentionally directed toward an alter ego" (162:144) form the broadest circuit of the social structural analysis. They are all characterized by an "alien attitude" (164:146), which, as with-worldly, is supposed to be a "You-attitude" (205:183, 208:187, 210:189, 220:199) and, as environmental—here Schütz operates with his narrower Thou concept—is supposed to be a "Thou-attitude" (182–183:164–165). In accordance with the circumstance that the "Thou" appears therein as a passive object, the Thou-attitude can also be one-sided (183:165). The reciprocal Thou-attitude, on the other hand, is the genuine *constituens* of the environmental, social *relation* (183:165, 186:167). "Social comportment" now stands out of the mass of lived experiences intentionally directed toward an alter ego through its spontaneous activity and "social behavior" (with which Schütz, as also Weber, is primarily concerned) on account of its prior projectedness—which enters into the spontaneity (162:144). With the social behavior that, in its turn, represents the preprojected social comportment most purely, the explicit projectedness of the alter ego itself is joined to its own prior projectedness. For this reason, Schütz calls it the "alien operation": "Under the in-order-to motive, specific lived experiences of the consciousness of the Other are to be brought about" (165:147). That with this the alien operation projects the "Thou" itself is not just my suspicion, but the opinion directly expressed by the author in *The Phenomenology of the Social World*. Indeed, the consciousness of the Thou is supposed to be "drawn into the projection of my operation" in the "environmental operational *relation*" (181:163). Schütz endeavors "to offer a description of that behavior of the I in whose projection the Thou and its lived experience are drawn in" (159:141).

From the vantage point of transcendental phenomenology, the intentional correlate of projection is, in the final analysis, the world. Correspondingly, with Schütz, the world also embraces the environmental relation, along with the with-worldly. However, the spatiotemporal world that is perspectivally centered upon my I counts as world (5:8, 116:165). The law of spatiotemporal perspectivity also determines what is with-worldly and what is environmental. This terminologically unfortunate distinction, whose misleading character is particularly evident in the antithesis of the with-world and cohuman being, is supposed to make it linguistically manifest that the social world experienced in the Thou-attitude is spatially and temporally distributed around me. So one can say straight off that my social environment is the social world, "with which the temporal and spatial community is connected" (160:142; see also 181–182:163–164, MR 543). It is defined through the factical presence of the Others. In this way, Schütz makes nothing of his single contribution to a substantially enriched and specific Thou concept. Such a contribution demands, so to speak, antithetically, the interpretation of the with-worldly alter ego as an anonymous, unindividual type (201–230:181–207). In opposition to this alter ego, the environmental Thou takes on the form of a nonrepeatable self (203:183, 208:188). For all that we read, "In the environmental Thou-attitude, I am even turned toward my neighbor in the streetcar and the 'man at the next table' " (197:177). I experience my neighbor on the streetcar as an environmental Thou, not because he encounters me in his unrepeatable self-being, but because he happens to be located in my neighborhood. Conversely, according to Schütz, the Other who is entrusted to me in his or her uniqueness, for example, my marital partner, is simply with-worldly, insofar and as long as he or she does not fulfill the condition of factical presence (200:179).

Since worldliness is imprinted upon all experience of alien subjects—the surrounding, as well as the with, after, and consequential—the general "theory of alien understanding" already necesarily relies upon it. The "surrounding-world/with-world" distinction anticipated by this theory is prefigured in the differentiation of the "signitive, symbolical representation," which Schütz sees the conception of alien psychic life, in its essential mediacy, as being. A symbolic sign of the psychic life of the Other is either the body of the Other or an "artifact" that refers to the Other as to its creator (110:100, 119:108). The experience of the alter ego through the medium of its body implies (as an experience of the factically present Other) surrounding-worldliness, which through the productively mediated experience of what is alien implies (as an experience of the factically absent Other) with-worldliness. In our view, however, what is important, above all, is that the mediacy of alien experience with Schütz, just as with Husserl, results in every case in a mediatedness through worldly beings.

The reiterated determinations of surrounding- and with-worldliness make clear what is at issue with the phenomenology of conversation put forth. One is not guilty of any simplification when one claims that this phenomenology moves exclusively in the field of that question-answer dialectic that Marcel cuts off from real dialogue. What Schütz manages to grasp is the reciprocal relatedness of question and answer, the going-out of the question toward the answer and the coming back of the answer toward the question. He thematizes its relatedness as a particularity of the relationship that binds every making cognizant (that is, the deliberate bringing-to-expression in distinction from the involuntary coming-to-expression) to a taking cognizance and every taking cognizance to a making cognizant (20:22, 129–130:119–120). Just as taking cognizance does in general present the "in-order-to motive" of making cognizant (146:135), so "the question is the because-motive for the answer, and the answer the in-order-to motive of the question" (180:162). Here we already find that Schütz conceives the question, like all making cognizant, as an alien operation. So making cognizant is also explicitly elucidated as such an operation (168:150). Consequently, it is represented as projection, and, indeed, in the first instance, as projection of the act in which the "Thou" signifies the meaning posited by me. I, as the one who posits the meaning, am, at the same time, the one "who anticipates the interpretation of the meaning through the Thou in projection" (145:130; see also 142:128, 166:147, 168:149, 178:160). Such an anticipation is an "expectation" (178:160; see also Weber 1913 257, 265–266, 279), but precisely of the kind that the dialogicians unmask as undialogical. It is, so to speak, the preenvisaged enactment of the alien life of consciousness. In this way, it presupposes the envisaged reenactment, through which alone the alien life of consciousness opens up to me in natural life (125–126:114–115). Schütz will not allow it to be confused with "empathy" (126–127:115–116). But the theory of empathy from which he distances himself is solely that of a naive psychology that, without knowledge of the transcendental constitution of the alter ego, yields *psychological* empathy as the originally disclosive access to the alien life of consciousness. On the contrary, Schütz separates himself from transcendental empathy so little that he grounds the envisaged reenactment upon it and characterizes it according to its image: "So we undertake, in a certain sense, an exchange of persons, in that we put ourselves in the position of the agent and, henceforward, in the event of just such an observed action, identify our life of consciousness with the alien life of consciousness" (126:115).

This basis hardly makes room for an actual experience of dialogical facticity. To be sure, Schütz is aware of the difference between my anticipation of the alien correspondence and its actual enactment: "The actual behavior" of the Other stands in relation to that awaited by me in the modus of fulfillment or nonfulfillment" (191:170). However, in a peculiar manner, he means that I, the one doing the speaking, in speaking to, project precisely the thatness of alien correspondence. In the case of the question, it is thereby a matter of the projection of the fact of the understanding of the Other just as well as the answer of the Other: "What is imaginatively envisaged and preprojected is *that* you will answer; *what* you will answer, of course, remains, within this meaning configuration (posing a question and hoping for an answer), undetermined and empty" (178:160). One is supposed to assume the reverse—that is, it is an open question whether you answer; from the content of the question and the "direction of the question,"[3] it is more or less prefigured what you will answer, if you answer. Now one could, perhaps, believe that in Schütz's sense, the preprojection of the that of the answer in no way encroaches upon its factical character, but simply says that I await your response. Meanwhile, in the opposition "imaginatively envisaged and preprojected"— undetermined and empty—we find the exclusion of openness from preprojection. The preprojection not only *provokes* the counteraction of the Other; it *produces* it. Only for this reason does the question have a right to the title "alien operation." The actual fulfillment of my project through the counteraction of the Other is itself still a matter of my project. That tendency of the "Thou," which is striven for in this way, does, according to Schütz, bring about, at its purest, the most authentic I-Thou relationship, the "environmental operational relation": "In a unitary and undivided stream, my duration (that is, my temporally flowing consciousness) comprehends the projection of your action and its actual fulfillment through your behavior as a unity" (192:171). This unity marks the most extreme point in the dialogical unity of action and passion. There, in dialogicalism, the alien act as alien is the indisposable ground of my own, which, accordingly, gives up its subjective act status. Here, however, my act, as mine and subjective, is the transcendental medium in which the alien act is dissolved.

In order to circumvent a misunderstanding that is still possible, it should in the end be emphasized that the proposed demarcation of Schütz's social ontology against the philosophy of dialogue does not in any way imply a depreciation of the work undertaken in this social ontology. Even less are we entitled to such a depreciation in that, from our limited perspective, we have not been able to survey any considerable part of the field exposed by Schütz. Had we examined it, we would undoubtedly have been confirmed in the conviction that *The Phenomenology of the Social World* deserves an exceptional place within the social philosophy of transcendentalism. The book has its place, more specifically, in the circuit of that personalistic attitude the analysis of which is furnished by Husserl in the second book of *Ideas*. Even there, linguistic communication appears on the foundation of empathy. Schütz similarly characterizes the operational relation with the help of that concept of "motivation" that guides Husserl's analyses (117–179:159–161). Admittedly, he does, at the same time, deepen the Husserlian account at several points. We should at least take note of two such points. At one point, Schütz transforms that temporal coexistence upon which Husserl reposes his entire theory of intersubjectivity into "simultaneity" in a quite specific sense (112–114:102–104, 181:163, 188:170; MR 543). This transformation implies, above all, an essential interiorization. With Husserl, temporal coexistence, generally speaking, only touches the external being-there-now of the Other. In contrast, Schütz's term "simultaneity" is directed toward the foundational state of affairs that I am able, even if only mediately, to take note of the lived experiences of the alien in their completion. At another point, Schütz contributes to the differentiation of the theory of alien understanding in that, in the first instance, he sharply separates the understanding of my own lived experiences by the alter ego and the understanding of the lived experiences of the alter ego (11:14), in order then to prove that the understanding of the lived experiences of the alter ego, the authentic alien understanding, is founded in the understanding of my own lived experiences by the alter ego (116:106, 119:109, 123–124:113–114). Indeed, the decisive role that this doctrine plays with Schütz attests to the tendency that he assumes in his efforts toward a deepening of the Husserlian approach in the direction of a still higher degree of mediacy. The last residue of dialogical immediacy in alien understanding is driven out of the alter ego through the presupposed reflection upon lived experiences. The "living intentionality" of the environmental social relation becomes the "intentionality of reflexive mirroring" (199:179; see also 189:170, 194:173, 230:118).

Appendix II
Between Transcendental Philosophy and the Philosophy of Dialogue: Karl Jaspers's Elucidation of Communication

Corresponding to a widely held belief, Hans Urs von Balthasar calls Buber and Jaspers "the two great dialogicians of our time."[1] In contrast, Löwith, just as well as Binswanger—the former with reference to the issue and the latter with reference to the person—have pointed out why the elucidation of communication developed by Jaspers does not, in the last analysis, belong to the philosophy of dialogue. As was already noted in the introduction, Jaspers's work does not immediately belong to it because, instead of starting out from the Thou, the second person of the personal pronoun in the strict sense, it starts out from "the Other itself." In line with everything that has been said, this is more than just a terminological difference. This distinguishes "the two great dialogicians of our time" even more fundamentally than the circumstance noted by Buber himself (DP 299–302), that Jaspers preserves the orientation of the Thou concept toward divine transcendence. For such a preservation follows, first and foremost, from the original distance from the Thou concept in general. In this way the decision on this issue, whether the Other is most genuinely a Thou or an Other self, regulates all further steps in the field of social ontology. Despite the difference posited therewith, we find essential similarities in this field and therefore in the sphere of life with human beings. So the elucidation of communication, although it is not itself a philosophy of dialogue, is to be found in its proximity. As was already emphasized in the introduction, it has its place in the space between transcendental philosophy and the philosophy of dialogue, but in such a way that its distance from the latter is much less than from the former. This place can be fixed under the following heads, in that we try to make out (1) in what the communicative analysis of "philosophy"[2] stands in agreement with the historically developed philosophy of dialogue, (2) what should be regarded as its original contribution to the unfolding of the dialogical principle, (3) to what extent it approaches the radicality of Buber's dialogic, and (4) in what way it stands in relation to transcendental philosophy.

1. Agreement between the philosophy of dialogue and the "elucidation of existence" rules, above all, in the thesis concerning the reciprocal constitution of the existentially communicating partners as a cipher for their descent from the event of the meeting. Jaspers represents the thesis as such with the greatest possible clarity.[3] "Existentiel" communication, in distinction to "*Dasein*'s communication," is nothing other than the "becoming actual" of its members, as becoming my self through the Other in conjunction with the self-becoming of the Other through me. But not only the real consequence of the thought of reciprocal constitution but even Jaspers's own statement leads toward this interpretation of the thesis as a cipher, in the same sense as in Buber's dialogic. For Jaspers himself emphasizes that this thought runs into a logical contradiction that can only be resolved if one recognizes the priority of the communicative relation vis-à-vis the existences standing in relation to one another (305–306:II 13–14). Only then will the difference of existentiel communication from *Dasein*'s communication also become clear—which last Jaspers calls "reciprocal interaction" because it presupposes its *relata* as fixed substances (305–306:II 13–14, 309:17). As meeting, the existential communication is, however, even for Jaspers, "will and grace" at one and the same time, as Buber would say, that is, in the language of existential elucidation, a nondisposable, nonmanipulable "gift" supported by a "conscious preparedness" that, in the form of "solitude," unifies the knowledge of the outstanding reality of self-being and the commitment to the meeting (347:II 56). Further, it appears, like the I-Thou relationship thematized by Buber and Binswanger, as the condition of an original experience of being. It is existentiel communication through which freedom "gets hold of being" (347:II 56).

2. Jaspers's original contribution to the unfolding of the "dialogical principle" consists, before all else, in the attempt to prove the *necessity* of the cooperation of the Other in self-becoming. The self-becoming that takes place in comunication is defined by Jaspers as the becoming-revealed-of-the-self-with-the-Other (350–351:II 59–60). This first makes possible revealedness vis-à-vis the Other and revealedness vis-à-vis one's self, both of which belong to existentiel communication (332:II 42; 255:I 296) but contribute nothing to its original genesis. Becoming revealed oneself is now necessarily a becoming-revealed-oneself-with-the-Other because I myself am that which is supposed to become revealed in becoming real. However, I am just as well the one to whom it is supposed to be revealed. Revelation cannot be conceived without just such an opposition of the revealed and the recipient of revelation. Only, I can perfectly well confront my existence (*Dasein* as Jaspers understands it), but not my self. So I can only become revealed to myself in that I become revealed to the Other. Self-revelation-together-with-the-Other means becoming revealed to oneself with the help of the Other, and this in its turn means becoming revealed to oneself through becoming revealed to the Other. Admittedly, this translation can hardly appeal to places that correspond to it literally in Jaspers. But it finds its justification in the further explication of self-becoming as calling-oneself-in-question (351–352:II 60–61). I myself cannot call myself in question because then the self that calls in question remains outside the calling-in-question. In order really to be able to call myself in question, I must, therefore, let myself be called in question by the Other, which shows once again that being-with-the-Other, which here receives the stamp of a "loving conflict," is the necessary condition of my self-being.

Here we shall document the agreement of communication analysis with the historical-factical philosophy of dialogue and its enrichment through an additional Jasperian thought, with reference to statements from within communications analysis itself. The proximity of this analysis to the philosophy of dialogue forces itself upon us still more immediately when one takes a look at the systematic connection between the elucidation of existence, whose first and foundational cornerstone constitutes the elucidation of existentiel communication, and the preceding world orientation. In abstraction from the *Dasein* of world orientation, communicative existence is disclosed as that swinging beyond the world that dialogic grasps Thou-saying as being.

More precisely, the transition from the level of world orientation to the sphere of existential elucidation is for Jaspers a leap from one mode of transcendence into another. The unity of the identity and the difference of *"Dasein"* and "consciousness in general" betrays what is at issue in the transcending observed in "world orientation." Jaspers identifies *Dasein* and consciousness in general[4] and yet separates them at most other places without reflecting upon the unity of identity and difference. Nevertheless, the unity is to be sought in the material thought out by him: in this, that *Dasein* can only realize itself in the transcending from itself to consciousness in general: "Inasmuch as I have discovered myself in my world as *Dasein*, from this moment of coming-to-myself and on, I was *no longer only this* Dasein. . . . I determine my own *Dasein* as that consciousness in general that is common to all men" (57:I 103). That identity of the different that is to be found here becomes evident when one makes clear the height upon which Jaspers situates *Dasein*. The *Dasein* that is directly thematized by him always already possesses complete I-consciousness (11–12:I 54–55). He only discloses retrogressively the "primitive" *Dasein* that is not conscious of itself. Indeed, in the end, he conceives of *Dasein* on the model of theorizing, scientifically active *Dasein*. The latter looks upon itself, on the one hand, as an "empirical" individual that, as a matter of fact, is present as an object among other objects in the world. So the natural scientist looks upon himself as a natural being, the humanist as a "historically isolated being"; for "as historically isolated I am one figure among thousands upon this theater" (658:III 358), upon the theater of world history. Similarly, everyday *Dasein* living therein, a *Dasein* whose I-consciousness is essentially "acceptive consciousness," is already confronted with itself, and so represents itself objectively in accordance with the image that the Others form of it: "When I ask what I mean when I say 'I,' the first answer is this: When I think about myself I have made myself into an object; I am this body as this individual, with an indeterminate self-consciousness in the mirror of my accepted status for my surroundings. I exist *as empirical Dasein*" (11:I 54). On the other hand, the *Dasein* that is conscious of itself, nevertheless, in the transcending of itself into a consciousness in general, adopts the standpoint of the superempirical and superindividual universal subject (9, 11–12:I 52, 54–55), which is "the one universal condition of all objective being" (513:II 223). As such a consciousness in general, it is not this isolated consciousness but "everyman" (343:II

51) just as, as the social I" which is taken up in acceptive consciousness, it is already at the same time "us all" (320:II 30).

This means, however, that *Dasein* is continually in conflict with itself. As *Dasein*, it is not what it is as consciousness in general, namely, pure universality. And as consciousness in general, it is not what it is as *Dasein*, namely, singular fact. This conflict is grounded in the constitution of that transcending appropriate to *Dasein*, a transcending through which *Dasein* is released from itself and still does not overcome itself. It is released from itself in that it abstracts from itself as an empirical individual. In spite of this, it does not overcome itself because it remains entrapped by the world. It surpasses itself solely as a being in the world in order to be conscious of itself as the condition of the worldliness of all worldly beings. The split in *Dasein* that resides therein is the motive that enforces the transformation of *Dasein* in existence. The transformation proceeds as a change in the mode of transcending. In place of the release from *Dasein*, we find a penetration or a clarification of it. But, in forcing its way through, the existentiel transcending overcomes *Dasein*, in that it forces its way out beyond the world as that which encompasses *Dasein* ontically and transcendentally. This transcending of the world falls together with the communicative self-revelation as the "apprehension and the overcoming of the sheerly empirically real" (350:II 59).

3. The sketch of the connection between world orientation and the analysis of communication, briefly set out here, obviously cannot lay claim to being accepted as the true reproduction of the textual material. Nevertheless, it has to be admitted that the sphere of world orientation coincides in large measure with that dimension in which the transcendental theory of intersubjectivity locates the Other. This coincidence clearly stands in relation to the coincidence in worldliness. However, it also proves to be more covert with regard to the idea of alter-ation. The transcendental event of alter-ation seems to be the basis (not properly set out by Jaspers) of the *Dasein* that is spread out between itself and consciousness in general. In that Jaspers reaches the level of existentiel communication in opposition to the sphere of world orientation, he, therefore, in the first instance, makes the same oppositional movement that characterizes the account offered by the philosophy of dialogue. However, his oppositional movement does not swing so far out. That the philosophy of existentiel communication

remains behind the radicality of "dialogicalism" is most clearly demonstrated by its negation of "immediacy" (353–354:II 67). In any case, an equivocation is to be found in Jaspers's attempt to prove the compatibility of existentiel communication and immediacy. In his view, what has to be negated is immediacy as nonmediatedness by the world. He hopes to be able to do away with it in that he discloses the breach that does, as a matter of fact, obtain between existentiel communication and the immediacy of the natural "contact" in sympathy and antipathy. This immediacy, which is actually negated, and that which has to be negated do not, however, have much more in common than the name. Indeed, in certain respects, they even relate to each other as opposites. For in the world unmediatedness, that which is most personal makes its appearance with the disappearance of the "material," whereas, according to Jaspers's own words, the natural unmediatedness of contact has "something impersonal and typical" about it. However this may be, it is certain that Jaspers wants to belie the world unmediatedness of the existentiel, communicative experience. In a more positive formulation, his thesis is one to the effect that existences meet in the world "only through the medium of contents," of "world contents." The antithetical stance of this thesis toward dialogic is only seemingly diminished by way of the ambiguous remark that "certainly it appears at times as though the contact were immediate." For even if one recognizes that for Jaspers at times immediacy really does hold sway between existences, one is not thereby by any means furnished with a proof for the restriction of his thesis. For, in Jaspers's sense, the momentary contact falls outside of existentiel communication (766:II 94), a circumstance that, moreover, is entirely suited to an elucidation of the separateness (resting upon the difference of "Thou" and "other self") of existentiel communication and the dialogicalistically interpreted I-Thou relation. World mediatedness may belong to existentiel communication. But the quite distinct relation between first and second person does not belong to it—in any case not at the stage of completion. Although the I-Thou relation is hardly able to save dialogicalism from the impermanence of the moment, the immediacy intended by it is in itself not merely such as to be made up of isolated moments.

4. If we take a closer look at Jaspers's justification for the exclusion of immediacy, we see that the same point that separates the analysis

of communication from dialogicalism establishes its connection to transcendentalism. Jaspers is of the opinion that without the mediation of world contents, an "impoverishment" of communication would occur (354:II 63). Behind this fear, we find the supposition that only world contents could preserve fullness, which, in its turn, ultimately means that the being of the self is empty. The being of the self is ultimately only the empty subject pole of the world. That the "being of the self and the world are correlated" in this way (354:II 63) is the reason for the reversion of the analysis of communication to the level of consciousness in general as well as to that sphere of being implied by transcendentalism. It is a matter here of more than just a peripheral phenomenon of the Jasperian conception. Only genuine fullness makes possible the real independence of the self and thereby the separation of existences. Where the existences are in themselves empty, they also flow together into one. In fact, Jaspers envisages momentary becoming-immediate as a momentary "becoming-one" (502:II 212; 504:II 214; 766:III 94). Becoming-one is supposed to be possible because world *Dasein* (*Weltdasein*) can sink down into moments. Consequently, according to Jaspers, *Dasein* is alone responsible for the separation of existences: "I and Thou, separate in *Dasein*, are one in transcendence" (356:II 65; see also 357–358:66–67). The momentary becoming-one is the mystical anticipation of transcendence as the goal toward which communication aspires but that, if it wants to be preserved as communication, it still can never reach (353:II 62; 357–358:II 66–67). For the separateness of the partner is constitutive for existentiel communication (348). It is out of this that it first becomes clear why, for Jaspers, momentary immediacy must fall outside existentiel communication: because it suspends the separateness and the "solitude" that results from it (348). But the separateness appropriate to *Dasein* is just as far removed from dialogical duality as the undivided unity of the "*corpus mysticum* of self-sustaining spiritual beings" (833; see also 245, 259). The duality thought out by the philosophy of dialogue is neither separateness in *Dasein* nor unity in transcendence, but the unity of separateness and inmost connection in self-being. However, because Jaspers also misses separateness in self-being along with unworldly fullness, he has to assign duality to *Dasein* and singularity to transcendence.

Postscript: The Transcendental Project of Social Ontology and the Philosophy of Dialogue

At the end of this voyage through the thicket of transcendental and dialogical social ontology the reader will expect a conclusive answer to the question, On which side does the truth really lie? Undoubtedly this question is all the more fitting since the value of the philosophy of dialogue, in particular, has been disputed. In the eyes of the wider public, the philosophy of dialogue has become like a coin in circulation. One speaks of the Thou and thinks one understands what one means. The concept of "meeting" circulates among theologians and pedagogues as a thoughtless catchword. "Conversation" counts as timely. In contrast, most of the counselors of academic philosophy show their disdain for dialogical thought in demonstrative gestures. The latter is, however, by no means the result of an in-depth discussion. Rather, the majority of Scholastic philosophers do not even make the attempt to assess its insightfulness. Instead, generally speaking, one withdraws to the transcendental position. In this way, one takes to be a secure possession what, to those who want to attribute the truth solely to dialogical thought, appears as a lifeless past made up of a cumbersome ballast of theories that have nothing to do with real life.

Even if the reader has not yet received the answer that he demands, one thing will have occurred to him in the course of the reading, that the present investigation neither unreservedly takes up the cudgels on behalf of the despisers of dialogical thought nor on behalf of those who adorn their ideologies with its insights. In accordance therewith, it neither joins in with the overhasty depreciation of transcendental philosophy undertaken by the latter nor with its unqualified apologists. Its stands decisively opposed to the former, in that it takes up Husserl's transcendental theory of intersubjectivity, as also its consequences, with unlimited seriousness; and it opposes the latter, in that it takes note of the criticism presented in the first part. But even the criticism here brought against transcendentalism is intended to be positive. In this—as in the critique of the philosophy of dialogue brought forward in the third chapter—it makes reference to the distance between the intention and the actual achievement or elucidates internal difficulties. For such a critique presupposes a recognition of the intention itself and therewith of the fundamental standpoint. In accordance with our guiding directive, the "transcendent" critique of Husserl, Heidegger, and Sartre is just as positive. For in the final analysis, its goal is the analysis of that social sphere that can be comprehended by transcendental philosophy. In order to be able to determine the scope of the transcendental project, it must, in any case, draw attention to what this project is *not* capable of comprehending. A transaction as negative as this is, however, still far removed from a depreciation. If it is directed against anything at all, then it is solely against that claim to absoluteness that transcendental social ontology raises precisely insofar as it thinks it can comprehend the entire social sphere and comprehend this sphere entirely, thanks to an identification of its model of the Other with the Other itself. For all that, a positive function still attaches to the polemic against the claim to absoluteness of modern transcendental philosophy. So the disclosure of that which lies outside the scope of transcendental philosophy is supposed to make room for the philosophy of dialogue. Indeed, it is dialogue that escapes the grasp of transcendental philosophy. For this reason, one can say straight out that, in the present investigation, the transcendental theory of intersubjectivity is criticized by the philosophy of dialogue. But that does not mean by any means, as should have become clear, that the philosophy of dialogue is taken as the truth and transcendental philosophy as the untruth.

The philosophy of dialogue is not the truth, but it has its definite component of truth. It concerns itself with a genuine phenomenon and, indeed, with one that cannot be thematized in an appropriate manner within the framework of transcendental philosophy, even as phenomenology. If the second part of the present investigation has at least succeeded in convincing the philosophically thoughtful, then it has fulfilled its most urgent task. The task of showing the object of dialogical thought to be a real phenomenon admittedly demanded more than just the assurance of its actual occurrence. It demanded the proof of the fact that it is a question here of a philosophically relevant phenomenon and thereby the clarification of ontological structures. Certainly, the attempt at such a structuration already provoked the suspicion of those who make dialogical thought out to be the truth without any qualification. Because they have devoted themselves to venturing opinions about existentially certified givens, they find its philosophical penetration not only superfluous but also harmful. They are of the opinion that, in this way, precisely that truth that is alone at issue, namely, the existentiel, gets overlooked. But the present investigation is not directed toward those who form judgments of this kind, but to the philosophically thoughtful. In that they protect the matter of dialogical thought against its disciples, they impel the philosophically thoughtful to make this matter their own.

Inasmuch as the structuring *interpretation* of dialogic already works against the dialogistical ideology, it really does so as a *critique* directed at the philosophy of dialogue. As the separation of intention and realization, it mostly reveals the impotence of dialogical thought in comparison with the power of the transcendental project. It therefore wants to demonstrate that the philosophy of dialogue, the phenomenon that dispenses with transcendental philosophy, can itself only be discovered in its essentials on the basis of transcendental philosophy. We have seen in what its dependence becomes known: in the drive toward the destruction of the schema of intentionality that is initially instated or in the merely negative contrasting of its object to that of transcendental philosophy, or even in that it carelessly applies transcendental means.

Still, critically emphasizing this lack rests upon just as affirmative a ground as does the critique of transcendental philosophy. For, in the first place, it is supported by the fundamental sympathy for any inventive thought. If philosophizing means risking failure by venturing upon the unthought, then the impotence of dialogical thought is in itself more philosophical than the power of transcendental philosophy, which arrives at less problematic results precisely because it is already less daring in its approach. I hope that the second part of this investigation, even in its critical features, has not lost the sympathy that follows from a recognition of this circumstance. On the basis of the belief that philosophizing at the frontier of thought is more philosophical than an inventory of indubitable possibilities for thought, it does, at any rate, become understandable that, in critically carrying through the philosophy of dialogue, more genuine "engagement" is to be found than in the interpretation of transcendental theories. This "engagement" does not attest to any partisanship, but rather to the character of the object: the unreadiness of a thought form that, precisely on account of its unreadiness, draws the interpreter more deeply into its movement than a complete, unequivocal doctrine ever could.

On the other hand, however, in the criticism of the second part of the investigation, an affirmative moment is also to be found because the dependence of the philosophy of dialogue upon transcendental philosophy is itself the expression of a positive state of affairs, in that in it the belonging together and the equal justification of both philosophies announces itself. That dependence is therefore only to be criticized to the extent that it prevents the philosophy of dialogue from handling its theme in its own way and speaking its own language. But the self-sufficiency to be hoped for is not independence in the sense of autarchy. The philosophy of dialogue is just as little entitled to raise a claim to absoluteness as the transcendental project of social ontology, and the fact that it cannot raise such a claim attests to its factical, and only partially self-conscious, dependence, which does not even allow it actually to take possession of what is its own.

Now, insofar as the present investigation wards off the claim to absoluteness on the part of the transcendental project of social ontology, and so establishes the impossibility of such a claim from the side of the philosophy of dialogue, it does, in the end, aim at *mediation*. But how is it supposed to be possible to envisage a mediation that does justice to both positions and is not established at the cost of one or the other? An approach to such an *apparent* mediation would seem to be furnished by modern transcendental philosophy just as well as by the historically developed philosophy of dialogue. Husserl's transcendental theory of intersubjectivity leaves room for dialogical communication in the sphere of the personalistic attitude. But the philosophy of dialogue cannot be satisfied with this place, since it starts out from the assumption that the Other is *originally* encountered as Thou. As we saw, Husserl belies the originality of this meeting in that he grounds dialogical communication upon the transcendental empathy of an alien I. Only in this way can he save the claim to absoluteness of his approach. Buber's dialogic, for its part, assigns a place in the sphere of the I-It relationship to transcendental alien experience. In this way, it seems to forgo the claim to absoluteness. Still, in starting out from the "two-foldness" of comportment, it places the "basic word I-It" alongside the "basic word I-Thou." But in the later destruction of the comportmental schema, this alongside-one-another is at the same time suspended, and in such a fashion that it accounts for "experiencing and utilizing" as a modus of alien understanding, and of an understanding of being in general that has been derived from the dialogical relation (DP 22–35). Consequently, transcendental philosophy can, conversely, hardly be satisfied with the place that the philosophy of dialogue assigns to it in its coordinate system. For it, too, must rely upon the originality of experience, on the basis of which its proponents say that they first constitute the Other as Other.

The conflict of the claims to absolutenesss accordingly consists in this, that the transcendental project of social ontology affirms as original what the philosophy of dialogue makes out to be futural, and that the latter attributes originality to that very phenomenon to which the transcendental project only ascribes a secondary significance. The rival claims to absoluteness are in themselves claims to originality. With this, therefore, the attempt at a mediation breaks down. As a result, it is now apparent that the easiest route to take is closed to such an attempt. On the one hand, it is impossible to accept without qualification the validity of the mutually exclusive conceptions of originality. For mediation is then excluded. On the other hand, however, it is equally impossible to sacrifice one of the conceptions to the other. For then mediation, like that proposed by the parties to the dispute themselves, remains entirely illusory.

In what follows, we shall try to point out the direction that leads between these two routes toward a real mediation. It most fruitfully starts off from the thesis in which the claim to originality on the part of the philosophy of dialogue finds its comprehensive expression. This thesis runs as follows: The event of the meeting, the "between," is earlier than those meeting each other. We aligned ourselves with this thesis with our presentation of the philosophy of dialogue, and accordingly the conclusive confrontation with transcendental philosophy has also to be aligned with it.

Corresponding to the method sketched out in the introductory remarks, the method of idealization of reflective positions there functions as the standard for the interpretation of dialogicalism, the doctrine of the derivation of the partner out of the between in its *most radical* form. In its most pointed formulation, it states that I and thou are brought into being *purely and simply* in the event of the meeting. We have, however, come up against several thinkers of the dialogical principle who advance this doctrine in a more moderate form. According to them, the between is only the origin of the self-being of the partner. They therefore fully recognize that the meeting presupposes that the ones meeting each other exist upon a particular being level, and concede to the between solely the power to transform the poles that impinge upon one another. Indeed, Buber often withdraws to this reduced standpoint. He occasionally restricts himself to the expression that the I becomes a "real self" in the meeting with the Thou (Gf 118), that the "individual" receives the mode of being of the person out of the between (DP 155; see also PM 163–164). With these concepts the other thinkers who reduce the dialogical principle to its minimal content also, for the most part, fix the *terminus a quo* and the *terminus ad quem* of the transformation effected by the between. In accordance with their nomenclature, a self is developed out of the purely subjective I and a person out of the individual. As deep-rooted, however, as this kind of a transformation might be, the assumption implicit in such a reduction prevents it from being an absolute creation, the assumption, namely, that the I as such, for example, as an individual, is already what it is without the between.

In contrast, Buber's *fundamental* approach concedes to the between an absolutely creative power in that it precisely excludes this assumption. He does this first by means of the theory touched upon above, the theory of the birth of the "basic word I-It" out of the "basic word I-Thou." For if the Thou-I is supposed to be more original than the It-I, then there remains no I any more that could precede the meeting. However, Buber also gives the principal dialogical thesis a radical interpretation through the unequivocal emphasis of the precedence of the "sphere of the between" over the "sphere of subjectivity." In this way, he forbids himself the retreat to the reduced standpoint. At the same time, he thereby legitimates the procedure of identifying the philosophy of dialogue, carried through in its extreme possibilities, with the unlimited affirmation of the originality of the between.

It is, however, illuminating that the reduction of the principal dialogical thesis to the significance of an expression about the dialogical self-becoming of the individual I would make possible a mediation between transcendental philosophy and the philosophy of dialogue. It would put us in a position to settle the conflict between the claims to originality by allowing us to grant to transcendental philosophy the originality of the beginning and to the philosophy of dialogue the originality of the goal, of the completed end. The beginning would be my individual I, the goal the self that proceeds from the meeting. Admittedly, the *termini* that fix the point of departure of the movement must be so broadly conceived as also to permit the subsumption of Heidegger's fundamental ontology under the beginning positions. To be sure, *Being and Time* does not describe a self-becoming of the I but only a becoming-I of the self, that is, of that *Dasein* structured like a self. But this *Dasein* falls under a concept of subjectivity that is only inadequately determined through the expressions "I" and "individual." From Heidegger's own standpoint, dialogical self-becoming would then be presented as a transformation of that *Dasein* structured like a self into an authentic self-being whereby the dialogically constituted self would be distinguished from the authentic self, in the sense of *Being and Time*, precisely in that it is dialogically constituted. Heidegger himself has such a transformation in mind when, at the end of the text *Vom Wesen des Grundes* [*On the Essence of Grounds*] (WG), a text in which, in correcting the transcendental position of *Being and Time*, he also entirely accepts a self-becoming of the I, he writes a sentence of which note has already been taken: "And only through the capacity for listening at a distance is *Dasein*, as a self, temporalized by the awakening of the answer of *Dasein*-with, in that being-with with which I-hood can be accorded, in order to win itself as authentic self."

Undoubtedly, this limitation of the central theorem of the philosophy of dialogue would essentially diminish its significance. If, in spite of the inadequacy of its realizations, the philosophy of dialogue is able to excite our interest, it is primarily because it brings into question not only the teleological but also the archeological originality of subjectivity. We therefore even now do not want to admit this restriction too hastily. Only the reasons that speak for it have first to be brought forward.

Two things speak for it, a positive circumstance and a negative circumstance. *Ex negativo*, it gets closer because the champions of the *radically* conceived form of the principal dialogical thesis hardly succeed in describing convincingly the genesis of *perspectivity* out of the nonperspectival reality of the between. Since perspectivity is the essential component of the subjectively constituted world, this means that they are not at all capable of validating their thesis. Indeed, they do not even bring the nonperspectivity of the initially affirmed reality and the perspectivity of the subjectively constituted world into any kind of relation with one another. On the other hand, just such a link is established—and this is the positive factor that recommends the restriction—by a few among those thinkers who envisage the emergence of the "I" out of the encounter with the Thou as the dialogical self-becoming of an individual that already exists before the encounter.

In conformity with their approach, they turn the rank ordering around; in their eyes, perspectivity stands at the beginning, and dialogical is for them the deperspectivalization of the initially subject-oriented world. In the third chapter of the present investigation, I cited Grisebach and Marcel as well as Buber in connection with the explanation of the perspectively I-centeredness of the It-world.[1] However, Grisebach and Marcel both remain behind Buber's radical approach, to the extent that they take the perspectivity of the world dominated by the subject for the basis upon which the I first arises in the meeting with the Thou. According to Grisebach, the dialogical present dislodges the I "from its standardizing role" (Gw 65), that is, "from the midpoint" of the subjectively constituted world (Gw 586). Even for him there follows from the meeting with the Thou, just as for Husserl out of the experience of the alter ego, a kind of "decentering" of the I. Only this decentering has a completely different character than that thematized by Husserl. Besides, on the basis of his purely negative criticism, Grisebach is not in a position to effect an affirmative development of the concept of dialogical decentering. For this reasoning he is just as little able to grasp its distinction from the objectifying decentering of transcendental sociology. Still, we become aware of the distinction as soon as we recall to mind Marcel's total project. This project is more complete than that of Grisebach because Marcel also thinks out the objectifying decentering. The dialogical advance beyond the initial centrality of the I is, according to him, an overcoming of the decentering that necessarily enters into the sphere of subjectivity, of the intentional "having," as soon as the Other arises. Consequently, the dialogical and the objectifying decentering are distinct stages. The objectifying decentering is an alteration, while the dialogical decentering is a self-becoming that takes place in the retreat from alter-ation. In the ontological history of mankind that Marcel depicts in fragmentary fashion, the transcendental relativization of the world is the first epoch, the mundanizing alter-ation of the relativizing subject the second, and the dialogical self-becoming is the third, conclusive epoch.

To a certain extent, this movement can be grasped in a Hegelian schema. It can be presented as the history of the human spirit, which comes out of its being-for-itself into otherness and eventually wins itself back again out of alienation through mediation with the Other. The three steps are therefore presented as thesis, antithesis, and synthesis. On the first step, the I is nothing but an I, on the second, it is with the Other in such a way that it itself becomes an Other; and on the third, it is with itself in being-with-the-Other. But the exposition with the help of the Hegelian dialectic conceals the fact that, in the history pursued by Marcel, the first two epochs fall into the same sphere, while human being leaves this sphere with the last. Only because dialogical self-becoming frees itself from objectifying decentering through the fundamental overcoming of the initial centrality of the I does it also appear for its part as decentering. The most essential distinction between the two modes of decentering lies precisely in this, that the objectifying, the alter-ation, is simply the dialectical counteraction against the transcendental ordering of the Other upon myself, whereas the dialogical raises human being to quite a different level.

This level is that of the between. At this level the I can no longer be thrown out of the center in the manner of objectivation because it no longer stands in the center. It is decentered in this fashion, in that it gives itself up to the Thou in *love*. Marcel characterizes as love the consummated end of the essential development that my relationship to the Other runs through, and he quite rightly contrasts this love to the "dialectic" from which it extricates itself. The dialectic is most deeply rooted in the conversion of the making own of the Other into the alter-ation of the own. On the basis of alter-ation, however, the human being who, as transcendental midpoint of the world, at first maintains his I against the Other does not turn back into his self through integration of the Other, but through the grounding of his self upon the Other. He discovers the Other as the basis of his capacity for self-being. This phenomenon of dialogical facticity, which is most easily found in the model of the constitution of address through the nondisposable correspondence of the Other, is, in its complete reality, personal love. That constitution demonstrates, in a fragmentary manner, the movement of dialogical self-becoming that realizes itself in love. It does this precisely to the extent that it is not constitution pure and simple, but is only the complete constitution, which we have opposed to the minimal constitution of address in the intention toward correspondence. For as complete constitution, it is fulfillment or completion, the coming-to-itself of address. The coming-to-itself of address is, however, the dialogical self-becoming of the I brought out in the singularity of the act and thereby in the one-sidedness of intentionality.

On the basis of this construction of the ontological history of mankind, one gains a concrete impression as to how the restriction of the genuine philosophical themes of dialogic makes possible its mediation with transcendental social ontology. The mediation that comes into view here seems satisfactory not only because, in the matter of transcendental social ontology, it accommodates the originality called for by the transcendental philosophers themselves; it proves its genuineness in this, too, that in its positive basic conception it relates both standpoints to each other. For, just as dialogical self-becoming is the positive idea of the I-Thou philosophy, so the theory of alter-ation makes up the affirmative kernel of the transcendental philosophy of the Other.

In that it links the positive sides of the objects of transcendental ontology and social ontology as moments of one and the same movement, the construction outlined above at the same time provides the mediation of the negative aspects. The philosophy of dialogue is the negation of the transcendental approach insofar as it belies the possibility of a subjective constitution of the originally encountered Other; conversely, the transcendental theory of intersubjectivity negates the approach of dialogical thought insofar as it denies the possibility of an immediate meeting with the Other. In this way, as we have seen, the supposition of the subjective constitution of the Other and the negation of immediacy belong together, just as do the protest against that supposition and the affirmation of immediacy. As subjectively constituted, the Other is precisely mediated through me and the world—through the world in the sense of worldly things, in the sense of my world horizon, and in the sense of the image that the Other forms of the world. The antithesis, in accordance with which the Other originally evades constitution, necessarily implies the assertion that he is encountered immediately. But whoever now tests the reality of human life without prejudice must recognize that the Other is *both* the one constituting in my world project *and* the one who evades subjective constitution, the sheerly mediate *and* the immediately encountered. No less certainly, he is the one who alienates me as well as the one who brings me to myself. He thrusts me into alter-ation and leads me back into my self. Only first on the basis of the distinction between the fellow human being who alter-ates me and the one who makes me into a self does it become clear, however, where the subjectively constituted, sheerly mediately experienced alien I and the immediately encountered Thou, which precedes all constitution, are to be appropriately located.

The mediacy of constitutive experience of what is alien has its validity in the world in which I have the Other before me as someone specific and am, for my part, "someone," one among the Others. This is the sphere of the *public* and of the social order that assigns specific roles to all human beings and relates each to the other as the bearers of roles. In contrast, the immediate encounter with the Thou takes place in the *intimacy* of that being-with-one-another in which One seeks that self of the Other who is never involved in function and role. An objection[2] has been raised against the modern philosophy of dialogue on the grounds that it limits the I-Thou relation to the "private." But this limitation,[3] which is by no means adopted everywhere, attests to a proper feeling for the confinement of the sphere of validity of the I-Thou relation. Only, one should not, in turn, restrict the multifold concept of the "private"—if it is to be useful in characterizing the sphere in which alone an immediate meeting is possible—to the meaning of the familial idyll. As the title for that sphere, it must at least embrace what Aristotle, in books VIII and IX of the *Nichomachean Ethics*, calls the complete friendship of those who love each other reciprocally for their own sake. This friendship with whose clarification Aristotle, through Plato, advanced the discovery of the "dialogical principle" to the frontiers of the doctrine of virtue,[4] reaches, on the one hand, far beyond that idyll and is, on the other hand, to be distinguished from the community of the polis, which it admittedly presupposes. The human being is involved in friendship not as ζωον πολιτικον but as αωον συνδυαστικον, as a being who by nature is fitted for the dialogical being-two and is indeed better adapted for it than for the political community: ανθρωπος γαρ τη φυσει συνδυατικον μαλλον η πολιτικον (1162a). The being-two of complete friendship is "intimate" and "private," to the extent that my partner has to be personally entrusted to me in it. He cannot be a stranger—neither someone unknown to me whom I cannot name nor the incidental someone whom I only know as a functionary of social institutions but not as a person.[5] Nevertheless, the alienness of public affairs can, from time to time, be converted into the intimacy of the personal, the completely dialogical relation. The Other can, at any moment emerge from his namelessness and reveal himself to me as a pure Thou. This change, which is accomplished with respect to him, then corresponds to my own retreat out of alter-ation into self-being.[6]

The place of the immediate meeting with the Thou is not only to be characterized as the intimacy of being-entrusted-to-one-another but also as *existentiel* praxis. Even this assigns immediacy to the stage of dialogical self-becoming. For by *existentiel* praxis I do not understand the social utilization and even less the everyday utilization of the Other or of one's own functioning for the Other. Rather, I understand by this solely the practical accomplishment of human existence, which circles around its capacity for self-being. The existentiel praxis of the immediate I-Thou relation is the practical accomplishment of existences that, in meeting each other, are brought out of alter-ation to themselves. So one cannot say straight off that the genuine sphere of mediate alien experience is the *theoretical* comportment. For to this sphere there also belongs all nonexistentiel modes of praxis, that is, those that are not directed toward self-being. In it there also takes place, for example, that substitution for perception of the praxis of concernfully solicitous dealings, a substitution undertaken by Heidegger and in which, according to Husserl, the Other is originally disclosed to me. For all that, mediate alien experience has a structure that conforms to theoretical knowledge in certain respects. The theory envisages its object, so to speak, from the outside; in order to be able to bring it before it, it has to hold it at that distance that first makes epistemological objectivity possible. The Other of mediate alien experience is given just as outwardly even when the latter is not itself a theoretical act. More precisely put: it is there always an intentional object. It is *intentionality* that makes mediate alien experience conform to theory. And since Heidegger does not want to overcome it, but simply to ground it through a regression to the specific facticity of human *Dasein*, it is also true to say of his analysis of being-with that it describes a comportment toward the Other that is structurally similar to the theoretical comportment. This similarity ceases when an immediate meeting with the Thou is developed out of the intentional relation to the alien I, for example, *Dasein*-with. For the meeting between me and you is immediate insofar as it has a nonintentional constitution. In the philosophy of dialogue, the concept of immediacy necessarily means the nonintentionality of the dialogical encounter, together with, at the same time, the nonconstitutedness of the Thou because intentionality is the vehicle of transcendental constitution. However, that the Thou is differently present in the nonintentional encounter than is the alien I of theoretical knowledge means concretely that I feel "at home" with him, and can feel at home with him because, as the nondisposable ground of my being, he is, despite his standing over against me in person—as Buber said—"nearer to me than is my I."

From here on we shall elucidate one of the reasons for which the philosophy of dialogue does not succeed in handling its theme as adequately as the transcendental theory of intersubjectivity handles its own. It is precisely the conformity that makes the mediate alien experience of theoretical behavior immediately accessible. In contrast, the immediate encounter, as existentiel praxis, and on account of its differently formed constitution, is withheld from the direct apprehension of theoretical exposition. We have learned to know the factical consequences quite well. They are to be differentiated in two directions from a fundamental viewpoint. Either the immediate meeting with the Thou is sought in its proper medium, that of the existentiel praxis of dialogical self-becoming, but not really analyzed, only conveyed— the theory then gives itself over to praxis and loses itself in edification— or the immediate encounter with the Thou is brought out into the sphere of intentionality, and then analyzed, but with inadequate concepts and with reference to insufficient models. The theory shrinks back from its task, the clarification of existentiel praxis, and displaces the object attributed to it in that element to which it is related. Both tendencies together make up the negativity of the historically developed philosophy of dialogue.[7]

With this conclusion, we have once again reached the starting point of our final observation, where it was a matter of characterizing our critique of dialogical thought. The reflections arrived at in this way have, at the same time, prepared an answer to that very question with which the reader has been repeatedly occupied during the reading of the third chapter of the investigation. Is the negativity of dialogic, in the opinion of the author, simply de facto, or is it also necessary?

In other words: Do we find revealed in this negativity only the *inadequacy of the historically developed philosophy of dialogue* or, rather, a *fundamental frontier of the philosophy in general?*

I cannot answer this without taking note of something personal. This final observation is a *post*script. I am writing it down a long time after the completion of the extant investigation, and an even longer time after its conception. In the course of the years, many insights have been sustained and have continually gained in certainty. A few convictions, however, have been shattered. Even my own stance toward the problem set out here has, on the one hand, been maintained and, on the other, been changed. At the beginning, and at the time at which the total view was being formed, it was entirely positive. In accordance with this approach, therefore, the extant investigation is supported by the belief that philosophy is in a position to overcome the de facto negativity of contemporary dialogic in every respect. This belief is not entirely broken, but only subsequently relativized, through a partial skepticism.

I will first set out what remains over from this belief. Even now I take it to be a realizable task of philosophy to think through the meeting conceptually as the dialogical self-becoming of the partner and to elucidate it from within. Therefore I still believe that the de facto negativity of dialogic can be overcome to the extent that the I-Thou relationship can be thematized even beyond the sphere of intentionality, in its very own element.

More generally conceived, the task only indicated above consists in the construction of a specific *theory of existentiel praxis.* When existentiel praxis first broke into consciousness, in the thinking of Kierkegaard, this task had already been envisaged, but had been rejected at the same time. It was rejected by way of the regression to the method of "indirect communication." This corresponds to the edifying objective of the Kierkegaardian existential dialectic, which theorizes about existentiel praxis, not for the sake of the theory, but for the sake of the existentiel praxis itself, that is, of that alien existence that it would like to lead in the direction of self-being. In addition, it appears as the natural reaction to the state of affairs depicted above, that the existentiel praxis is withheld from the "direct apprehension" of the theory. Where no direct theorizing is possible, the indirect seems, in fact, to be the only way out. The historical development, which is connected with Kierkegaard, has nevertheless shown that, in the last analysis, this way out is a flight from theory pure and simple. Certainly, Kierkegaard still discovers structures of existence, but not only like Heidegger, as existential characteristics of human *Dasein*, but as the inner lawfulness of existentiel behavior itself. He actually carries out, even if only in places, an indirect theorization of existentiel praxis. Jaspers, on the contrary, has practically no theory any more. It has given way to an appeal to, and a gathering together of, so-called "phenomena." I have quite intentionally placed the short appendix on the elucidation of communication presented by Jaspers at the end of the investigation. In a certain respect, it forms a transition to what has been said in this postscript on the subject of the ontological history of mankind. With Jaspers, we find many building blocks for the construction of this history. For all that, no theory joins the individual parts together architectonically, and the fragmentary assemblage that the Jaspers appendix ventures upon already unavoidably awakens the impression of a heavy-handed systemization. The same refusal of theory characterizes the later publications of Buber and Marcel. In Buber's *I and Thou*, an implicit ontology does at least still lie concealed under the forbidding garb of pseudo-poetic language, an ontology whose explication was attempted here. His subsequent presentations of the "dialogical principle" have, however, lost more and more of their speculative power. Even from the earlier works of Marcel, published in diary form, that genesis of the completed meeting cannot simply be read off from alter-ation as it can off the contributions of other authors to dialogic.[8] It can, however, be intimated as the latent sense connecting the individual thought experiments. In contrast, the work of the aging Marcel hardly furnishes any usable material toward its constitution and toward a theory of dialogue in general. Certainly, from the very beginning, the theory did not stand in any way in the foreground of modern dialogicalism; in the meantime, however, it has entirely given up on a praxis that is supposedly totally inaccessible to reflection in favor of a merely indicative appeal.

So a *theory* of existentiel praxis is considered not only by the ideologizing consumers of dialogic, but even by the producers themselves, as untimely. It is also even more untimely with regard to the philosophical (or such as declare themselves to be philosophical) currents that aspire to replace the dying "philosophy of existence" and the ontological thinking of late Heidegger,[9] which is closely bound up with dialogic in many respects, without admittedly being permeated by its problems or even having simply taken them up. There, on the one side, we find sociologism, which, where it possesses philosophical relevance, also wants to be a theory of praxis, but a theory of *social praxis*. Sartre has of late demonstrated that such a theory can even integrate *existentiel* praxis within itself, that the latter must, indeed, be founded in it. But, in Germany, sociologism only very rarely reaches the level of Sartre's new anthropology. Much more commonly, it, too, follows the tendency to ignore the matter of the "existentiel" along with the catchword. Where it breaks out of philosophy altogether, it is also directed against the theory of existentiel praxis, to the extent that it is theory. For then it does not want to be anything other than social praxis. The antithesis of this is, on the other side, a logicism that has spread abroad powerfully and that is getting ready to restrict philosophy to *pure* theory and to remove from its thematic circle any kind of praxis insofar as it is not that of scientific theory itself. Although its representatives lack insight into this issue and so depreciate as "irrationalism" the philosophy of self-being and of being itself, they are nevertheless among those who speak of the "existentiel" without being able to elucidate it, in the conviction that only the *exclusively* conceptual and the logically resolvable should be a possible theme for philosophical theory. As a matter of fact, the latter is the predominant object of critical, self-responsible thought, and it is good that the philosophy of our day has once again accepted pure theory as its principal business. But unless it also holds fast to the task of providing a theory of praxis, it does not respect the task that it inherits from its own tradition. This task of providing a theory of praxis is only a part of a more comprehensive task with which philosophy has been especially preoccupied since German idealism: the task of thinking "reality." According to Schelling, this reality, the facticity of being, is "the inapprehendable basis of reality, the never absorbed remainder, that which can never be resolved into understanding, even with the most strenuous exertion."[10] Existentiel praxis is just as resistant to logical resolution. But that does not mean that it is entirely inaccessible to thought. Only, one should not expect from a theory of existentiel praxis what can justifiably be demanded from a pure theory. It is not entirely capable of transforming darkness into light. It is, however, in a position to carry the light of understanding into the darkness. And that is a great deal. For if "progress" is to be found at all in philosophy, it is certainly due not a little to this, that, in probing its scope, thought succeeds in extending even further the sphere of rational illumination, in that it gains upon the surrounding darkness, bit by bit.

It still has to be said to what extent the factical negativity of the modern philosophy of dialogue is essential. After long hesitation I have arrived at the view that the incapacity of dialogic to account for the origin of the I *purely and simply* out of the meeting with the Thou attests to a fundamental limitation of the philosophy. The philosophy fails, or so it seems to me, at the *extreme* point of the doctrine of the originality of the between.

We have borne in mind the possibility of a reduction of this thesis to a statement about dialogical self-becoming because it opens up the prospect of a mediation between transcendental philosophy and the philosophy of dialogue. In this way, however, the reduction would not be carried out at all. Those reasons that recommend it would simply be presented. Thereby it has by no means been already proved that the general thesis of the philosophy of dialogue is true solely in its reduced form. Insofar as the reduction was supported simply by the fact that dialogic can relate to the transcendental project, in a manner that does justice to this project, exclusively in its most moderate and not in its radical formulation, the decisive motive turned out to be the incapacity on the part of the radical approach to accommodate verification, but not, however, its untruth. And if I now make the supposition that the empirically confirmable incapacity of the philosophy of dialogue is that of philosophy in general and as such, I do not explain as untrue what is removed from philosophy. On the contrary, I would rather suggest that behind the representation of the unconditioned precedence of the between over subjectivity in all its forms, a determinate truth lies concealed, though one that cannot be reached by philosophy. Admittedly, one does not get beyond suppositions at this point. Still, even suppositions have their grounds. And to finish, I shall take account of them.

Just as with the question concerning the necessity of a restriction of the problematic thesis, so, too, it is here essentially a question of two grounds, and indeed, once again, of a positive one and a negative one. Negatively speaking, the supposition of the truth of the radical approach of dialogic can perhaps be justified by saying that originality, in the sense of *the initial*, is also lacking in certain respects from the sphere of that understanding of the Other that is sustained by transcendental subjectivity. At this point, we cannot repeat *in extenso* the indications of such an apparent deficiency, indications that were furnished in the first part of the work. Only the essential trait to be found in all this should once again be brought out. My transcendentally verifiable relationship to the Other appears not to be a genuine beginning because it presupposes the relationship of the Other to me. In order that I should be able to understand the Other *as* Other, that is, as something different from things, the Other must already be encountered by me as only he and never a thing can be encountered. Should I be in a position to go up to him, he must therefore have already come up to me. This coming-up-to-me of the Other is then only to be distinguished from the mode of encounter of things if it constitutes me inwardly, that is, in the final analysis, in my being and consciousness. For outwardly even things can come up to me. A stone can fall on my head; an avalanche can roll over me; a speck of dust can get into my eyes. Sartre's earlier social ontology has performed the great service of having presented convincingly the priority of that relation of the Other to me that is constitutive of me inwardly, as against my relation to the Other, at least in individual analyses. If Sartre, nevertheless, remains captivated by the transcendental project then, among other things, it is because he does not trace the constitution of the I in the Other (as does dialogic for its part) back to the constitution of the I *and* the Other out of the between, and so does not attempt to think it in its originality. That it is supposed to be thought out in its originality seems precisely to be what has to be denied. For all that, no one can prevent this negation from casting doubt upon the nonprimordiality, or better, the "nonoriginality," of that which—immanently considered—can be conceived with complete evidence.

But not only the suspicion with regard to the noninitiality of the transcendental understanding of the alien supports the supposition of the truth of the radical dialogical approach. Rather, in support of this supposition, a positive argument can also be brought forward, an argument that is itself taken from the dialogical approach. The primordiality that, as completedness, one is entitled to attribute to the matter of dialogical thought, seems to imply originality. Dialogic looks at the completing end insofar as it thinks the self-becoming of the I out of the meeting with the Thou. Self-becoming has, as its return home out of alter-ation, the character of a turning back to the beginning. I become myself—this means that I become what at bottom I am: I become what initially I already was. However, dialogical self-becoming is not a turning back to that I that, as the transcendental origin of the world, stands at its midpoint. It is not such a turning back even in the sense of an authenticating repetition or an unfolding of the still implicated beginning. For then the self that, in the end, I receive from the Other would only be the *true* world midpoint. It is, however, something completely different, namely, being in and out of the between. Since dialogical self-becoming must, nevertheless, be a turning back to the beginning, it refers from out of itself to the between as to a beginning that still precedes the transcendentally accessible point of departure, the constitution of the world out of subjectivity. This thought is certainly formal. But it is confirmed through the concrete experience of those who help each other reciprocally to get to themselves. Its substantive foundation is the living consciousness of the partner, to have found once again, in being out of the between, an origin that was already lost when the I directed itself toward that "solitude" out of which it constitutes the world as its own.[11]

The loss of this origin would explain why philosophy is not able to think the absolute genesis of subjectivity out of the between. Over and beyond that, its recognition would also permit us to maintain, in modified form, that mediation of the transcendental and the dialogical approach that appeared to be endangered by the recent direction of our thought experiment. For, among its presuppositions, the transcendental project of social ontology held to the originality of the beginning as much as to the reality discovered by it, a reality that *for us* would be initial. For us—this means, more exactly: for the human beings of historical world time; even more exactly: for the "adult" human beings of this time. The child still lives—or so it appears—near to the lost origin, and so legitimates, in a certain manner, the attempt on the part of dialogic to describe the absolute genesis of subjectivity out of the between as the awakening of the childlike consciousness. Admittedly, this awakening is not that genesis. However that movement that is aimed at the being in between may be presented as the search for the lost origin, its goal itself lets it be known that the origin is not the childlike consciousness. Only a dreamy and spiritually weary romantic who disregards the exertion of self-being can falsify the toward which of the movement in such a fashion. Because it would like to take flight from the historicality of the spirit in the hiddenness of nature, it is also deprived of the possibility that the loss of origin that occurs in separate individuals only represents the repetition of an event that history, as the history of the world and of the spirit, has first instantiated. However, if one envisages the loss of the origin as a historical fact, then one must concede that for us there is no other reality than that which is transcendentally attainable. This transcendentally attainable reality remains the beginning to the extent that we, who have established a reflective relationship to ourselves and to our surroundings, find it alone as the world, in our historical situation.

For ages philosophy has only been able to hint at the beginning that *precedes* this world, in that it either leaped out of the logos into the mythos or explained what the Judeo-Christian tradition knew how to assess. Neither pagan myths nor the speculative interpretation of biblical revelation should be appealed to here as testimony for the truth of the radical approach of dialogic. Still, it is worthy of mention that many of them have interpreted that initial human nature that got lost through guilt in an approach of a corresponding kind.

The finest example of a philosophical myth about the origin of the individual out of the unity that precedes duality but already implies it, an example that Binswanger discusses, is the fanciful story of Aristophanes in Plato's *Symposium* (189c–193d). Admittedly, the story is only fanciful in the light of the grotesque details with which it is adorned and because it projects an inner, spiritual reality in the exteriority of the bodily. However, this, combined with the fact that Plato even puts the myth in the mouth of the comic poet, is simply dialectical wrappings for that seriousness that is necessary because the reality to be taken seriously is no longer a reality. In any case, this is indicated by the repeatedly (193b, 193d–193e) expressed request of Aristophanes not to cast ridicule upon his speech (κωμωδεῖν), that is, to take as a simple joke something that, according to its content, ought to be taken seriously. Above all, this is confirmed by the fact that Aristophanes, as the foremost of the speakers, touches upon the *essence* of that eros that the participants at the banquet extol—even if only from a limited perspective.[12]

How he explains eros is well known. Originally there were not only a masculine sex and a feminine sex as there is today, but also a third, masculine-feminine, sex (ἀνδρόγυνον). However, just as androgenous human being was an original unity of that which is separated into man and woman in the humanity living now, so the human beings belonging to the two other sexes—seen from today—were double beings whose halves were both either masculine or feminine. Only as a result of an injustice (αδικια), of a hybrid rebellion, to which the first sexes were led on by their strength, have all human beings been divided into two parts by God, in which form they must exist henceforth.

According to Plato, this separation is the historical condition of the possibility of eros. For, since then, each seeks his other half. The man who was only human in conjunction with a woman is driven by longing for the woman, while those men who are "a piece from a man" tend toward the masculine and to that feminine made up of the remaining half of the once entirely feminine being. The driving force of love is accordingly a longing for the reinstantiation of the initial nature of human being: "So for a long time back now love for one another has been innate in human being and seeks to lead us back to our initial nature and to make one out of two and to heal human nature" (191c–191d). The initial nature is then once again restored when all have found not just any complementary half of their sex, but the very human being with whom they were once united. This situation removes Plato into a future that can only be assigned to mankind when it piously serves the deity. In our age, on the other hand, only a few are fortunate enough to meet the Thous united with them earlier. To them, admittedly, it will now be revealed that eros refers back beyond itself to the lost origin. For that for whose sake they strive to be always together is certainly not the common enjoyment of love (η των αφροδισιων συνουσια). Indeed, they are incapable of even saying what they really want from one another. This not knowing attests to the loss of the origin. At the same time, however, the origin is disclosed in the yearning (μαντευεσθαι) that takes the place of knowledge. For it is through yearning that the partners discover that they want to be together, because only in this way can they be again what they were initially.

The thought of the androgenous constitution of human being originally was kept alive in Christian times. In particular, German Romanticism got carried away by it.[13] In the *Philosophy of Mythology* even Schelling reaches out for it (*Werke* XII 156–157) in order, with its help, to describe the structure of the "originary consciousness in its original condition" (XII 159). More than this, however, it should interest us that Schelling, in the *Philosophy of Revelation*, interprets the biblical fall from grace as the "catastrophe" of the overthrow of the initial creation in that very world that transcendental philosophy alone can reach. As that "original fact of history" (XIII 360; see also XII 153) that can never be proved a priori, but that can be known, from its dreadful consequences, as the "unforeseeable act, without which there would not be a history at all" (XIII 385), the fall from grace is, according to Schelling, a "second beginning" (XIII 360). It is this insofar as "human being now first becomes the midpoint" (XIII 353) that centers the world upon itself, that world projected outside of the divine. It centers the world upon itself—this means that it constitutes the world in the transcendental sense, in the sense of Fichte's transcendental idealism: "Human being can boast of being the originator of this external world. In this sense Fichte is right . . . human being is the instator of the world" (XIII 352).

At no point does Schelling come so close to the modern philosophy of dialogue as here. At the beginning of the third chapter, we indicated that and how the most speculative dialogician, Franz Rosenzweig, was connected with it. Ebner, however, who could hardly have read the acute thinker of German idealism, also repeats, to a certain extent, Schelling's interpretation of the transcendental world interpretation in the horizon of the fall from grace when he states that the "solitude" of the world-constituting I is "no original fact," but a consequence of the fall from grace (WR 21–22).

However, a philosophy that does not, like Plato's, construct myths or, like Schelling's, expound the biblical history of the fall from grace in a speculative fashion is not only closed to the lost original reality; it cannot even throw light upon the loss of this reality as a genesis of the transcendentally projected world. In that the originality of the between in the sense of initiality is withheld from philosophical thought, the lapse of the reality presiding in the between into the world, as the sphere of subjectivity, is similarly concealed from it.

However, something else, and perhaps the most important thing, is still to be found as a result of the withdrawal of the "first" beginning beyond the scope of philosophical thought. As a result of its fundamental incapacity to grasp the absolute constitution of the I on the basis of the meeting with the Thou, it follows, by necessity, that dialogic does not make possible any understanding of the creation of Man through God. It furnishes no suitable means for the philosophical elucidation of the *theology of creation*. For all that, we do not mean by this to deny to it any kind of theological relevance. Buber's "theology" of the between does seem to possess a certain truth content. Its philosophical validity is to be limited, however, from two sides. In the first place, it is to be restricted in just the way that, in the present investigation, the title of the final chapter does it, in that it characterizes the "theology" of the between as the goal of dialogic, one that *transcends philosophy*. To be sure, this characteristic does not localize it entirely outside philosophy, but nevertheless demotes it to the level of a mere perspective, one that opens up in the purely philosophical penetration of the dialogical principle. I have in this manner deliberately drawn the line between pure philosophy and *philosophical* theology more sharply than Buber, whose own supposedly thoroughly philosophical thought can be sufficiently clearly distinguished from the theology of *revelation* alone. But over and beyond that, one must, in my opinion, also undertake a reduction of the *content* of Buber's "theology" of the between.

According to our interpretation, Buber grasps God as the existent reality of the between, as that in which the very being that, from the standpoint of worldly beings, is deemed to be "nothing" itself exists. It would be philosophically as well as theologically less problematic if one were to address this reality—the "medium" that links all relations with one another—as the "domain of God." That expression of Jesus handed down by Luke (17:21), which Luther renders as "The kingdom of God is inside of you," reads in another, and today almost universally recognized, translation, "The kingdom of God is *in the midst of you*." It exists *between* those human beings who are called to it, as a present future. Presumably, that reality that the dialogic of the between shows itself to be from a theological viewpoint is *the* side of the kingdom of God that philosophically can be taken account of at all: the side not of "grace," but of the "will." The will to dialogical self-becoming belongs to the striving after the kingdom of God in such a way that its future is promised in the present love of human beings for one another. Even Buber catches sight of this at times, though Ebner does so most immediately when he writes, "The kingdom of love is also the kingdom of God. And Jesus has said that this dwells inwardly in man. A few now want the *entos hymon* of the original German text translated into the German as 'in the midst of you' and understood as such. They are right. For the kingdom of God is not in human being in the inner solitude of its existence, in the solitude of its I, but lies in this, that the I has been disclosed to the Thou in the word and in love, and in the word and in the act of loving—and then it is also 'in the midst of us' as the community of our spiritual life" (WR 183). As "theology," the philosophy of dialogue, like all great philosophy of religion since Kant, can only be the philosophy of the kingdom of God. But the kingdom is not God. In it, that thought that admittedly thereby already surpasses itself has an intimation of the splendor of God or of the Holy, which latter is revealed in the Thou without its revelation being able to be such as would permit philosophy to become genuine theology, or discourse about God Himself.

Notes

Scope and Method of the Investigation

1. Rosenstock-Huessy (Soz. 152–153). At the back of the book are listed abbreviations for frequently cited works.

2. Husserl (K 70–71) [pp. 69–70 in the translation].

3. Volkelt (1920 117, 121). Scheler (1926 244–307) [pp. 213–264 in the translation].

4. Löwith (1928 138). Binswanger (1942 192), a criticism of Jaspers.

5. Löwith (1928 129–131), a criticism of Scheler. See also Bonhoeffer (1954 29–31) [pp. 36–37 in the translation]. For dialogicalism against Scheler see Buber (DP 298).

6. Ortega y Gasset (1957). For the influence of this book through Husserl see Schütz (1959 91–93).

7. Volkelt (1906 45–48).

8. Volkelt (1920 118–121).

9. Shortly after the flowering of dialogicalism in the twenties, John Cullberg (1933) handled the "Thou-Problem in Contemporary Ontology." I shall occasionally refer back to this work. On the other hand, we can leave out of account the philosophically unsatisfactory work of Schröder (1951). For the totality of the social ontology of the twentieth and also of the nineteenth centuries, see Laín Entralgo (1961), I.

10. Besides the present work, see also the historical expositions of the dialogicalists themselves. For Hegel and Feuerbach see especially the already mentioned *Habilitation* of Löwith (1928). For Hegel and the stream flowing from him, see Dieter (1958/1959 141–144) and (1957), especially pp. 538–539. For Fichte see Weischedel (1939).

11. The author hopes that he will be able to set out his studies on the theory of intersubjectivity of German idealism in another publication. [See the introduction to this translation.]

12. Vierkandt (1923), especially pp. 302, 403.

13. Wiese (1933).

14. For the choice of model text for Sartre's social ontology see section 10 in chapter 6 of the present work.

15. In this work the social-ontologically relevant statements in the still unpublished posthumous works of Husserl are not taken into account. They are abundantly evaluated by Toulemont (1962). It seems to me that they do not decisively alter the picture offered by the published work. However, the problem of historical-absolute intersubjectivity sketched out in a few supplements to *Crisis* (especially XXIV and XXV), with whose exposition the Husserlian theory would be overthrown, ought to be developed in greater depth in those notes that still await publication. For this reason, I have held back from the detailed analysis of this problem. See the suggestions in Theunissen (1963 357-360).

Chapter 1

1. Husserl (CM 181) [p. 155 in the translation].

2. Here and in what follows, italics in the original text will only be reproduced when they do not disturb the context in which the citation is introduced.

3. Fink (1938/1939 241, 243-244) and (1934 30). Helmust Plessner offers a different view in Plessner (1959 15-16, 19).

4. Husserl (K 81, 118, 218-219) [pp. 79, 115, 214-215 in the translation].

5. Husserl (FTL 208) [p. 235 in the translation].

6. See also Landgrebe (1949 51) and Diemer (1956 22, 23).

7. Husserl (Id.III 159).

8. Husserl (Id.I 89, 130) [pp. 127, 164 in the translation].

9. Toulemont (1962 300). Since this book first became available to me after the completion of the present investigation, I unfortunately could not take account of its views. It represents an important addition to the Husserl interpretation offered here, not only because it considers the unpublished manuscripts on the problem of intersubjectivity but, above all, because it primarily follows up the constitution of social relations, guided by an original sociological interest.

10. This escapes Hermann Ulrich Asemissen (1957) in his otherwise acute book. Asemissen is only able to call the phenomenological reduction a "reduction from the de facto to the pure I" (pp. 37, 39, 43) because he equates the de facto I with the mundane-factical I and misinterprets the "pure" as that which is purified of all facticity. A great part of the criticism that Asemissen brings against Husserl suffers from this misunderstanding.

11. Husserl (Id.II 298-300).

12. See Husserl's letter to George Misch of 16 November 1930, printed as an appendix to Diemer (1956 393-394): ". . . the finally real and concrete subjectivity in the whole fullness of its being and life. . . . : the absolute subjectivity in its historicity."

13. This reply admittedly does not claim to exhaust Husserl's concept of the "absolute" in *all* its meanings. For an analysis of the multiplicity of these meanings see Boehm (1959a). However, our interpretation supplements Boehm's exposition in that the meaning of the concept indicated here does not find expression there.

14. Heidegger (SuZ 114) [p. 150 in the translation].

15. At least the originary I that Husserl talks about in *Crisis*. With regard to the originary I thematized in Husserl's later posthumous manuscripts, see Brand (1955), especially pp. 61-66, which considers unpublished manuscripts of Husserl.

16. The constituting being gives the intentionality thematized by Husserl its specific meaning, even in contrast to Brentano's concept of intentionality. See Landgrebe (1949 59-61). With Husserl it is a matter of "operative," or, as Fink says (1938/1939 266), "functioning intentionality."

17. Fisch (1942 117-118).

18. That the transcendental problem of the world stands for the basic problem of phenomenology has been accentuated most emphatically in the article by Fink (1933), which has become a classic.

19. The distinction between transcendental subjectivity qua constituting consciousness and the transcendental subject or I that, as transcendence in immanence, is itself constituted, has been brought out in particular by Funke (1957 9-11, 22, 33, 35 inter alia).

20. Brand (1955 18-20).

21. Fink (1933).

22. The textual basis for following interpretation is the first chapter of the second section of *Ideas*, book I, 57-59. In *Ideas*, book I, as also in the *Cartesian Meditations*, Husserl pursues the "Cartesian" way to the reduction, which already in the second part of *Erste Philosophie*, from 1923/1924, he supplements with the "phenomenologicopsychological" way, and in *Crisis* he eventually gives up in favor of the latter. At the end of a later section I go briefly into that distinction between the two ways that bears upon the problem of intersubjectivity.

23. Fink (1933 366) and Seebohm (1962 76).

24. For this reason the transcendental reduction to which Husserl repeatedly refers back can only be correctly carried out as *universal*. See Landgrebe (1949 106-107).

25. For the preceding see also EP.II 77-78. That the phenomenological reduction as the "placing out of account of the world . . . is at the same time a placing out of account of my self-mundanizing apperception" (EP.II 78), and so is the suspension of my humanity, is not brought out strongly enough in the chapter of book I of *Ideas* examined in the present work.

26. See the letter to George Misch published in Diemer (1956), in which Husserl speaks of "transcendentally relativizing phenomenology."

27. The letter B after the page number indicates here, as also in what follows, that the citation is taken from a manuscript published as an appendix.

28. Kern (1962), especially pp. 314, 315, 322, 323.

29. For a fundamental interpretation of this work, see Landgrebe (1961).

30. In what follows our interpretation is based on *Cartesian Meditations*, §34, pp. 103–106:69–72; see also *Phänomenologischen Psychologie*, §9, pp. 72–87.

31. Langrebe (1949 22–24) also sees it this way.

32. The highly regarded article by Schütz (1957) has also raised the question how transcendental intersubjectivity can be thought about together with the *eidos*, the "transcendental ego in general." The reflections that follow may well contribute a little to answering this question. Schütz limits himself—here as well as in his article as a whole—to working out problems that in his opinion have not been mastered.

33. Fink (1933 264–265) takes it to be "a naiveté—initially advocated by Husserl, but later revised—to carry over, with regard to objective being, the developed eidetic method to 'consciousness' and its connection with objects." Unproductive for the solution of the problem under study here is Eley (1962).

34. Drüe (1963) devotes a paragraph to the "relation of the reductions to one another" (pp. 219–223), but fails also to achieve any complete clarity on this point.

35. By a completely different route Landgrebe (1949 53) also arrives with Husserl at the insight that, in the final analysis, "the antithesis of fact and essence is suspended."

36. Of course Wolters (n.d.) is right when he remarks that the individuality of the phantasma is "different from that of the perceived, insofar as its concreteness, its differentiation, is not so rich" (p. 23).

37. This thesis contradicts the conception of Theodore W. Adorno, who writes, "Through variation, the I is no longer 'mine'—means, no longer I" (1956 236). Adorno errs nevertheless in the supposition that Husserl would make the pure I into a mundane I in that he calls it "mine."

38. Besides A. Schütz, Johannes Thyssen has also presented the problem of eidetic intuition in connection with the problem of intersubjectivity in a small but exceedingly significant study. See Thyssen (1953). Even Thyssen arrives at the conclusion that the introduction of the "*eidos* ego" does not suspend the Cartesian approach with regard to my de facto ego (pp. 191–192). However, according to Thyssen, this is not the case only because the *eidos* ego does not present a real supraindividual subject and so cannot emerge as a constitutional source. Thyssen holds fast to this; that with the orientation of attention toward the *eidos* ego, the realm of my de facto ego is surpassed.

39. Eigler (1961 87).

40. As model text I take as my basis *Cartesianische Meditationen*, §§17–19, pp. 77–89 [pp. 39–53 in the translation]. As a supplement to a few main points treated here only briefly, reference should be made to Theunissen (1963).

41. Sinn (1958 2).

42. FTL 215 [p. 243 in the translation] and Id.III(postscript) 150n2.

43. Alfred Schütz at the beginning of his previously mentioned article (1957) provides a comprehensive presentation of statements distributed throughout book I of *Ideas* toward a theory of intersubjectivity.

44. Id.II(introduction of the editor) XV.

45. Husserl gave up the publication of this book because in his opinion he had not succeeded in solving the problem of intersubjectivity. See Schütz (1959 88).

46. Zeltner (1959) rightly refers to the fact that in the question concerning intersubjectivity, Husserl did not reach a specific answer once and for all but tackled the problem from ever new vantage points.

Chapter 2

1. Husserl speaks of "primordinal" as often as of "primordial." Although "primordial" is linguistically more correct, I have, for the sake of consistency, chosen "primordinal," the word much more commonly employed by Husserl.

2. CM 125 [p. 93 in the translation] et passim; see also ID.III 125 B and EP.II 176.

3. Schütz (1959 87) rightly takes the equation of animals and human beings as I-like life forms as "entirely thinkable." In what follows I have bracketed out that problem of the constitution of animals, which is not sufficiently explained by Husserl. See also Schütz (1957 91) Toulemont (1962 77–79).

4. I do not go into the difficulties that lie in Husserl's theory of the constitution of the lived body in order not to repeat what has already been said about it. See especially K. Hartmann (1953). However, I cannot accept fully Hartmann's thesis that the peculiar placement of the body as a phenomenon that is posited and at the same time apodictically given would lead the phenomenological reduction into absurdity and make Husserl's separation between transcendental meaning and concrete reality questionable (p. 9). It seems to me that Hartmann has not sufficiently distinguished between the transcendental and the psychophysical I.

5. See section 9 in chapter 4 of the present work (especially note 12) for the concept of the person.

6. Reference should be made to K. Hartmann's thesis (1953 28–29).

7. The remark within quotation marks is mine.

8. For Husserl's concept of apperception see Diemer (1956 91–92) and Uygur (1958/1959 444).

9. Schütz (1957 90).

10. K. Hartmann (1953 35) criticizes this "paralleling of the psychic and the transcendental." According to him the alien subject is still not encountered with the alien psyche. Admittedly Hartmann pays too little attention to the change of attitude that, according to Husserl, comes about in the transition from the psychological to the transcendental viewpoint.

11. For supplementation see K. Hartmann (1953 34–36).

12. Diemer (1956 283) distinguishes three modes of empathy corresponding to the empathic constitution of the Other as a psychic, a personal, and a transcendental I.

13. It is well known that the concept of empathy played a major role in the philosophical and psychological discussions at the beginning of the century. Close to Husserl stand the commanding works of Theodore Lipps: *Aesthetics*, I (1903). Lipps, who, like Husserl, heavily criticizes the representation of the analogy inference (1907 694–696), grasps empathy as an instinctive knowledge put together out of the imitative drive and the life expression drive (1907 713–715).

The thoughts with which Lipps anticipates certain essential features of the Husserlian account will be especially noted in what follows. From the standpoint of Husserl, Edith Stein (1917) comes to terms with Lipps, but also with Volkelt, Meinong, Witasek, Munsterberg, Scheler, and others. Stein, whose work, according to her own report, proceeded at the instigation of Husserl, but before insight into *Ideas*, book II, was available, does not in principle move beyond her teacher in her positive analysis.

14. K 234 [p. 231 in the translation]; see also Id.II 200 ("mediately susceptible to empathy"), Id.III 112 B.

15. Sinn (1958 70).

16. For the following see especially CM 157-158 [129-130 in the translation] and Id.II 169:242-243.

17. See also the presentation in Id.II 170-171.

Chapter 3

1. See posthumous manuscript K III 18, p. 26: The Others are mediators "for my self-knowledge as an object in the world," cited by Uyger (1958/1959 448).

2. Id.II 228, 240, 249n, 250n, 270, 280.

3. See Section 1 in chapter 1.

4. Prior to Husserl, Theodor Lipps already envisaged empathy as an "alteration of our self" (1912 13), through which we lose the uniqueness of our I-being and become "one" I among others (1907 73-75; 1906 34-36).

5. According to Schütz (1957 100), that constitution of the Other through me and of me through the Other described in the "Fifth Cartesian Meditation" is not capable of grounding the transcendental community of monads, the transcendental we. In fact, between the thought of that constitution and the idea of transcendental communalization, there arises a gap that can only be bridged through the construction laid down in this chapter.

6. Filippini (1960), especially pp. 222-223.

7. Theodor Lipps speaks in much the same way of a "multiplication of my self" (1906 37).

Chapter 4

1. In spite of this, it is, in fact, as Zeltner says (1959 294), "a genuine service on the part of Husserl" to have followed up the reference of the world to intersubjectivity. But as with every revealing, this one is also—to speak with Husserl himself—a "revealing-concealing" (K 53) [p. 53 in the translation] in one. In addition, even Zeltner comes to the conclusion that through the thesis that all human community is "determined by the common belief in a common reality of the world," Husserl abbreviated the phenomenon of sociality (1959 311).

2. Schütz (1957 87) poses this question without answering it.

3. K. Hartmann (1953 36, 47n2, 77, 98, 103, 106) brings out the fact that, according to Husserl, the Others are encountered as world objects. Nevertheless, with my attempt to lay out the

presuppositions of the Husserlian theory of intersubjectivity, I am going after something different from Hartmann's critique. Hartmann brings against Husserl's theory the objection that at bottom it is incapable of rendering intelligible the givenness of the Other as a subject. I do not raise this objection. Conversely, Hartmann would apparently have no objection to the simultaneity given in advance by the transcendental clue, to whose limitations I make reference, if Husserl were only entitled to this simultaneity. How different the standpoints are is made clear by the fact that Hartmann takes Heidegger's analysis of being-with and Sartre's doctrine of alien existence as the norm for a phenomenologically legitimate social ontology.

4. Husserl describes it more extensively in EU 188-194 [pp. 255-261 in the translation].

5. K. Hartmann (1953 82-83) shows that from the point of view of Husserl's presuppositions this is not nearly so easy in reality.

6. At this point reference is still being made to G. Funke's attempt to explicate the problem of language and comprehension on the basis of Husserl's phenomenology; see Funke (1957 107-147).

7. In Husserl's ethical investigations, which Alois Roth has presented with regard to the lecture manuscripts (1960), intersubjectivity plays a decisive role. Only in §§21, 54 does the problematic of intersubjectivity move more strongly into the foreground; but even here Husserl contents himself with vague remarks partly inspired by Scheler that hardly contribute anything toward the fundamental clarification of the question concerning the significance of the ethical for the transcendental laying of the foundation of intersubjectivity.

8. Szilasi (1959 104).

9. In what follows, when we speak of the factical-everyday as the "natural" alien experience, we are distinguishing a different nuance in the meaning content of the concept "natural" than in the preceding chapter. There we were preoccupied with naturalness primarily as the naiveté that is overcome in the regress to the transcendental sphere of origin. Here we are now interested in the natural in its positive sense as that "life-wordly phenomenon" that Husserl understands it as being when already early on (followed up further by Heidegger) he poses the task of "achieving a natural world concept." We characterize as "transcendental" experience of the alien, in contrast to that mode of "transcendental experience" that corresponds to the object of research "alter-ego," a mode of experience in accordance with which, in Husserl's opinion, the theoretical analysis of phenomena has to be carried out.

10. See the distinction between "home-world" and "alien-world" that Landgrebe brings out (1949 115) as the characteristic trait of the life-world; on this see also Toulemont (1962 184-186).

11. Unless otherwise indicated, the page numbers given in what follows, up to section 7, are from this book.

12. With regard to this experience one can also say quite rightly what Landgrebe (1949 175-176) affirms unreservedly: that the Other is, according to Husserl, encountered "quite immediately" and that his givenness "is much more original than that of a mere thing."

13. Together with the insight into the original unity of the personalistically interpreted fellow human being, the acknowledgment of communicative immediacy is also primarily a valuable contribution of book II of Ideas. But it is not limited to this. It already comes to expression in the exposition in book I of Ideas on the "World of the Natural Attitude": "Animals, for instance, human beings, are immediately there for me; I look at them, I see them, I hear their coming, I grasp them by the hand, in speaking with them I immediately understand what they perceive and think, what kind of feelings are aroused in them, what they wish or want" (Id.I 57) [p. 101 in the translation]. In the winter term of 1923/1924, Husserl states no less

clearly, "The perception of an alien (organic) body is a perception insofar precisely as I grasp the being of this body as being itself immediately there. And in just the same way the other human being is there for me perceptibly as a human being. Indeed, I emphasize this perceptible immediacy most strongly in that I say: a human being stands here before me in bodily form . . . it is not thinkable that I could experience him still more immediately"(EP.II 62).

14. On this see also Husserl (1928a), II/I, §7: "Die Ausdrücke in Kommunikativer Funktion" ["Expressions in Their Communicative Function" in the translation].

15. Diemer (1956 65, 69-69, 126-127, 260, 292-293) brings out the great significance that Husserl's posthumous manuscripts accord to interpersonal "love." He sees an influence of Scheler therein. The texts that he brings in, however, leave it doubtful whether Husserl, as Diemer openly avows, really situates love in the sphere of the transcendental constitution of the Other. See also Toulemont (1962 245-247, 253-255), Uygur (1958/1959 456-457).

16. See the particularly indicative descriptions from the initial and the conclusive phase of Husserl's reflections on the problem of intersubjectivity: Id.I 61-62, 63 [pp. 105, 106 in the translation], K 149, 239 [pp. 146, 236 in the translation]. In between we find work in *Ideas*, book II, that brings out communicative immediacy. But already in the passage noted above from *First Philosophy* in which Husserl takes it to be "quite unthinkable" that I "could experience my fellow human beings more immediately" than I actually do, this immediacy is taken back again right away: "And yet a certain mediacy is included in the sense of this perception" (EP.II 62). See also EP.II 187: "But looked at more closely this immediacy is precisely only a relative one."

17. See also Lauer (1955 379).

18. In any case, the concept of introjection is somewhat ambiguous; see 175-176.

19. See especially section 3, chapter 2, 211-280.

20. Toulemont (1958 135-151).

21. See §2: "The Scientific Attitude as Theoretical Attitude."

22. See, for example, Id.II 325, Id.III 66, K 30 [p. 32 in the translation], EU 189 [p. 163 in the translation].

23. For a contrasting view, see Uygur (1958/1959 443).

24. I have given up the idea of an extensive presentation of this problem, which has played a significant role in the context of the theory of intersubjectivity, since it has already been provided and is superfluous to the progress of the investigation. See Diemer (1956 294-306), Sinn (1958 108-120), Paci (1960 319-321), and, more recently, Witschel (1964 43-45).

25. From the standpoint of the basic norm of my humanity even animals are constituted as anomalies: CM 154 [p. 126 in the translation].

26. Besides the "Fifth Cartesian Meditation," see Id.III 109 B, EP.II 492 B, and 494 B.

27. See the note in EP.II 483 B: "Transcendental clarification of the distinction of the mode of being of things and of other human beings and the difference of their transcendence."

28. On the critique of this theory of analogizing see Lain Entralgo (1961), I, pp. 167-169.

29. Even on this point reference should be made to the parallel in Lipps. According to Lipps, the alien I is given to me through the "multiplication of my self" (1906 37). It is therefore

"the result of a projection, a mirroring, a streaming in of my self" (1912 17). The alien personality is nothing other than "one's own personality modified in such and such a way" (1912 13–14).

30. Diemer (1956 102–103).

31. K 175 [p. 17 in the translation]: "As temporalized, it, the actual momentary I, can also traffic with its past, and so no longer actual, I, discourse with the latter, criticize it, like an Other."

32. According to Seebohm (1962 148) the passage cited refers to a conception of the constitution of the alter ego not otherwise represented by Husserl whereby the latter is not secondarily constituted but constituted in unity with the self-constitution of my stream of experience. On the basis of our discussion, it is clear that the statement introduced here points precisely in the opposite direction and makes the Husserlian conviction about the origination of alien constitution out of self-constitution look particularly clumsy.

33. Ms. C7I, p. 5, cited in Brand (1955 99).

34. Ms. C7I, p. 6, cited in Brand (1955 99).

35. Ms. C17I, p. 42, cited in Brand (1955 98).

36. Fink (1933 362n).

37. It is for all that certainly possible that from here on the "mundanizing self-apperception" can be clarified as that which Husserl grasps as the constitution of my "personal" as the "psychophysical" I in the context of the problem of the primordinal reduction (CM 130) [pp. 99–100 in the translation]. This mundanization cannot really be a mundanization in the sense of an integration in the world. For then it would need the Other from whose constitutional operations the primordinal reduction abstracts. However, is it not then perhaps that very mundanization that my transcendental ego experiences out of the habitual collapse of its continual constituting of the worldly? That statement that introduces the concept of mundanizing self-apperception may be taken this way. I carry out the latter in that I, as transcendental ego, "have constituted and am continually further constituting the world existing for me (as correlate)." In this way it would also legitimate that characterization of the primordinal as the personal I that is left ungrounded by Husserl. Nevertheless, we cannot really respond to our question in a demonstratively affirmative manner. For in the text Husserl actually describes the mundanizing self-apperception as the conception of my self as a worldly being. Of course, in order to understand this circumstance, we have to take account of the fact that he says I carry out a mundanizing self-apperception "under the title I in the usual sense of the human-personal I." Looked at in this way, the latter is in fact a mundanizing (which presupposes the Other). But the question circumvented by Husserl is, in what sense one can still talk about a mundanizing self-apperception when it is precisely not a matter of the constitution of the "human personal" I, but of the constitution of *that* personal I that has still not been comprehended together with its body in the unity "human being"?

38. On this concept see Brand (1959 71–72).

39. Although immanent alter-ation, as recollection, enters into that empathy through which the objective world is constituted, it is still for itself not capable of effecting a constitution of the objective world. For it stands under the law of successiveness, not under that of the "simultaneity of the I pole" (K 175) [p. 172 in the translation] or of temporal coexistence, which must count as that condition of the constitution of the objective world that is only fulfilled by intersubjectivity. What it achieves is simply an identification that corresponds analogically to the intersubjective (CM 159 [p. 127 in the translation], K 166 [p. 63 in the translation]). But

the intersubjective identification is only the presupposition of objectivation, not the objectivation itself. In the sphere of immanent alter-ation, therefore, the latter has nothing corresponding to it. Admittedly, even here, Husserl speaks occasionally of objectivity (Id.II 83). But he is clear about this, that, in contrast with the intersubjective, the latter is an inauthentic objectivity. Only in the stage prior to the construction of the theory of intersubjectivity does he set forth the conception that real objectivity is constituted through the identification of a past lived experience in the repetition of reproducing acts (1928b 54-56). There the basic principle is still valid: "All objectivation is carried out in time consciousness."

40. Despite its significance I refer only briefly to this presupposition because its questionable character has already been repeatedly established by critics of the theory of intersubjectivity. See, in particular K. Hartmann (1953 77) and Schütz (1957 105-107). Seebohm (1962 147-148) does not stand opposed to the thought of a constitution of the Other as such, but to this, that this constitution is described by Husserl as simply secondary on the basis of already constituted temporality. In this way he modifies Thyssen's position (1953 190, 192), following which Husserl does not actually attain the intended transcendence of the Other because he tries to reach it out of the primordinal lower layer. Of course, in that Thyssen in addition criticizes Husserl's representation of the disclosedness of alien transcendence through the operations of my I, from the standpoint of "realism" (1953 190), in principle he also holds to that position of constitutive transcendental philosophy defended by Seebohm.

41. Fink (1952) and Schütz (1957 106-107). According to Schütz, the concept of constitution first took on the meaning of creation in the course of the development of the Husserlian philosophy.

42. Similarly, Biemel (1959 200-201), Levinas (1949 40-42), Funke (1956 362). On Husserl's concept of constitution see also Toulemont (1962 43-45).

43. See also Toulemont (1962 301).

44. He also speaks against the thesis presented Landgrebe (1949 177, 181, 191, 194-195, 204) and taken over by Uygur (1958/1959 449-450) to the effect that Husserl has in mind the precedence of the evidence of the Thou, prior to the I-experience. According to Landgrebe, there opens up, on the basis of Husserl's theory of intersubjectivity, the possibility of thinking divine transcendence as an addressing Thou. In contrast, I am sympathetic to Zeltner's conception (1959 310), in accordance with which transcendental phenomenology does not make possible any "transition from the relationship 'I and the Others' to an original I-Thou relationship." On Husserl's question concerning God see Hohl (1962 83-85), Strasser (1945), and Toulemont (1962 273-275).

45. Together with the problem of constitution it is this question that has most fruitfully preoccupied those interpreters of the theory of intersubjectivity represented up to now and that, for the most part, has been answered in the negative. But it is the distinction between my absolute, unique ego and my transcendentally communalized ego, a distinction presented previously in a fundamental way, that first lays bare the innermost ground of that ambiguity that attaches to the very attempt at an overcoming. According to K. Hartmann (1953 106-107) and Thyssen (1953), Husserl remains stuck in solipsism. Theodore Celms (1928), who, supported by book I of *Ideas* and the lecture manuscripts, has furnished the first contribution to the critique of the theory of intersubjectivity (387-405), arrives at the conclusion that, instead of an overcoming of solipsisms, Husserl only succeeds in extending monistic into pluralistic solipsism (404). Moreover, according to Celms, the basis of pluralistic solipsism is the metaphysical, phenomenologically undemonstrable supposition of a preestablished harmony between my representation of the alien I and the alien I "itself" (399). Strasser (1945) refrains from taking up a detailed critical stance. To be sure, he interprets the "perhaps" as a basic feature of Husserl's solution characterized by "one-sided immanentism," but praises, nonetheless, its one-sidedness and absolutely consequential character (18). Lauer (1955 388) is of the opinion that the theory of intersubjectivity really does disarm the objection of solipsism.

Chapter 5

1. Page numbers in this chapter not preceded by any letters giving title abbreviation refer to this book. [Those in parentheses are from the German edition (SuZ); those in square brackets, from the translation.]

2. The connection between Heidegger's analysis of being-with and Husserl's theory of inter-subjectivity has not hitherto been explained. In what follows it is not so much a matter of the disclosure of a historical dependence as it is the demonstration of substantive correspondences. Without doubt, however, one is entitled to work on the assumption that at the time of writing of *Being and Time*, Heidegger knew Husserl's theory of intersubjectivity in that form that Husserl gave to it in later publications; see note 38. It is of especial importance that Heidegger examined Id.II 47n1.

3. A short and explicit critique is to be found in *Being and Time* (47-48 [73]). That *Being and Time* is, nevertheless and as a whole, determined by an unspoken confrontation with Husserl Heidegger himself has said clearly enough. See his preface to Richardson (1963 XV): "In the meantime, Phenomenology in Husserl's sense was developed into a specific philosophical position, predelineated by Descartes, Kant and Fichte. . . . The question of being unfolded in *Being and Time* is set up against this philosophical position, and this on the basis of a substantially correct, as I still believe today, adherence to the principle of phenomenology."

4. On this see Pöggeler (1963 72). Boehm (1959) rejects Heidegger's reproach as unjustified.

5. In his remarks on Husserl's article in the *Encyclopaedia Britannica*, published in a critical appendix to Husserliana IX, pp. 600-602. Brief as they are, these remarks belong to the most significant documents on the philosophical-historical place of *Being and Time*. See Biemel (1950b).

6. On Heidegger's criticism of the traditional concept of the subject see Marx (1961 93-108).

7. See also Lubbe (1960).

8. Heidegger (WG 42).

9. Landgrebe (1949 97-99).

10. One may talk of such a determination in spite of Heidegger's disapproving stance—emerging clearly after World War I—toward Husserl's "transcendental turn." At bottom this negation is directed only toward the attempt to seek the source of world constitution in an I. On Heidegger's initial attachment to transcendental phenomenology, see Lehmann (1964).

11. Here and in what follows one must bear in mind that Heidegger's concept of horizon does not coincide with Husserl's. To be sure, it too has its origin in pure phenomenology, but Heidegger ontologized Husser's concept of the world horizon in that he distinguished the ontic moment that modified the latter into a synonymous expression for the universe. Where, in the course of the investigation, I talk of "horizon," I understand this word in Heidegger's sense.

12. Herewith, according to Heidegger, the self also precedes the "Thou" as the correlate of the "I": "Only because *Dasein* is as such determined through selfhood is an I-self able to relate to a Thou-self. Selfhood is the presupposition for the possibility of I-hood, which is always only disclosed in the Thou. Selfhood is, however, never related to the Thou, but—because it first makes all that possible—is neutral" (WG 35). The paragraph in which this statement stands evidently contains a concealed answer to Löwith's critique. In it Heidegger now also carries

the restricted I concept from *Being and Time* over to the Thou—which is at least as problematic as the I concept itself.

13. Richardson (1963 97–99).

14. Not only has the Heidegger literature taken no notice of the back reference of the analysis of being-with to the theory of intersubjectivity; it has accomplished astonishingly little even for the immanent elucidation of the analysis of being-with itself. Even in critical contributions of some importance one hardly finds more than what was brought to expression in the second part of our investigation. We shall, on the occasion of the interpretation of this thinker, refer also to later works by authors who, in principle, take up the same position as Löwith, Binswanger, and others. Although we agree with this criticism in its essentials, still, in Heidegger's case, as well as with Husserl, the analysis is primarily oriented with regard not to criticism but to laying out the—in any case necessarily one-sided—model. However, we take up a decisive distance from the apologists of Heidegger, insofar as they advance the thesis that, under the title of "authentic being-with-one-another," Heidegger has left room for the I-Thou meeting. See Uslar (1959). On the other hand, the notion advocated by Wiplinger (1961 365–367), that a dialogical moment is to be found in the being-thought of late Heidegger, seems to us to be substantively grounded. But one cannot get there from the analysis of being-with.

15. In the unpublished lectures on logic of the 1925/1926 winter term, in which Heidegger conveyed essential parts of the analysis of *Dasein*, being-in-the-world and being-with are for the most part still contrasted in this manner as two equiprimordial basic modes of *Dasein*. It is, however, also significant for the mastery of worldliness, to be considered below, as the exclusive horizon of being-with-one-another, that Heidegger, in the edited text of *Being and Time*, conveniently avoids such formulations. Nevertheless, Heidegger says that *Dasein* is "concernful being-in-the-world and being-with with Others" (280).

16. Waehlens (1948 71n1) also supposes that Heidegger's critique of the theory of empathy is aimed a Husserl.

17. Heidegger also discovers this in his criticism of Husserl. See Pöggeler (1963 74–75).

18. Macquarrie (1960 90) overlooks this.

19. See the German edition of the present work, pp. 418–419.

20. Cullberg (1933) expresses this state of affairs in this way: With Heidegger, "the 'cohuman being' is a moment in the a priori with-world." This critique, brought up in the same way by Grisebach, we find again in Sartre.

21. On this concept and on Heidegger's "with" in general as a "basic word," see Schöfer (1962 60, 75).

22. For this reason it seems to me naive to think that Heidegger's "notion of encounter" stands in an essential proximity to theology. This is Heinrich Ott's opinion (1959 63–65). In all likelihood, the "way of Martin Heidegger," to the extent that it is that of fundamental ontology (and Ott is thinking of this in the present context), and the "way of theology" are nowhere more remote from one another than in the concept of "encounter."

23. Filippini (1961 215) speaks of the Heideggerian "They" as Heidegger speaks of the We. See in the present work chapter 4, section 4.

24. See in the present work the examples in chapter 4, section 5.

25. In the same way that Heidegger speaks of the We—see in the present work chapter 4, section 5—Husserl also speaks of the They. But while Husserl's concept of the They does not

coincide with his concept of the We, but only characterizes a segment from the whole of it, Heidegger's They concept finally corresponds to Husserl's We concept in its broadest scope, to the extent that the latter relates to the human-personal community. Admittedly, the We thematized by Husserl and taken up by Heidegger under the title of the "They" does not comprehend all possibilities of We-being. We shall get to know others in the following chapter. The basic feature of the Husserlian We, which Heidegger sharpens, is the lack of distinction among their members, who are neither ontologically separated from one another nor go to make up a totality with one another.

26. Heidegger himself announces the correspondence of everydayness, qua inauthenticity, on the one hand, and naturalness, on the other, when he instates the "natural I-talk" as an equivalent expression for "everyday I-saying" (321–322).

27. Gründer (1962), especially p. 318.

28. The natural I with which the inauthentic-everyday self should be compared is the I of the natural attitude just as well as an objective I.

29. On the problem of the identification of inauthenticity and everydayness see section 7.

30. On the problem of the fundamental-ontological relationship of death and *Dasein*-with, see the critical and very acute exposition of Sternberger (1934 32–75).

31. See Löwith's critique in the German edition of the present work, p. 419.

32. When Heidegger says here that "everyday being-with-one-another" maintains itself *between* the two extremes of solicitude, he presumably confers upon the concept of the "everyday" the meaning to be discussed below of an "indifferent proximally and for the most part" (43 [68]), so that there results no contradiction in the identification of leaping-in and inauthentic solicitude, on the one hand, and leaping-ahead and authentic solicitude, on the other. Moreover, the passage over solicitude is in no way unambiguous (121–122 [157–158]). Although inauthentic solicitude is supposed to be essentially "dominant," Heidegger writes, "In such solicitude the Other *can* become dependent and dominated." Although it is supposed to be continually directed toward the instrument to be concernfully employed, in accordance with another statement, it confronts *"for the most part* the concern with the present-at-hand." Even the remark that the leaping-ahead solicitude does "not so much" leap in for the Other as rather anticipate him has the bizarre result that leaping-ahead and leaping-in solicitude are, according to Heidegger, extremes. However, Heidegger leaves it to the reader to bring the statement that everyday being-with-one-another maintains itself between "the two extremes of positive solicitude" into accord with the thesis "that proximally and for the most part *Dasein* maintains itself in the deficient modus of solicitude." It is certainly not to be assumed that "bypassing one another, not-being-involved with one another," provides that mean between the solicitude of leaping-in and leaping-ahead. In order to clarify the connection, Heidegger's remark may be brought in to the effect that a "being-with-one-another that arises out of the fact that one pursues the same thing" for the most part appears "in the modus of distance and reserve." Following this, the solicitude that leaps in would already be impelled from itself to bypass the Other because it is not genuinely preoccupied with the Other but with the instrument to be concernfully employed by him. Whereby, admittedly, only the genesis of the indifference of being-without-one-another would be explained, but not the origination of the counter-to-one-another that Heidegger, to all appearances, still counts among the deficient forms of solicitude. (Italics in the citations are mine.)

33. Theunissen (1958 73–83).

34. That authentic being-with-one-another in Heidegger's sense is sheerly indirect can also be expressed in this way: the authentic self is not constituted in it. *Dasein* achieves its authentic

self without the positive cooperation of *Dasein*-with. Against this see WG 50: "And only through the capacity for listening at a distance is *Dasein*, as a self, temporalized by the awakening of the answer of *Dasein*-with, in that being-with with which I-hood can be accorded, in order to win itself as authentic self." The contradiction of the two conceptions has to be seen against the background that Heidegger, in the essays immediately following upon *Being and Time*, more or less takes issue with the criticism of his major work that appeared in the meantime, in the course of which confrontation he undertakes in part a correction of the position assumed in *Being and Time*. Clearly the conception of being-with-one-another also falls under this correction, a conception to which Heidegger now, together with positive authenticity, also accords an immediate ontological function of disclosure, and indeed in phenomenal regions that are covered over in *Being and Time*. See Heidegger (1951 28): "Another possibility of such a revelation (that is, of being in totality) is to be found in joy at the presence of the being— not of the simple person—of a loved one."

35. Just as Husserl calls his idealism a "transcendental solipsism," so Heidegger also talks of "existential 'solipsism' in connection with individualization" (188 [233]).

36. Müller-Lauter (1960 67–83), who keeps the problematic of being-with for a later discussion, has furnished one of the most important contributions to the critical clarification of fundamental ontology.

37. Müller-Lauter (1960 72).

38. It does not, as one might expect, correspond to the triad of state of mind, understanding, and discourse, but to that of discourse, sight, and interpretation as original modes of understanding. Therein we find Heidegger's centering of being-in-the-world upon the transcendental project or upon understanding as the "basic form of all human disclosure" (170 [214]).

Chapter 6

1. When not otherwise noted, page numbers in this chapter not preceded by any letters giving title abbreviation refer to the French edition of this work *L'Etre et le néant* (En). On Sartre's *Critique de la raison dialectique*, vol. I: *Théorie des ensembles pratiques* (Crd), see section 10 later in this chapter.

2. Schütz (1948/1949) gives a brief but precise presentation of Sartre's critique of Husserl, Hegel, and Heidegger. It is noteworthy that Schütz, the distinguished connoisseur of Husserl's theory of intersubjectivity, agrees with Sartre's criticism of this theory (192–194, 195). In brief, he supports Sartre's thesis that Husserl points out a relation between empirical subjects, but not the significant relation between transcendental subjects. Confirmation of this comes from a position that Schütz himself defends, namely, that Husserl is not capable of rendering intelligible the constitution of the transcendental alter ego or that of the transcendental community. The positive relation between Sartre's social ontology and Husserl's theory of intersubjectivity is just as little explicated in Schütz (1948/1949) as in the remaining literature. On Sartre's Hegel critique, which I must decline to treat here, together with his entire relationship to Hegel, see Kopper (1960/1961).

3. Holz (1951 63–64) overlooks the radical transcendence of the world of the originally encountered Other in his exposition of Sartre's phenomenology of shame.

4. Biemel (1950a 88–89) rightly objects to Sartre's affirmation that Heidegger would not be able to reach the ontically concrete level from the ontological level of being-with, on the grounds that Sartre already distinguishes the ontological structure of being-with through the description "level" in a way that Heidegger does not at all.

5. Sartre's critique of Heidegger reproduces in almost every point Lain Entralgo (1961), I, pp. 266–267).

6. K. Hartmann (1963 4, 110, 112).

7. K. Hartmann (1963 33).

8. This thought, which also plays a decisive role in Karl Jaspers's elucidation of communication, was certainly first formulated in a sharp and penetrating manner by George Simmel; see Simmel (1908), especially pp. 81, 84, 85–86. Simmel has, in general, anticipated numerous theorems of Sartre. In connection with the concept of the "third," I shall point out one of the outstanding parallels. Over and beyond that, however, the basic theme of Sartre's social ontology is already announced in Simmel: that being that is identical with itself (and thereby distinct from my being-for-me) and that the Other accords to me in that he makes me into his object. Simmel even speaks of the "look of the Other" in the context of the passages quoted here. In connection with the thesis that we, as those who are never entirely at one with their being, represent fragments, he says, "This fragmentary character, however, extends the look of the Other into what we never are purely and wholly" (1908 34). Admittedly, a distinction exists between Simmel's conception and that of Sartre: for Sartre, I am not for myself what I am because I exist beyond myself; for Simmel, because I remain behind myself. Accordingly, with Sartre, the Other throws me back upon my factical being, while, with Simmel, he leads me out beyond my factical being.

9. The rather cheap criticism of Sartre by those who reproach him for having forgotten, on the subject of the description of the social-conflict situation, the "encompassing horizon"— for example Möller (1959)— or the "harmony"—for example, Desan (1960)—is itself forgetful of the substantive justification that flows from the separation, affirmed by Sartre, out of *interiorité*. Moreover, the "objective" breaks decisively into the viewpoint of an "encompassing unity"—see K. Hartmann (1963 108)—and validating ontology at only one point in Sartre's doctrine of alien existence: where Sartre attempts to consider the irreducible facticity of the multiplicity of individuals together with the presupposed totality of consciousness (358–363). But even there he only recognizes an "incomplete totality." We can dispense with an exhaustive presentation of this truly questionable metaphysical theory in our framework; reference should be made to K. Hartmann (1963 108–110) and Salvan (1962 77–79).

10. With Sartre, embodiment is closely tied in with the facticity of being-for-itself. One can say straight off that in that dimension in which it exists for me, my body is my original facticity (see especially 389–393 [pp. 407–409 in the translation]. Although Sartre's analysis of the body belongs in the framework of his social ontology, I shall not consider it at length because its interpretation would require too much space. Kopper (1960 61–81) interprets Sartre's social ontology in the horizon of the problem of embodiment. See also Maier (1964 1–20).

11. Sartre (1947 31–35). According to Simone de Beauvoir (1960 141–142), Sartre had already become acquainted with Husserl in 1932 through a reading of E. Levinas. He read Husserl himself (as also Scheler, Heidegger, and Jaspers) a year later in Berlin (Crd 34.) His *L'Imagination* 1936) is already wholly and entirely determined by Husserl. Liselotte Richter (1961 32) records that he had also heard Husserl's last lectures in Freiburg.

12. This is exemplified by the above-mentioned connection between facticity and embodiment, the question concerning the embodied character of the body. Sartre takes up a problem that played a major role in Husserl's phenomenology and that in Heidegger has almost entirely faded into the background. But he answers this question with the help of the concept of that facticity that, in its turn, assumes a fundamental significance in Heidegger's analytic of *Dasein* and that is not seen by Husserl. Another example: According to Sartre, worldly reality offers itself to us neither primarily as an object of perception—as for Husserl—nor as an instrument— as for Heidegger—but as an "instrumental thing," as "chose-ustensile." What, however, at

first looks like a mere synthesis turns out, on closer examination, to be the adoption of an existential-ontological cognition with a view to a more original repetition of the Husserlian account. For, in the conclusively decisive positions of *Being and Nothingness*, Sartre goes back to the perceptual world established by Husserl as the foundation. Evidence for this is the emphasis upon perspectivity as a "nécessité ontologique" (371; see also 379–381). So the model that Sartre adopts as the basis of his social ontology is then also wholly and entirely determined by the perspectival spatiality of the perceptual world.

13. On Sartre's grounding of Husserlian egology see also Sartre (1936/1937).

14. Already at the threshold of the twentieth century Hugo Munsterberg—in the continuation of the theory of intersubjectivity of German Idealism, above all that of Fichte—makes the concept of recognition the basic concept of the entire social ontology. With him, too, as with Sartre, the way out from recognition is connected with the way back to the "immediacy" of my consciousness of the Other. He too arrives at this immediacy through the conversion of my traditional thematic relation to the Other into my-being-approached-by-the-Other. Moreover, with him it is not a matter of the recognition of my object-I constituted by the Other, but of that of the alien subjectivity itself. But the recognition of the requirement with which the Other approaches me is supposed first to disclose the Other as such. Munsterberg arrives at this view through the radical deconstruction of concealing, in particular scientific, theories and through the orientation toward the "world of valuation," which is even more original than the world of perception. That I encounter the Other itself immediately through recognition means negatively: originally I do not perceive his physical body and do not at all discover him in the world as a spatial object. In this way Munsterberg, who today is quite unjustly almost forgotten (and was already ignored at the time of the German school of psychology and philosophy), changes the transcendental theory of intersubjectivity even before it can be established. However, he changes it by going in the same direction that Husserl and Heidegger open up: in the direction of a phenomenology of the life-world. For Husserl also names him as a forerunner of his theory of the personalistic attitude (Id.II 173). See Munsterberg (1900) and Laín Entralgo (1961), I, pp. 93–97.

15. The concept of "petrification" appears frequently even in the *Critique of Dialectical Reason*. So, according to Sartre, with the exploitation of the Peruvian gold mines through the Spaniards of the sixteenth century, gold becomes a "petrifaction of action" (Crd 240 [p. 171 in the translation]). Corresponding to the change in the concept of alienation (see section 10), the subject of petrifaction, the petrifying, is here not the Other but that matter mediated through the Other.

16. Barnes (1959 114).

17. Schütz (1948/1949 196) refers to a really confusing equivocation in Sartre's object concept: the object is, on the one hand, as here, the in-itself; on the other hand, it is the *cogitatum* in its appearing-to-me.

18. See Sartre's exposition of this state of affairs with regard to the model of my relationship to the object-Other (409).

19. See section 3.

20. See Sartre's description of the change that the world of the soldier undergoes when the latter turns to flight (356).

21. Sartre (1956).

22. Jameson (1961 188), Salvan (1962 69–70).

23. On Sartre's concept of love see Arntz (1960). Arntz also throws light upon the ontological presuppositions of Sartre's doctrine of alien existence (given with the distinction of In-itself and For-itself).

24. To be sure, the subject-we is the only form in which I as subject can be together with Other as subjects. But precisely not in opposition. This opposition is also formed here by objects, materially the worldly things. The Others amalgamated in the subject-we with me and among each other into an undifferentiated community in perception, judgment, and concernful intercourse are related to them. Under the title subject-we Sartre therefore creates a place for Heidegger's "They." He does this expressly as long as the proximity to Husserl's we remains concealed from him. In spite of the reference to Husserl's idea of the intersubjective constitution of the world, he ascribes the transformation of the social model from "frontal opposition" into a "lateral dependence" to fundamental ontology (302 [p. 331 in the translation]). Therefore the place of the They in the totality of the Sartrian theory of alien existence is also of an entirely subordinate significance. It stands at least as far from the position of the "object-we" as, upon the singular level, the being-for-me of the Other stands to my being-for-the-Other. For the two forms of the we should correspond exactly to the "l'être-regardant" and the "l'être-regardé" in the relationship of the individual to the Other (486:537). At bottom, however, the experience of the "subject-we" is, for Sartre, still less original than it should be in the role of a plural counterpart to my experience of the object-Other. Sartre is not weary of stressing "that the experience of the subject-we does not at all possess the value of a metaphysical disclosure" (500:553), that it is "a purely psychological and subjective proceeding" (497:541) incapable of even approximately fulfilling the ontological claim of "being-with" as a constitutive moment of being-in-the-world. Moreover, the frequent assertion of this circumstance betrays the absence of a genuine grounding. In any case that very state of affairs that principally supports the merely empirical relevance of the subject-we—the dependence upon the singular experience of the Other—is equivalently valid of the object-we, in whose experience "the disclosure of a real dimension of existence" (502 [p. 555 in the translation]) takes place.

25. The concept of the "third" has been developed above all by Simmel in his "sociology" (1908), especially pp. 96–123. Even he proceeds upon the assumption that the introduction of the third qualitatively alters the social situation (1908 96); in his view too the original conflict of both partners is as a rule converted into solidarity (1908 102). Indeed, he anticipates Sartre's theory of the constitution of class consciousness. Following him, the partners of the initial "bilateral bond" achieve a "feeling of status" with regard to the dominant third" because the common elements can now only be sought on the side of the comrades and, of course, are only to be found in them, which makes up the antiantithesis of both to the common superordinate" (1908 99). From Simmel the concept of the third has been taken up by Litt (1924 111–114), according to whom, the present of the third first makes possible "the conscious apprehension of the being-for-one-another of two beings," which—even in this thesis he follows that insight of Simmels formulated in the same way by Sartre—cannot be found in the I-Thou relationship because "I" only have "Thou" there before me and not the relationship itself.

26. Thyssen (1954/1955 166) misunderstands these words when he takes them as proof of the resolution ostensibly intended by Sartre of alien reality into my own.

27. Admittedly, in accordance with the double role of the Sartrian ontology as completion and as transformation of the transcendental approach, being-seen is also ambiguous. Conceived in itself primarily as sensible being-perceived, it is at the same time steeped in the medium of the ethical. In particular, that experience through which I principally realize my being looked at falls into the sphere of the ethical, namely, shame. Shame occupies so preeminent a place because I am essentially object for the Other as "object of valuation" (326:358). Indeed, the look of the Other first makes my being in general ethically relevant. In my being-for-myself I have absolutely no qualities and thus no ethical qualities. The qualities, however, with which the alien subject endows me are, in the first instance, of a moral nature (332–333:365). That

they as well as the subjective reactions to my being-seen—like shame and that pride (351–352) interpreted as "conceit"—are almost entirely negative corresponds to the theory of the disempowering of my consciousness and the negative constitution of my ownmost self.

28. All page references in this section, unless otherwise indicated, refer to this work.

29. This is clearly the view of Albérès (1960 139–143). For an opposing view see Zehm (1964 175–193).

30. Zehm (1964 187–189).

31. Even and precisely in the sphere of the group and the collective Sartre finds multiple modes of alter-ation. Thus every member of a group is alter-ed in that he is constituted as an inessential part of a purely objective, substantial totality with respect to those who are Other to this group, therefore "not grouped" (553–561; see also 635–641). The concept of "être-autre" (being-other), which goes back to that of "autre-être" (other-being) in *Being and Nothingness*, is one of the basic concepts with which Sartre operates in this sphere (see, inter alia, 302n:248, 398:366, 419:393, 440:420, 443:424, 541:549, 561:575, 637:670, 640:674). On serial alter-ation, "alterity" as "ratio of the series," see especially 312–314:260–262.

Chapter 7

1. Here are the writings that I shall principally take into consideration alongside those of Buber: H. Cohen, *Religion der Vernunft aus der Quellen des Judentums* (RV); F. Rosenzweig, *Der Stern der Erlösung* (SE), *Kleineren Schriften* (KS), and *Briefe* (1935); H. Ehrenberg, book I of *Disputation* (Disp.I); E. Rosenstock-Huessy, *Angewandte Seelenkunde* (AS), *Der Atem des Geistes* (AG), and books I and II of *Soziologie* (Soz.I, II); F. Ebner, *Das Wort und die geistigen Realitäten* (WR) and *Wort und Liebe* (WL); G. Marcel, *Journal metaphysique* (Jm) and its continuation, *Être et avoir* (Ea); E. Grisebach, *Gegenwart* (Gw); and K. Heim, *Glaube und Denken* (GL). I do not bring into the center of the investigation the work of those Protestant theologians influenced by the philosophy of dialogue who themselves set store by the affirmation that they speak as theologians and not as philosophers, even if occasional references should throw light upon their relation to the philosophy of dialogue. In this manner I make reference to F. Gogarten, *Ich glaube an der dreieinigen Gott* (1926) and *Glaube und Wirklichkeit* (GW); E. Brunner, *Wahrheit als Begegnung* (WB); and the second part of the third volume of K. Barth, *Kirchlichen Dogmatik* (KD III/2). In contrast with these dogmatic-theological contributions, I bring the above-mentioned treatises of Heims directly into the presentation because Heims, although a theologian by name, himself considers these treatises to be philosophical attempts at a religious-philosophical laying of the foundation of dogmatics (GL 438). That theological dialogicalism that is laid out not only in the so-called "dialectical" theology but, for example, also in the thought of Paul Tillich and Reinhold Niebuhr proceeds, when it is not connected to Grisebach, almost entirely from Buber's dialogic. On this see especially Cullberg (1933) and Friedman (1955 268–280).

2. The last study of the collection of articles by Herrigel goes into the essay by Rosenzweig also treated here (1928 228–230). On Herrigel's book see Grisebach (1929/1930). The critical stance that Grisebach adopts toward all other representatives of "new thought," and at the bottom of which we find the opinion that only he goes far enough into the destruction of the old thought, is here directed against the thought, characterized by Herrigel as new, that it is solely a "system of opposition." Thereby the critical accent is placed upon "system." That the really new thought stands in opposition is also precisely Grisebach's conviction. Moreover, he agrees with Herrigel, who brings forward his objections to the "present" in the critique of "fundamental thought"; see Herrigel (1928 166–206) and Grisebach (1929/1930 169).

3. Buber (DP 288), a postscript.

4. Steinbüchel (1936). Hans Kohn characterizes Buber's dialogic as "new thought" (1961 229–230).

5. Löwith (1958). On Rosenzweig's biography, see Glatzer (1961). Baeck depicts the form of consciousness (1958 43–50).

6. On Rosenzweig's connection to Schelling see (KS) 371, 383; 1935 298–299. Also see Freund (1955).

7. Since the *Star of Redemption*, unlike all the other works that will be introduced in the present section, is supposed to offer a "system of philosophy" (KS 374), it needs a coherent interpretation. Such an interpretation would, however, overstep the frame of our investigation. For this Freund (1955) should be referred to.

8. For other examples of Grisebach's critical attitude toward Heidegger, see Gw X 40 (implicit), 93, 281 (implicit), 555n, 589–590. See also Grisebach (1930). This article was stimulated by the same discussion (during the week at Davos in spring 1929) between Heidegger and Cassirer to which Rosenzweig—informed by Herrigel's report in the *Frankfurter Zeitung* of 22 April 1929—appeals with his interpretation of fundamental ontology as a contribution to "new thought."

9. Rosenstock-Huessy (GU 149–159). On the basis of the fact that it starts out from a "duality" of basic words, Buber's dialogic is here branded as a gnostic heresy. The heresy of which it is guilty appears, of course, as a falling away from Rosenstock-Huessy's own "doctrine on Thou and Me."

10. Centering the Buber interpretation upon *I and Thou* is justified on the grounds that in this writing Buber not only translates his "experience of faith" into philosophical language for the first time but does so in a way that is determinative for all later writings. Of the later writings of a philosophical character, we shall primarily take account of *Zwiesprache*, 1930; *Das Problem des Menschen* (PM), 1942; *Urdistanz und Beziehung* (UB), 1951; and *Elemente des Zwischen-menschlichen*, 1953. I cite the first- and last-named treatises as well as *I and Thou* as *Schriften über das dialogische Prinzip* (DP).

11. That at the time of the setting down of the *Metaphysical Diary* he knew nothing about German dialogicalism is confirmed by Marcel himself; see Marcel's "Ich und Du bei Martin Buber" in Levinas (MB 35). See also Friedman (1955 162n).

12. The question whether Buber hit upon the dialogical principle in dealing with the Hasidic doctrine or did not rather see Hasidism in the horizon of the dialogical principle cannot be decided here. It is also certainly not to be answered in the sense of a simple either-or.

13. Buber (CB 127–131).

14. Friedman (1955 51n) draws attention to still earlier expressions of Buber's dialogic.

15. Ebner (1963 I 800–819, especially 801) for his part confirms this.

16. See Cohen's similarly named work from the year 1915.

17. Weizsäcker, later known, together with Buber and Wittig, as one of the three editors of the magazine *Die Kreatur*, already was in close contact with Rosenzweig, who clearly owed much to him from the winter of 1906/1907 (1935 36, 251). Just before reading Cohen's late work, Rosenzweig read an unpublished book of Weizsäcker (1935 281). See also the recollections of Rosenzweig and Buber in Weizsäcker (1949 10–19, 25–31). Testimony to the early orientation of Weizsäcker toward dialogical thought is the remarks on the "personal relationship between God and Man" in Weizsäcker (1963 104)—lectures on natural philosophy held in 1919/1920—and Weizsäcker (1923), especially pp. 12, 14, 20.

18. Reprinted in Rosenstock-Huessy (1963), vol. I, pp. 739–810.

19. On both these concepts see H. Ehrenberg (1911).

20. Here we are only concerned to throw light upon the connections, and the lack of connections, among the founders of the modern philosophy of dialogue. Grisebach, for example, no longer belongs to them. A prior work on the "present" only furnishes from among Grisebach's early writings the book *Die Grenzen des Erziehers und seine Verantwortung* (1924). In contrast, in *Wahrheit und Wirklichkeit* (1919), the relation between truth and reality is still not seen in that perspective that is determinative for his work *Present*. Admittedly, it is quite a different matter with Heim, who had already laid the ground for his fundamental account of *Glaube und Denken* (GD) in the investigation *Glaubensgewissheit* [*Certainty of Faith*] (Gg), written in 1916 but cited according to its fourth edition, 1949. After Rosenstock-Huessy had in the same year drawn Rosenzweig's attention to the second edition (1935 657; see also 675), Rosenzweig, conversely, promised his spiritual companion on 26 November 1917 that he would send him Heim's *Certainty of Faith*. He read this treatise immediately after writing down the "original germ" and "found that everything was much more cleanly and better expressed there, although almost everything is in fact the same" (1935 261; see also 268). Still, as is his wont, Rosenzweig sees a greater degree of sameness than is actually present. We are going to see that, with that very feature of his thought that already comes to prominence in the *Certainty of Faith*, Heim distances himself from the center of the philosophy of dialogue.

21. Through H. Ehrenberg (1922), Ebner (1963 I 646–647, 800) was made aware of Feuerbach's I-Thou philosophy.

22. Friedman (1955 48) also names George Simmel as a spiritual father of the Buberian I-Thou philosophy and refers to numerous passages in Simmel's work *Die Religion*. See also Faber (1962 24–27). Here we are only going to refer to the prefiguration of a theme of Buber's dialogic in Simmel's *Soziologie* [*Sociology*] (1908). The significance of this genial book for the unfolding of the dialogical principle lies primarily in the explicit regress to the presocial interhuman relations that have still not crystallized into "objective formations" (see especially 18–20). In this way Simmel brings fundamental phenomena of the dialogical life to light. Only the explication of the problem that imposes the simultaneity of radical independence and the I relatedness of the Thou will be mentioned (30): the descriptions of intimacy (84–85), of trust and gratitude (581–583), as well as of giving (464, 488); the working out of the specifically dialogical superempirical trust as "the basic category of human behaviour" (346–347, 373); the reference to looking at oneself as the highest concretion of dialogical immediacy and reciprocity (647–649); as well as finally the definition of the ethical as the "devotion of the I to a Thou" (206). It is admittedly worth bearing in mind that Buber himself did not include Simmel, who was one of his teachers, under the rubric of his dialogic. Rosenzweig, who had heard Simmel in the winter term of 1907/1908, only speaks of the Berlin philosopher with scorn and contempt (1935 56, 152–154, 156, 181, 230), even if he has to admit that Simmel's service is "the creation of a truly original method in sociology" (1935 153). However, Rosenzweig is struck not so much by the substantive differences as by the superficial mode of thought and the personal implausibility of Simmel. Substantively, however, Simmel may have remained estranged from radical dialogic because he holds to the starting point in the "individual" and seeks the social mediation of the individual, in spite of every emphasis upon immediacy, in the "notion" that one makes of the other—see, in particular, "Appendix to the Problem: How Is Society Possible?" in Simmel (1908 27–29). The dialogical account of his sociology is only one among many that were in part continued in the opposite direction. The return of Simmel's themes in Sartre's social ontology is not accidental.

23. The principal thesis of the Buber interpretation that follows develops in a briefer form Theunissen (1964).

24. Buber (1962 1111–1113).

25. Marcel (1963 36), also cited as Levinas (MB 36). On Buber's clarification of the concept of the between, see Levinas (MB 604–605).

26. Cohen (RV 103,105), Pfuetze (1961 201).

27. Levinas heads a section of his contribution to MB in this way: "Martin Buber and the Theory of Knowledge"; see Levinas (MB 119–134, especially 124–125). I agree with him not in his criticism, to be sure, but in the general tendency of his interpretation of Buber. Even Levinas tries to see Buber in the context of the philosophical endeavors of the twentieth century. However, he brings dialogic back too closely to fundamental ontology and does not distinguish sharply enough between Buber's attempt at an overcoming and Heidegger's attempt at a grounding of intentionality.

28. That the interpretation of the "sphere of subjectivity" with the help of Husserlian terminology is not arbitrary and irrelevant is confirmed by Levinas, who insists that it is "characterized in Buber by the same expressions that Husserl utilizes for the designation of the intentional object" (MB 122).

29. Pfuetze (1961 154), Faber (1962 79–82). Faber rightly emphasizes that Buber's concept of immediacy does not mean the uncontrolled and unreflected nature of feeling.

30. Buber (H 291).

31. Buber (W). See also Cohen (RV 84).

32. Buber's concept of relation—moreover, merely a "skeleton word" (MB 603–604)—corresponds to the central concept in the late work of Cohen: that of "correlation"; see Rosenzweig (KS 346).

33. Rosenstock-Huessy also speaks here of mutuality [Gegenseitigkeit] (AG 59, 72; Soz. I 158, 168, 170) as an indispensable moment of the dialogical relation (AG 77, 299; Soz. I 289–290, 294, 297), Rosenzweig, as well as Buber himself in the postscript to the new edition of I and Thou, of alternation [Wechselseitigkeit] (KS 335), and Cohen of reciprocity [Reciprocität] (RV 103). In this context, what has to be considered is that parity in the socioethical sense that is regarded by the latter as the essential condition of genuine correlation. Cohen has the ideal of such a parity in mind when he seeks to prove that the Old Testament concept of the Other (Rea) means not only the "nearest" in the sense of the colleague but also and precisely the farthest in the sense of the alien. In addition to Cohen's Religion of Reason, see also Cohen (1924 182–195, 306–330). Since the present investigation is directed not so much at the social-ethical problematic as at the social-ontological, the late work of Cohen cannot be evaluated in its framework. Reference should be made to the distinguished exposition in Hommes (1963), especially pp. 332–338.

34. We shall see that in the world complete mutuality is only possible between human beings. However, complete mutuality is also not always actual between human beings. Indeed, there are interhuman I-Thou relations (for example, between teacher and pupil or the psychotherapist and his patients) that, from their very essence, can never be developed into complete mutuality. Nevertheless, they are what they are only thanks to mutuality; see the postscript to the new edition of I and Thou in Buber (1960 470–472).

35. Buber (EC 19).

36. See Weizsäcker's similarly universal concept of the "mutuality of life" in (1951 342—352) and (1956 172–343).

37. Buber (Gf 151).

38. Above all, Ebner also conceives and formulates his thesis about the precedence of the Thou over the I in this way (WR 21, 36, 112–113, 152, 176–177); see also Ebner (1963 I 32, 648, 668–669, 762–763, 764; II 40). See also Buber's critical reply to Levinas (MB 596).

39. That I first really become an I in being-addressed, this is the meaning of the statement about the primacy of the Thou in comparison with the I in Rosenstock-Huessy. There the "Thou" is related to me in just the same way as the "I." Thou is what the Other says to me in speaking-to-me (AS 25, 35–36, 39; AG 68, 85, 88, 265; GU 157). Buber elucidates his thesis that "I" first becomes real in being-addressed in the critical reply to Levinas: "I owe my I to saying Thou not to the person to whom I say Thou" (MB 596).

Chapter 8

1. This extension of the Thou concept beyond the interhuman realm is certainly the most criticized point in Buber's dialogic, which has found little response even within dialogicalism. Goldschmidt, for example, calls Buber a mystic and poet on account of his unrestricted use of the Thou concept (1946 73–76).

2. Cohen distinguishes Thou and He as "Fellow" (Mitmensch) and "Neighbor" (Nebenmensch). It should be an ethical duty to transform the neighbor into the fellow (RV 132, 159, 169–170). The same distinction is to be found in Ebner (WL 200), who calls for making the Other into a fellow (WL 209).

3. Brown (1962 98–99, 113).

4. Many representatives of the philosophy of dialogue agree in this. According to their most essential and most universal determination, the philosophy of dialogue is, as Rosenstock-Huessy says, a "linguistic philosophy" (AC 26, 37), a "higher" (AG 35, 53, 82; Soz. I 157) or "deeper grammar" (AG 69; Soz. I 285, 313). Rosenzweig calls the new thought a "grammatical" or "linguistic thought form" and calls himself a "linguistic philosopher" (KS 387). Similar expressions are to be found in the other dialogicians. See Freund (1955 132–154).

5. On the inner relation of "language" and "between" see also Buber (1962 443). ("Das Wort, das gesprochen wird" and "Dem Gemeinschaftlichen folgen"). Since Buber grasps the between as the reality, language is for him also one with reality. This unification is to be found just as well in Rosenstock-Huessy and Marcel. Rosenstock-Huessy calls language the "life of life" (AG 20, 64; see also 51, 81; Soz. I 200). Marcel says that the living duality of discourse and response is "quite certainly at the center of the real: all spiritual life is essentially a dialogue" (Jm 137). The expression "spiritual life" as the "word" exchanged between I and Thou is used at the same time by Ebner himself (WR 190). Ebner then also explains the word like Buber in terms of the between itself (WR 12–13, 17–18, 77, 89, 158). See also for a similar viewpoint H. Ehrenberg: "Speech is the true reality of the life of the spirit" (Disp.I 183); as such, speech is "between us and things" (Disp.I 175; see also 176–177, 182–184).

6. In contrast is Schroers (1949), according to which genuine dialogicity can in the end only be ascribed to discourse.

7. Feuerbach, Grundsätze der Philosohie der Zukunft (1950 144, 168–169). See also H. Ehrenberg (Disp.I 174, 178).

8. See also Rosenstock-Huessy (1955b 31n).

9. According to Marcel (Jm 137:138), "When I talk to someone in the third person I treat him as independent—as absent—as separate." See also Wittig (1927/1928 423).

10. See also on the totality of the problematic sketched out here the exposition of Reinach's phenomenology of the addressing act in the German edition of the present work, pp. 379–381.

11. Rosenstock-Huessy (1952 83–104), "Datives Denken," especially pp. 83–84.

12. This immediacy lends the vocative its unique place in dialogical life. Humboldt has already seen this too. He grounds his thesis in accordance with which the vocative as the "case of the second person pronoun" is lifted "right out of the series of remaining cases," with the reference to the fact that in opposition to these other cases, which serve "objective discourse posited outside of the subject," the vocative binds the speaker "immediately" with his counterpart (*Gesammelte Schriften* VI/1 172). Ebner draws attention to the fact that the Thou "is nothing other than a vocative" and that the whole "personal pronoun of the second person . . . essentially has the meaning of the vocative" (WR 120). The vocative is, or so he says, "the nominalization of the second person, the substantialization of the Thou" (WR 118). Rosenstock-Huessy also endorses the above-mentioned thesis of Humboldt. In his opinion, the vocative is "not a case at all" (Soz. I 155). It is not a case, however, because, as the original modus of the discovery of the Thou and as the presupposition of conversation, it precedes all cases that are first possible within conversation: "Vocatives form the presupposition for all reciprocal communication; on the other hand, nominatives and other cases are in place within communication. The vocative provokes conversation" (Soz. I 155–156; see also II 195; GU 154–155, 157).

13. Pfuetze (1961 259).

14. In contrast, we already find in Buber's text *Ereignisse und Begegnungen* (1917): "Each thing and each being has twofold qualities: the passive, admissible, exploitable, divisible, comparable, connectable, rationalizable, and the other, the active, inadmissible, unexploitable, indivisible, incomparable, unconnectable, unrationalizable. The latter is the confrontational, the essential, the offering character of things." Friedman says (1955 49), quite rightly, that this text presents the connecting link between Buber's philosophy of realization (*Daniel*) and his dialogic.

15. This difference, moreover, explains the difference in the attitude toward the problem of discourse in *I and Thou* and in *Dialogue*. Out of *I and Thou*, where Buber describes the essential facts, the foundation of silence in discourse can be clearly understood. In *Dialogue*, a text that envisages the phenomenon more psychologically and "with regard to examples" (DP 131), a case is brought forward in which, from the very outset, silence reigns over I and Thou and in which no word introduces the meeting (DP 128–129).

16. See the exposition—in part inappropriate to Buber's intention—on this theme in Kummel (1962 41–43).

17. Marcel depicts the dialogical counterpossibility to this, and, indeed, with regard to that situation of my being-for-other that was also seen by Sartre as original. With reference to his thesis that I am able to transcend every true judgment about myself, Marcel asks, "What do I mean by this exactly? That all judgment with respect to myself is directed toward someone who, by definition, cannot coincide with myself; the one for whom I am Thou goes infinitely far beyond these judgments even if he adheres to them; he opens up for me, in loving me, a sort of credit" (Jm 216).

18. The suspension of the future is not to be found, as Hammerstein (1958 45) believes, in this at all.

19. Buber (1955 59).

20. On the basis of the difference between the dialogically open and the fixed foreknown future, Buber grasps the distinction of prophesy and apocalypse (1962 49–51). For a critique, see Taubes (1963 389–413, especially 400–407), also cited as Levinas (MB 389–413).

21. That language is originally conversation, and that each speaking, to the extent that it needs "the presence of an other human being," can only be part of a conversation or the core of one, is already emphasized by Hirzel (1963 I 7–8). As an example of an extremely antidialogistical philosophy of language, see Vossler (1923).

22. Rosenzweig (1935 33, 376, 384), Rosenstock-Huessy (AG 195), Grisebach (Gw 77, 150–151, 341, 507–509, 575, 577–579).

23. Ebner (1963 I 772): "the Thou is not and is nothing, but-Thou art." Behind this statement stands Ebner's entire doctrine of the radical difference between the being expressed in the "am" and the "art." See also Ebner (1963 I 32–33, 754–756, 820–858; II 233–234, 236). The state of affairs so fundamental for dialogic and to which Buber's and Ebner's words are directed is one that Humboldt probably has in mind when he says that the I and the He are "really different objects" and that with them everything is "really exhausted," so that, on the contrary, the Thou does not fall in the "sphere of all beings," but belongs to another sphere, "that of an action with a common mode of operation" (Gesammelte Schriften VI/1 26).

24. That grammar also speaks in the case of the second person pronoun shows to what an extent it stands under the sway of the interpretation of language as representation of objectivity. On this see Humboldt (Gesammelte Schriften VI/1 161): "Now, since our universal grammar proceeds entirely from the logical, the pronoun that is an analytical part of discourse is placed in it differently than in the present development, where we look for an analytical part of language itself. Here it precedes everything else and is seen as self-depicting; there it first follows the completed explanation of the principal parts of the sentence and essentially bears, as its name also indicates, a representative character in itself." According to Humboldt, "pronouns certainly belong to the oldest words" (VI/1 302). See the quite similar expressions of Jakob Grimm introduced by Ebner (WR 85, 157). Ebner, most strongly influenced by Humboldt and Grimm, writes, "It has a special connection with the pronouns I and Thou. In concrete usage, they are not substitutes for a substantive in the sentence, not the representatives of a name in general or the name of a person in particular, but stand 'immediately' for the 'person' itself in that spiritual sphere formed and objectified by the 'word' " (WR 18; see also 1963 I 773; II 252–253). Even the I can, for this reason, "never be expressed without contradiction in the third person" (WR 109). According to Ebner, this, admittedly, only concerns the living I, which is what it is solely in the relationship to the Thou.

25. Marcel (Ea 219—230:151–152). The realm of the It or the order of having is "the order of predication itself or again of the characterizable." In contrast, the Thou is that which cannot be characterized.

26. Buber here finds himself in complete agreement with Marcel, who also works with the concept of "totality" (Jm 157:158): "In reality, the one I love does not possess qualities for me; I grasp him as a totality, which is why he is resistant to predication." According to Marcel, this is admittedly valid just as much of "personal" being pure and simple, and therefore not only of the Thou but also of my self as a (understood in a specifically dialogical sense) "Person" (Jm 196:199, 203:207, 215:220).

27. Rosenstock-Huessy's Applied Soul Science advocates the worldliness of the It and the world-transcending character of the Thou even more sharply than Buber's I and Thou. Accordingly, that human being taken in the third person is "human being in the world sense" (AS 51), and the theme of science is "the life of the world in the third person, as world space, as past" (33). The indicative that, according to Rosenstock-Huessy, stands for the modus coordinated with the third person is, at the same time, the form in which " 'something' can be said about the world" (29; see also 56). It fixates "outside the speaker in world space" (30), subjugates what "is released in the world" (29). That love, on the other hand, in which the Thou is present "oblivious of the world" (30). Accordingly, Rosenstock-Huessy opposes the philosophy of the Thou to philosophy as "world view" (30). The same opposition of "Thou" and "World" is to be found in Ebner (WR 92, 156).

28. With Grisebach, too, the objective is that which is "fitted into" the world, and the Thou is that which is withheld from any such "integration" (Gw 152, 356, 586). Marcel defines the It as the thing "that is thought to be 'categorizable' " (Jm 162:163). Judging corresponds to it on the act side. Judging is, however, nothing other than integration: "To judge is to classify" (Jm 161:162).

29. Rosenzweig, who posits the essence of love in momentariness (SE II 92-93; see also Soz. II 571) and speaks of "grasping all beings in the immediacy of a moment" (KS 397; see also SE I 85), reproduces the phenomenon of this momentariness itself with the concept of "non-continuity" (SE II 197). Grisebach identifies dialogical momentariness with "reality" (Gw 177, 189).

30. Faber (1962 97-100, especially 98-99) notices, quite correctly, a certain tension between this thesis about the pure actuality and momentariness of the Thou, which already in the next moment has to become an It, and the insight expressed elsewhere, that the dialogical relation is realized in the interchange of "actuality and latency."

31. On Buber's working out of the concept of realization in *Daniel* see Friedman (1955 31-39).

32. Alongside Dilthey, Friedman also names Nietzsche and Kierkegaard (1955 34-35).

33. Faber (1962 30-32).

34. R. Ehrenberg (1927/1928 139): "An unresolvable simultaneity of activity and passivity, of wanting and being wanted, of going out and being received, is the sole reality of all life."

35. The insertion of the totality of my being into the act carried out by me is a phenomenon of dialogical life that is posited by Buber in a fundamental way. Buber also means nothing other than this when in a general sense he speaks of "Belief." The determination of belief as that very act that my entire being goes into is more original than the distinction between the "two modes of belief" that is made in the work of this title. Its validity extends to that belief (represented by Jewry) whose roots lie in an ungrounded trust, as well as to that belief (represented by Christianity) that recognizes something just as ungrounded as truth (1962 653). Even the distinction between good and evil has its place here according to Buber; see his *Bilder von Gut und Böse* (1962 643). See also Friedman (1963), also cited as Levinas (MB 153-179). According to Friedman (1955 11-15, 59-60, 74), the problem of evil is precisely the unifying root of Buber's philosophy of dialogue.

36. Diamont (1960 47-48) and (1963), the latter of which is also cited as Levinas (MB 208-219). On Buber's reaction, see Levinas (MB 599).

37. For this reason, as Marcel remarks (Jm 137-138:137-138, 196:196), I only direct a question from the very outset at that which I take to be answerable.

38. The command, the order, or the request is that claim to which Rosenstock-Huessy accords the greatest originality (AS 26, 30, 33, inter alia). The Thou is that "hearer of the request that is thrown out into the future" (Soz. I 157). To it there corresponds the precedence of the imperative, which, indeed—as already mentioned—represents for Rosenstock-Huessy the verbal form of the authentic future, present in the Thou. In the field of conjugation, Rosenstock-Huessy wants to give the imperative, just like the vocative, its "leading character" in grammar (AG 89). For "the Thou is only rooted in the imperative" (Soz. I 159), in the "Thou form of the imperative" (AS 26), through which the Thou initially becomes accessible to me (AS 30), and that also "subdues my soul" when the command reaches me (AS 35; see also Soz. I 301; Soz. II 59-60; GU 102). See also R. Ehrenberg (1927/1928 137).

39. See also the formula with which Laín Entralgo in his religious metaphysics of the loving meeting expresses what is meant here (1961 II 192).

40. That my freedom is surrounded by destiny is also affirmed by Nikolai Berdiaev (1951 194). In this book, essential pieces of Buber's dialogic, which Berdiaev cites frequently (125, 136–137), are explored. Berdiaev himself says that what he calls "object" corresponds to Buber's "It" (136). Over and beyond this, however, other theses and concepts of Buber are brought back here: the concept of "participation," which Berdiaev opposes to the concept of (dialogically understood) of communication (79–80, 87–88, 141–142); the intuition of the universality of the I-Thou relationship (144–145); the conception of the It as temporally and spatially localized being (176–177), and the corresponding conception of the unworldliness of the Thou (209); and, finally, the thesis that the We is grounded in the correlation of I and Thou (238, 346). In spite of this, Berdiaev falls short of the basic approach of dialogic. To be sure, he too grasps the relation to the Thou as "transcending," but for him the latter is not the swinging beyond of the world, but the surpassing of the I toward the "Thou" (77–78, 155–156), whereby he equates the Thou with the "other I" or with the "alien subject" (90, 122, 125, 151, 238). To be sure, he too distinguishes the fixed foreseeable future and the dialogically open future, but he quietly transforms the latter into the space of that creative activity freed from all passivity that he can set over against the future that simply happens to me (167, 172, 184, 201). Behind this alteration of the dialogical principle, we find negatively the renunciation of the starting point from the between and positively the fundamental affirmation of the original givenness of the I (see especially 113, 124, 205).

41. When Sborowitz (1955) compares the doctrines of Buber with those of Jung, and contrasts determination as "relationship to one's self" with relation as "relationship to the Thou," he does not operate with Buber's concept of determination. Therewith, the belonging together of relation and determination affirmed by him is also something different from the one intended in the following citation.

Appendix I

1. Those page references of this appendix not supplied with initials relate to Schütz, *Der sinnhafte Aufbau der sozialen Welt* [*The Phenomenology of the Social World*] (1932). In addition, I draw on Schütz (MR).

2. See especially Weber (1913). This informative article is reprinted in Weber (1922). On Weber's concept of understanding see principally Dieter (1952), especially pp. 6–8.

3. On this concept see Rombach (1951 146–147).

Appendix II

1. Balthasar (1958 15); see also (1956 60).

2. The page references to the appendix on Jaspers relate to the second edition of *Philosophie* (1948), especially pp. 338–396.

3. See especially (16, 45, 231, 244:I 59, 89, 275, 288; 301–302, 355–356, 365, 664–665:II 9–10, 64–65, 73, 374–375).

4. Such an identification is to be found, for instance, at the beginning of the "Elucidation of Existentiel Communication" (347:II 56). Jaspers speaks there first and foremost of the "solipsism or universality of *Dasein*" and then of "solipsism and . . . the universality of consciousness in general," doubtless in the belief that it comes down to the same thing. If one reflects upon the difference contained in this identify, solipsism is ordered more toward *Dasein* as the singular

individual and universalism more toward consciousness in general as to everyman, that is, to the universe of world-constituting subjects. Solipsism and universalism, however, both belong to the movement of self-seclusion, and are thus characterized as the opposite of the communicative self-revelation.

Postscript

1. See chapter 7, section 4.

2. Schulz (1962 20-21). See also Schulz (1955 236n), where reference is made, quite rightly, to the unsubstantiated character of the attempt to carry through the philosophy of being-with-one-another *against* German idealism.

3. In particular, Rosenstock-Huessy does not do this. Indeed, he seeks the dialogical primarily in the sphere of the public. Even there, where he considers it as love, it is, in the final analysis, a matter of the behavior in which it—for instance, in the marital tie—is given over to the public and thereby, in his opinion, fulfills itself as love: "For all love would like to declare itself publicly" (Soz. II 630). Rosenstock-Huessy, who is from the ground up a jurist, sociologist, and historian, characterizes the authentic medium of this publicity as law, society, and history. Depositing the dialogical in this medium belongs to his attempt to overcome the negativity of dialogic through an "extension to permanence." As a jurist, Rosenstock-Huessy hopes for the permanence of the dialogical from the binding character of the law, as a sociologist from the spiritual substantiality of institutions, to which the entire last part of book II of *Sociology* is dedicated, and as a historian from the "time-worn" relations in which the later generation has to meet the claims of the earlier. All this is expressed particularly clearly in the work that appeared last, which could well be regarded as Rosenstock-Huessy's legacy: *Die Sprache des Menschengeschlechts. Eine leibhaftige Grammatik in vier Teilen* (Heidelberg), volume 1 of which was published in 1963 and volume 2 in 1964. Unfortunately, this work cannot be satisfactorily treated in the present investigation.

4. Gadamer (1961 270-271). On the premodern history of the "dialogical principle" see also Berlinger (1962), especially pp. 70-76, 216-237.

5. I am using the concept of the person not in the sense of Löwith and Binswanger, but with the meaning that it has for, for example, Buber, and in accordance with which it means the "self." For Löwith and Binswanger, the person is precisely a functionary, since this characterizes the individual in his "being-as." In contrast, I adopt that very meaningful and fruitful distinction between "person" and "function" that M. Müller (1962) makes.

6. I hope that I am not suspected of wanting to bring back to life that distinction between community and society drawn by Tönnies (1912) with the distribution of mediate alien experience and the immediate Thou encounter to the spheres of the public and the intimate. Therein, community is defined as familial-homely connectedness and society as the public (p. 4). But the opposition between transcendental experience of the alien and dialogical understanding is by no means the one that principally concerns Tönnies, with his distinction between community and society, that is, the opposition between "real and organic life" and "ideal and mechanical construction" (p. 3). The genuine I-Thou relationship is certainly no mechanical aggregate, but just as little is it an organic connection. Its "immediacy" (a dangerously ambiguous concept) is not that of the naturalness that belongs essentially to community according to Tönnies. In his system, the whole of sociological organicism has no place at all for dialogical understanding. Othmar Spann too (1930) ignores the duality of I and Thou in that he takes the difference between individualism and universalism to be an unavoidable alternative. It is precisely the special social-philosophical goal of Buber's dialogic to overcome this alternative.

7. This is an appropriate place to remind the reader once again of the method of the present investigation. In the introductory remarks, our method was characterized as the attempt to formalize extreme reflective positions. When therefore we speak of the "immediate meeting with the Thou," we mean the Thou in its *most extreme* form, precisely that in which it is immediately encountered. Every Thou is certainly not encountered in such an immediate manner. The distinction between the mediately experienced alien Thou, for example, *Dasein*-with, and the immediately encountered Thou does not suffice in and of itself. The Thou, for its part, emerges once again in a twofold form, as mediately and as immediately encountered. This differentiation of the Thou itself—brought into play by Marcel himself and reproduced on the basis of phenomenology following, Marcel's intentions, by Rombach and by Löwith with a certain modification—I take to be extremely important. An investigation that does not proceed as does the present in a radical fashion could, with good reason, set out the mediately encountered Thou as the concrete truth of the "Other." The "mediation" that we seek would then be left over for it because the mediately encountered Thou already in itself represents the mediation of the intentional and the dialogical. The place of this substantial mediation, its medium, is language as the dialectic of question and answer. In my opinion, too, the philosophy of dialogue does not fall short of its goal in that it too seeks the Thou in this middle ground, but only to the extent that it transposes the categories of intentionality, which are still partly valid in this middle ground, to the immediate encounter with the (completed) Thou—that it grasps "the Thou" in a leveled-down fashion according to the model of the mediately encountered Thou, if not entirely according to that of the purely mediately experienced alien Thou.

To the extent that the specific structure of the dialogical encounter and the intentional constitution of alien experience are found together in the realm of the medium, that praxis that has still not become genuinely existentiel can also be reconciled with the theory. Gadamer has done this in a convincing manner in a problem area which has been entirely ignored by me, that of a humanistic hermeneutics. In his book *Wahrheit und Methode, Grundzüge einer philosophischen Hermeneutik* (1960), especially pp. 340—367, Gadamer takes the dialogical relation, which he very carefully unravels into distinct relationships of higher or lower degrees of Thou proximity, as the archetype for the anlysis of "hermeneutical experience." In his view, such an archetypal character is possible because the tradition is also encountered by me as the partner of communication. I can only understand a text when I take up the questions that confront me out of this text and when I envisage it itself as an answer to a question. So the task of interpreting is an "entering into a conversation with the text" (p. 350). In this way, the hermeneutic experience is an analogue to living conversation, above all, because this conversation, when it stands upon what is for Gadamer the highest level of interhuman experience, is characterized by "openness to the Thou," which as "openness to the tradition" also determines the highest level of hermeneutic experience, the "historically effective consciousness." But Gadamer also interprets the completed conversation as question-answer dialectic. In accordance with his conception, conversation possesses purely and simply "the necessary structure of question and answer" (p. 349). With the same necessity, every openness for the Thou is limited by, namely, the question *horizon*, which first makes the question into a directed questioning (p. 346). Admittedly, Gadamer demonstrates the sureness of his phenomenological outlook by adding that a question *comes* to us rather than *being posed* by us. It is "more something that we undergo than an action" (p. 348). Consequently, we do not so much conduct a conversation as fall into one (p. 361). This description accords precisely with the "ambiguous" essence of that speaking to be found in the middle ground of the question-answer dialectic that is still charged with intentionality, but essentially reaches out beyond so that intentionality is posited as the vanishing moment.

8. Löwith thematizes the movement from alter-ation to dialogical self-becoming as an inner-dialogical occurrence: as the transformation of the I-Thou relationship, which, thanks to its reflexive dialectic, leads to alter-ation, into the relationship of an I self and a Thou self. In a similar fashion Marcel also already integrates alter-ation into the theme of the philosophy of dialogue. In contrast, in any complete construction of the ontological history of mankind, the entire phenomenon of alter-ation must be taken into account, and therefore, above all, the

transcendentally original event that, according to Husserl, brings about the lapse of the originary I into the world. Thus far Berdiaev has gone furthest in this direction. He not only sets up a connection between dialogical self-becoming and alter-ation, which he envisages under the title "socialization," but also derives from this socialization, more explicitly than Marcel, the objectivation of the world. See Berdiaev (1951 38, 47, 79–80, 103, 116, 127).

9. As noted in chapter 5, section 1, Wiplinger has already referred to dialogical moments in the late work of Heidegger. Heidegger's thought of being stands particularly close to the universal, nonanthropologically restricted dialogic of Buber—in spite of its inappropriate critique of Heidegger and in spite of Heidegger's depreciation of the entire philosophy of the Thou. Between Buber's talk of the over against one another of all beings and Heidegger's talk of the over against one another of earth and heaven, mortals, and divinities, one cannot even find verbal correspondences. Even the substantive proximity of Heidegger's thought of being to dialogical thought in general is unrecognizable. It is given in such a way that here, just as there, it is a matter of linguistic philosophy. To be sure, the dialogical philosophical reversal of the traditional rank ordering of thought and language in a certain respect simply reproduces the opposition of Hamann against Kant. Still, it prepared Heidegger's "way to language." Its philosophical-historical significance already becomes clear out of this. Perhaps *its* significance will be more correctly estimated when it is at last seen that the approach of Heidegger's late philosophy, which is mistaken in its execution, carries more weight than the approach of fundamental ontology, whose execution is more successful precisely because it attempted less.

We should still bring in here a remark on the method of the Heidegger interpretation in the present investigation: What was thematized was not the correspondences between Heidegger's late thought and dialogical thought, but those correspondences lying on the side of transcendental philosophy between Heidegger's early thought and Husserl's theory of intersubjectivity. In this way, the general method of the working out of extreme reflective positions required not merely the renunciation of all that which already corresponds to dialogical thought in *Being and Time*. Rather, this renunciation was also, and above all, necessary because the positive relation of fundamental ontology to the philosophy of dialogue is not to be met with on the level of the analysis of being-with, but at the higher level of the question of being. The question of being, which guides and encompasses everything in *Being and Time*, must, however, for its part be given up, in order not to extend without limit the interpretation. Admittedly, there follows therefrom a sort of perspectival foreshortening; while I consider Husserl's transcendental philosophy principally in its futurally significant aspects, I question Heidegger's fundamental ontology with regard to its past. The former I follow up forward, the latter backward. It is clear that, in this way, *Being and Time* cannot be fully evaluated.

10. Schelling (*Werke* VII 360).

11. From this consciousness a new light is thrown, moreover, on Binswanger's characterization of the "space" of love as "home."

12. Jaeger (1944 256). See also Krüger (1948 119–130). Of course, the application of this myth to dialogic is not to be associated with the affirmation that the Platonic Aristophanes reproduces Plato's conclusive also superseded by ve conception of eros. As with all preceding interpretations, the myth of Aristophanes is also superseded by Socratic discourse. Still, the decisive recognition of Socrates that eros is love as ιεα του αγαθου is prepared by Aristophanes in line with its negative side, and indeed, in particular, through the remark that the loved ones at bottom do not seek the enjoyment of love and do not know what they want from each other when they lapse into sheer physicality.

13. Franz von Bader has tried to ground it in a scientific manner; see Huch (1920 202).

Abbreviations for Frequently
Cited Works

AG	E. Rosenstock-Huessy, *Der Atem des Geistes*
AS	E. Rosenstock-Huessy, *Angewandte Seelenkunde*
CB	M. Buber, *Die chassidischen Bücher*
CM	E. Husserl, *Cartesianische Meditationen*
Crd	J. Sartre, *Critique de la raison dialectique*
Disp.I	H. Ehrenberg, *Disputation. Drei Bucher vom Deutschen Ideal-ismus. I: Fichte*
DP	M. Buber, *Die Schriften über das dialogische Prinzip* (includes *Ich und Du, Zwiesprache,* and *Elemente des Zwischenmenschlichen*)
Ea	G. Marcel, *Être et avoir*
EC	M. Buber, *Die Erzählungen der Chassidim*
En	J. Sartre, *L'Être et le néant*
EP	E. Husserl, *Erste Philosophie*
EU	E. Husserl, *Erfahrung und Urteil*
FTL	E. Husserl, *Formale und transzendentale Logik*
GD	K. Heim, *Glaube und Denken*
Gf	M. Buber, *Gottesfinsternis*
Gg	K. Heim, *Glaubensgewissheit*
GL	K. Heim, *Glaube und Leben*
GU	E. Rosenstock-Huessy, *Das Geheimnis der Universität*
Gw	E. Grisebach, *Gegenwart*
GW	F. Gogarten, *Glaube und Wirklichkeit*
H	M. Buber, *Hinweise*

Abbreviations

Id.I	E. Husserl, *Ideen*, I
Id.II	E. Husserl, *Ideen*, II
Id.III	E. Husserl, *Ideen*, III
Jm	G. Marcel, *Journal metaphysique*
K	E. Husserl, *Die Krisis der europäischen Wissenschaften und die transzendentale Phänomenologie*
KD	K. Barth, *Die Kirkliche Dogmatik*
KS	F. Rosenzweig, *Kleinere Schriften*
MB	E. Levinas, ed., *Martin Buber*
MR	A. Schütz, "On Multiple Realities"
PM	M. Buber, *Das Problem des Menschen*
PP	E. Husserl, *Phanomenologischen Psychologie*
RV	H. Cohen, *Religion der Vernunft aus den Quellen des Judentums*
SE	F. Rosenzweig, *Der Stern der Erlösung*
Soz.	E. Rosenstock-Huessy, *Soziologie*
SuZ	M. Heidegger, *Sein und Zeit*
UB	M. Buber, *Urdistanz und Beziehung*
W	M. Buber, *An der Wende*
WB	E. Brunner, *Wahrheit als Begegnung*
WG	M. Heidegger, *Vom Wesen des Grundes*
WL	F. Ebner, *Wort und Liebe*
WR	F. Ebner, *Das Wort und die geistigen Realitäten*

References

Adorno, Th. W.
(1956). *Zur Metakritik der Erkenntnistheorie. Studien über Husserl und die phänomenologischen Antinomien.* Stuttgart. [Translated as *Negative Dialectics* (New York).]

Albérès, R.-M.
(1960). *Jean-Paul Sartre.* Paris.

Arntz, J. Th. C.
(1960). *De Liefde in de Ontologie van J.-P. Sartre.* Nijmegen.
(1961). "De verhouding tot de ander in het Oeuvre van J.-P. Sarte." In *Tijdschrift voor Philosophie* XXIII, 237–274.

Asemissen, H. U.
(1957). *Strukturanalytische Probleme der Wahrnehmung in der Phänomenologie Husserls.* Cologne.

Baeck, L.
(1958). *Von Moses Mendelssohn zu Franz Rosenzweig. Typen jüdischen Selbstverständnisses in den letzten beiden Jahrhunderten.* Stuttgart.

Bagot, J.-P.
(1958). *Connaissance et amour. Essai sur la philosophie de Gabriel Marcel.* Paris.

Balthasar, H. W. U.
(1836). *Die Gottesfrage des heutigen Menschen.* Vienna/Munich. *Einsame Zwiesprache. Martin Buber und das Christentum.* Cologne/Olten.

Barnes, H. E.
(1959). *The Literature of Possibility.* London.

Barth, K.
(KD). *Die Kirchliche Dogmatik.* III:2. Zurich, 1948.

Beauvoir, S. de
(1960). *La Force de l'âge.* Paris.

References

Berdiaev, N.
(1951). *Das Ich und die Welt der Objekte.* Darmstadt.

Berlinger, R.
(1962). *Augustins dialogische Metaphysik.* Frankfurt am Main.

Biemel, W.
(1950a). *Le Concept de monde chez Heidegger.* Louvain/Paris.
(1950b). Husserl's *Encyclopaedia Britannica* article and Heidegger's notes on it. In *Tijdschrift voor Philosophie* XII, 246–280.
(1959). "Die entscheidenden Phasen der Entfaltung von Husserls Philosophie." In *Zeitschrift für philosophische Forschung* XIII, 187–213.

Binswanger, L.
(1922). *Einführung in die Probleme der allgemeinen Psychologie.* Berlin.
(1947). *Ausgewählte Vorträge und Aufsätze.* I. Bern.
(1942). *Grundformen und Erkenntnis menschlichen Daseins.* Zurich.
(1956). *Drei Formen missglückten Daseins.* Tübingen.
(1957a). *Der Mensch in der Psychiatrie.* Pfullingen.
(1957b). *Schizophrenie.* Pfullingen.
(1960). *Melancholie und Manie.* Pfullingen.

Boehm, R.
(1959a). "Zum Begriff des 'Absoluten' bei Husserl." In *Zeitschrift für philosophische Forschung* XIII, 214–242.
(1959b). "Zijn en tijd in de philosophie van Husserl." In *Tijdschrift voor Philosophie* XXI, 243–276.

Bonhoeffer, D.
(1954). *Sanctorum communio.* Munich. [Translated as *The Communion of Saints* (New York).]

Boss, M.
(1954). *Psychoanalyse und Daseinsanalytik.* Bern.

Brand, G.
(1955). *Welt, Ich und Zeit. Nach unveröffentlichten Manuskripten Edmund Husserls.* The Hague.

Brown, J.
(1962). *Kierkegaard, Heidegger, Buber and Barth: Subject and Object in Modern Theology.* New York.

Brunner, E.
(WB). *Wahrheit als Begegnung.* Berlin, 1938.

Buber, M.
(1913). *Daniel. Gespräche von der Verwirklichung.* Leipzig.
(1917). *Ereignisse und Begegnungen.* Leipzig.
(CB). *Die chassidischen Bücher.* Berlin, 1928.
(EC). *Die Erzählungen der Cassidim.* Zurich, 1949.
(UB). *Urdistanz und Beziehung.* Heidelberg, 1951.
(W). *An der Wende. Reden über das Judentum.* Cologne/Olten, 1952. [Translated as *At the Turning* (New York).]
(GF). *Gottesfinsternis. Betrachtungen zur Beziehung zwischen Religion und Philosophie.* Zurich, 1953. [Translated as *Eclipse of Gods* (New York).]
(H). *Hinweise. Gesammelte Essays.* Zurich, 1953.
(DP). *Die Schriften über das dialogische Prinzip.* Heidelberg, 1954.
(PM). *Das Problem des Menschen.* Heidelberg, 1954.
(1955). *Sehertum. Anfang und Ausgang.* Cologne/Olten.

References

(1960). "Ich und Du. Von der Wechselseitigkeit in den Ordnungen des Seins." In *Sinn und Sein*. Ed. R. Wisser. Tübingen, 465–474.
(1962). *Werke*. I: *Schriften zur Philosophie*. Munich/Heidelberg.
(1963). "Antwort." In *Martin Buber*. Ed. P. A. Schilpp and M. Friedman. Evanston/Stuttgart, 589–639.

Celms, Th.
(1928). *Der phänomenologische Idealismus Husserls*. Riga.

Cohen, H.
(1915). *Der Begriff der Religion im System der Philosophie*. Geissen.
(1924). *Jüdische Schriften*. I. Berlin.
(RV). *Religion der Vernunft aus den Quellen des Judentums*. Frankfurt am Main, 1929.

Colin, P.
(1951). "Christlicher Existentialismus." In *Christlicher Existentialismus: Gabriel Marcel*. Warendorf, 16–133.

Cullberg, J.
(1933). *Das Du und die Wirklichkeit. Zum ontologischen Hintergrund der Gemeinschaftskategorie*. Uppsala.

Desan, W.
(1960). *The Tragic Finale*. New York.

Diamont, M. L.
(1960). *Martin Buber*. New York.
(1963). "Dialog und Theologie." In *Martin Buber*. Evanston/Stuttgart, 208–219.

Diemer, A.
(1956). *Edmund Husserl. Versuch einer systematischen Darstellung seiner Phänomenologie*. Meisenheim.

Dieter, H.
(1952). *Die Einheit der Wissenschaftslehre Max Webers*. Tübingen.
(1957). "The Concept of Beauty in Schiller's Aesthetics." In *Journal for Philosophical Research* 11, 527–547.
(1958/1959). "Hegels Theorie über den Zufall." In *Kant-Studien* L.

Dilthey, W.
"Beiträge zur Lösung der Frage vom Ursprung unseres Glaubens an die Realität der Aussenwelt und seinem Recht." In *Gesammelte Schriften*. V, 90–138.

Drüe, H.
(1963). *Edmund Husserls System der phänomenologischen Psychologie*. Berlin.

Ebner, F.
(WR). *Das Wort und die geistigen Realitäten. Pneumatologische Fragmente*. Regensburg, 1921.
(WL). *Wort und Liebe*. Regensburg, 1935.
(1963). *Schriften*. Munich. I: *Fragmente, Aufsätze, Aphorismen. Zu einer Pneumatologie des Wortes*. II: *Notizen, Tagebücher, Lebenserinnerungen*.

Ehrenberg, H.
(1911). *Die Parteiung der Philosophie*. Leipzig.
(1922). "Einleitung." In *Ludwig Feuerbach, Philosophie der Zukunft*. Stuttgart.
(Disp.I). *Disputation. Drei Bücher vom Deutschen Idealismus*. I: *Fichte*. Munich, 1923. (III: *Hegel*. Munich, 1925).

References

Ehrenberg, R.
(1926/1927a). "Glaube und Bildung." In *Die Kreatur* I, 3–16.
(1926/1927b). "Gottesreich und organisches Leben." In *Die Kreatur* I, 370–408.
(1927/1928). "Gewissen und Gewusstes." In *Die Kreatur* II, 135–147.

Eigler, G.
(1961). *Metaphysische Voraussetzungen in Husserls Zeitanalysen.* Meisenheim.

Eley, L.
(1962). *Die Krise des Apriori in der transzendentalen Phänomenologie Edmund Husserls.* The Hague.

Faber, W.
(1962). *Das Dialogische Prinzip Martin Bubers und das erzieherische Verhältnis.* Ratingern.

Feuerbach, L.
(1950). "Grundsätze der Philosophie der Zukunft." In *Kleine philosophische Schriften.* Ed. M. G. Lange. Leipzig.

Filippini, E.
(1960). "Ego ed alter-ego nella 'Krisis' di Husserl." In *Omaggio a Husserl.* Ed. E. Paci. Milano, 213–225.
(1961). "Nota su Husserl e Heidegger." In *Rivista di filosofia* LII, 212–216.

Fink, E.
(1933) "Die phänomenologische Philosophie Edmund Husserls in der gegenwärtigen Kritik." In *Kant-Studien* XXXVIII, 319–383.
(1934). "Was will die Phänomenologie Edmund Husserls?" In *Die Tatwelt* X, 15–32.
(1938/1939). "Das Problem der Phänomenologie Edmund Hussernls." In *Revue internationale de philosophie* I, 226–270.
(1952). "L'analyse intentionelle et le problème de la pensée spéculative." In *Problèmes actuels de la phénoménologie.* Ed. H. L. van Breda. Bruxelles, 53–87.

Fisch, I.
(1942). *Husserls Internationalitäts- und Urteilslehre.* Basel.

Freund, E.
(1955). *Die Existenzphilosophie Franz Rosenzweigs. Ein Beitrag zur Analyse seines Werkes* "Der Stern der Erlösung." Hamburg.

Friedman, M. S.
(1955). *Martin Buber. The Life of Dialogue.* London.
(1963). "Die Grundlagen von Martin Bubers Ethik." in *Martin Buber.* Evanston/Stuttgart, 153–179.

Funke, G.
(1956). "Mundane Geschichte, ontologische Erfahrung und transzendentale Subjektivität." In *Philosophisches Jahrbuch der Görres-Gesellschaft* LXIV, 361–371.
(1957). *Zur transzendentalen Phänomenologie.* Bonn.

Gadamer, H.-G.
(1960). *Wahrheit und Methode. Grundzüge einer philosophischen Hermeneutik.* Tübingen.
(1961). "Hermeneutik und Historismus." In *Philosophische Rundschau* IX, 241–276.

Glatzer, N. N.
(1961). *Franz Rosenzweig: His Life and Thought.* New York.

References

Gogarten, F.
(1926). *Ich glaube an den dreieinigen Gott.* Jena.
(GW). *Glaube und Wirklichkeit. Gesammelte Aufsätze.* Jena, 1928.

Goldschmidt, H. L.
(1946). *Hermann Cohen und Martin Buber.* Genf.
(1948). *Philosophie als Dialogik.* Affoltern.
(1964). *Dialogik. Philosophie auf dem Boden der Neuzeit.* Frankfurt am Main.

Gollwitzer, H.
(1963). *Die Existenz Gottes im Bekenntnis des Glaubens.* Munich.

Graumann, C. F.
(1960). *Grundlagen einer Phänomenologie und Psychologie der Perspektivität.* Berlin.

Grisebach, E.
(1919). *Wahrheit und Wirklichkeiten.* Halle.
(1924). *Die Grenzen des Erziehers und seine Verantwortung.* Halle.
(Gw). *Gegenwart. Eine kritische Ethik.* Halle, 1928.
(1929/1930). "Altes und neues Denken." In *Die Kreatur* III, 29–37.
(1930). "Interpretation oder Destruktion? Zum kritischen Verständnis von Martin Heideggers 'Kant und das Problem der Metaphysik.' " In *Deutsche Vierteljahrsschrift für Literaturwissenschaft und Geistesgeschichte* VIII, 199–232.

Gründer, K.
(1962). "M. Heideggers Wissenschaftskritik in ihren geschichtlichen Zusammenhängen." In *Archiv für Philosophie* XI, 312–335.

Hammerstein, F. v.
(1958). *Das Messiasproblem bei Martin Buber.* Stuttgart.

Hartmann, K.
(1953). "Husserls Einfühlungstheorie auf monadologischer Grundlage." Thesis, University of Bonn.
(1963). *Grundzüge der Ontologie Sartres in ihrem Verhältnis zu Hegels Logik.* Berlin.

Hartmann, N.
(1931). *Zum Problem der Realitätsgegebenheit.* Berlin.
(1949). *Metaphysik der Erkenntnis.* Berlin.

Heidegger, M.,
(WG). *Vom Wesen des Grundes.* Frankfurt am Main, 1949.
(1951). *Was ist Metaphysik?* Frankfurt am Main.
(SuZ). *Sein und Zeit.* Tübingen, 1953. [Translated by Macquarrie and Robinson as *Being and Time* (New York, 1962).]
(1957). *Identität und Differenz.* Pfullingen.

Heim, K.
(GL). *Glaube und Leben. Gesammelte Aufsätze und Vorträtze und Vorträge.* Berlin, 1926.
(Gg). *Glaubensgewissheit.* Berlin, 1949.
(GD). *Glaube und Denken.* Hamburg, 1957.

Henrich, D.
(1952). *Die Einheit der Wissenschaftslehre Max Webers.* Tübingen.
(1957). "Der Begriff der Schönheit in Schillers Ästhetik." In *Zeitschrift für philosophische Forschung* XI, 527–547.

References

(1958/1959). "Hegels Theorie über den Zufall." In *Kant-Studien* L, 131–148.

Herrigel, H.
(1928). *Das neue Denken*. Berlin.

Hildebrand, D. v.
(1955). *Metaphysik der Gemeinschaft*. Regensburg.

Hirzel, R.
(1963). *Der Dialog*, I, II. Hildesheim.

Hohl, H.
(1962). *Lebenswelt und Geschichte. Grundzüge der Spätphilosophie E. Husserls*. Freiburg/Munich.

Holz, H. H.
(1951). *Jean-Paul Sartre*. Meisenheim.

Hommes, U.
(1963). "Das Problem des Rechts und die Philosophie der Subjektivität." In *Philosophisches Jahrbuch* LXX, 311–343.

Huch, R.
(1920). *Die Romantik*. I: *Blütezeit der Romantik*. Leipzig.

Humboldt, W. v.
Gesammelte Schriften (Akad. Ausgabe). VI/1.

Husserl, E.
(1928a). *Logische Untersuchungen*. Halle. [Translated by J. N. Findlay as *Logical Investigations* (Philadelphia, 1970).]
(1928b). *Vorlesungen zur Phänomenologie des inneren Zeitbewusstseins*. Ed. M. Heidegger. Halle.
(FTL). *Formale und transzendentale Logik*. Halle, 1929.
(EU). *Erfahrung und Urteil. Untersuchungen zur Genealogie der Logik*. Ed. L. Landgrebe. Hamburg, 1948. [Translated by Churchill and Ameriks as *Experience and Judgment* (Evanston, IL, 1973).]
(CM). *Cartesianische Meditationen und Pariser Vorträge*. Ed. S. Strasser. Husserliana I. The Hague, 1950. [Translated by D. Cairns as *Cartesian Meditations* (The Hague, 1960).]
(Id.I). *Ideen zu einer reinen Phänomenologie und phänomenologischen Philosophie*. I: *Allgemeine Einführung in die reine Phänomenologie*. Ed. W. Biemel. Husserliana III. The Hague, 1950.
(Id.II). *Ideen zu einer reinen Phänomenologie und phänomenologischen Philosophie*. II: *Phänomenologische Untersuchungen zur Konstitution*. Ed. W. Biemel. Husserliana IV. The Hague, 1952.
(Id.III). *Ideen zu einer reinen Phänomenologie und phänomenologischen Philosophie*. III: *Die Phänomenologie und die Fundamente der Wissenschaften*. Ed. W. Biemel. Husserliana V. The Hague, 1952.
(K). *Die Krisis der europäischen Wissenschaften und die transzendentale Phänomenologie*. Ed. W. Biemel. Husserliana VI. The Hague, 1954. [Translated by D. Carr as *The Crisis of European Sciences and Trancendental Phenomenology* (Evanston, IL, 1970).]
(EP). *Erste Philosophie* (1923/1924). II: *Theorie der Phänomenologischen Reduktion*. Ed. R. Boehm. Husserliana VIII. The Hague, 1959.
(PP). *Phänomenologische Psychologie* (1925). Ed. W. Biemel. Husserliana IX. The Hague, 1962.

Jaeger, W.
(1944). *Paideia*. II. Berlin.

Jameson, F.
(1961). *Sartre, The Origins of a Style*. New Haven/London.

References

Jaspers, K.
(1962). *Philosophie*. Berlin. 1948. [Translated by A. Ashton as *Philosophy* (Chicago, 1970).]

Kern, I.
(1962). "Die drei Wege zur transzendental-phänomenologischen Reduktion in der Philosophie Edmund Husserls." In *Tijdschrift voor Filosofie* XXIV, 303–349.

Knittermeyer, H.
(1952). *Die Philosophie der Existenz*. Vienna.

Kohn, H.
(1961). *Martin Buber*. Cologne.

Kopper, J.
(1960). *Die Dialektik der Gemeinschaft*. Frankfurt am Main.
(1960/1961). "Sartres Verständnis der Lehre Hegels von der Gemeinschaft." In *Kant-Studien* LII, 159–172.

Krüger, G.
(1948). *Einsicht und Leidenschaft. Das Wesen des platonischen Denkens*. Frankfurt am Main.

Kümmel, F.
(1962). *Über den Begriff der Zeit*. Tübingen.

Laín Entralgo, P.
(1961). *Teoria y realidad del otro*. I: *El otro como otro yo/Nosotros, tú y yo*. II: *Otredad y projimidad*. Madrid.

Landgrebe, L.
(1949).*Phänomenologie und Metaphysik*. Hamburg.
(1961). "Husserls Abschied vom Cartesianismus." In *Philosophische Rundschau* IX, 133–177.

Lauer, Q.
(1955). *Phénoménologie de Husserl. Essai sur la genèse de l'intentionnalité*. Paris.

Lehmann, K.
(1964). "Metaphysik, Transzendentalphilosophie und Phänomenologie in den ersten Schriften Martin Heideggers (1912–1916)." In *Philosophisches Jahrbuch* LXXI, 331–357.

Levinas, E.
(1949). *En découvrant l'existence avec Husserl et Heidegger*. Paris.
(MB). *Martin Buber*. Evanston/Stuttgart, 1963.

Lipps, Th.
(1903). *Ästhetik. Psychologie des Schönen und der Kunst*. I: *Grundlegung der Ästhetik*. Hamburg/Leipzig.
(1906). *Leitfaden der Psychologie*. Leipzig.
(1907). "Das Wissen von fremden Ichen." In *Psychologische Untersuchungen*, I. Leipzig, 694–722.
(1912). *Die ethischen Grundfragen*. Leipzig/Hamburg.

Litt, Th.
(1924). *Individuum und Gemeinschaft*. Berlin.

Löwith, K.
(1928). *Das Individuum in der Rolle des Mitmenschen*. Munich.
(1958). "M. Hiedegger und F. Rosenzweig, ein Nachtrag zu 'Sein und Zeit.'" In *Zeitschrift für philosophische Forschung* XII, 161–187.

(1960). *Gesammelte Abhandlungen*. Stuttgart.

Lübber, H.
(1954). "Das Ende des phänomenologischen Platonismus. Eine kritische Betrachtung aus Anlass eines neuen Buches (Wilhelm Schapp, In Geschichten verstrickt)." In *Tijdschrift voor Philosophie* XVI, 639–666.
(1960). "Die geschichtliche Bedeutung der Subjektivitätstheorie Edmund Husserls." In *Neue Zeitschrift für systematische Theologie* II, 300–319.

Macquarrie, J.
(1960). *An Existentialist Theology*. London.

Maier, W.
(1964). *Das Problem der Lieblichkeit bei Jean-Paul Sartre und Maurice Merleau-Ponty*. Tübingen.

Maihofer, W.
(1954). *Recht und Sein. Prolegomena zu einer Rechtsontologie*. Frankfurt am Main.

Marcel, G.
(Jm). *Journal métaphysique*. Paris, 1927. [Translated by B. Wall as *Metaphysical Diary* (London, 1952).]
(Ea). *Être et avoir*. Paris, 1935. [Translated as *Being and Having* (London).]
(1945). *Homo viator*. Paris.
(1951). *Le Mystère de l'être*. Paris.
(1963). "Ich und Du bei Martin Buber." In *Martin Buber*. Evanston/Stuttgart, 35–41.

Maringer, S.
(1936). *Martin Bubers Metaphysik der Dialogik im Zusammenhang neuerer philosophischer und theologischer Strömungern*. Cologne.

Marx, W.
(1961). *Heidegger und die Tradition*. Stuttgart.

Michel, E.
(1946). *Der Partner Gottes*. Heidelberg.

Möller, J.
(1959). *Absurdes Sein?* Stuttgart.

Müller, M.
(1962). "Person und Funktion." In *Philosophisches Jahrbuch* LXIX, 371–404.

Müller, W. H.
(1956). *Die Philosophie Edmund Husserls*. Bonn.

Müller-Lauter. W.
(1960). *Möglichkeit und Wirklichkeit bei Martin Heidegger*. Berlin.

Münsterberg, H.
(1900). *Grundzüge der Psychologie. I: Allgemeiner Teil—Die Prinzipien der Psychologie*. Leipzig.

Ortega y Gasset, J.
(1957). *El hombre y la gente*. Madrid.

Ott, H.
(1959). *Denken und Sien. Der Weg Martin Heideggers und der Weg der Theologie*. Zurich.

References

Otto, R.
(1923). *Das Heilige*. Stuttgart.

Paci, E.
(1960). "Sul problema dell' intersoggettività." In *Il Pensiero* V, 291–325.

Pfuetze, P.
(1961). *Self, Society, Existence. Human Nature and Dialogue in the Thought of George Herbert Mead and Martin Buber*. New York.

Philipps, L.
(1963). *Zur Ontologie der sozialen Rolle*. Frankfurt am Main.

Plessner, H.
(1953). *Zwischen Philosophie und Gesellschaft. Ausgewählte Abhandlungen und Vorträge*. Bern.
(1959). *Husserl in Göttingen*. Göttingen.

Pöggeler, O.
(1963). *Der Denkweg Martin Heideggers*. Pfullingen.

Reinach, A.
(1913). *Die apriorischen Grundlagen des bürgerlichen Rechtes*. Halle.

Richardson, W.
(1963). *Heidegger. Through Phenomenology to Thought*. The Hague.

Richter, L.
(1961). *Jean-Paul Sartre*. Berlin.

Rombach, H.
(1951). "Über Ursprung und Wesen der Frage." In *Symposion. Jahrbuch für Philosophie* II, 135–236.

Rosenstock-Huessy, E.
(AS). *Angewandte Seelenkunde*. Darmstadt, 1924.
(AG). *Der Atem des Geistes*. Frankfurt am Main, 1951.
(1952). *Heilkraft und Wahrheit*. Stuttgart.
(1955a). *Der unbezahlbare Mensch*. Berlin.
(1955b). *Des Christen Zukunft oder Wir überholen die Moderne*. Munich.
(Soz.). *Soziologie*. Stuttgart. I, 1956; II, 1958.
(1957). *Zurück in das Wagnis der Sprache*. Berlin.
(GU). *Das Geheimnis der Universität. Aufsätze und Reden aus den Jahren 1950 bis 1957*. Ed. G. Müller. Stuttgart, 1958.
(1963 & 1964). *Die Sprache des Menschengeschlechts. Eine leibhaftige Grammatik in vier Teilen*. Heidelberg: I, 1963; II, 1964.

Rosenzweig, F.
(1935). *Briefe*. Berlin.
(KS). *Kleinere Schriften*. Berlin, 1937.
(SE). *Der Stern der Erlösung*. Heidelberg, 1954. [Translated by W. Hallo as *The Star of Redemption* (New York, 1971).]

Roth, A.
(1960). *Edmund Husserls ethische Untersuchungen*. The Hague.

Salvan, J.
(1962). *To Be and Not to Be. An Analysis of Jean-Paul Sartre's Ontology*. Detroit.

Sartre, J.-P.

(1936). *L'Imagination*. Paris.

(1936/1937). "La Transcendance de l'ego." In *Recherches philosophiques* VI, 85–123. [Translated by Williams and Kirkpatrick as *Transcendence of the Ego* (New York, 1957).]

(En). *L'Être et le néant*. Paris, 1943. [Translated by H. Barnes as *Being and Nothingness* (New York, 1953).]

(1947). *Situations*. I. Paris.

(1956). *Der Leib*. Stuttgart. [Extract in German from *L'Être et le néant*.]

(Crd). *Critique de la raison dialectique*. I: *Théorie des ensembles pratiques*. Paris, 1960. [Translated by S. Smith as *Critique of Dialectical Reason*. I: *Theory of Practical Complexes* (London, 1976).]

Sborowitz, A.

(1955). *Beziehung und Bestimmung. Die Lehren von Martin Buber und C. G. Jung in ihrem Verhältnis zueinander*. Darmstadt.

Schapp, W.

(1930 & 1932). *Die neue Wissenschaft vom Recht*. Berlin: I, 1930; II, 1932.

(1953). *In Geschichten verstrickt*. Hamburg.

(1959). *Philosophie der Geschichten*. Leer.

Scheler, M.

(1926). *Wesen und Formen der Sympathie*. Bonn. [Translated by P. Heath as *The Nature of Sympathy* (London).]

Schelling, F. W.

Werke. Ed. K. F. A. Schelling. VII, XII, XIII.

Schleiermacher, Th.

(1957). "Ich und Du. Grundzüge der Anthropologie Ferdinand Ebners." In *Kerygma und Dogma* III, 208–229.

(1962). *Das Heil des Menschen und sein Traum vom Geist. Ferdinand Ebner, ein Denker in der Kategorie der Begegnung*. Berlin.

Schöfer, E.

(1962). *Die Sprache Heideggers*. Pfullingen.

Schröder, G.

(1951). *Das ich und das Du in der Wende des Denkens. Untersuchung zum Problem der Ich-Du-Beziehung im philosophischen Denken und in der Theologie der Gegenwart*. Göttingen.

Schroers, G.

(1949). *Die Rede als Lebensform*. Bonn.

Schulz, W.

(1958). *Die Vollendung des deutschen Idealismus in der Spätphilosophie Schellings*. Stuttgart.

(1962). *Johann Gottlieb Fichte. Vernunft und Freiheit*. Pfullingen.

Schütz, A.

(1932). *Der sinnhafte Aufbau der sozialen Welt*. Vienna. [Translated by Walsh and Lehnert as *The Phenomenology of the Social World* (Northwestern U. Press, 1967).]

(MR). "On Multiple Realities." In *Philosophy and Phenomenological Research* V (1944/1945), 533–576.

(1948/1949). "Sartre's Theory of the Alter Ego." In *Philosophy and Phenomenological Research* IX, 183–187.

(1957). "Das problem der transzendentalen Intersubjektivität bei Husserl." In *Philosophische Rundschau* V, S. 81–107. [Reprinted in Schütz's *Collected Papers* (The Hague, 1962), I.]

(1959). "Husserl's Importance for the Social Sciences." In *Edmund Husserl 1859–1959*. The Hague, 86–98.

References

Seebohm, Th.
(1962). *Die Bedingungen der Möglichkeit der Transzendental-Philosophie.* Bonn.

Simmel, G.
(1906). *Die Religion.* Frankfurt am Main.
(1908). *Soziologie.* Leipzig.

Sinn, D.
(1958). "Die transzendentale Intersubjektivität mit ihren Seinshorizonten bei Edmund Husserl."
Thesis, University of Heidelberg.

Spann, O.
(1930). *Gesellschaftslehre.* Leipzig.

Spörri, Th.
(1934). "Soziologische Positionen in der Theologie Karl Heims." In *Wort und Geist, Festgabe für
Karl Heim zum 60. Geburtstag.* Berlin, 283–299.

Stavenhagen, K.
(1925). *Absolute Stellungnahmen.* Erlangen.
(1957). *Person und Persönlichkeit.* Ed. H. Delius. Göttingen.

Stein, E.
(1917). *Zum Problem der Einfühlung.* Halle.

Steinbüchel, Th.
(1936). *Der Umbruch des Denkens. Die Frage nach der christlichen Existenz erläutert an Ferdinand Ebners
Menschdeutung.* Regensburg.

Sternberger, A.
(1934). *Der verstandene Tod.* Leipzig.

Strasser, S.
(1945). Het vraagstuk van het Solipsisme bij Edmund Husserl." In *Tijdschrift voor Philosophie* VII,
3–18.

Szilasi, W.
(1959). *Einführung in die Phänomenologie Edmund Husserls.* Tübingen.
(1961). *Philosophie und Naturwissenschaft.* Bern.

Taubes, J.
(1963) "Martin Buber und die Geschichtsphilosophie." In *Martin Buber.* Evanston/Stuttgart,
398–413.

Theunissen, M.
(1958). *Der Begriff Ernst bei Søren Kierkegaard.* Freiburg/Munich.
(1962). "Sören Kierkegaard." In M. Landmann, *De Homine.* Freiburg/Munich, 496–510.
(1963). "Intentionaler Gegenstand und ontologische Differenz. Ansätz zur Fragestellung Heideggers in der Phänomenologie Husserls." In *Philosophisches Jahrbuch* LXX, 344–362.
(1964). "Bubers negative Ontologie des Zwischen." In *Philosophisches Jahrbuch* LXXI, 319–330.

Thurnher, F.
(1954.) "Das Sprachdenken Ferdinand Ebners." In *Ammann-Festgabe.* II. Innsbruck, 20–33.

Thyssen, J.
(1953). "Wege uas dem geschlossenen System von Husserls Monadologie." In *Actes due XIème
congrès international de philosophie.* Amsterdam, 188–194.

References

(1954/1955). "Vom Gegebenen zum Realen." In *Kant-Studien* XLVI, 68–87, 157–171.

Tönnies, F.
(1912). *Gemeinschaft und Gesellschaft. Grundbegriffe der reinen Soziologie.* Berlin.

Toulemont, R.
(1958). "La spécificité du social d'après Husserl." In *Cahiers Internationaux de sociologie* XXV, 135–151.
(1962). *L'Essence de la société selon Husserl.* Paris.

Troisfontaines, R.
(1951). "Der Begriff der Gegenwärtigkeit bei Gabriel Marcel." In *Christlicher Existentialismus: Gabriel Marcel.* Warendorf, 277–300.
(1953). *De l'existence à l'être. La Philosophie de Gabriel Marcel.* Namur.

Tymieniecka, A.-T.
(1962). *Phenomenology and Science in Contemporary European Thought.* New York.

Uslar, D. v.
(1959). "Vom Wesen der Begegnung." In *Zeitschrift für philosophische Forschung* XIII, 85–101.

Uygur, N.
(1958/1959). "Die Phänomenologie Husserls und die 'Gemeinschaft.' " In *Kant-Studien* L, 439–460.

Vierkandt, A.
(1972). *Gesellschaftslehre. Hauptprobleme der philosophischen Soziologie.* Stuttgart.

Volkelt, J.
(1906). *Die Quellen der menschlichen Gewissheit.* Munich.
(1920). *Das ästhetische Bewusstein. Prinzipienfragen der Ästhetik.* Munich.

Vossler, K.
(1923). "Sprechen, Gespräch und Sprache." In *Deutsche Vierteljahrsschrift für Literaturwissenschaft und Geistesgeschichte* I, 665–678.

Waehlens, A. de
(1948). *La Philosophie de Martain Heidegger.* Louvain.

Weber, M.
(1913). "Über einige Kategorien der verstehenden Soziologie." In *Logos* IV, 253–294.
(1922). *Gesammelte Aufsatzen zur Wissenschaftslehre.* Tübingen.

Weischedel, W.
(1932). *Versuch über das Wesen der Verantwortung.* Freiburg.
(1939). *Der Aufbruch der Freiheit zur Gemeinschaft. Studien zur Philosophie des jungen Fichte.* Leipzig.
(1960). *Wirklichkeit und Wirklichkeiten. Aufsätze und Vorträge.* Berlin.

Weizsäcker, V. v.
(1923) "Einleitung." In *Kant, Der Organismus.* Stuttgart.
(1949). *Begegnungen und Entscheidungen.* Stuttgart.
(1951). *Der kranke Mensch. Eine Einführung in die Medizinische Anthropologie.* Stuttgart.
(1956). *Pathosophie.* Göttingen.
(1963). *Am Anfang schuf Gott Himmel und Erde. Grundfragen der Naturphilosophie.* Göttingen.

Wiese, L. v.
(1933). *System der Allgemeinen Soziologie als Lehre von den sozialen Prozessen und den sozialen Gebilden der Menschen (Beziehungslehre).* Munich/Leipzig.

References

Wiplinger, F.
(1961). *Wahrheit und Geschicklichkeit. Eine Untersuchung über die Frage nach dem Wesen der Wahrheit im Denken Martin Heideggers.* Freiburg/Munich.

Witschel. G.
(1964). "Zwei Beiträge Husserls zum Problem der sekundären Qualitäten." In *Zeitschrift für philosophische Forschung* XVIII, 30-49.

Wittig, J.
(1927/1928). "Das Geheimnis des 'Und.' " In *Die Kreatur* II, 419-425.

Wolf, E.
(1958). *Recht des Nächsten. Ein rechtstheologischer Entwurf.* Frankfurt am Main.

Wolters, J. B. Th.
(n.d.). "Eidos. Das Universale im Lichte der Philosophia Pereniss mit besonderer Rucksicht auf Edmund Husserl." Thesis, University of Freiburg.

Zehm, G. A.
(1964). *Historische Vernunft und direkte Aktion. Zur Politik und Philosophie Jean-Paul Sartres.* Stuttgart.

Zeltner, H.
(1959). "Das Ich und die Anderen. Husserls Beitrag zur Grundlegung der Sozialphilosophie." In *Zeitschrift für philosophische Forschung* XIII, 288-315.

Index

439

Index